Shakespeare's ROYAL SELF

SHAKESPEARE'S
Royal Self

JAMES KIRSCH
Foreword by Gerhard Adler

*Published by G. P. Putnam's Sons, New York, for
the C. G. Jung Foundation for Analytical Psychology*

To the members of my Shakespeare's seminars in Los Angeles, California, in 1960, 1961 and 1962, for the inspiration, love and devotion which they gave so generously in the exploration of Shakespeare's depth.

ACKNOWLEDGMENTS

I would like to express my appreciation to the following publishers, institutions and individuals for their permission to quote herein from copyrighted material:

To the Bollingen Foundation for the several excerpts from the Collected Works of C. G. Jung;

To the British Academy for passages from *Hamlet, the Prince or the Poem* by C. S. Lewis;

To the Cambridge University Press for the material from J. Dover Wilson's *What Happens in Hamlet,* the New Shakespeare editions of *Hamlet* and *Macbeth,* and *Shakespeare Survey 1960;* the University of Chicago Press for passages from H. C. Goddard's *The Meaning of Shakespeare;* the Harvard University Press for those from W. H. Clemen's *The Development of Shakespeare's Imagery* and from the Arden edition of *Macbeth* and *King Lear;* the Louisiana State University Press for *Shakespeare's Philosophical Patterns* by W. C. Curry; the Oxford University

Press for *The Tibetan Book of the Dead* and for *The Dream of Learning* by D. G. James;

To Macmillan, Ltd. for the extract from Edith Sitwell's *A Notebook on William Shakespeare;* the Blaisdell Publishing Co. for material from the Kittredge editions of *Hamlet, King Lear* and *Macbeth;* the Thomas Y. Crowell Co. for *The Heart of Hamlet* by Bernard Grebanier; the Humanities Press for Olav Lökse's *Outrageous Fortune;* Meridian Books for G. Wilson Knight's *The Wheel of Fire;* W. W. Norton for the passages from *Hamlet and Oedipus* by Ernest Jones; Scott, Foresman & Co. for James C. Coleman's *Abnormal Psychology and Modern Life;*

To Edward Arnold, Ltd. for the lines from John Russell Brown's *Shakespeare: The Tragedy of Macbeth;* E. & S. Livingstone for R. R. Simpson's *Shakespeare and Medicine;* Longman's for *Explorations in Shakespeare's Language* by H. H. Hulme; Methuen & Co. for T. S. Eliot's *The Sacred Wood* and G. Wilson Knight's *The Imperial Theme;* Routledge & Kegan Paul for *Shakespeare's Poetics* by Russell Fraser; Jonathan Cape for the passages by Edmund Blunden in *Shakespeare Criticism 1919-1935;* Chatto & Windus for *Explorations* by L. C. Knights;

To Rowohlt Verlag for a passage from their bi-lingual edition of *Hamlet;* to Konrad Triltsch for material from Ingeborg Gurland's *Das Gestaltungsgesetz von Shakespeares "König Lear";*

To the legatees of the Brill Testamentory Trust for material from *The Basic Writings of Sigmund Freud,* as translated and edited by Dr. A. A. Brill; to Basic Books and to Sigmund Freud Copyrights Ltd., Mr. James Strachey and The Hogarth Press Ltd. for permission to quote from *Some Character Types Met With in Psycho-Analytic Work,* Volume XIV (1914-1916) of the Standard Edition of *The Complete Psychological Works of Sigmund Freud;*

And to Dr. George B. Wilbur for the excerpts from David B. Barron's "The Babe that Milks."

J. K.

FOREWORD

Side by side with religion it is in art that man has expressed his deepest concern with himself as man. And here again it is in art using language as its medium that this concern is most clearly formulated. Here creative man has tried from time immemorial to discuss and define the riddle of his existence. Here and in religion in the widest sense (including for instance the realm of mythology) he has confronted a primal vision of cosmic dimensions, a vision which has constantly led him to the limits of his understanding of himself and into the depths of transcendental images which could be rendered only in the language of the symbol.

The enigma of creativeness, rooted in the irrational, indefinable matrix of man's timeless and limitless psyche has held eternal fascination for him, and has helped to produce the most memorable justification of his status as man. It is here that the dance of Shiva has found its human counterpart.

Thus it is not surprising that for Western man it is on the one hand in the Bible, on the other hand in Shakespeare that the supreme formulations of the confrontation with the eternal can be found. It may seem arbitrary if we choose Shakespeare as a counterpart of the Bible—there is Homer, Dante, there are the Greek tragedies, or *Faust*. Naturally they all form part of a human opus with an immense phenomenology. If we single out Shakespeare as the greatest representative of written art in the West it is because he has given us the most varied, the most complete, and the most dramatic representation of man's nature and the enigma of his soul. There seems no limit to the poetic expression of man's inner world and of the endless inner conflict of passions and emotions, of the tragedy of failure as well as the achievement of mastery, and of man's suspense between his own extremes that express the paradoxical mystery of the primal vision.

No wonder that this immense cosmos of Shakespeare's opus, and the enigmatic figure of its creator, have given rise to an endless number of commentaries and interpretations. And among his dramatic personalities none has aroused more fascination than the figure of Hamlet. With each generation the focus of interpretation has varied, each generation projecting its own riddle into the riddle of Hamlet.

In our own times we have seen a new approach arising out of the new discoveries of depth psychology. It started with Freud's remark in his *Interpretation of Dreams,* taken up by Ernest Jones in his *Hamlet and Oedipus,* a book which has become a kind of psychoanalytic classic. In accordance with the prevailing psychological climate of the times, we find in both cases an approach based exclusively on a personalistic psychology. It tries to explain the enigma of Hamlet from his personal antecedents, from the child's unsolved riddle of the sphynx, the Oedipus conflict.

Fascinating and revealing though the results of this psychological approach may be with regard to the personal history of the hero, it is bound to leave out the transpersonal mystery of the tragedy—the mystery of man as such, and most of all the problem of the impersonal power of the creative daimon. It is here that we may find a much more adequate and subtle instrument in the psychology of C. G. Jung, who has opened up completely new vistas. With his concept of the primordial archetypal images and symbols he has given us new tools for the interpretation of those depths of human psychology which transcend the purely personal layer of man's psyche. Books like Dr. Esther Harding's *Journey into Self,* an interpretation of *Pilgrim's Progress,* or Erich Neumann's *Art and the Creative Unconscious,* prove the fruitfulness of this new approach.

Dr. Kirsch's book supplies further evidence of the value and importance of Jung's concepts for an understanding of artistic creativeness. His book is a most valuable contribution to the problem of *Hamlet,* and of the two other tragedies which he has chosen as complementing Hamlet's enigma, *Macbeth* and *King Lear.* Dr. Kirsch, a personal pupil of Jung's and a highly experienced psychologist, has applied his knowledge of Jung's work and his own knowledge of the human psyche to a new and fascinating interpretation of these three great dramas of human conflict, failure, and redemption.

Hamlet, the riddle of man *qua* man, Macbeth, the riddle of man as the victim of his superhuman passions, Lear, the riddle of man's redemption through extreme suffering—the three together cover a wide range of man's paradoxical existence. To all three Dr. Kirsch contributes new insights. I am not a Shakespearian scholar and cannot speak as such. But to me as a psychologist, who for over three decades has tried to apply himself to man's psychological problems, Dr. Kirsch's interpretations and comments are of the greatest value, with regard both to the problem of suffering and redemption and of creativeness. In addition the insights into the place these tragedies occupy in Shakespeare's own psychological pattern seem highly relevant. Dr. Kirsch's book is a most rewarding study of all these subjects and I recommend it warmly to all those interested in these fields.

GERHARD ADLER

London, November 1965

CONTENTS

FOREWORD BY GERHARD ADLER : ix

INTRODUCTION : xvii

HAMLET: A DRAMA OF HAUNTED MAN : 3

KING LEAR: A PLAY OF REDEMPTION : 185

MACBETH'S DESCENT INTO HELL
AND DAMNATION : 321

The text used in the illustrative quotations
is that of the Oxford Shakespeare,
edited by W. J. Craig, 1954.

INTRODUCTION

Art, by its very nature, is not science, and science is essentially not art; both provinces of the mind, therefore, have a reservation that is peculiar to them, and that can be explained only from themselves. Hence when we speak of the relation between psychology and art, we are treating only of that aspect of art which without encroachment can be submitted to a psychological manner of approach. Whatever psychology is able to determine about art will be confined to the psychological process of artistic activity, and will have nothing whatever to do with the innermost nature of art itself.

What contribution can analytical psychology make to the root-problem of artistic 'creation,' that is, the mystery of the creative energy? . . . Inasmuch as 'no created mind can penetrate the inner soul of Nature,' you will surely not expect the impossible from our psychology, namely a valid explanation of that great mystery of life, that we immediately feel in the creative impulse. Like every other science psychology has only a modest contribution to make towards the better and deeper understanding of the phenomena of life; it is no nearer than its sisters to absolute knowledge.

C. G. JUNG

Although every work of art remains essentially a mystery, Jung's discovery of the objective psyche as an empirical phenomenon has opened new pathways for the understanding of art, especially of poetry and drama. Jung was able to demonstrate that all *great* art springs from that part of the soul to which he gave the name "collective unconscious," and which he also frequently described as "objective psyche," in contrast to the much more limited field of personal consciousness.

William Shakespeare's work is characterized by its objectivity and universality, rooted in his experience of the human soul. It seems as if his personality disappears behind his work—that, like God, he breathes life into his characters and they then move on their own, independently of their creator. But they all carry the seal of Shakespeare's unique individuality. It would be difficult to state in distinct terms the qualities which made this man of the Renaissance period such a unique dramatist, a poet "not of an age, but for all times" (Ben Jonson). Yet Shakespeare's work does reveal some of the secret. It lies in his astounding, almost unlimited knowledge of the human heart, in his ability to articulate so much of the highest and the lowest in man, the gentlest and the most violent, *all* passions, and in so much thought. He was one of the few men who not only experienced *sections* of human life, but the whole mystery of human life. His plays are at the same time the hot lava and the outflow of this experience. They are the confession of his "royal self."

I chose three plays out of the canon as significant steps in Shakespeare's inner development because in each of them the unconscious appears as a separate factor, as a dramatic figure (Ghosts, Witches), or because the consciousness of the hero is for a time concentrated on the unconscious and characteristically changed by it (King Lear). While I limited myself to three plays, I found it necessary, on the other hand, to analyze each of them with the greatest possible detail in order to demonstrate the *whole* process of individuation. I could not afford to limit myself to certain high points in the drama. I had to follow every step in the development of the hero and other important figures, every change in the psychological, political and general climate of the environment. In other words, I treated each play in the same way that a dream has to be analyzed, giving full attention to each detail of its structure and sequence, but always holding on to the story, and thus arriving at its meaning as a whole.

If my reader follows this procedure, he will read the work as a running psychological commentary on the three plays. In this way he might reexperience them as Shakespeare's grand opus, by which the playwright liberated himself from "original sin" [1] and gained his royal self.

[1] In contrast to Hamlet's statement to Ophelia: "For virtue cannot so inoculate our old stock but we shall relish of it." (III.i.120)

Shakespeare's ROYAL SELF

Hamlet

A DRAMA OF
HAUNTED MAN

*Hamlet's true hero is man—haunted man—man with his mind on
the frontier of two worlds, man unable either quite to reject or
quite to admit the supernatural, man struggling to get something
done as man has struggled from the beginning, yet incapable of
achievement because of his inability to understand either himself
or his fellows or the real quality of the universe which has
produced him.*

C. S. LEWIS

For more than three centuries Shakespeare's play, *Hamlet,
Prince of Denmark,* has fired the imagination of many and has
produced continual and varied interpretations—so that Brandes,
in his 1907 edition of *Hamlet,* could remark that the literature
on *Hamlet* was larger than the national literature of some of the

smaller European nations. Since 1907 the literature has probably doubled. This speaks for the vitality of the play and indicates that as a whole it has become a genuine symbol—something which expresses a universal truth of the human psyche. This play has created as much intellectual and emotional interest through the centuries as is usually generated only by religious dogma. It is therefore of the greatest importance to find out what the play is about, what Hamlet's character is, what particular philosophy Shakespeare expresses in the play, and what the other, subsidiary themes are.

Although modern scholarship has attempted, insofar as it is possible, to establish a correct text of *Hamlet,* the one that Shakespeare himself intended, these efforts have led to the conclusion that such a text cannot be established for every word. But we know where the cruxes lie and where there are textual uncertainties. Thus scholarship has provided a text as reliable as possible considering the conditions under which Shakespeare's play was printed.

Beyond this technical, though very necessary work, scholars and poets have of course given us their interpretations and evaluations. As could only be expected, *Hamlet* has been considered by most to be a great play, a magnificent work of art, even Shakespeare's greatest play. However, there have also been other opinions by men of considerable stature. For example, T. S. Eliot says:[1]

> The play (*Hamlet*) is most certainly an artistic failure. . . . Shakespeare tackled a problem which proved too much for him.

And along the same lines, W. F. Trench writes:[2]

> We find it hard, with Shakespeare's help, to understand Hamlet: even Shakespeare, perhaps, found it hard to understand him: Hamlet himself finds it impossible to understand himself. Bet-

[1] *The Sacred Wood: Essays on Poetry and Criticism* (Methuen & Co., Ltd., London, 1920), pp. 98, 102.
[2] *Shakespeare's Hamlet: A New Commentary* (Smith, Elder & Co., London, 1913), p. 115.

ter able than other men to read the hearts and motives of others, he is yet quite unable to read his own.

It is almost impossible to deal with literary and textual problems in Shakespeare without introducing psychological viewpoints and, unavoidably, the scholar's and poet's own psychology enters deeply into such considerations. It has been said of Coleridge, for example, that in analyzing Hamlet he described himself much more than he did Hamlet. There are modern Shakespearean scholars who are fully aware of the new insights which modern depth psychology has afforded and have introduced them into their interpretations, achieving thereby a deeper understanding of the plays as a result of their research into the unconscious. Chief among such scholars is Wolfgang Clemen, who remarks that, from our modern viewpoint, we are much more aware of the complexities and contradictions of the human psyche than was the nineteenth century.[3]

And yet, representatives of modern depth psychology have dealt comparatively little with *Hamlet*. There are a few important remarks in Freud's *Interpretation of Dreams*. Claiming that

[3] Rowohlt's bilingual edition of *Hamlet* (Hamburg, 1957), p. 237: "Vom Blickwinkel gegenwärtiger Seelenkunde aus, die von der Widersprüchlichkeit und Komplexität des menschlichen Charakters mehr weiss als das 19. Jahrhundert, sind wir vielleicht heute eher imstande, auf eine Festlegung von Hamlets Charakter nach dieser oder jener Richtung hin ganz zu verzichten und Shakespeares Geheimnis in der Darstellung dieses Charakters gerade darin zu sehen, dass er selbst eine solche Fixierung vermieden hat, um uns desto mehr durch die Wahrheit des einzelnen Eindrucks zu überzeugen, uns zu fesseln durch die Lebendigkeit, mit der sich in den verschiedenen Situationen der Charakter aus einer jeweils neuen Lage heraus äussert und entwickelt." ("From the standpoint of contemporary psychological knowledge, which knows more about the contradictions and complexities of the human character than did the nineteenth century, we are today perhaps in a better position to put aside any attempt to ascertain Hamlet's character with finality in accordance with this or that line of thought, and to see that the secret of Shakespeare's portrayal of this character resides precisely in the fact that he himself avoided anything so hard and fast in order that we may be the more convinced by the truth of each single expression and in order to hold our attention by means of the lifelikeness with which, in different situations, his character is expressed and developed through each new development of the plot.")

his interpretation referred exclusively to the deepest layer in the soul of the creative poet, Freud wrote:[4]

> In *Hamlet* (the basic wish-phantasy of the child) remains repressed, and we learn of its existence . . . only through the inhibitory effects which proceed from it. . . . Hamlet is able to do anything but take vengeance upon the man who did away with his father and has taken his father's place with his mother —the man who shows him in realization the repressed desires of his own childhood. The loathing which should have driven him to revenge is thus replaced by self-reproach, by conscientious scruples, which tell him that he himself is no better than the murderer whom he is required to punish.

Ernest Jones, Freud's disciple and biographer, has written a learned book, *Hamlet and Oedipus,* elaborating Freud's ideas. Jones says: [5]

> It is but fitting that Freud should have solved the riddle of this Sphinx, as he has that of the Theban one.

Although Jones is not inclined to speak of Hamlet in clinical terms, he nevertheless diagnoses him as a "severe case of hysteria on a cyclothymic basis." Further:[6]

> What must have operated in Hamlet's infancy is *still operating.* . . . Hamlet had in years gone by, as a child, bitterly resented having had to share his mother's affection even with his own father, had regarded him as a rival, and had secretly wished him out of the way so that he might enjoy undisputed and undisturbed the monopoly of that affection. If such thoughts had been present in his mind in childhood days they evidently would have been "repressed," and all traces of them obliterated, by filial piety and other educative influences. The actual realization of his early wish in the death of his father at the hands of a jealous rival would then have stimulated into activity these "re-

[4] Sigmund Freud, *The Interpretation of Dreams* (Modern Library edition, Random House, New York, 1950), pp. 163-164.
[5] W. W. Norton, New York, 1949, p. 22fn.
[6] *Ibid.,* pp. 69-70.

pressed" memories, which would have produced, in the form of depression and other suffering, an obscure aftermath of his childhood's conflict. This is at all events the mechanism that is actually found in the real Hamlets who are investigated psychologically.

Jones's final thought is:[7]

> It is only fitting that the greatest work of the world-poet should have had to do with the deepest problem and the intensest conflict that have occupied the mind of man since the beginning of time—the revolt of youth and of the impulse to love against the restraint imposed by the jealous eld.

It seems to me that the Freudian theory only provides a Procrustes bed for Shakespeare's play. The great value of Freud's and Jones's statements is in their emphasis on the incest complex as an important portion of Hamlet's psychology. We shall see, however, how this insight has to be integrated with other, larger aspects of the play.

Analytical psychology is especially interested in drama as a form of expression, because of its relationship to "active imagination," a method developed by C. G. Jung to bring unconscious material into consciousness.[8] In order to clarify certain problems, contents of the unconscious are *personified* and dramatically confronted with each other. Discussions and interactions occur between and among such imaginary figures who, though they move with a certain autonomy, are experienced as being part of one's own psyche. The individual enters the discussion with these figures, with the result that his conscious ego and the personified contents of his unconscious are mutually affected. If one reads examples of such active imagination, and particularly if they happen to be written in poetic language, one is struck by their similarity to a play that is accepted as a work of art. As a

[7] *Ibid.,* p. 179.
[8] See "The Technique of Differentiation between the Ego and the Figures of the Unconscious," *Two Essays on Analytical Psychology,* Vol. 7 of the Collected Works (New York, Pantheon Books [Bollingen Series XX], 1953), p. 210.

rule, however, active imagination has no artistic value; its purpose is to enliven the unconscious and make internal conflicts conscious. One of the important differences between active imagination and a stage play is that in active imagination the conscious ego is involved and interacts with the figures in the *drame interieur.* The experiences which analytical psychologists have had with active imagination, on the other hand, open a particular door to Shakespeare's creative life.

It has been noted that Shakespeare dealt with important problems of existence in each of his plays. An author like S. L. Bethel,[9] for instance, assumes that when writing a play Shakespeare dealt with a problem of existence. In other words, the writing of a play must have had the same function for Shakespeare as active imagination does for a modern man, and must have had a tremendous effect on his own psychology. Many of his plays represent an *Auseinandersetzung* (confrontation and clarification) with figures from the objective psyche. His work becomes art because a consciously creating will gives a meaningful order to the characters, events, ideas and emotions. (In active imagination, no attempt at order or quality of expression is made.) The objection that Shakespeare wrote plays for the theater, for an audience, and therefore would not express in them his own problems can be met by the fact that whatever he wrote would have been a projection, a throwing-out of something from his own soul (not necessarily of his own ego). The long-lasting significance of Shakespeare's plays rests on the fact that in dealing with his own problems through the medium of art, he also dealt with universal problems of the human soul in one of the most compelling of art forms.

Active imagination is always accompanied by a sense of participating in a mystery, because the unconscious contents rise autonomously and never fully reveal their meaning. It can be said without exaggeration that most of Shakespeare's plays convey the quality of mystery; in *Hamlet* mystery is the essence of the play. Hamlet is deeply concerned with the mystery of his own soul. He himself says to his friends:

[9] *The Winter's Tale: A Study* (Staples Press, London, 1947), p. 118.

> You would play upon me; you would seem to   (III.ii.387)
> know my stops; you would pluck out the heart of my mystery.

Ernest Jones considers this mystery to be a "sphinx," but to him a sphinx is like a mathematical riddle which can be completely solved. In this sense there is no mystery in *Hamlet* that can be totally translated into rational terms. I believe that Freud and Jones pointed in the right direction, but their views appear limited and not always warranted by the text. There is no indication in the text that childhood fantasies play any role.

Other commentators have made significant contributions. Bernard Grebanier, in his *The Heart of Hamlet,*[10] clarifies in many details whole scenes of the play, but he fails in his attempt at understanding the mystery because he feels that everything in the play can be explained. The result is not the heart of Hamlet, but a dry and somewhat lifeless copy. Harold C. Goddard's essay on *Hamlet* in *The Meaning of Shakespeare*[11] is much more satisfactory because he includes the unconscious in his analysis. Unfortunately, he also makes occasional dogmatic statements about the play (although not to the extent of Grebanier) and thereby reduces its mystery. Many other books and articles on *Hamlet* convey a great deal of insight into certain aspects and details of the play, but only a few authors have allowed the mystery of the play its full effect. I will not attempt to explain the mystery in *Hamlet,* but rather circumambulate it and emphasize one feature which, because it is psychic, increases the mystery rather than reduces it.

Hamlet is a mystery in the sense that a quality of the soul is conveyed which, although it can be experienced, can only approximately be translated into conscious language. Like every other work of art, *Hamlet* is a symbolon, an organic whole. Through its action and imagery it expresses a meaningful sequence of events but, perhaps to an even greater extent, it points to an unknown and possibly unknowable reality from which all events and all actions spring. Saying it another way, it is a living

---

[10] Thomas Y. Crowell Co., New York, 1960.
[11] University of Chicago Press, Chicago, 1951. Vol. 1, p. 331.

Gestalt that receives its life from a mysterious center which gives permanent meaning to all its words and actions. It lives in Hamlet's soul, expressing itself in his environment and in dramatic action. The two factors which are emphasized again and again throughout the play are the incestuous marriage of Claudius and the phenomenon of the Ghost. They throw a strong light on the mystery in the play and from them an understanding of Hamlet's personality can be achieved.

For centuries the discussion has raged around the nature of Hamlet's character. *Character* refers to static, habitual behavior.[12] I do not believe, however, that Hamlet's character can be described in any definite manner, because drama in general, and this play in particular, deals with a dynamic *process*. There is a continuous change in Hamlet's psychology. Some modern psychological conceptions define character as a dynamic process; only in this sense is it possible to speak of Hamlet's character. I will therefore make limited use of this term. From the dramatic point of view, the dynamic *development* of Hamlet's personality is what interests reader and audience. The key to Hamlet's "character" rests in its complexity. Any simplification—as was done in the *Hamlet* film by Sir Laurence Olivier who, in his introduction declared Hamlet "the man who could not make up his mind"—violates the essence of the play.

Act One

i

Heinrich Heine stated:[1]

> The exposition in Shakespeare's tragedies is admirable. In the first introductory scenes we are taken out of our profane work-

---

[12] See Hans Bender, "Charakter und Schicksal," *Neue Wissenschaft*, II. Jahrgang, 1962/63, Heft 3, p. 97: "We define character as the personal, individual essence of a human being (*Wessenart*). It is that which is relatively constant in the essence and behavior of a person."

[1] *Shakespeares Mädchen und Frauen* (H. Delloye, Paris, 1839), p. 146.

aday feelings and professional thinking, and are transported into the myth of those immense events with which the poet intends to shake and purify our souls.

It is also a rule in the interpretation of dreams that the first sentence of the dream brings the exposition of the problem with which the dream is dealing. There is a deep kinship between the unconscious and the drama. Every longer dream is a fully developed drama, and theatrical drama satisfies us best when it places on the stage those inner conflicts which have been going on eternally in the human heart. We would therefore not go too far in assuming that the first scene, possibly even the first line, in one of Shakespeare's plays has a particular importance. Harry Levin, in his book, *The Question of Hamlet*,[2] takes the first line, "Who's there?" as the theme for a collection of valuable essays on the play. This line fittingly introduces us to the problem. The vast literature on the question of Hamlet's character certainly proves that we are never quite sure who is really there. The atmosphere of mystery and dread immediately strikes us. C. S. Lewis has described it beautifully:[3]

> The mystery is not in Hamlet's motives but rather in that darkness which enwraps Hamlet and the whole tragedy and all who read or watch it. It is a mysterious play in the sense of being a play about a mystery.

The mystery is immediately deepened by brief remarks about the "bitter cold" and the "quiet guard." Francisco is called an "honest soldier," and the dread that we feel in these men standing the midnight watch is increased when Horatio enters, at first only dimly seen. He asks the question:

What, has this thing appeared again to-night?   (I.i.21)

[2] Oxford University Press, New York, 1959.
[3] *Hamlet, the Prince or the Poem,* Annual Shakespeare Lecture of the British Academy (Humphrey Milford Amen House, Great Britain, 1942), p. 11.

With this, the theme of the play is plainly announced. This "thing" is a ghost.[4] It is of greatest importance to realize that this first scene is devoted to an extensive and dramatic discussion of the Ghost, and that we see Prince Hamlet only in the second scene. In other words, the exposition of the play deals exclusively with the Ghost and with circumstances elaborating on general and particular aspects of the Ghost. First, the watchers discuss whether this Ghost is a reality or a fantasy. Marcellus, who *has* seen the Ghost, says of Horatio:

> Horatio says 'tis but our fantasy,   (I.i.23)
> And will not let belief take hold of him.

In their further dicussion, just as Bernardo begins to tell of his experience with it, the Ghost enters. It looks exactly "like the King that's dead." Marcellus wants Horatio to speak to it because he is a scholar, but doubting Horatio reacts with: "It harrows me with fear and wonder." Horatio then addresses the Ghost, but his repeated attempts to make it speak have no effect. The Ghost walks silently away. Bernardo says, "See, it stalks away."

Fear and wonder are emotions characteristically associated with the appearance of an unconscious content in consciousness, which on account of its particular nature overwhelms consciousness.[5] These emotions always indicate that an archetype is contacting consciousness. Such experiences are called "numinous" experiences. Everything in this scene emphasizes the numinosity of the occurrence. The loneliness, the icy cold, the time (midnight) make everyone susceptible to the entrance of uncon-

---

[4] From R. A. Schröder's literary and political viewpoint, the Ghost is the only tragic hero in *Hamlet,* because he is the only continually acting and advancing tool of fate, who is driven at the same time by his desire for vengeance. In achieving his vengeance, he also destroys his royal house, and his throne is taken over by the son of that king whom he had subjected in his lifetime. *Gesammelte Werke II* (Suhrkamp Verlag, Berlin, 1952), p. 295.

[5] See C. G. Jung, *The Archetypes and the Collective Unconscious,* Vol. 9 (1) of the Collected Works (Pantheon Books [Bollingen Series XX], New York, 1959), p. 39.

scious contents. After the Ghost leaves, Bernardo is perfectly
justified in asking Horatio:

> . . . you tremble and look pale.   (I.i.53)
> Is not this something more than fantasy?
> What think you on't?

Horatio, a skeptic and a rationalist, who at the beginning of this
scene had humorously presented himself as not being complete
("a piece of him"), has to admit the reality of the experience:

> . . . I might not this believe   (I.i.56)
> Without the sensible and true avouch
> Of mine own eyes.

With this frank admission by Horatio, the reality of the Ghost is
firmly established. This line convincingly refutes the assumption
made by some scholars that the Ghost in *Hamlet* is nothing
more than a theatrical trick. On the contrary, it is of the essence
of the play that psychic reality, and in particular the world of the
dead, is as valid as the world of the living. It is also immediately
understood that such an invasion by the dead into the world of
the living indicates an unusual condition—the existence of an
illness. Therefore, Horatio draws the proper conclusion when he
says:

> . . . in the gross and scope of mine opinion,   (I.i.68)
> This bodes some strange eruption to our state.

Among its different meanings the term "eruption" has a medical meaning for Shakespeare, as can be seen from *The First Part
of King Henry IV* (III.i.28): "Diseased nature oftentimes
breaks forth in strange eruptions." Caroline Spurgeon[6] has
shown that images of disease occur frequently in *Hamlet*. Disease is emphasized not only in the dramatic events but in the
language itself, which is permeated with this quality. We are

[6] *Shakespeare's Imagery and What It Tells Us* (Cambridge University
Press [American edition by Beacon Press, Boston], 1958).

constantly reminded that Shakespeare wanted to express the inner process in Hamlet as an illness, a contagion, which affects individuals as well as the collective situation. Here in the first scene, Horatio gives a careful, condensed description of the political condition of the country, the result of the conflict between "our valiant Hamlet" and Fortinbras of Norway. He sees the appearance of the Ghost as causally connected with the political situation, an "eruption" of a disease which afflicts "our state." The world of political life and the world of the psyche are intimately connected. The Ghost is an indication of a serious disease existing in the state of Denmark. The idea is amplified by Horatio's comparison of the apparition with conditions in the "most high and palmy state of Rome" before Julius Caesar's murder:

> . . . the sheeted dead (I.i.115)
> Did squeak and gibber in the Roman streets.

Horatio believes that the return of the dead has something to do with a serious disturbance in the state, and sees them as:

> . . . precurse of fierce events, (I.i.121)
> As Harbingers preceding still the fates.

The Ghost silently reappears. Again Horatio, gathering his courage, decides to confront it.

> I'll cross it, though it blast me. Stay, illusion! (I.i.127)
> If thou hast any sound, or use of voice,
> Speak to me;
> If thou art privy to thy country's fate,
> Which happily foreknowing may avoid,
> O! speak.

But the Ghost seems to move quite suddenly from place to place. The "cock crows" and it disappears. The three, Marcellus, Bernardo and Horatio, deeply moved by what they have just experienced, discuss the apparition. Marcellus fears they did it "wrong, being so majestical, to offer it the show of violence." For it is a psychic content: it is "as the air, invulnerable." Marcellus believes that it wanted to speak but that the crowing of the cock prevented it.

Horatio accepts this explanation and even amplifies it. However, he also believes that "it started like a guilty thing." They are not sure what to call it. For Marcellus, ghosts belong to the realm of evil spirits. They cannot make an appearance at times when "our Savior's birth is celebrated." Such "nights are wholesome" in contrast with this one. With the disappearance of the Ghost, the skeptic in Horatio gains the upper hand and so he says:

So have I heard and do in part believe it. (I.i.165)

They decide to inform Prince Hamlet of their experience "as needful" in their "loves" and "duty."

Before they have a chance, however, there is a scene in which Claudius discusses the political situation from his point of view as king, and in which Hamlet appears. We will postpone our inquiry into the nature of this "thing" (the Ghost, which Horatio calls "illusion") until Horatio and Marcellus tell Hamlet of their experience and Hamlet himself has his encounter with the Ghost.

ii

Hamlet has been called one of the "slow" plays of Shakespeare because there is a great deal of meditation and reflection; the principal deed is interfered with quite often and delayed for some time. The scene in which the Ghost appears to Marcellus, Bernardo and Horatio, and the scene in which it appears to Hamlet and reveals its murder, are separated by a long scene in which King, Queen, Attendants—among them Polonius and Laertes—and also Hamlet make their first appearance. Its function is to introduce us to most of the important characters in the play and to describe the condition of consciousness at the court.

The King remarks on the collective condition of the country

which has come about as a result of King Hamlet's recent death. In those days of the feudal state, the well-being of a country depended to the highest degree on the condition of the king. King and country were almost identical. For Shakespeare, the king had a particular mana and, in his psychological meaning, approached the quality of a god. King and god were not quite identical as in old Egypt, but in many respects the king was lifted high above ordinary human beings, even above his vassals. Therefore, the death of a king was always an event which shook the fundaments of the entire country. In his speech from the throne, King Claudius refers to this situation and says that as a result of the recent death of the old king, young Fortinbras of Norway considers Denmark weak.

> Holding a weak supposal of our worth, (I.ii.18)
> Or thinking by our late dear brother's death
> Our state to be disjoint and out of frame,

Fortinbras feels that he could force

> . . . the surrender of those lands (I.ii.23)
> Lost by his father, with all bands of law,
> To our most valiant brother.

The King speaks of the former king as "dear brother" and of his newly-married queen as his "sometime sister, now our queen." Neither the grief over his brother's death, nor the joy over his marriage to his late brother's wife comes from the heart. His feelings are something that he can manipulate:

> . . . that it us *befitted* (I.ii.2)
> To bear our hearts in grief.

He tries to express his emotions in a manner most suitable for the occasion. In so doing, he uses pairs of words whose meanings actually cancel each other out. They are so-called oxymora, and in this particular situation they jar our feelings. For example:

Have we, as 'twere with a *defeated joy,*   (I.ii.10)
With an *auspicious* and a *dropping* eye,
With *mirth in funeral* and with *dirge in marriage* . . .

Although his wedding followed the funeral of the late king in quick succession, the emotion of mirth cannot ordinarily arise at a funeral, nor would a dirge be sung in marriage. This imagery immediately gives away the insincerity and falseness of the King's feelings and shocks our ears. This king has something to hide; he is a divided personality.

Kittredge says:[7]

> This speech (1-39) deserves careful study with reference to the character of Claudius, which is often misconceived. Its artificial style and balanced antithesis are not the effects of hypocrisy, but merely of ceremony. Being the King's first speech from the throne since his coronation, it is formal and dignified, especially so through 1.16—the end of the King's acknowledgment of the aid of his advisers. Then follows, in a style still dignified but less stilted, an account of the business for which this particular council has been assembled. Lines 17-25 sum up facts already known to the Council, and the rest of the speech concerns the dispatching of Voltemand and Cornelius as ambassadors to Norway. The whole address is appropriate, skilfully constructed, and even eloquent. It gives the audience a high idea of the intellectual powers of the King, whom we as yet have no reason to suspect or to dislike.

I agree with Kittredge's emphasis on the formality and ceremony of this speech, the "artificial style and balanced antithesis," but the speech nevertheless reveals the insincerity of Claudius' feelings and his attempt to suppress his emotions.

While he is still delivering his royal address, Voltemand and Cornelius enter. Politically, Claudius is clever. Like a good statesman, he sends these two to Norway as ambassadors. In a letter he hands over to them, he instructs them to prevent any threat to Denmark:

[7] *Hamlet,* Edited by George Lyman Kittredge (Ginn & Company, New York, 1939), p. 139.

> . . . we have here writ   (I.ii.27)
> To Norway, uncle of young Fortinbras,
> Who, impotent and bed-rid, scarcely hears
> Of this his nephew's purpose, to suppress
> His further gait herein.

Now the King gives his attention to Polonius and Laertes. A father-son relationship is revealed, in which the son displays absolute obedience to the father, and also to the King. Young Laertes cannot leave the country without the express permission of his father and of the King. After hearing Polonius pronounce in a long, tortuous sentence that he has given *his* consent, the King easily and happily agrees. This incident places in strong relief the very different relationship between the King and Hamlet. Hamlet also wishes to leave the country, but when Claudius turns to him, addressing him as "my cousin Hamlet, and my son," Hamlet bursts out with a puzzling and many-faceted line —the first words he speaks in the play:

> A little more than kin, and less than kind!   (I.ii.65)

This is the first inkling we have of the complex, profound nature of Hamlet and of his conflict. Because of his hostility toward Claudius, he resents being called even "cousin," a term which in Elizabethan England meant a close relative, more distant than brother or sister and most frequently referring to nephew or niece. Hamlet implies that by his mother's marriage to Claudius he has become much more than just a close blood relative of the King. He has become a son, and yet he is less than affectionate and loving. "Kind" taken as a noun means that he is also different in his natural disposition or character; he is a totally different species (kind) from Claudius.

Both the King and Queen have noticed Hamlet's melancholy. The King refers to it in an image:

> How is it that the clouds still hang on you?   (I.ii.66)

Hamlet, taking the image literally, replies with an ambiguous image: "I am too much in the sun." As Kittredge explains:[8] "More in the position of a *son* than I wish I were!" J. Dover Wilson[9] adds that "in the sun" is a reference to the proverb:

> "Out of God's blessing into a warm sun,"—from an exalted, or honorable, state or occupation to a low or ignoble one.

In another place he explains it as:[10]

> "Out of house and home, outlawed, disinherited."

Kittredge further comments:[11]

> Before Claudius can reply, the Queen interposes and thus gives him a chance to ignore Hamlet's taunt. He is glad to let it pass, for he is determined, for her sake, to be on friendly terms with his stepson.

The Queen begs her son to "cast thy nighted color off," as if a depression were something that could be put on or off like a coat. She emphasizes the common fate of man:

> All that lives must die,   (I.ii.72)
> Passing through nature to eternity.

Hamlet agrees, so the Queen questions:

> If it be,   (I.ii.74)
> Why seems it so particular with thee?

Hamlet picks up the word "seems":

> Nay, it *is;* I know not "seems."   (I.ii.75)

In contrast to the King, whom it "befitted to bear (his heart) in grief," Hamlet shows that he is *really* grieving, that one cannot judge from his "inky cloak" alone:

[8] *Ibid.,* p. 143.
[9] *New Shakespeare Hamlet* (Cambridge Univ. Press, 1957), p. 286.
[10] *Ibid.,* p. 150.
[11] *Op. cit.,* p. 143.

> 'Tis not alone my inky cloak . . . (I.ii.77)
> Together with all forms, moods, shapes of grief
> That can denote me truly. These indeed seem,
> For they are actions that a man might play;
> But I have that within which passeth show—
> These but the trappings and the suits of woe.

In this context, so early in the play, Hamlet emphasizes his true grief in contrast to the seeming and formal grief of the royal couple. He frankly declares that there is a genuine human quality in himself, something that *truly* grieves—something not defined yet—as opposed to the "trappings and the suits of woe." He points to a contrast between true being and make-believe.[12] He is convinced that he is true and that the others put a cloak around their true feelings. He sees it as a contrast, not yet a conflict. It is, however, a first indication of a far deeper conflict, not about feelings and the show of feelings, but about the question of his true nature. How does he react to the situation which he finds at the court and in the whole country? What feelings, thoughts and emotions are aroused by it? How does it influence him? And, finally, can he maintain that within which "passeth show"?

We now see that the King misunderstands Hamlet. Is it because he cannot understand Hamlet at all, that they are too different in their kind? Or does the King not want to understand? At any rate, he continues in the same old vein, speaking of "mourning duties," as if Hamlet were grieving just because it is the custom to mourn the death of one's father. In his long speech, Claudius criticizes Hamlet severely, speaks of "unmanly grief," as if Hamlet—or, for that matter, anyone—could change true grief by will. He is obviously irritated by Hamlet's attitude and, in some heat, says:

> . . . We pray you throw to earth (I.ii.106)
> This unprevailing woe.

12 See Wolfgang Clemen, "Sein und Schein," *Kommentar zu Shakespeares Richard III* (Vandenhoeck & Ruprecht, Göttingen, 1957), p. 201; Theodore Spencer, *Shakespeare and the Nature of Man* (Macmillan Co., New York, 1942).

He asks Hamlet to think of him "as a father," promises him a wonderful position at court, assures him of his love—and yet refuses to give Hamlet permission to leave the country to go "back to school in Wittenberg."

Hamlet seems unconvinced. His mother addresses him in a very different vein than Claudius. She utters her request as prayers. Hamlet consents to stay at court out of obedience to his mother, not to the King. Claudius, who has just used the strongest means of forceful persuasion, refers to Hamlet's obedience as:

> This gentle and unforced accord of Hamlet   (I.ii.123)

and finds it good reason to celebrate with drink and cannon:

> And the King's rouse the heaven shall bruit again,   (I.ii.127)
> Re-speaking earthly thunder.

Hamlet is now left alone. His conflict, dimly revealed in his "more than kin and less than kind," is now spelled out in his first monologue. He is deeply depressed, wishes that his existence would dissolve "into a dew." He would even like to commit suicide, but his profound religious belief ("the Everlasting had . . . fix'd His canon 'gainst self-slaughter") prevents that. His depression is not pathological. It is a reactive depression, that is, one that is caused by external facts or a situation. In such a case the depression is proportionate to the factor which causes the depression and is therefore justified by the condition in which the ego finds itself, and is psychologically understandable. In Hamlet's case, the depression is perfectly justified by the situation he finds at court on his return from Wittenberg:

> That it should come to this!   (I.ii.137)
> But two months dead! nay, not so much, not two:
> . . . and yet, within a month—
> . . . married with my uncle,
> My father's brother.

Every depression represents a condition in which the ego is depressed to the level of the unconscious. In a pathological depression the contents are usually of a bizarre nature. In a psychological depression the contents are well associated with each other, follow an inner logic and have a corresponding feeling tone. They are always psychologically understandable. Functionally, a depression has the same significance for the psyche as a fever for the biological organism. It is a state which assists healing. Psychologically, this healing is made possible by bringing contents out of the unconscious, or enabling consciousness to receive and work upon contents of the unconscious which otherwise would not be accessible. In the case of Hamlet, his consciousness is confronted with a very unpleasant and highly emotion-charged situation, and the depression helps him to appreciate fully the complex of affairs at the court and to gain clarity about it. This influx of unconscious contents, with their powerful accompanying emotions, can overwhelm the ego and threaten to dissolve it. In Hamlet, a firm nucleus of strength remains in the ego because of his acknowledgment of the Divine, and so the disastrous dissolution of ego cannot occur. But the libido is withdrawn from the world; it seems to Hamlet "weary, stale, flat, and unprofitable." It is to him like an "unweeded garden." And then he reveals the reason for his melancholy: the severe shock he has suffered at the recent marriage of his mother. Up to that moment, his father and mother had appeared as exceedingly wonderful people, and their relationship as having been filled with an ideal love—"and yet, within a month" after his father's death, this most wonderful mother had married his father's brother. It is obvious that Hamlet's world had been represented by his parents and that he had had an ideal image of them. However, the reality of his parents could not agree with this image. His mother's remarriage forced him to withdraw suddenly that wonderful projection and, with that, woman became a questionable entity for him: "Frailty, thy name is woman!"

To Hamlet, this marriage is a great crime, a serious disturbance in the universe. His own inner world trembles like an earthquake because the image of his mother, who carried for him the feminine principle, has suddenly turned from shining white to stark black. Even worse for him, however, is that he, "who passeth show," is forced to "hold his tongue." The whole situation fills him with dread for the future:

> It is not, nor it cannot come to good.   (I.ii.158)

This monologue gives us perfectly good reasons why a highly intelligent and sensitive young man of native integrity should be thoroughly depressed to the edge of suicide. He is confronted with facts that are known to everyone at court. Evidently everyone else has accepted the marriage without qualms; it appears that for political reasons the counselors have even approved of it. Hamlet alone is repelled by the situation. In this condition, he cannot vent his feelings or consider any line of action. In his own psychology, the greatest trauma is the breakdown of the anima image. Up to this time it has been projected upon the mother; now he sees only the dark, incestuous and immoral side of it. With this sudden change, the possibility of a trusting relationship with any woman has become impossible.

A depression always indicates that libido has sunk into the unconscious and has there activated images of the unconscious; they will appear on the inner stage. It is natural that the image of the father, who to Hamlet represents in many ways an ideal, would then appear on this inner stage. It is at this moment that his friends, Horatio, Marcellus and Bernardo, visit Hamlet. Evidently he has not seen them for a long time and so, naturally, he asks them, "What is your affair in Elsinore?" Some bitter remarks are then made about his mother's wedding, and when Horatio says that he came to see Hamlet's "father's funeral," Hamlet responds with:

> My father, methinks I see my father.   (I.ii.184)

This innocuous remark, which is the natural result of Hamlet's meditation, astonishes Horatio because, for a moment, it must have struck him as a possibility that Hamlet might also have seen the Ghost. So he asks, "O! where, my lord?" Somewhat taken aback, Hamlet answers, "In my mind's eye." In this way, Horatio finds a natural entree for cautiously bringing up the subject of the Ghost:

> My lord, I think I saw him yesternight. (I.ii.189)

It is Hamlet's turn to be astonished. Calling upon Marcellus and Bernardo as witnesses, Horatio then describes the appearance of the Ghost:

> A figure like your father, (I.ii.199)
> . . . Goes slow and stately by.

He speaks of the two men's "oppress'd and fear-surprised eyes," and tells Hamlet how on the third night he kept watch with them and saw this phenomenon himself. Again, he calls it "the thing" and "the apparition."

Here perhaps is the best opportunity to discuss the Ghost from a psychological point of view. The Elizabethans certainly had a strong belief in ghosts, spirits, fairies, etc.[13] The clearest proof is James I's book on demonology. Such things were accepted as reality in those days. Shakespeare shared these ideas but he evidently had personal experience of them also. In *Hamlet,* as well as in *Macbeth* and other plays, he went far beyond the concepts of his time. He did not represent ghosts simply as objective phenomena but as psychic reality with a decisive and transforming effect on the individual.

The ghost phenomenon and its effect upon Hamlet agree very closely with the findings of analytical psychology in regard to the autonomy of complexes and archetypes. Briefly one could characterize these findings in this way: the ghost is a *psychic* phenomenon which is experienced by certain individuals as having an objective existence. We have no way of proving objectively

[13] Sherman Yellen, "The Psychic World of William Shakespeare," *International Journal of Parapsychology,* Vol. IV, No. 3, 1962; Louis Lavater, *Of Ghostes and Spirites Walking by Night* (London, 1572).

the existence or non-existence of ghosts. All we have are statements of certain individuals that they have had such an experience. The ghost behaves like a psychological complex. It appears that it has more autonomy than ordinary psychological
complexes. Such ghost complexes usually develop after the
death of some close relative. Besides their autonomy—that is,
their independent behavior—they also have definite effects on
the personality of the living, varying in many ways. One possibility, for example, is a more or less intense possession of the victim's consciousness by the ghost. Accordingly, the principal result of ghost-possession is an identification of the living person
with the personality of the dead, which in its intensity differs
from case to case. At any rate, such ghost-possession tends to
make the living person more unconscious and subject to uncontrolled impulses and affects. The ghost is also related to the phenomenon of double personality. In a case of ghost-possession it
is as if two personalities were living in one body—the personality of the living and the personality of the dead. The two personalities can be in conflict with each other or coexist without too
much tension.

There are usually two psychological conditions necessary for
the invasion of a person by a ghost. One condition is that a great
similarity or unconscious identity, though latent, exists between
the personality of the living and that of the dead. The other condition is a state of dissociation. In the case of Hamlet, we find
that the marriage of his mother has caused a depression and
evoked ambivalent feelings in regard to her. His love for his
mother is mingled with intense loathing and hatred for her incestuous marriage.[14] His intuition tells him that something more is
wrong than this criminal marriage, which the counselors and
electors of state have condoned and even approved. Thus the
two typical conditions for the appearance of a ghost are present
in Hamlet—a dissociation due to wildly conflicting emotions,

[14] J. Dover Wilson explains that in Elizabethan times the marriage of a
woman with her deceased husband's brother "would of course be regarded as no marriage at all by the Church whether Protestant or Catholic."—*What Happens in Hamlet* (Cambridge Univ. Press, London, N.Y.,
1951), p. 292.

and an unconscious identity with his beloved father. His father, however, is not only his personal father, but also the King, and therefore with his death all those difficult problems arise which have always attended the change from an old king to a new one. Their nature is necessarily collective, and the transition from one king to another has been accomplished in all primitive societies, and also in high civilizations such as Egypt, by particular rites which ensure that the mana of the old king will be renewed and properly conferred on the new king. Even in our democratic society, the inauguration of a new president is a solemn occasion and God's blessing is invoked by representatives of different religions. In the case of Hamlet, the Ghost is clearly characterized as the archetype of the King. The King, as Jung has shown, always carries the archetype of the Self, and also the royal insignia of the Self—the crown, the scepter and the orb. Therefore, Hamlet's meeting with the ghost of his father also means meeting his own Self, compelling Hamlet to face himself. The encounter with the Ghost has a meaning transcending by far Hamlet's personal psychology, but this added archetypal quality also makes it more difficult for him to deal with the Ghost adequately.

Taking up the thread of the play again, we recall Hamlet's remark that he had seen his father "in (his) mind's eye." Informed that the Ghost has appeared, he now becomes highly interested and excited, and the suspicions which had been troubling his mind become focused:

> My father's spirit-in-arms? All is not well.   (I.ii.254)
> I doubt some foul play.

Yet he admonishes his soul to "sit still." He asks intense questions of his friends; it is almost an interrogation. He wants to know minute details. For instance: "What! look'd he frowningly?" "Pale or red?" He must assure himself that it was a numinous experience.

HORATIO: It would have much amaz'd you.   (I.ii.235)

("Amaz'd" is used in the Elizabethan sense of shocking astonishment.) Hamlet is most anxious to meet the Ghost himself and
swears his friends to secrecy:

> If you have hitherto concealed this sight,   (I.ii.247)
> Let it be tenable in your silence still.

iii

Before Hamlet's wish to see the Ghost is fulfilled, Shakespeare
gives us a scene which introduces Polonius and his family, a
group of characters who will have an important effect on Hamlet's life. Scene 3 of Act I begins with a conversation between
Laertes and Ophelia. Everything is ready for Laertes' departure, and he takes this opportunity to bring up the subject of his
sister's relationship to Hamlet. His speech shows that he does
not understand in the least what goes on in the girl's heart. He
naïvely assumes that his ideas and attitudes toward life and the
court must also be Hamlet's ideas. He emphasizes Hamlet's
royal position, speaks in terms of common sense and gives her
moral advice, discredits Hamlet's love for her, poisons her with
his misconstruction of the whole relationship, and instills fear
into her:

> . . . but you must fear,   (I.iii.16)
> His greatness weighed, his will is not his own.

He shatters her. Few women could stand such a destructive attack. Yet she has the strength to ask: "No more but so?"
—whereupon Laertes answers in a conciliatory way, "Perhaps
he loves you *now*," but insinuates more doubts about the genu-
ineness of Hamlet's love and gives her diplomatic advice which
destroys the natural character of her own feelings.

The same problem which Hamlet has between *is* and *seems,*
between inner truth and appearance, is shown here. In regard to
her love, Laertes advises Ophelia to undo what she is and to
appear to be what she is not. She and Hamlet truly love each
other; it is her only vital concern, the only thing which raises her

above the mire of the conditions in her home, the moral depravity of which is revealed in later scenes. This love is her strongest
value and promises a future, and is thus representative of her
emotional security. There *is* love, but Laertes persuades her that
it only *seems* so. Worldly wisdom is set against the wisdom of
the heart. Being a prince, says Laertes, Hamlet would not be his
own master in making his choice. Laertes teaches Ophelia *his*
wisdom:

> . . . so far to believe it (I.iii.25)
> As he in his particular act and place
> May give his saying deed.

He warns Ophelia not to lose her virginity ("your chaste treasure"). He even uses military imagery, exclaiming:

> Fear it, Ophelia, fear it, my dear sister, (I.iii.33)
> And keep you in the rear of your affection,
> Out of the shot and danger of desire.

Four times he uses the term "fear." He even ends by telling her:

> Best safety lies in fear. (I.iii.43)

Ophelia does not contradict or raise objections to Laertes'
long sermon. She even promises to keep "the good lesson"—but
with some humor she points out that *he* should keep this lesson
as well. She clearly knows her brother, and admonishes him to
"reck . . . his own rede." Nevertheless, Laertes' words destroy
Ophelia's trust in Hamlet, and the love which could have been
her fortress is deeply shaken. She gives up being what she truly
is—a loving woman. It is at this early stage that her consciousness begins to slip from its moorings. Here begins a process
which finally leads to a complete breakdown of consciousness,
that is, to psychosis.

At this moment Polonius enters. Wishing Laertes good luck
on his journey and giving him his blessing, he then addresses a
sermon to his son. It has become one of the most famous pas-

sages in the play. Practically every English-speaking youngster has to learn it by heart. It has been taken to express Shakespeare's moral philosophy. It is a philosophy which excellently expresses Polonius' character, but otherwise does not make much sense. How can any man live, for instance, without giving his "thoughts . . . tongue"? How can he make friends (try "their adoption") if he does not speak with them? His ideas about "proper dress" are certainly most conventional. How can anyone maintain friendly relationships without ever lending or borrowing money? It is strange that the central idea of the play — ("to thine own self be true") should be expressed by Polonius. *His* concept is surrounded by the truisms and half-truths of a dotard and, in the context, probably have nothing but a material meaning. It should be noted that the image which accompanies this advice—"as the night the day"—is particularly flat and empty. Grebanier says:[15]

> Listened to carefully, however, though containing a few acceptable platitudes, it turns out to be admirable enough as precepts for getting on in the world; but the man who followed it would certainly be cheated of experience's richest rewards. Yet the phraseology of this speech has echoed down the centuries—for no good reason. What has been the point of mouthing "And it must follow as the night the day" as though it were the sublimest instead (as Shakespeare intended) of the emptiest of images, a perfect reflection of the obvious-mindedness of the dotard who speaks it? . . . "This above all: to thine own self be true" sounds noble enough—until you realize that in context it can only mean, "Be true to your own material advantage; see to it that you line your pockets well."

But in Shakespeare, words and lines often have to be understood on different levels. I agree with Grebanier that in the context and in the manner in which Polonius relieves himself of this platitude, it has only a materialistic meaning. Nevertheless, in a perverse way, it also expresses the old Greek truth of the Delphic oracle: "Know thyself," and therefore has had so much

[15] *Heart of Hamlet,* pp. 284-285.

appeal through so many generations. Polonius certainly does not take himself seriously. He is not true to himself. He *is* a "time server." Grebanier characterizes him perfectly when he says:[16]

> He is devoid of warmth, humanity, and affection (except for his son), and gives symptoms of never having known a spiritual impulse in his life. A career of making all his acts subservient to self-advancement has in the end deadened even his practical cunning.

How difficult it is in life to be oneself is dramatized in this play by the tragic deaths of Hamlet, Polonius and Ophelia, each death the result of the individual *not* being true to himself. Hamlet takes great pains to demonstrate to Opehlia, Polonius, Claudius and his mother, in different ways, how they are not true to themselves—but he does not see where he is also a traitor to himself. Ophelia's true nature is expressed in her love for Hamlet, but she weakly accepts Laertes' and Polonius' doubts and obeys their demands to sever her relationship with him. She acts as an obedient tool of others, dividing herself from herself. Her love continues, of course, to be the center of her self and makes her conduct a complete betrayal of her life. This conflict between her true being and her actions prepares for her mind's ultimate breakdown.

We see this in the conversation immediately following between Ophelia and her father. As soon as Laertes has left, Polonius brings up the subject of "Lord Hamlet." This seems to be the first occasion on which they discuss this relationship. He is a father who does not know what is going on in his own daughter. " 'Tis put on me, and that in way of caution," he remarks, as if there were something between Hamlet and Ophelia that should shun the light of day. His suspicion is, of course, that the intimacy of the relationship has been physical, or that if it has not she has at any rate seriously endangered her reputation. Again, he uses ambiguous words about self-knowledge: "You do not understand yourself so clearly as it behoves my daughter and your honour." In this context, "understand yourself" refers to

16 *Ibid.,* p. 283.

her social position, her reputation—in other words, it has a
purely social meaning. But it also refers to her love for Hamlet.
Her feeling for Hamlet is undoubtedly strong. She has accepted
many "tenders" of Hamlet's affection, but she has not reflected
upon her love or upon the problems which would arise in regard
to her position at court. Polonius draws his conclusions from his
own psychology. To him, Hamlet's love cannot be anything but
lustful fire; in Hamlet's position as prince, and as probable future king, nothing could come of this relationship. Polonius assails her love and her self-respect. He uses military terms, just as
Laertes did:

> Set your entreatments at a higher rate   (I.iii.122)
> Than a command to parley.

With all the strength at her command, Ophelia affirms her own
as well as Hamlet's love, but she has to admit, "I do not know
. . . what I should think." Her love has no support from reflection. Therefore, Polonius' attack is successful and she un-
conditionally surrenders:

> I shall obey, my lord.   (I.iii.136)

iv

As planned, Hamlet visits Horatio and Marcellus on their night-
watch, near midnight. The icy atmosphere and the loneliness on
the platform before the castle are strikingly characterized in a
few words. The stillness of the night is interrupted only by a
flourish of trumpets and a discharge of guns, in contrast to the
expectant calm of the night air. The castle is filled with carousing
and "wassail." Hamlet profoundly resents the King's love for
wine and the bad reputation the Danes have gained because of
it. It leads him to declare:

> So, oft it chances in particular men,   (I.iv.23)
> That for some vicious mole of nature in them,
> As, in their birth . . .
> Carrying, I say, the stamp of one defect . . .

Shall in the general censure take corruption
From that particular fault: *the dram of eale*
Doth all the noble substance of a doubt,
To his own scandal.

While Hamlet is right in criticizing the King and court for this weakness, his words are also a description of his own psychology. He is a man of high virtues, great achievements—but there is some "vicious mole of nature" in him, and *his* "noble substance" will be destroyed by the "dram of eale." In other words, he has projected his own psychology upon the King and his followers. So far, Shakespeare has not given us insight into what this "vicious mole" could be in Hamlet's personality. Will his encounter with the Ghost perhaps give us a hint or a possible explanation?

Hamlet has just made this keen observation on the "dram of eale" and its deleterious effects when the Ghost makes an appearance and is seen by all three men. Hamlet, who has previously seen his father in his mind as a memory image he could revive at will, is now confronted with the Ghost as an objective phenomenon which moves and acts according to its own laws. Shakespeare uses this dramatic possibility in a manner completely consistent with Elizabethan ideas of ghosts.

Modern parapsychological literature contains many reports of psychic phenomena which have been observed by more than one person. As noted before, such statements do not prove the concrete reality of ghosts but only that two or three people have had the same experience, and that for these people it is a mutually shared experience and to that extent has objectivity for them. In our clinical work we observe "ghosts" as dream figures which have reality for the dreamer only as long as the dream lasts, and this experience is not shared with anyone else. Ghosts make their appearances in dreams most frequently shortly after the death of a close relative. Sometimes the dreamer is aware in the dream that the person is dead; sometimes he dreams that the dead has returned from a far country. This is the reason the French calls ghosts *les revenants* (the returning ones).

Psychologically speaking, a ghost is an autonomous complex

which as a rule has a negative effect upon the personality of the living. Corresponding to the ghost complex as pictured in the dream, there occur definite changes of the personality. The most frequent symptom is a tremendous feeling of guilt, usually in the form of a conviction on the dreamer's part that it is his fault in one way or another that his relative has died. Furthermore, we find that people assume to a degree certain characteristics of the dead—they think, feel and behave in a fashion similar to that of the deceased. In some cases it as if the personality of the dead would possess the living one, as if an alien psychology would permeate the living one. In psychotic conditions, we find that quite often such a complex (the image of the dead relative) is externalized and that such a patient is firmly convinced that the personality of the dead one, the ghost, is "in the other room," "knocks on the wall," "speaks to me," "accuses me," or "shouts curses at me." Occasionally one sees reports that individuals in a waking state have seen the ghost sitting in a chair or walking in a room. In all those cases which I have observed, the ghost was always seen by one individual only. In one of these cases, for instance, my patient had a number of dreams about her father who had recently died, in which she saw him as a ghost—and so did her two sisters. But it was only my patient who in a waking state once saw him sitting in a chair. I have never observed a case in which more than one person had the experience of the ghost at the same time.

This field of borderline experience has suffered so much from fraud that no scientifically proven conclusions can as yet be drawn. The reality that is referred to in all these phenomena is psychic reality, not material reality. Therefore this field has rightly been called *para-psychology;* it is a branch of psychology and the phenomena experienced are psychic. Jung, in discussing the flying saucer phenomena,[17] states that the only way we have of declaring any object or event a reality is by the concensus of more than one person, or by the *concensus omnium*. In discuss-

[17] "Flying Saucers: A Modern Myth of Things Seen in the Skies," *Civilization in Transition,* Vol. 10 of the Collected Works (Pantheon Books [Bollingen Series XX], New York, 1964), p. 307.

ing what reality is to us, he mentions that on two different occasions certain phenomena had been observed by several persons simultaneously and were therefore taken as objective reality. Later on it was proven that there was nevertheless no *material* reality to the observations.

Our practical experience demonstrates to us that the ghost is an autonomous complex and, like other complexes, radiates certain effects on consciousness, thus bringing about a change in the personality; for the individual in the grip of his experience, the ghost has an unquestionable reality. In Scene 2, Shakespeare allows us to see Hamlet's psychology before he has the ghost experience. His meeting with the Ghost then deserves our closest attention in order to see what changes occur in Hamlet as a result of the confrontation. It is a numinous experience. Hamlet instinctively calls for divine grace—"Angels and ministers of grace defend us!"—because he realizes that he is in great danger. He tries to discover the nature of this ghost, to find out from the apparition itself what its true meaning is:

> Be thou a spirit of health or goblin damn'd,   (I.iv.40)
> Bring with thee airs from heaven or blasts from hell,
> Be thy intents wicked or charitable . . .

The question facing Hamlet in this numinous experience is whether this vital content of the unconscious brings health, sanity—or insanity. Are the thoughts ("airs") creative or destructive, the intent friendly or hostile? The Ghost comes in such questionable shape. "Questionable" in the Elizabethan sense means "arousing questions." Irrespective of the Ghost's benevolent or malevolent intent, Hamlet's overwhelming desire is to *know*. Therefore, without any further doubt, he announces:

> I'll call thee Hamlet,   (I.iv.44)
> King, father; royal Dane . . .

and insists on knowing why the King, breaking all the laws of physical nature, has returned to "shake our disposition," disturb our limited consciousness ("We fools of nature"—we who only know what nature conveys to us).

When a numinous content suddenly presents itself, thoughts burst into consciousness which are "beyond the reaches of our souls." Hamlet asks:

> What may this mean,   (I.iv.51)
> That thou, dead corse, again, in complete steel,
> Revisits thus the glimpses of the moon,
> . . . we fools of nature
> So horridly to shake our disposition
> With thoughts beyond the reaches of our souls?

It is this attitude of Hamlet's which gives the play its unfathomable depth and unending fascination. C. S. Lewis says:[18]

> As soon as I find anyone treating the ghost as merely the means whereby Hamlet learns of his father's murder . . . I part company with that critic . . . Hamlet for me is no more separable from his ghost than Macbeth from his witches, Una from her lion, or Dick Whittington from his cat. The Hamlet formula, so to speak, is not a "man who has to avenge his father" but a "man who has been given a task by a ghost."

Hamlet is deeply shaken. In spite of, or *because* of its fascination, he insists on questioning the Ghost:

> Say, why is this? wherefore? what should we do?   (I.iv.57)

The Ghost beckons; Hamlet wishes to follow him to a "more removed ground." Both his friends, Horatio and Marcellus, are afraid to go deeper into this experience, but Hamlet is not afraid. On the contrary, his courage in following this experience to the end is utterly reckless. Given the possibility of knowing something about the after-death state—the *Bardo,* as the Tibetans would say—Hamlet's life means nothing to him:

[18] *Op. cit.,* p. 11.

> Why, what should be the *fear?* (I.iv.64)
> *I do not set my life at a pin's fee.*

He is supported in this imprudence by the metaphysical conviction that the soul is "immortal." A ghost, being also immortal,
cannot do Hamlet any harm. Metaphysical statements, as is well
known, can neither be proved nor disproved. The psychological
truth, however, is that the human soul can be affected for better
or for worse by contents of the unconscious. Horatio immediately counters Hamlet's foolhardy belief with a powerful warning:

> What if it tempt you toward the flood, my lord, (I.iv.69)
> Or to the dreadful summit of the cliff
> That beetles o'er his base into the sea,
> And there assume some other horrible form,
> Which might deprive your sovereignty of reason
> And draw you into madness? think of it;
> The very place puts toys of desperation,
> Without more motive, into every brain
> That looks so many fathoms to the sea
> And hears it roar beneath.

Clinical experience quite often provides us with psychological
situations in which the unconscious floods consciousness, overwhelms it with images and creates dangerous conditions. It is
not too unusual that such an inundation announces the beginning of a psychosis. The invasion of the Ghost opens the flood-
gates of the unconscious. Horatio is quite right when he says
that it might deprive Hamlet of the "sovereignty of reason" and
"draw (him) into madness." The "very place," that is, the extreme and unprotected exposure of the ego to the numinous contents of the unconscious, puts "toys of desperation . . . into
every brain that looks . . ." Those fears which Hamlet represses can very well reappear with highly intensified strength.
But Hamlet's fascination by the Ghost is uninterrupted. He is
determined to follow it. When *reason* fails, his friends try to use
physical force to stop him. How absolute Hamlet's resolve to
know the unknowable is can be seen from his exclamation:

My fate cries out,   (I.iv.82)
And makes each petty artery in this body
As hardy as the Nemean lion's nerve.
Still am I called.

and from his threat to kill his friends.

Of course one cannot object if someone feels that his fate cries out, that he is *called* to encounter a ghost. As psychologists, we would probably act as Horatio and Marcellus did. We would warn somebody, we would point out the dangers resulting from a certain course of action. But if the person felt it to be his fate, felt it as a "call"—then we must allow him to live his fate, whatever it is. Hamlet disregards the warnings of his friends and defiantly exposes himself to this peril of the soul. As a result, all those things of which Horatio warned him necessarily occur. The dramatic action of the play reveals how the flood of the unconscious reaches him, overwhelms and finally destroys him. It is the particular purpose of this analysis of *Hamlet* to describe the different stages of Hamlet's transformation, which are caused by the infiltration of the ghost complex into Hamlet's consciousness.

This scene ends with a few remarks by Hamlet to his friends, who in the darkness of the night have lost sight of him— remarks which clearly indicate the tremendous excitement with which Hamlet follows the Ghost. And so we come to the decisive encounter.

v

It appears that the fears of Hamlet's friends are not fully justified. His first words, addressed to the Ghost, "Whither wilt thou lead me? speak, I'll go no further," show that Hamlet is not willing to follow the Ghost absolutely. His ego has maintained some strength and this at last forces the Ghost to speak, so that a genuine confrontation between ego and numinous content can take place. I make this remark because it is a frequent occurrence in analytical work that fate compels the human being to confront a numinous content. Such contents are usually anima

or animus, or the Self.[19] Confrontations with ghosts are most
unusual. In the case of Hamlet, the intense numinosity of the
Ghost derives from the fact that it represents not only Hamlet's
father, but also the King, and consequently also the archetype of
the Self. The tremendous fascination which the Ghost has for
Hamlet is the result of his meeting his own Self. Psychologically,
the Ghost also represents a challenge to Hamlet to be himself
and to accept his destiny as King of Denmark, to mature from a
prince to a king. But first he has to hear more about the psychology of the Ghost. The Ghost tells him:

> My hour is almost come,   (I.v.3)
> When I to sulphurous and tormenting flames
> Must render up myself.

According to Elizabethan lore, this means that King Hamlet is
now in purgatory. This is confirmed by his later lines:

> Doom'd for a certain term to walk the night,   (I.v.10)
> And for the day confin'd to fast in fires,
> Till the foul crimes done in my days of nature
> Are burnt and purg'd away.

Hamlet's pity is aroused, but the Ghost wants none of it. He is
out for serious business; he wants revenge; and then he introduces himself: "I am thy father's spirit." But he will tell Hamlet
no more about the post-mortal state. His refusal to reveal such
secrets is accompanied with exceedingly terrifying pictures.
Hamlet's curiosity about the after-death state, which he wants
most of all to know about, is never satisfied. As we will see later,
it calls up all kinds of speculation in him. Hamlet, however, is
most anxious to receive accurate information about his father's
death. It is murder, performed in a most unusual way. It is the
perfect crime. It could never have been discovered without the
dead himself returning to tell the tale:

> 'Tis given out that, sleeping in mine orchard,   (I.v.35)
> A serpent stung me; so the whole ear of Denmark

[19] Cf. Jung, *Two Essays.*

Is by a forged process of my death
Rankly abus'd; but know, thou noble youth,
The serpent that did sting thy father's life
Now wears his crown.

Hamlet's immediate reaction is utter eagerness and readiness to "sweep to (his) revenge." The Ghost naturally is very gratified with Hamlet's willingness for revenge. He describes his brother as a lustful and extremely gifted man who, with "witchcraft of his wit . . . won to his shameful lust the will of (the) most seeming-virtuous queen." He describes himself as extremely virtuous, and his love for the Queen as having the greatest dignity. We cannot but help wonder about this self-righteous description. What were the crimes he speaks about; what were those "foul crimes done in my days of nature"? Are they, as Kittredge says:[20] "The ordinary sense of mortality which now appear to him in a more serious light than when he was alive"? Or are they crimes of "intemperance," as J. Dover Wilson says? [21] Whatever they were, Hamlet's image of King Hamlet appears at least as one-sided:

So excellent a king; that was, to this,   (I.ii.139)
Hyperion to a satyr.

Discussing the medical aspects of the murder, as described in lines 59-64, Dr. R. R. Simpson,[22] who goes into great detail, says that "a number of poisons can be and are absorbed through the intact ear." He also says:

Shakespeare's description of the action of the poison may not be scientifically accurate but it is surely the most vivid and poetical description in the whole of toxicology.

Simpson arrives at the conclusion:

[20] *Op. cit.*, p. 167.
[21] *Hamlet*, p. 160.
[22] *Shakespeare and Medicine* (E. & S. Livingstone, Ltd., Edinburgh and London, 1959), p. 138.

It would seem, therefore, that here we have the almost perfect crime. No clues were left and death was attributed to the serpent's bite, as it might well have been. No suspicion was aroused in the minds of the people. We are left to decide on the evidence supplied by the Ghost. Shakespeare almost produced the perfect crime—if it had not been for that Ghost!

This statement by a modern physician indicates that King Hamlet's murder was quite possible in the manner described by Shakespeare.

Nevertheless, the symbolic meaning of this murder is of even greater significance. In the Adam and Eve story in Genesis, the serpent is considered to be a symbol of evil, and Shakespeare uses it as such in different places. For example, Lady Macbeth tells her husband, "Be the serpent under't" (I.v.74), a reference which the commentators relate to Virgil's statement, *"anguis latet in herba."* The image in the Ghost's report is of a vicious hidden sting inflicted by the evil intentions of his brother. The sting's effect is heightened by the image of a poison instilled in the ear. It describes clearly the Ghost's influence on Hamlet himself: words, opinions, misunderstandings and misapperceptions penetrate his ear and poison his mind.

The Ghost wants revenge and asks Hamlet to take it upon himself to eradicate the evil in the royal couple:

> Let not the royal bed of Denmark be   (I.v.82)
> A couch for luxury and damned incest.

In spite of this, he also makes a contradictory demand:

> Taint not thy mind, nor let thy soul contrive   (I.v.85)
> Against thy mother aught. Leave her to heaven
> And to those thorns that in her bosom lodge
> To prick and sting her.

Finally the Ghost leaves, with the words: "Remember me."

How could Hamlet ever forget this numinous experience? The Ghost has invaded him and instilled in him a thirst for revenge.

It is a dark instinct which, heretofore, has been alien to Hamlet. Now, suddenly, he finds himself committed to pursue revenge under most difficult circumstances. He is a changed personality. The logical conclusion would therefore be that the Ghost is an evil spirit. Nevertheless, Hamlet's image of his father remains most positive. Although he has asked himself before whether the father-spirit is a devil or a good spirit, now that the father presents him with the facts, he overlooks the evil aspect because of the love and pity in him for his father, and because he already has such a dark picture of his mother. So, in spite of the evidence, he holds on to the ideal image of the father. Therefore, he cries out:

> O all you host of heaven! O earth! What else?   (I.v.92)
> And shall I couple hell? O fie! Hold, hold, my heart!

At the first appearance of the Ghost, Hamlet had cried out, "Angels and ministers of grace defend us!" Now he calls out again for the "host of heaven," but realizes that he must have the help of all three realms, which are traditional in the Christian trichotomy of the metaphysical world: heaven, earth and hell. What disturbs him is that he has to set hell in motion as well. He knows he can never forget the Ghost; on the contrary, stirred to the depths, overwhelmed by emotions of love and pity, he now surrenders completely to the Ghost's demand for revenge:

> And thy commandment all alone shall live   (I.v.102)
> Within the book and volume of my brain.

In spite of Hamlet's appeal to the "angels and ministers of grace," his own emotions and the numinosity of the experience have rendered him unconscious. He, the artist, philosopher and genius, accepts revenge as his filial duty. It is here that tragedy and inevitable fate begin their ominous course.

It is a psychological truth that one becomes what one fights. (Thus Hamlet is already changed. He accepts attitudes which are against the grain of his personality.) For example, the conquest of Greece by the Romans had the effect of Hellenizing Rome. One may also observe it on an individual level whenever someone attacks philosophies or attitudes very strongly and then later, and unknown to himself, adopts them. Hamlet's acceptance of the task of avenging his father's murder makes him immediately decide to attack Claudius. In the course of the play he then assumes more and more of the characteristics of Claudius, especially in his attitude to murder. The most astounding evidence of this change later on in the play is the cold-blooded manner in which Hamlet has Rosencrantz and Guildenstern killed:

> . . . the bearers put to sudden death,   (V.ii.46)
> Not shriving-time allow'd.

—just as the Ghost had complained of having to die

> Unhousel'd, disappointed, unanel'd,   (I.v.77)
> No reckoning made, but sent to my account.

Now that Hamlet has allowed the Ghost's desire for revenge to take complete possession of him, he also becomes fully involved with all the aspects of his mother's marriage. By now the negative image of woman is firmly fixed in his mind:

> O most pernicious woman!   (I.v.105)

And Claudius is seen as:

> O villain, villain, smiling, damned villain!   (I.v.106)

He comes to the conclusion:

> That one may smile, and smile, and be a villain.   (I.v.108)

Again, the contrast between what is and what seems to be—or, psychologically speaking, the contrast between the psychological fact of Claudius' guilt and the mantle of dignity and gaiety he shows to the world—is uppermost in Hamlet's mind. He is deeply struck by the fact that someone could commit such a crime, be so guilty, and yet act as if nothing were wrong.

What Hamlet does not see at this point is that by surrendering completely to the commandment of his father, he betrays that within him which "passeth show." Accepting his father's need for revenge, making it his own, places him in the same position as Claudius: he must "show" something which he is not and cover up what he really is. He treats the appearance of the Ghost as a secret (it may not be going too far to say a *guilty* secret). He does this because he has received the knowledge through a revelation of the unconscious and because it relates to the King who, irrespective of how he became king, is considered divine and therefore untouchable by Hamlet as well as by society. The way in which this information has come to him prevents him at first from telling even his closest friend, Horatio, that Claudius is a murderer. (Later, he *does* tell him:

There is a play to-night before the king;   (III.ii.80)
One scene of it comes near the circumstance
Which I have told thee of my father's death.)

Far less would it be possible for Hamlet to tell the court and the people and to convince them of the crime committed against his father unless he has some material proof of the King's crime. Under any circumstances, it is very difficult for any human being to contain secrets, keep them to himself. For instance, doctors who have to keep many secrets undergo characteristic psychological changes because secrets function like complexes—they become repressed contents which in an indirect way exert specific and disturbing influences on consciousness and behavior. Similar psychological changes have been observed in members of the Secret Service. To have such secrets and to be psychologically affected by them does not mean that such people become insane, but that in some way their consciousness will be under the influence of these secrets: for example, there will be an urge to reveal the secret to someone and a conscious effort must be exerted to subdue the urge.[23]

When the Ghost disappears into the "matin air," Horatio and Marcellus find Hamlet again. It would have been the most natural thing for Hamlet to have informed them at once about everything that had happened between him and the Ghost. King Hamlet had not asked for absolute secrecy. The wildness of Hamlet's emotion after the tremendous experience with the Ghost overflows and almost compels him to reveal the secret, for he exclaims:

> There's ne'er a villain dwelling in all Denmark,   (I.v.123)
> But he's an arrant knave.

After all, these friends had seen the Ghost first and had kept the secret very well. There is no reason for Hamlet to believe that they would betray the secret. It would be an act of friendship to tell them what the Ghost had said, and he would gain their help by doing so. But Hamlet wants to keep the secret to himself. He wants to get rid of his friends as quickly as possible:

> And so, without more circumstance at all,   (I.v.127)
> I hold it fit that we shake hands and part.

Naturally, Horatio is quite upset over Hamlet's rude behavior, which is not what one would expect from a friend. Hamlet apologizes for the offense, then lifts the veil of his secret just enough to say:

> Touching this vision here,   (I.v.137)
> It is an honest ghost, that let me tell you.

---

23 C. G. Jung: "Such invasions (of the unconscious) immediately constitute a painful personal secret which alienates and isolates (one) from his surroundings. It is something that we 'cannot tell' anybody. We are afraid of being accused of mental abnormality—not without reason, for much the same thing happens to lunatics. Even so, it is a far cry from the intuitive perception of such an invasion to being inundated by it pathologically, though the layman does not realize this." *Psychology and Alchemy*, Vol. 12 of the Collected Works (Pantheon Books [Bollingen Series XX], New York, 1953), p. 49.

But he then insists on utmost secrecy and makes Horatio and Marcellus, these tried friends, swear three times with the most solemn oaths, that they will not so much as whisper a word about what has happened.

It is of great significance that this oath has to be given at three different places. Up to this point, Hamlet's ego has been stable, but with the invasion by the Ghost, his ego, his "frame of nature," has been "wrench't from its fix'd place." (*Lear*—I.iv.290)

The Ghost supports Hamlet in this secrecy—but Hamlet's attitude toward the Ghost has also changed. He calls the Ghost "true-penny . . . this fellow in the cellerage." His most significant term of description, however, is:

> . . . old *mole!* canst work i' the earth so fast?   (I.v.162)
> A worthy pioner!

—because by now the Ghost has become a complex which digs and digs, and undermines him like an "old mole."

This is perhaps an opportune moment to consider the question of the nature of Hamlet's tragic flaw—the "stamp of one defect"—a question which was raised on page 32. Grebanier gives a short review of what other commentators have considered Hamlet's "tragic flaw":[24]

> . . . according to Goethe (it) is extreme sensitivity; according to Coleridge and Schlege, excessive intellectualization; Bradley, melancholia; Ulrici, moral scrupulosity; the psychoanalysts, a complex.

Grebanier himself says:

> How are we then to describe his tragic flaw, the *hamartia* which will hurl him to destruction? We have already identified it as a species of rashness. . . . So far from being the hero who cannot whip himself into action, he is the tragic figure that can act readily, but who must not—until the moment be ripe.

[24] *Op. cit.,* p. 260fn.

I agree with Grebanier that it is a species of rashness. I believe, however, that Shakespeare himself has given us a hint, or more than a hint, of the cause of this rashness.

In Hamlet's speech while awaiting the arrival of the Ghost, he spoke of the unfortunate drinking habits of the Danes and declared that:

> . . . for some *vicious mole* of nature in them, (I.iv.24)
> . . . the stamp of one defect . . .
> Shall in the general censure take corruption
> From that particular fault.

It is certainly no accident that here, in the swearing scene (I.v.162), Hamlet uses the same word with a different meaning, this time referring to the Ghost as an "old mole." The ghost complex has become an encapsulated complex which, like a mole in the earth, burrows in Hamlet's psyche and causes a gradual destruction of Hamlet's consciousness. It makes him unconscious, brings rashness of action, forces him into compensatory attitudes, sharpens his wit and makes him speak frequently in terms with double meanings. He himself notices it when he tells his friends:

> As I perchance hereafter shall think meet (I.v.171)
> To put an antic disposition on.

"Antic disposition" has frequently been interpreted as madness. Grebanier quotes the Oxford English Dictionary, Vol. 1, pp. 365-366, showing that the common denominator for "antic" is "grotesque." He says:[25]

> Hamlet . . . is saying no more than that he may find it necessary to behave in a way that will hereafter perhaps appear absurb, ludicrous, bizarre, grotesque.

I quite agree with Grebanier that:[26]

[25] *Ibid.*, p. 147.
[26] *Ibid.*, pp. 145-146.

Hamlet does not imply by "As I perchance hereafter shall think meet to put an antic disposition on" that he may hereafter decide to play the madman.

Rather than to "find it *necessary*" I would say that Hamlet might find it *opportune* to "play the madman." It might suit his purpose, "find it meet." The *purpose* is to hide the manner in which he attains this knowledge and to get material proof of Claudius' crime. That would certainly not mean that Hamlet would now feign madness. And we can refer here to Grebanier's ideas which I find persuasive. *Antic disposition* clearly describes the mood in which Hamlet finds himself as a result of the strange influence of the ghost complex.

When the oath is finally concluded, Hamlet tries to make amends for his rude and ungentlemanly demands on his friends by assuring them of his love. Though psychically isolated, he nevertheless decides to "go in together." He now has an exaggerated sense of mission. He feels that he alone has to straighten things out. He is *out of joint,* but he feels like an unwilling savior:

> The time is out of joint; O cursed spite,   (I.v.188)
> That ever I was born to set it right!

As we see throughout the play, Hamlet is a genius, an artist, a philosopher—but not a warrior. Grebanier says:[27]

> Hamlet, unquestionably, has been a soldier; but we do not see him operating in that profession during the course of the play.

There are two indications that he *is* a soldier. At the very end, when Fortinbras says:

> Let four captains   (V.ii.406)
> Bear Hamlet, like a soldier, to the stage.

[27] *Ibid.,* p. 148.

And when Ophelia says:

> O, what a noble mind is here o'erthrown! (III.i.158)
> The courtier's, soldier's, scholar's, eye, tongue, sword.

This, to my understanding, means that Hamlet, along with many other qualities, also had the virtues of a soldier in that he fought for a good cause, courageously, like a soldier. He is a gentleman in the best Elizabethan tradition. His father was a *warrior* who, although a loving husband and father, committed, in the interest of power (*Realpolitik*), a number of crimes ("the foul crimes done in my days of nature") and possibly in a way merited his fate—being murdered by a brother who coveted his power. Father and son were most dissimilar in their true natures, but Hamlet, although no longer a youth, unconsciously was still identified to a certain extent with both his parents. Fate gave him an opportunity to clarify the image of father and mother in himself. It came as a shock to him to discover dark and evil qualities in his mother, but he did not take into account his father's crimes and power psychology, and did not see that he was essentially different from his father. He was royal too, but his royalty was more of the spirit, his father's of power. Hamlet's kingdom was the inner world, his father's that of politics. Under the shock of discovering his mother's licentiousness and the murder of his own father, Hamlet surrendered to the Ghost and, in doing so, surrendered also to the past and to the psychology of his father. Possessed by the ghost complex, Hamlet was led upon a path not truly his own. It set up a conflict between his true nature (the artist, the man of spirit, the philosopher in the best sense of the word) and the man of the world. Submitting to primitive instincts, he became a divided personality. This division is so sharp and uncanny because the father complex speaks with a voice from beyond the grave, and is associated with the archetype of the father. This man who was in so many ways capable of profound reflection about himself, who from the beginning asked himself whether this ghost was a good or evil ghost, never realized that the ghost—though an "honest" ghost—

came from purgatory, even though the ghost told him so. Hamlet appeals to the "angels and ministers of grace" to defend him —that is, to the highest and best in himself—but he is reckless with his own life and his own soul:

> . . . what should be the fear?   (I.iv.64)
> I do not set my life at a pin's fee;
> And for my soul, what can it do to that,
> Being a thing immortal as itself?

Fear is a most natural instinct, given by nature to warn us of dangers, internal as well as external, and usually sets up a reaction in our psychic and physical organism to meet the danger as suitably as possible. We know for instance that fear injects adrenalin into the bloodstream and thus sharpens our senses and quickens and strengthens our reactions. To know and to accept fear is the sign of the truly courageous man. This is particularly true in meeting psychological dangers, in all encounters with powerful inner complexes. An absence of fear is characteristic for certain types of psychosis. In the Rorschach test, the absence of color disturbance, for example, is one of the factors which speak for psychosis. In Hamlet's case, one cannot say that fear is absent. He *disregards* it. He is reckless in exposing himself to the ghost complex and thus opens himself to invasion by the unconscious. In primitive rituals, for instance in puberty rites in which the young man meets the "ancestors," a careful ritual is performed in order to enable the youth to confront the activated contents of the unconscious. In primitive societies, funeral ceremonies are of an elaborate character, since primitive man is well aware of the danger that issues from the spirit of a dead person. Primitive man has always been aware of and careful with the so-called perils of the soul.[28] Hamlet, however, who has already been brooding about the speedy and incestuous marriage of his mother, throws caution to the winds, is fatally attracted by the numinosity of the unconscious, and is in no way

[28] See Sir James George Frazer, "The Perils of the Soul," Part II of *The Golden Bough* (Macmillan & Co., London, 1951).

prepared for a proper meeting with the Ghost. His friends warn him. Instead of reflecting on the wisdom of their objections, he becomes angry and threatens them with violence. *It is this rash and unreflected manner in regard to the perils of the soul which can be called Hamlet's "tragic flaw."* He is therefore quite wrong when he says:

> . . . for my soul, what can it do to that,   (I.iv.68)
> Being a thing immortal as itself?

It may be true that, in a universal sense, the soul of mankind is immortal, but the soul of an individual man can die. Jung says (in a footnote explaining "the dangerous water," a parable used in a particular case he is describing):[29]

> The stream, though small, is "most dangerous." The servants say they have once tried to cross it, but "we scarcely escaped the peril of eternal death." They add: "We know too that our predecessors perished here." The servants are the alchemists, and the stream or its water symbolizes the danger threatening them, which is clearly the danger of drowning. The psychic danger of the opus is the irruption of the unconscious and the "loss of soul" caused thereby. I have in my possession an alchemical MS. of the 17th cent., showing an invasion of the unconscious in a series of pictures. The images produced bear all the marks of schizophrenia.

Psychosis is the death of the soul. In Hamlet's case one cannot speak of a psychosis (called madness in the play), but Hamlet's encounter with the Ghost sets up a conflict in him between the "angels and ministers of grace" and the "blasts from hell"— between the creative and *life-giving forces* and those of *death* and destruction. At one point, Hamlet even makes an attempt to unite these two opposing forces which on this level cannot be united:

[29] C. G. Jung. *Mysterium Coniunctionis,* Vol. 14 of the Collected Works (Pantheon Books [Bollingen Series XX], New York, 1963), p. 121.

O all you host of heaven! O earth! what else?   (I.v.92)
And shall I couple hell?

His inherent weakness, to give up what is best in himself and to
surrender to another's will, was already indicated when, at his
mother's request, he so easily agreed to remain in Denmark.
Hamlet recognizes the problem of what *is* and what *seems* in
other people, but does not see it in himself. Shakespeare created
a situation in Hamlet's environment which gave the Prince ample opportunity to project onto others his own problem—the
fact that he is not himself, that he is possessed and governed by
his father complex and all it entails.[30] Laertes, Ophelia and Fortinbras obey their fathers and try to follow in their footsteps.
Rosencrantz and Guildenstern obey the King—and so does Polonius. It is only Horatio who has no dependency on the father
and is therefore the most balanced personality in the play. He
proves to be a true friend to Hamlet, though he seems to be too
identified with Hamlet when he wants to die together with him:

I am more an antique Roman than a Dane   (V.ii.352)
Here's yet some liquor left.

Hamlet holds Horatio's friendship very highly, but does not accept his advice or his warnings for moderation in dealing with
the Ghost.

As mentioned earlier, is is difficult for me to speak of Hamlet's character as a static entity. It appears evident however that
the drama develops out of Hamlet's unconsciousness of his *own*
being, out of the fact that the Ghost with his desire for revenge
takes full possession of Hamlet's consciousness ("thy commandment all *alone*") and thus starts a dynamism which neces-

[30] C. G. Jung: "The self . . . is an archetype that invariably expresses
a situation within which the ego is contained. Therefore, like every archetype, the self cannot be localized in an individual ego-consciousness, but
acts like a circumambient atmosphere to which no definite limits can be
set, either in space or in time. (Hence the synchronistic phenomena so
often associated with activated archetypes.)"—*Aion*, Vol. 9 (ii) of the
Collected Works (Pantheon Books [Bollingen Series XX], New York,
1959), pp. 167-168.

sarily leads to a tragic end. This fact—the invasion and possession by the ghost complex—is the poison which permeates Hamlet's psyche and slowly kills him; kills first his integrity and later his physical body. Poison is the outstanding symbol in the whole play. The King was murdered by poison "dropped into his ear." The unnamed "foul crimes" were the cause of his death and they did not die with his death. They continue to have their subtle, insidious and malign influence (poison!) by reappearing in Hamlet's unconscious as a ghost, and calling up in Hamlet the primitive instinct of revenge. By the law of fate, they bring about first King Hamlet's own murder and later his wife's incestuous marriage to his brother. Just as King Hamlet hid his own crimes, so must Claudius hide the murder *he* committed. The attempt to conceal it makes it doubly poisonous. Gertrude did not know Claudius' crime, so must believe, like everyone else, that her husband died a natural death.

Hamlet is the only one at the court who carries in himself an image of the divine order of things. He possesses the greatest integrity. The *tragedy* is that he is also poisoned by the Ghost. Through his reckless attitude toward the Ghost, he becomes psychologically changed. He therefore cannot handle wisely this admittedly difficult and rotten situation. He is drawn back into the father's psychology and profoundly contaminated with the late King's spirit of crime and revenge. Now called to action, he cannot act in a manner corresponding to the true Hamlet, the man of spirit. The Ghost demands an impossible thing of him:

> But, howsoever thou pursuest this act,   (I.v.84)
> Taint not thy mind, nor let thy soul contrive
> Against thy mother aught. Leave her to heaven,
> And to those thorns that in her bosom lodge
> To prick and sting her.

The very fact that Hamlet has contact with the Ghost and surrenders his consciousness unreservedly already affects and "taints" Hamlet's mind. Furthermore, it burdens him with an uncertainty regarding the extent of his mother's knowledge of, even her participation in, the murder of his father. The accusations of the Ghost against the mother refer only to the fact that the Ghost's brother Claudius, "that incestuous, that adulterate beast," had sexual relations with his wife in his own lifetime.

> With witchcraft of his wit, with traitorous gifts— (I.v.43)
> O wicked wit and gifts, that have the power
> So to seduce!—won to his shameful lust
> The will of my most seeming-virtuous queen.

The Ghost accuses the mother only of having fallen victim to the magical powers of Claudius' intelligence and his other fascinating gifts, having thereby entertained an illicit relationship. By these words of the Ghost, Hamlet's mind is poisoned in two ways: one, the father's personality, with its desire for revenge, has become part of him; and, two, he is beset with a vexing problem in regard to his mother's possible participation in the murder. Thus, Hamlet is now alienated from himself, in conflict with himself. There are two personalities in him—his and the Ghost's. Were he the true Hamlet, a philosopher (understood in the medieval sense[31]), he would handle this situation in a very different way than by revenge and might find other ways to satisfy his filial duty without violating his integrity. Harold C. Goddard points out, for example, that, handled differently, Claudius might have confessed his crime and abdicated. Since, psychologically speaking, Hamlet is now both he and his father, he will have to accomplish the revenge in a way that satisfies his father. This, however, absolutely contradicts his own integrity. Furthermore, the information he has about the murder has come to him in a strange way. It has been conveyed to him by "a power beyond the reach of his soul," or, to use a modern term, by an extra-sensory intuition. He will have first to convince *himself* by other means that the Ghost's report of his own murder is true, and later on he will have to convince the court by material evidence that Claudius really murdered the King. The murder was

[31] A person seeking the "philosopher's stone," the greatest value contained in the human soul.

done in secret and there were evidently no witnesses to the fact. What chance does he have ever to prove the murder? It is this problem of translating his intuitive knowledge into factual evidence which has so often been understood as a paralysis of the will. But in fact, throughout the play, he always acts forcefully and decisively, even rashly. As Grebanier showed very clearly,[32] Shakespeare lays no emphasis on the course of time in the play, and it depends on the position that we, as spectators and readers of the drama, take whether we assume that Hamlet delayed the killing of Claudius or not.

Naïvely we assume that it was Hamlet's duty to accomplish his revenge immediately by killing Claudius. A personality like Laertes might have acted thus—that is, a person who was not himself but simply a younger edition of his father. If we take Hamlet as he was *before* he became involved in the dark aspects of his mother's marriage, that is, Hamlet as the artist, philosopher, he would not have acted out of a need for revenge but in a way that would allow divine justice to take its proper course. Since he tried to satisfy both needs, he attempted something impossible and it was only a question of which side in him would eventually win.

Hamlet's weakness shows up clearly and significantly when his ego is confronted with the will of the Ghost, that is, the directed consciousness of an archetypal complex. In this case, it is fateful, because any encounter with an archetype constellates fate.[33] After the encounter with the Ghost, Hamlet is never again quite the true Hamlet, and since he never takes an attitude against the Ghost it is only a question of time until the unconscious content, the Ghost with its primitive desire for revenge, will overwhelm him. Shakespeare's interest in the play was in demonstrating this conflict and the gradual and complete destruction of Hamlet's personality by the Ghost.

Furthermore, one has to consider the fact that this whole complex—the numinous experience of the Ghost, coupled with the knowledge of a hidden crime and the necessity to hide this

---

[32] *Op. cit.,* pp. 177-180.
[33] See Jung on the fate-producing anima, *Aion,* p. 21.

knowledge—creates a tremendous tension in him which overflows and, under the proper stimulation of the complex, makes him say too much, almost gives him away. But all these conditions, although they establish an intense and highly unusual psychology and puzzle everyone at court, do not allow us to consider Hamlet insane in any way. He maintains his rational qualities at all times. He is always aware of the situation and even perceives intuitively very much more than does anyone else among his friends and enemies. Only twice does he misinterpret the situation (in regard to Ophelia, and to Rosencrantz and Guildenstern), but this is fully understandable considering the unusually difficult task he has in acquiring evidence about the murder of a king.

Hamlet is frequently placed in situations in which, due to the conflict, he cannot execute his revenge, or where he is pushed by it into rash and totally unreflected actions. Beset with the complex produced by the Ghost experience and forced to provide evidence under impossible circumstances, his sorrowful exclamation is quite understandable:

> . . . O cursed spite (I.v.189)
> That ever I was born to set it right!

If one wishes to apply a clinical term to Hamlet's psychic condition, one can only call it a neurosis. Neurosis is defined as a condition in which a conflict exists of which the individual is largely or completely unconscious. This diagnosis most aptly fits the case of Hamlet. From the moment of his mother's marriage he is brought into a sharp conflict between the best in him and the necessity to adjust to the conditions at the court. It is actually a conflict between the creative and destructive forces within him. The meeting with the Ghost deepens and sharpens this conflict to the extreme and tips the scales powerfully in favor of the destructive.

Hamlet and Claudius are the two antagonists of the play, but Hamlet's inner conflict has ample opportunity to project itself on two different figures. On the "good" side is Horatio. On the destructive side is Polonius. Then there are characters like Laertes, Ophelia, Rosencrantz and Guildenstern who, in the course of the dramatic action, receive varying projections, mainly from Hamlet, and then symbolize destructive qualities in Hamlet's character.

Polonius' psychology, and that of his family, characterize very well the moral atmosphere at the court. No brutal crime like murder or incest is perpetrated in this family, but there has been murder of a much subtler nature through the profound doubts that Laertes and Polonius instill in Ophelia about her love for Hamlet. It is evident that Ophelia has been in love with Hamlet for some time and that a considerable amount of intimacy has existed between them—although because Ophelia is a "nice girl," a consummation of this love has probably never taken place. Ophelia's love for Hamlet is deep and genuine, but quite unreflected. Her mind is simple and under the pressures in her home she has never developed ideas of her own. One wonders how Hamlet could have fallen so deeply in love with her. The answer is that it is just such simplicity and vacuousness which attracts men of high caliber, because this emptiness allows a man to project the anima image into such a woman. In turn, Ophelia has responded to Hamlet with a great feeling of love. As long as no conflict entered into the relationship from the outside it could flourish and certainly was satisfying, because it gave Ophelia great intellectual stimulation and was the only ray of light penetrating the dark and dismal atmosphere in her home. For Hamlet, her femininity was just the vessel to receive his feeling.

The exposition as given in the first act states the problem then as between truth and semblance (*Sein* and *Schein*). Hamlet, Laertes and Polonius, on different levels, make statements about being true to oneself. Laertes and Polonius immediately demonstrate that they are *not* true to themselves—that they put on an appearance, but in fact are something quite different. Hamlet quite genuinely believes that he is what he appears to be. He and Ophelia, by obeying the commandments of their fathers, betray themselves and rob themselves of their true natures.

Two parties are clearly set up against each other. On one side is Hamlet, on the other Claudius and Hamlet's mother—both sides pretending something which they are not, and using other characters for their purposes: Laertes, Ophelia, Polonius. Claudius hides the guilty secret of the murder; the Queen successfully forgets King Hamlet and his love for her; Hamlet hides his ghost experience and the fact that he has full, though unsubstantiated, knowledge of their crime.

In conclusion, we can say that in Act I Shakespeare has given us a wonderful exposition of the play. All the characters bearing a name have appeared, with the exception of Rosencrantz and Guildenstern, Fortinbras, and the two minor figures, Reynaldo and Osric. Hamlet's psychology, his conflict and his "tragic flaw" have been clearly established. The moral decay of the environment has been painted in dark colors, providing all the conditions in which the conflict of the tragic hero is mirrored. What gives this play its extra dimension is that, through the inclusion of a ghost, our main interest and our difficulty in understanding the play is squarely placed within the psychological processes of Hamlet. It will now therefore be my particular concern to show how Shakespeare, in a supremely masterful way, creates dramatic situations in order to unfold, amplify and deepen Hamlet's insoluble problem.

Act Two

i

The first dialogue in the second act serves to characterize Polonius even more clearly, but contributes nothing to the action of the play and is therefore frequently omitted in performances. It is a conversation between Polonius and Reynaldo, a servant, which shows Polonius' low opinion of his own son. He plans to send Reynaldo to Laertes in Paris, orders him to spy on Laertes, to plant rumors in order to give Laertes a bad reputation, thinking that such belongs to a gentleman. He even orders Reynaldo

to tempt Laertes into immorality. Since the principal characters
are not themselves, but play roles, wear masks and take the
masks for their true being, they must project these false images
on each other. The scene for misunderstanding has already been
set.

After Reynaldo leaves, Ophelia bursts into the room. She is
quite upset and visibly so. She tells her father an amazing story
about Prince Hamlet, and this moves the action of the play forward quite strongly. The story she tells has puzzled commentators:

> . . . as I was sewing in my closet, (II.i.77)
> Lord Hamlet, with his doublet all unbrac'd;
> No hat upon his head; his stockings foul'd,
> Ungarter'd, and down-gyved to his ankle;
> Pale as his shirt, his knees knocking each other;
> And with a look so piteous in purport
> As if he had been loosed out of hell
> To speak of horrors, he comes before me.
> . . .
> He took me by the wrist and held me hard;
> Then goes he to the length of all his arm,
> And, with his other hand thus o'er his brow,
> He falls to such perusal of my face
> As he would draw it. Long stay'd he so;
> At last, a little shaking of mine arm,
> And thrice his head thus waving up and down,
> He raised a sigh so piteous and profound
> As it did seem to shatter all his bulk
> And end his being; that done, he lets me go,
> And with his head over his shoulder turn'd
> He seemed to find his way without his eyes;
> For out o' doors he went without their help,
> And to the last bended their light on me.

We have to decide whether Ophelia's story is true, or is a
product of her imagination. If it did happen, it would show
Hamlet in a peculiar light and we would have to revise some of
the opinions we have formed about him. If all this is a product of
her fancy, we must conclude that Ophelia is an extremely cun-

ning girl to have invented such a plot, or that this fanciful report is the first symptom of her beginning insanity.

Grebanier believes that the account she gives is true, that Hamlet forced his way into her room in order to see her because she had broken off all communication with him. He says:[1]

> Can we not conceive him, torn between his complicated worries over the Ghost's revelations and his bitterness at Ophelia's unexplained renunciation of him at a time when he most needs her love, flinging himself upon his couch without bothering to disrobe (though naturally without his hat on his head!), tossing about in anguished uncertainty—and then suddenly, with characteristic impulsiveness, jumping up, resolved to find out at once by confronting Ophelia without warning, whether or not she is such another as Gertrude?

J. Dover Wilson says:[2]

> In this condition of extreme distress Hamlet seeks out Ophelia, the woman he loves, in the hope of finding consolation and help in her presence. But she has nothing for him; and though, as she tells us, "He falls to such perusal of my face as a' would draw it," her face reflects fear alone, the fear that is still upon her as she relates the story to her father.

Kittredge says:[3]

> It is at this moment that Hamlet decides that he must renounce Ophelia and give up all thought of marriage and happiness. To involve an innocent girl in such a revenge as he contemplates would have been a crime.

Olav Lökse, in his book *Outrageous Fortune*,[4] tries to solve certain puzzles in Shakespeare's plays by discussing the ways in which the characters and situations were represented in the

[1] *Op. cit.,* p. 198.
[2] *What Happens in Hamlet,* pp. 111-112.
[3] *Op. cit.,* p. 178.
[4] Oslo Univ. Press (Humanities Press, New York, 1961), pp. 46, 52.

Hamlet plays preceding Shakespeare's. He devotes a whole chapter, "The Decoy and the Mad Lady," essentially to Ophelia's report, starting with the question:

> What sort of girl did the Elizabethan audience expect to be presented on the stage when watching a ghost-revenge play on the Hamlet story from *Saxo* and *Belleforest?*

(Lökse assumes, probably correctly, that the audience was well acquainted with these pre-Shakespeare Hamlet plays.) If we accept his basic assumption:

> However much *Hamlet* differs from other ghost-revenge plays, it fundamentally adheres to the conventional pattern of such plays as known by the audience.

—then his conclusions about the figure of Ophelia are compelling. We would have to accept her as the *"bad* lady from *Saxo* and *Belleforest."* Then Shakespeare's hint to the audience, through the mouth of Polonius in Act I, Scene 3:

> 'Tis told me, he hath very oft of late   (91)
> Given private time to you; and you yourself
> Have of your audience been most free and bounteous

could not be broader. Consequently, we must accept Ophelia's report as a product of her imagination and not as fact. Everything she tells then corresponds to the theory which the Elizabethans had about madness. To Lökse:

> Ophelia succeeds in delivering a story that makes Hamlet terribly mad, and mad in full accordance with contemporary theories of madness because of thwarted desire. And in order to make clear to the audience what kind of a story this is, Shakespeare makes Ophelia include the typical number three that is so significant to fiction, particularly when it is included in a story that is delivered in a very fluent way and which so glibly fits the theory: "And thrice his head thus waving up and down."

It is Ophelia who sets in motion the theory that Hamlet is mad for love. Her plot is then to propound the idea that Hamlet would be cured by marrying her. Thus she would overcome the obstacle against a morganatic marriage of a royal prince. Lökse's sharp eye sets the lines of I.iii.132-134:

> I would not, in plain terms, from this time forth
> Have you so slander any moment's leisure,
> As to give words or talk with the Lord Hamlet.

side by side with the lines of II.i.108-110:

> No, my good lord, but as you did command,
> I did repel his letters and denied
> His access to me.

Says Lökse:

> Ophelia actually falsifies what Polonius has said to her in order to make her answer fit the implications of Polonius's question. Further, she now relates that Hamlet has been in her closet in spite of the fact that her father had prohibited this.

To my mind, his final conclusion is incontrovertible:

> The moment comes when Ophelia turns to the man whom she has described only recently as being present in her closet, even taking her by her arm and looking her in her face, and asks him the fatal question: ". . . Good my lord, how does your honour for this many a day?" Ophelia has been lying from beginning to end. Ophelia's report is the report episode from Saxo and Belleforest making its way into Shakespeare's play.

The only valid conclusion we can draw in regard to Hamlet is that some peculiar change in his behavior has taken place. It must have set the courtiers' tongues wagging. No one knew the true reason. Such a condition is most suitable for creating all sorts of rumors, because ignorance sets all kinds of fantasies in motion. Jung, in "A Contribution to the Psychology of Rumour," [5] describes in great detail such a case, in which he was able to examine all those portions of a rumor which had been contributed by each individual of a class of young girls. We have just seen how Ophelia filled in the gaps in her knowledge. It was of course just that which would best satisfy her frustrations. The story itself seems quite plausible. Polonius falls for it, and many commentators have believed her also. The audience in this case knows the reasons for Hamlet's strange behavior. His encounter with the Ghost has profoundly shaken him, has given him a taste of hell. A violent conflict is raging in him. Is the Ghost really the spirit of his dead father—or is it the devil in disguise? Is what the Ghost told him really true? He tries all the means which his superior mind possesses in order to integrate the numinous experience. First, he carries it alone, but, as we hear later, he relates everything to Horatio. He might have wanted to communicate it to Ophelia also, but just at that point she has unaccountably withdrawn from him. His mind dwells uninterruptedly on the phenomenon of the Ghost, and on the Ghost's command to take revenge. This condition has on him the effect of an *idée fixe* and must consequently make him depressed. When Ophelia says that he looked as if he had been loosed out of hell, she uses this image as a metaphor, while for Hamlet it is a reality. In saying he has been loosed out of hell, she has picked up the essence of his condition, not realizing how true it is. I have had patients tell me about a friend, or about another patient, exclaiming: "He is crazy!" and yet without realizing that this was literally true—a fact of which I, as a psychiatrist, was aware.

But Ophelia's story, evidently told with strong emotion, sets Polonius' mind on a new track. Obviously he has been concerned with Hamlet's strange behavior. Hearing his daughter's story, he immediately arrives at the conclusion she is hoping for:

Mad for thy love? (II.i.85)

[5] *Freud and Psychoanalysis,* Vol. 4 of the Collected Works (Pantheon Books [Bollingen Series XX], New York, 1961), p. 35.

He becomes quite apologetic, admitting that he has underestimated the seriousness of Hamlet's love for her, and excuses his misjudgment by reason of his age and the usually bad mores of younger people. It appears to him that his new theory of love-madness:

> This is the very ecstasy of love,   (II.i.102)
> Whose violent property fordoes itself
> And leads the will to desperate undertakings
> As oft as any passion under heaven
> That does afflict our natures,

is the key to Hamlet's strange behavior, and that there is an unexpected windfall in it which might improve to the utmost his position at court. Therefore he decides to take her at once to the King:

> Come, go we to the king;   (II.i.117)
> This must be known; which, being close, might move
> More grief to hide than hate to utter love.
> Come.

If the break in the love relationship had been the cause for Hamlet's disturbance ("ecstasy"), everything would have been well once he was again permitted to see Ophelia. But since Hamlet's real problem is to deal with the King's guilt and the Ghost's command, Ophelia's breaking of their relationship can only be seen by him in that context. The damage to their relationship is irrevocably done. Hamlet would naturally have liked to make Ophelia his confidante as he had Horatio, but breaking the relationship at just this essential moment raises strong suspicions about her collusion with her father. Furthermore, as we saw before, his mother's incestuous marriage has profoundly affected his anima image and filled him with distrust of women altogether. This behavior of Ophelia's only confirms such a negative opinion of women in general.

ii

The next scene introduces two new characters, Rosencrantz and
Guildenstern. The King receives them as two old friends and
former schoolmates of Hamlet. Hamlet's strange behavior has
become a very important fact at the court, and Claudius is deeply
concerned about it. For reasons that we can guess, he must wonder in the depths of his heart whether, against all probability,
Hamlet might have chanced to discover something about the
murder. At least his conscience must gnaw at him in this respect.
He cannot approach Hamlet directly. Therefore he wants to use
these friends of the Prince to try to find the reason for the
change in Hamlet's disposition. And so he tells them, speaking
not of madness, but of Hamlet's "transformation":

> . . . so I call it,   (II.ii.5)
> Since nor th' exterior nor the inward man
> Resembles that it was.

The King admits that it must be something "more than his father's death." He asks Rosencrantz and Guildenstern to spy on
Hamlet, presenting as a motive for such dishonesty his *paternal
desire* to help Hamlet.

The Queen supports the King in this attitude and promises
rewards:

> For the supply and profit of our hope,   (II.ii.24)
> Your visitation shall receive such thanks
> As fits a king's remembrance.

It is important to understand that Rosencrantz and Guildenstern accept this offer only because they believe that the King's
and Queen's concern for Hamlet is genuinely motivated by their
desire to cure him of his strange affliction. As friends they are
eager to see Hamlet restored to his former happy self. To serve
in this matter, as requested by the King and Queen, would be
not only an act of friendship, but of duty. Both King and Queen

ask for their services in the form of an entreaty, but the two gentlemen accept it as a royal command:

> . . . by the sovereign power you have of us,　　(II.ii.27)
> Put your dread pleasures more into command
> Than to entreaty.

The relationship of the two young courtiers to the King and Queen falls into the same pattern as that of the other characters in the play. They all accept obedience as the proper attitude. Hamlet says to the Ghost:

> And thy commandment all alone shall live　　(I.v.102)
> Within the book and volume of my brain.

Polonius, of Laertes:

> He hath, my lord, wrung from me my slow leave　　(I.ii.58)
> By laboursome petition, and at last
> Upon his will I seal'd my hard consent:
> I do beseech you, give him leave to go.

Ophelia:

> I shall obey, my lord.　　(I.iii.136)

As soon as Rosencrantz and Guildenstern leave, Polonius enters with news that the King's ambassadors are "joyfully return'd" from Norway, and, before going on to any business he might want to discuss with Claudius, he expresses the same sort of obedience to the King:

> I hold my duty as I hold my soul,　　(II.ii.44)
> Both to my God and to my gracious king.

According to his words, he has to obey the King as devoutly as he obeys God.

Then he springs his surprise on the royal couple, when he suddenly says:

> I have found   (II.ii.48)
> The very cause of Hamlet's lunacy.

In using the term "lunacy" Polonius already designates Hamlet's behavior as something more than love-madness. The King wants to hear about it at once. It is even more important to him than the political news he expects from the returning ambassadors. But Polonius keeps the King on tenterhooks. He will talk of Hamlet only after the affairs of state have been taken care of. He goes out to fetch the ambassadors, Voltimand and Cornelius. This gives the King an opportunity to tell Gertrude that Polonius has "found the head and source of all your son's distemper." Again we see that the King uses a much weaker term for Hamlet's condition than Polonius has used. The Queen does not expect any particular revelation. She has formed a definite opinion:

> I doubt it is no other but the main,—   (II.ii.57)
> His father's death, and our o'erhasty marriage.

The ambassadors enter and report on their successful mission to Norway, asking that free passage through Denmark be given to Fortinbras. When they leave, Polonius begins to tell what he has discovered about Hamlet. He is long-winded (although he himself claims that "brevity is the soul of wit"). He repeats his opinion of Hamlet. He categorically declares:

> Your noble son is mad.   (II.ii.92)

—and defines madness by a tautology (not that modern psychiatry has much better definitions of insanity). His silly, senile talk irritates the Queen, but this only gives him an opportunity to continue with more of the same kind of comments which are supposed to be sophisticated but are truly asinine. After this long, garrulous speech, he startlingly produces, like a bolt from the sky, a letter which Hamlet has written to Ophelia. Knowing Polonius, we can surmise that this letter has fallen into his hands by less subtle means than he professes. But we can believe that Ophelia handed it to him because it would support her maidenly plot to force Hamlet somehow into marrying her. On the other hand, we must also conclude that this indiscreet act represents an outright betrayal of Hamlet. It is certainly significant for the understanding of future events that at this early point she has made herself a tool of her father's plans. Hamlet of course knows nothing of this. All he can know is that for unaccountable reasons she has broken off all contact with him. It must arouse all kinds of suspicion in him. Polonius interrupts his own reading of the letter by criticizing its literary quality: " 'beautified' is a vile phrase." The Queen is astonished at the letter and asks, "Came this from Hamlet to her?" She is no doubt less concerned with the literary qualities of the letter than she is with the nature of the relationship. It cannot be determined from the text what the real reason may be for her astonished question. The most probable reason, in my opinion, is that she considers Hamlet's relationship to Ophelia a typical Elizabethan flirtation, a sexual affair in which no deeper feelings or serious intentions are involved, and it is a most unexpected revelation to her that Hamlet would pour out such profound, and at the same time, poetical feelings to a girl who was at best a flirt. Polonius, on the other hand, is certainly interested in showing off his daughter as a virtuous woman. To prove this, he emphasizes her filial obedience and claims that she has told him everything that has gone on between the two lovers. We know, of course, from Act I.iii.91-93, that he is lying.

Obviously, the King shares the Queen's opinion of Ophelia and Polonius knows what the King thinks. The King cannot ask outright, "Have they had an affair?" so he asks:

But how hath she received his love? (II.ii.128)

Polonius counters with:

What do you think of me? (II.ii.129)

The King, driven into a corner, must of course answer in a positive yet noncommital way:

> As of a man faithful and honorable. (II.ii.130)

His integrity and honor having been questioned, Polonius goes again into a long-winded speech. We cannot help but feel that "the lady doth protest too much":

> No, I went round to work, (II.ii.139)
> And my young mistress thus I did bespeak.

He then reports that she took the "fruits of his advice," and that the result of her repulsion of Hamlet's love (according to his senile way of reasoning) is the true cause of Hamlet's so-called madness:

> Into the madness wherein he now raves, (II.ii.150)
> And all we mourn for.

Remembering his own guilt, the King doubts this, but the Queen, who only a few moments before still considered old Hamlet's death and her hasty marriage as the probable cause, is now inclined to believe it.

Nevertheless, the King decides to put this new theory to a test and Polonius, in his subservience, is most willing to use his daughter for the purpose:

> I'll loose my daughter to him.[6] (II.ii.163)

The King is sure of her cooperation since she has handed Hamlet's letter over to her father. The plan is for Polonius and the King to hide behind an "arras" and spy on Hamlet.

---

[6] Dover Wilson edition of *Hamlet*, pp. lvii-lviii: "The expression 'loose,' notes Dowden, 'reminds the King and Queen that he has restrained Ophelia from communicating with Hamlet'; but it has also another meaning, still connected with the breeding of horses and cattle, which would not be missed by an Elizabethan audience."

It is sad to reflect on Ophelia's submissiveness to her father in agreeing to being used for such a sinister purpose, but she has an unlimited belief in her father's wisdom and, like Rosencrantz and Guildenstern, believes that the end justifies the means.

Hamlet now enters, reading a book, apparently not aware of anyone's presence. Polonius asks the King, Queen and others to leave immediately so that he can talk to Hamlet alone. The following scene between the two men can only properly be understood if we realize the premises under which they meet. Polonius is convinced of Hamlet's insanity and treats him as if he were completely "gone" and had lost all orientation in reality. Hamlet is under the pressure of the ghost complex and aware of the disturbance of his relationship with Ophelia. He guesses that her father is at the root of this trouble. He cannot speak openly but must speak in images. Polonius begins, like a modern psychiatrist who tests a psychotic patient's orientation in time and space:

Do you know me, my lord?   (II.ii.173)

Hamlet perceives what Polonius is up to and uses Polonius' belief as a shield. Madmen can, of course, say anything they like; they are not subject to the usual conventions of polite society and cannot be held responsible. His first answer, therefore, "You are a fishmonger," taken literally would mean that he mistakes the man he knows very well. Kittredge comments:[7]

There is of course a symbolic meaning of which we, with the passage of time, cannot be quite sure.

According to J. D. Wilson[8] the symbolic meaning is a "flesh monger," a "bawd."

According to Coleridge:[9]

[7] *Op. cit.*, p. 185.
[8] *Hamlet*, p. 170.
[9] Kittredge *Hamlet*, p. 185.

Hamlet means "You are sent to fish out the secret!"

Hamlet's intention is to let Polonius know that he knows how Polonius treats his daughter and tries to use her for his purposes. He really answers Polonius' question, "Do you know me?" much more fully and in a different sense than Polonius expected. Polonius only tried to find out whether Hamlet knew his identity, but Hamlet manages to tell him in a symbolic way what sort of man he really is:

> Then I would you were so honest a man.   (II.ii.177)

His images are so obscure that neither Polonius nor we can fully grasp them:

> For if the sun breed maggots in a dead dog,   (II.ii.183)
> being a good kissing carrion,—

Wilson states that:[10]

> 'God' and 'good' are sometimes confused in this and other quarters . . . the two versions give different meanings, both convenient to the context.

Without entering into the scholarly discussion of the precise meaning of this and the following lines:

> Let her not walk i' the sun; conception is a   (II.ii.187)
> blessing; but not as your daughter may conceive.

we can be sure they indicate that Hamlet knows Polonius very well as a fawning sycophant. The image could go as far as meaning that Ophelia is a flirt, or possibly even a harlot, but it is unclear whether this is Hamlet's real opinion or whether he attributes this opinion to Polonius.

Hamlet speaks in a superior and symbolic manner, punning

---

[10] *Op. cit.*, p. 172.

and letting off steam by verbally attacking Polonius. Polonius, not understanding, takes Hamlet literally and is more than ever convinced that he is completely mad:

> . . . he is far gone, far gone.   (II.ii.196)

Their conversation continues in the same vein, Hamlet telling Polonius indirectly that he is an old, impotent and senile man. Polonius reacts as if he had an inkling that his conception of Hamlet's insanity was just too crude:

> Though this be madness, yet there is method in't.   (II.ii.208)

He cannot help but see that Hamlet's replies are sometimes "pregnant" but, with a sort of perverse reasoning, believes that it is just Hamlet's insanity that sharpens his wits.

In this conversation, Hamlet has managed to tell Polonius indirectly, through allusions, that he considers him a dishonest man. Although this is certainly true of Polonius, Hamlet does not see his own dishonesty. As we know, he must hide and defend his secret, and this effort to conceal his true feelings and his grim knowledge forces him into a bitter verbal attack. Polonius is not bothered in any way by questions of truth and honesty. He is intellectually unable to comprehend what Hamlet is driving at. His limited mind can only take all these allusions as a further proof of Hamlet's insanity. Since Hamlet has asked about his daughter, he cannot but conclude:

> . . . in my youth, I suffered much extremity for love.
>   (II.ii.188)

Polonius continues the conversation—or, better, the psychiatric interrogation. He wants to prove to himself beyond the shadow of a doubt that Hamlet is insane. Hamlet, with his superiority and agile intelligence, cannot relate to Polonius as a human being. Under the dominance of his own conflict, and irritated by the childish manner in which Polonius tests his sanity, he answers Polonius' questions in an unexpected manner; yet his words are prophetic. When Polonius asks:

> Will you walk out of the air, my lord?   (II.ii.211)

Hamlet answers, "Into my grave?" He does not want to reveal his secret, yet still he gives too much away. When Polonius ends the conversation with formal, conventional address:

> My honourable lord, I will most   (II.ii.222)
> humbly take my leave of you.

Hamlet says:

> You cannot, sir, take from me any thing that   (II.ii.223)
> I will more willingly part withal; except my life,
> except my life, except my life.

He knows he is fighting for his life, but why tell Polonius this? Fortunately, Polonius does not understand it and Hamlet's reaction to this whole conversation is:

> These tedious old fools!   (II.ii.227)

On his part, Hamlet has probably also not understood that Polonius' theory of madness due to love might have further consequences for him.

Now Rosencrantz and Guildenstern enter and Hamlet receives them with all the feelings and attitudes of friendship and camaraderie that evidently have existed among them for a long time. They exchange joking banter, but the mood changes immediately after Rosencrantz uses the word "honest" and soon Hamlet's suspicions are aroused. The talk turns to the condition of Denmark, which Hamlet considers "a prison." Again Hamlet says too much:

> O God, I could be bounded in a nut-shell,   (II.ii.260)
> and count myself a king of infinite space,
> were it not that I have bad dreams.

Obviously, through the visitation of the Ghost, Hamlet's unconscious has been disturbed and it is most natural that he has had "bad dreams."

In our modern psychological approach we do not believe that there are such things as *bad* dreams. The dream has a compensatory function; it adds knowledge which either is not yet known to consciousness, or has been repressed by consciousness. Therefore, every dream is *good* in the sense that it enlarges consciousness and furthers life. Of course, consciousness is frequently unable to integrate certain contents which a dream has brought up, rejects them and reacts to them with negative affects: fear, disgust, etc.

Hamlet certainly refers to his dreams as bad because in some way they probably deal with the murder of his father and with the effect that the Ghost's revelation has had on him, and show that he is not handling the problem in a way that would be compatible with his true nature. Awakening from them would leave him in a bad mood. When Hamlet then says, "A dream itself is but a shadow," Shakespeare's probable meaning is that it is an image without substance. Hamlet's conscious attitude and treatment of Polonius have already revealed his inability to integrate what the unconscious was telling him, and his remark to Rosencrantz and Guildenstern ("I could be bounded in a nut-shell . . ." etc.) indicates that he feels his freedom is seriously limited by a disturbing content of the unconscious. His problem is still as insoluble as ever.

So, after some more of this friendly, witty—but spiked—bantering, Hamlet asks a most natural question:

> . . . what make you at Elsinore?   (II.ii.277)

Rosencrantz answers:

> To visit you, my lord,

but adds:

> no other occasion.

It is this small unnecessary remark that immediately puts Hamlet on guard. Thanking them profusely for their visit, he gives vent to his suspicion:

> Were you not sent for?   (II.ii.282)

They are somewhat flustered; their embarrassment immediately conveys to Hamlet that he is on the right track, so he tells them outright that he knows they were summoned. They play this game of hide-and-seek a little further, trying to act dumb:

> To what end, my lord?   (II.ii.292)

Hamlet responds:

> That you must teach me.

and implores them to be "even and direct" with him. They whisper with each other, and so Hamlet knows now for certain that they were sent for, and then they admit it. Hamlet tells *them* why, in his opinion, they were summoned to court and gives them an explanation which is a masterpiece in covering up what really concerns him. It is the truth, but not the whole truth.

By their admission, Rosencrantz and Guildenstern have now given up working for the King and are really Hamlet's friends. But Hamlet still considers them in the service of the King and therefore his enemies. Again he tells them something which, to a large degree, is true; it betrays some of his secret but also carefully protects the secret. He speaks of his depression, the mood he is in:

> I have of late,—but wherefore I know not,—   (II.ii.314)
> lost all my mirth.

The retraction of the libido from objects is so intense and:

> . . . it goes so heavily with my disposition   (II.ii.316)
> that this goodly frame, the earth, seems to
> me a sterile promontory.

He describes the majestic beauty of nature, the infinite capacities of man in unequaled prose, saying that all this has become meaningless to him; he cannot delight in it; and neither man nor woman can please him any more.

To cheer him, Rosencrantz and Guildenstern tell Hamlet of the arrival of the Players, evidently remembering that he was very fond of the theater. Hamlet evidences great familiarity with it, and shows the true interest of an artist in this discussion, a fact which has been frequently commented on from the literary point of view. From the psychological point of view it shows that in spite of his depression he can discuss at length and in great detail a subject seemingly remote from his immediate problem (further proof that this depression is purely psychological).

Again, his concern with the King and his contempt for him shows up in Hamlet's remarks:

> . . . my uncle is king of Denmark, and those that   (II.ii.388)
> would make mows at him while my father lived,
> give twenty, forty, fifty, a hundred ducats
> apiece, for his picture in little.

And once more Hamlet tells too much for his purpose, but since a flourish announces the arrival of the Players, we do not hear whether Rosencrantz and Guildenstern have caught any of Hamlet's insinuations. Nothing in the later course of the play gives us reason to believe that they have. Hamlet's remarks about the King's picture, therefore, are typical reactions issuing from his complex and so have the character of a monologue, while the preceding discussion was a genuine dialogue.

Hamlet greets the Players in his friendliest manner but again he cannot resist speaking out of his complex when he ends his speech with:

> You are welcome; but my uncle-father   (II.ii.396)
> and aunt-mother are deceived.

Guildenstern eagerly takes up this remark, hoping to find Hamlet's secret, and Hamlet, taking his schoolfellows to be double-dealing knaves, feeds and at the same time denies their notion that he is mad:

> I am but mad north-north-west; when the wind   (II.ii.405)
> is southerly, I know a hawk from a handsaw.[11]

Polonius enters and Hamlet at once attacks him verbally. Using Polonius' belief in his madness as a protection to say the cruelest things about him, he harps, as before, on Polonius' use of his daughter, when he exclaims, seemingly out of context:

> O Jephthah, judge of Israel, what a   (II.ii.431)
> treasure hadst thou!

—referring to a ballad well known in Shakespeare's time. The ballad was based on a story in Judges (Ch. 11, v. 30-40) in which Jephthah, the Judge, had made a vow unto the Lord "that whatsoever cometh forth of the doors of my house to meet me . . . I will offer it up for a burnt offering." The Lord gave Jephthah victory, so when he saw his daughter coming out of the house to meet him "he did with her according to his vow," and she "knew no man." In quoting this ballad, Hamlet implies that, like old Jephthah, Polonius is willing to sacrifice his daughter— not to the Lord but to the King.

Polonius cannot help but admit:

> If you call me Jephthah, my lord, I have a   (II.ii.439)
> daughter that I love passing well.

Hamlet, quick-witted, puns on the word *follows,* when he says, "Nay that follows not." He uses the word in the two meanings:

---

[11] One assumes that this is a misprint and that "handsaw" is a bird (heron).

as a sequence in the ballad, and as a conclusion to be drawn. Polonius, of course, takes this identification of himself with Jephthah as a further sign of Hamlet's madness, since it happens that insane people occasionally do not recognize persons but mistake them for some figure in their imagination. Still, Polonius cannot grasp the meaning of Hamlet's comparison, especially since Hamlet misleads him by taking *follows* in the sense of *sequence in the ballad,* namely, that he is sacrificing his daughter to the King's wishes.[12] In brief, Hamlet sharply perceives Polonius' mercenary and panderous attitude to his daughter, but does not notice his own destructive treatment of Ophelia—that he too makes her a pawn in his game.

The following scene of the arrival of four or five Players and of Hamlet testing them has been commented upon so often that nothing more need be said. The language is intentionally archaic and highly dramatic, telling of vengeance, blood and murder, expressing beautifully the hidden atmosphere at the Danish Court. From a psychological point of view, it is significant that these Players give Hamlet the idea of using them for some form of projective technique, as we would say today. He wants them to perform the play, *The Murder of Gonzago,* and add an extra dozen lines that he himself would write. It is at this point not clear exactly what Hamlet's purpose is in planning this. The soliloquy which immediately follows, however, clarifies his intentions. There we listen in on his most secret thoughts and complex emotions. He is deeply stirred by the ability of the actors to express emotions which are not their own but of a character they only impersonate:

> Is it not monstrous that this player here,   (II.ii.585)
> But in a fiction, in a dream of passion,
> Could force his soul so to his own conceit
> That from her working all his visage wann'd;
> . . . his whole function suiting

[12] Kittredge, p. 196, on "that follows not": "Polonius understands this to mean 'That doesn't *logically* follow,' and takes the remark for mere insanity. There is no deep meaning in the passage: Hamlet is talking madly."

With forms, to his conceit? . . .
For Hecuba!
What's Hecuba to him, or he, to Hecuba,
That he should weep for her?

What would the actor do in Hamlet's circumstances?

He would drown the stage with tears   (II.ii.596)
And cleave the general ear with horrid speech,
Make mad the guilty and appal the free,
Confound the ignorant, and amaze indeed
The very faculties of eyes and ears.

The truth is, however, that Hamlet is not an actor. For him it is
not simply a question of acting out his emotions and impulses.
He contrasts himself with the actor: for the actor, the motives
are not his own, he personifies an imaginary figure, therefore he
can give direct and full expression to his emotions and act accordingly. At this point, Hamlet does not even know whether the
Ghost's report is true, nor is he sure whether the Ghost was a
devil or a good spirit. He is in conflict between himself and the
command of the Ghost. His better nature would not want to
submit unreflectedly to the Ghost's primitive desire for revenge.
On the other hand, he must do something about Claudius. He
seeks a way out of this conflict which will be compatible with the
best in him. His bitter veiled attacks on Polonius have already
demonstrated that his usually friendly, open nature has been
affected by this violent inner disunion. In the following long
monologue, he identifies with the side in him which thinks that
his duty is to fulfill his father's command. He attacks his better
nature, misinterprets his own best motives, blames himself, calls
himself:

    . . . a rogue and peasant slave . . .   (II.ii.584)
    A dull and muddy-mettled rascal, peak,
    Like John-a-dreams . . .
    . . . a coward . . .
    But I am pigeon-livered, and lack gall.

That he feels that he is

> Prompted to my revenge by heaven and hell   (II.ii.621)

agrees with this attitude. We can see the change of attitude here. Before meeting the Ghost, Hamlet had asked the "angels and ministers of grace" to defend him. We know that he was prompted then only by heaven, but now he believes that he is prompted by heaven *and* hell.

Hamlet now very clearly expresses what the purpose of the play will be:

> About, my brains! hum, I have heard   (II.ii.625)
> That guilty creatures sitting at a play
> Have by the very cunning of the scene
> Been struck so to the soul that presently
> They have proclaimed their malefactions;
> For murder, though it have no tongue, will speak
> With most miraculous organ.

The plan which has emerged in his mind during the meeting with the Players takes definite shape. He wants to use it for two purposes. One, to prove decisively whether "The spirit that I have seen may be the devil,"

> and the devil hath power   (II.ii.636)
> To assume a pleasing shape; yea, and perhaps
> Out of my weakness and my melancholy—
> As he is very potent with such spirits—
> Abuses me to damn me.

And, secondly, to establish the guilt of the King. Therefore, he concludes this monologue with:

> . . . the play's the thing   (II.ii.641)
> Wherein I'll catch the conscience of the king.

It might not be superfluous to discuss further Hamlet's intentions in presenting the play. As we noted before, he wants to use this play as a test. In modern language it would be called a projective test, something like the thematic apperception test, which would allow him to recognize the hidden guilt of the King by the affects and reactions the King would have while viewing the play. It would give Hamlet, so he hopes, adequate *psychological* proof for the King's guilt. But beyond that, he hopes that, though the murder was a hidden one, it will speak with "miraculous tongue" and force the King to confess his guilt. In contrast to his first unconditional surrender and his gullible acceptance of the truth of the story, he now gives full consideration to the possibility that the Ghost may have been an evil spirit and may be using the "rotten" situation to destroy him.

Therefore, the presentation of the play appears to Hamlet as an excellent solution. If the King would *really* confess, then a clear course could be pursued. Justice would be served and the best in Hamlet's nature could find its true expression. We must remember that this is the attitude which Hamlet intends to assume, and to compare it with his behavior during and immediately after the play. If he could maintain the attitude he proposes:

> . . . I'll observe his looks;   (II.ii.633)
> I'll tent him to the quick.

he probably would succeed in his purpose: "to catch the conscience of the king."

Harold C. Goddard discusses this situation very clearly:[13]

> The first two acts of *Hamlet,* up to the coming of the players, make plain the character of the burden that has been placed on Hamlet's shoulders and what he ought *not* to do to discharge it. His soul cries out over and over: Do not obey your father. Do not kill the King. . . . Like his creator's, Hamlet's heart of hearts is in dramatic and poetic art.

What I call "better nature," Goddard puts in beautiful terms:

[13] *Op. cit.,* pp. 360-362.

His evil spirit had told him to kill the King. His good angel tells him to show the King to himself by holding up the mirror of art before him. The dagger or the play? That is the question. It is God's Hamlet who chooses the play.

The end of the second act leaves us with great tension. Will our expectation for the success of Hamlet's plan be fulfilled? Or will intervening events, or a change of attitude in Hamlet, distort the issue?

Act Three

i

The third act opens with a talk between the King and Queen and the two gentlemen—Rosencrantz and Guildenstern—in the presence of Polonius and Ophelia. We enter into a conversation which has evidently been going on for a little while. The King asks Rosencrantz and Guildenstern if in their meeting with Hamlet they were able to discover the reasons for what he, Claudius, now calls Hamlet's "confusion." Only the day before he had spoken of Hamlet's "transformation"; now it has become "turbulent and dangerous lunacy." Rosencrantz and Guildenstern tell him quite truthfully that Hamlet feels depressed ("he feels himself distracted") but that he will not reveal the cause. Guildenstern reports on Hamlet's resistance to being spied upon, and speaks of his behavior as "crafty madness." He again refers to Hamlet's defense against revealing his true state of mind:

> . . . keeps aloof (III.i.8)
> When we would bring him on to some confession
> Of his true state.

Rosencrantz and Guildenstern complete their report on Hamlet by speaking of his interest in the Players. If they understand anything of Hamlet's hints, they certainly do not mention them. Although they are quite truthful in their report, they do not betray Hamlet. Polonius then conveys Hamlet's invitation to the King and Queen "to hear and see the matter." The King joyfully responds, taking it as an indication of an improvement in Hamlet's condition.

After Rosencrantz and Guildenstern depart, the King asks the Queen to leave so that he and Polonius can pursue their plan alone. Ophelia, however, is present when this odious plan is discussed. They intend to have Hamlet meet Ophelia by accident, as it were, and to observe what happens between them, claiming that as parents they are justified in this distasteful action:

> Her father and myself, lawful espials. (III.i.32)

They want to find out if the "affliction of his love" has produced his condition, and the Queen repeats the same attitude of other characters (Ophelia, Laertes; cp. p. 51):

> I shall obey you. (III.i.38)

Now she calls Hamlet's attitude "wildness." She can never call it *madness* or *lunacy,* as the King and Polonius do. Both the King and Queen consider Hamlet's condition an illness; their psychological reactions, however, are very different. The Queen wants to help Hamlet, while the King's actions, and those of Polonius, are obviously due to murkier motives.

Polonius advises Ophelia to "colour" (disguise) her true intentions by reading a book, obviously a prayer book or something devotional. Grebanier[1] points to the use of the word "colour," in Hamlet's time, as "allegeable ground or reason." I believe that, as Shakespeare so often did with words in the play, he used this word in different meanings. Polonius' next line:

> . . . with devotion's visage (III.i.47)
> And pious action we do sugar o'er
> The devil himself.

[1] *Op. cit.,* p. 234.

proves that it was not only meant as a prop, but also as a disguise, thus showing clearly that he knows that his present action is a devilish thing. Unwittingly, he frankly describes an important aspect not only of his personal psychology, but of the whole play, one to which Hamlet has reacted with much disgust and revulsion in Act I:

That one may smile, and smile, and be a villain. (I.v.108)

The King, hearing this, is cut to the quick. We see that he himself suffers from his guilt and the need to "paint" over it (another example of *Sein* and *Schein*). This insight, however, does not prevent him from doing a devilish thing right now: he goes ahead with his spying.

Hamlet enters, oblivious at first of Ophelia's presence. There follows the famous and the most misunderstood monologue which begins with the words, "To be, or not to be: that is the question." We hear Hamlet's thoughts in the monologue, of which Grebanier says:[2]

. . . celebrated (and most completely misunderstood) of his soliloquies . . . too celebrated for its own good, despite the majesty of its utterance.

I regret that it was not I who also said:

As we approach consideration of the "To be or not to be" soliloquy we are overwhelmed with concern: what apology can serve our turn for having the temerity to offer a new account of this celebrated passage? Well, to our business—*nec deus intersit nisi dignus vindice nodus!*

Grebanier discusses at great length a large number of interpretations by many commentators of this monologue. I cannot discuss all of his valuable work in this respect. However, since he has given so much attention to this particular passage, it would

[2] *Ibid.*, pp. 203, 205, 208, 209.

appear very helpful to mention his own viewpoint. I fully agree
with him that Hamlet does not meditate suicide. Grebanier starts
with the important question: What is the dramatic fact behind
the present soliloquy?

> Tonight "The Murder of Gonzago" will surely "catch the con-
> science of the King" if he is guilty. If he prove so, Hamlet must
> outline at once a plan of action that will enable him to avenge
> his father. The Prince now stands on the very threshold of the
> crisis of his problem. The closer the great event approaches,
> the harder it is for him to wait. He speaks, therefore, somewhat
> from impatience; but he also speaks somewhat from awareness
> that beyond tonight's test of Claudius lie, it may be, heavy
> deeds for him to do—deeds of blood and death.

In Grebanier's opinion, the famous words "To be or not to be"
are *colorless* and *abstract:*

> They are, we have said, colorless and abstract. Shakespeare
> wanted them so. There is no warrant for paraphrasing the first
> line into anything more concrete than "Is it (or, possibly, is
> this thing) to be or is it not to be—that is the question." What
> is this *it* or this *thing?* There can be no warrant for identifying
> it as more than some conclusion or decision Hamlet has just
> come to.

Grammatically, one is required to add "it" or the "thing" to
arrive at Grebanier's conclusions. So Grebanier asks what *is* this
"it" or this "thing"?

Goddard's understanding of the play, which I feel is most
akin to mine, leads him to believe that the question in the monologue is *whether to be a murderer or not.* He has *also* added an
"it"—for him, the murderer.

By adding a grammatical object ("it" or a "murderer"), *to be*
becomes an auxiliary verb and changes the meaning of the line.
Though even the greatest scholar cannot with the greatest cer-
tainty pretend to know exactly what Shakespeare meant
("Shakespeare wanted them so"), I believe that we are not per-

mitted to change the text from "To be or not to be" to "To be something or not to be something." My instinct and that of most commentators rejects such an assumption. I do not feel that Shakespeare meant these words as "colorless and abstract." Considering the whole philosophical trend in Hamlet's thinking, I am inclined to believe that "To be or not to be" is the most important question in the play, dramatically in the center of its structure, and pivotal in Hamlet's philosophy. It is *the* question of existence or non-existence. In support of this opinion, I can adduce Hamlet's answer to the Queen's question:

> All that live must die;   (I.ii.72)
> . . . If it *be*,
> Why *seems* it so particular with thee?

To which he replied:

> Seems, madam! Nay, it is; I know not 'seems.'

Before Hamlet encountered the Ghost, the question for him was between *to be* and *to seem*. Putting the lines side by side is evidence by analogy that Shakespeare is here discussing the question of existence and non-existence. Now, *after* meeting the Ghost and having reflected on him and the vistas that confrontation opened on the nature of life, the question for him has changed from *to be* or *to seem* into *to be* or *not to be*.

As Grebanier correctly pointed out, this monologue reveals a conflict between two different attitudes toward handling Claudius. One is: "In the *mind* to suffer the slings and arrows of outrageous fortune," that is, to wait patiently until the situation clears up, until the King, forced by circumstance and evidence, proclaims his guilt and until Hamlet has properly integrated the experience of the Ghost in his mind. In the second attitude, being pushed by his ghost complex and the impulse for revenge, he would give in to them and act. In that case he knows he would surely be killed as well. Having seen the Ghost returning from hell ("thou, dead corse, again, in complete steel, revisits thus the glimpses of the moon"), he quite naturally asks himself what death (the state of non-being, "not to be") would mean. He considers the possibility (based on his experience of the Ghost) that physical death would not necessarily mean the end of everything, that—as we would say in modern language—the activity of the unconscious would continue after death:

> . . . To die,—to sleep;—   (III.i.64)
> To sleep! *perchance to dream!* ay, there's the rub;
> For in that sleep of death *what dreams may come,*
> When we have shuffled off this mortal coil,
> Must give us pause; there's the respect
> That makes calamity of so long life.

The threat of something *after* death "puzzles the will" of Hamlet. As Coleridge has already pointed out, the phrase, "The undiscovered country from whose bourn no traveller returns," does not contradict this. It refers to a man's own house, his own living body. Of course, no one ever returns to his own body, but as Hamlet knows from his ghost experience, a non-material psychic condition does continue after death. He reflects on this after-death state: the uncertainty of what terrible things one might suffer there makes one rather stay alive and "bear those ills we have than fly to others that we know not of." I agree with Grebanier that these "ills" Hamlet refers to have a most personal meaning in his particular situation. It is, however, this consciousness ("conscience" in the Elizabethan sense of the word) of a Bardo and its terrible sufferings:

> GHOST: Doom'd for a certain term to walk the night   (I.v.10)
> And for the day confined to fast in fires,
> . . . I am forbid
> To tell the secrets of my prison-house,
> I could a tale unfold whose lightest word
> Would harrow up thy soul, freeze thy young blood,

which "makes cowards of us all":

> And thus the native hue of resolution   (III.i.84)
> Is sicklied o'er with the pale cast of thought.

Hamlet's numinous experience has opened up in him thoughts beyond the "reaches of our soul" which have widened his consciousness immensely, but the time has been rather short (two months) for him to deal with it adequately. Furthermore, nothing exists in western culture which teaches him that all these phenomena are the embodiment of his own mind, or as we would say in modern psychological language: they arise in the unconscious psyche. They are not products of consciousness, nor of the ego, but are *autonomous* manifestations of one's own psyche. Hamlet did not have such advice as is given in *The Tibetan Book of the Dead:* [3]

> Fear not that. Be not awed. Know it to be the embodiment of thine own intellect.

Consequently, Hamlet has no chance to integrate the ghost experience. He can make conscious whatever the Ghost conveyed to him about the after-death state, but the nature of the Ghost and its character remain largely unconscious. Thus a ghost complex is formed in him; by its very unconsciousness, it infects him. In psychological terms, the autonomous unconscious complex contaminates him. It instills in him the desire for revenge, but at the same time he feels the paralyzing effect of the ghost complex:

> . . . enterprises of great pith and moment   (II.i.86)
> With this regard their currents turn awry,
> And lose the name of action.

As this monologue shows, the conflict in Hamlet is between patiently waiting for a clarification of the situation and a bal-

---

[3] Edited by W. Y. Evans-Wentz (Oxford Univ. Press, London, 1957), p. 137.

anced and satisfactory integration of the ghost experience (an attitude which requires great tension capacity)—and the impulse for revenge which he is driven to by the command of the Ghost. Hamlet is hit in the core of his existence by the invasion of unconscious material. The ghost complex has become a "boil" in his being. He is thrown into a profound conflict by it and therefore is unable to follow a clear course. Earlier, in the second scene of Act II, he still thought:

> . . . if he but blench   (II.ii.626)
> I know my course.

But, in the meantime, the insidious infection by the Ghost has made progress. Now, in the monologue of the first scene in Act III, Hamlet's conscious attitude has changed. Reflection, thought and consciousness are deprecated:

> Thus conscience does make cowards of us all.   (83)

He realizes his incapacity for clear decision:

> . . . the native hue of resolution   (III.i.84)
> Is sicklied o'er with the pale cast of thought.

In short, by contamination with the Ghost, Hamlet's desire for action and revenge have become stronger than his patience to deal carefully with the complicated inner and outer situations. The course of the tragedy is determined by this "boil" in Hamlet's psyche.

If Hamlet could have arrived at a realization that the Ghost was part of his own psyche, it would have been possible for him to integrate this complex and he would have acted very differently than he does in the play. (Of course, we would then also have no play!) In that case, "conscience" (consciousness) would have received the highest value. I speak about this from my experience as a psychotherapist. I have seen a number of cases in which a person was contaminated by a ghost complex, and in which consciousness, a full realization of the nature and character of a ghost, a proper confrontation with the problems "beyond the reaches of our soul," allowed an integration of this strange content, brought a healing (making whole), and consequently an enriched vitality. In this connection I would like to point to W. H. Clemen's discussion of this passage, in which he rejects the customary interpretation of it as "reflection hinders action." In his *The Development of Shakespeare's Imagery,*[4] he says:

> Here the image does not serve the purpose of merely casting a decorative cloak about the thought; it is much rather an intrinsic part of the thought. . . . Hamlet sees this problem under the aspect of a process of the human organism. The original bright colouring of the skin is concealed by an ailment. Thus the relation between thought and action appears not as an opposition between two abstract principles between which a free choice is possible, but as an unavoidable condition of human nature. The image of the leprous ailment emphasizes the malignant, disabling, slowly disintegrating nature of the process.

It is due to Hamlet's essentially introspective nature and to his intuitive capacity that the unconscious flows easily into his consciousness. By its very nature, the unconscious expresses itself mostly in images, and it is this direct perception of the inner theater that quite naturally presents itself as images. Therefore, Hamlet does not speak in similes ("like") but as a truly intuitive personality. Imagery becomes the suit of his thoughts. This form of expression is much more adequate in formulating the complexity of his thought processes, but it is also much more difficult for the rational mind to understand. It explains the dilemma of the other characters in the play (and of many critics) in understanding Hamlet, and as so often in life, if one does not understand a thought or a person, human nature is inclined to declare it or him "crazy" or "stupid." [5]

[4] Harvard Univ. Press, Cambridge, 1951, pp. 111-112.
[5] Jung, *Psychology and Alchemy,* p. 52: "The experience of the unconscious is a personal secret communicable only to a very few, and that with difficulty."

In particular, this image of the "leprous distilment" (I.v.64) expresses most comprehensively the nature of the ghost complex in Hamlet. Its "malignant, disabling, slowly disintegrating nature" is due to its unconsciousness; consequently, it is projected on other persons, specifically the King, the Queen and Polonius. Since the Ghost is of an archetypal nature, too, it also expresses itself in the situation and is part of the psychology of other individuals—again, King, Queen—but, in addition, of the collective atmosphere of Denmark ("something is rotten in the state of Denmark").

Returning now to the analysis of the play itself, we find that Hamlet's thoughts, as expressed in this monologue, are at this moment interrupted by Ophelia. His love for her instinctively speaks:

> Soft you now!   (III.i.88)
> The fair Ophelia! Nymph, in thy orisons
> Be all my sins remember'd.

She addresses him rather formally. Hamlet reacts also rather formally. And then, unexpectedly, Ophelia proposes to return some little presents (which it is customary and charming for lovers to exchange). This to Hamlet indicates a rejection, especially at this moment when he had been prevented from seeing her for some time. Actually, this is Ophelia's weak feminine attempt to reestablish contact with him and regain his love.

Hamlet is rather flustered, denies that he ever gave her anything. Taken aback, Ophelia thinks that Hamlet has deserted her, has given up his love for her, and is even accusing her of unkindness. But mostly she thinks that he must be crazy to deny such an obvious fact. He misunderstands her weak feminine play. Kittredge says:[6]

> From this point Hamlet talks as insanely as he knows how. Ophelia replies with the gentle firmness which one might use

[6] *Op. cit.,* p. 211.

to a refractory child, until Hamlet's feigned madness grows so
distressing that she can only pray to heaven for his relief. No
doubt Hamlet suspects that somebody is listening, and he
cannot afford to take chances. Whether or not Ophelia is acting
under instructions, it is necessary that she should share the
general opinion that he has lost his mind. Indeed, it is far more
merciful to her to confirm that impression than to let her think
that he is sane and does not love her.

J. Dover Wilson has a very different opinion:[7]

> Ophelia has overplayed her part: it was not he who had jilted
> her but she him, at her father's command; her little speech,
> 'sententious' and 'couched in rhyme, has an air of having been
> prepared' (Dowden); finally, though he meets her 'by accident'
> she is ready with her trinkets. Hamlet is now on his guard; he
> knows that both the King and Polonius are listening; and what
> he says for the rest of the scene is designed for their ears.

How would Hamlet know of the plot of the King and Polonius? There is the possibility that at this moment he becomes
aware of Polonius hiding behind an "arras." The very fact that
he asks:

> Are you honest? . . . Are you fair? (III.i.103)

demonstrates that Hamlet is not insane. These questions appear
out of context. They are discourteous, to say the least, but in
this situation his suspicion has been aroused. He must have won-
dered why she had the trinkets ready when she was supposed to
be meeting him by accident. She does not understand the purpose of these offensive questions, but *his* answer is obviously
sensible:

> That if you be honest and fair, your honesty (III.i.107)
> should admit no discourse to your beauty.

[7] *Hamlet,* p. 193.

—further proof that Hamlet is not insane.

Ophelia then asks a most obvious and understandable question:

> Could beauty, my lord, have better (III.i.110)
> commerce than with honesty?

Hamlet's answer is somewhat complex, and he admits that what he says is "sometimes a paradox." He is probably thinking here of his mother. His thought is directed by the ghost complex and his mother's remarriage, for which he has not yet any clear answer. The anima image which had already been injured by his mother's incestuous marriage is now utterly negative. He tries to disguise his secret and to lead Ophelia and the listening Polonius onto the wrong track. He tells Ophelia that he did love her *once,* then in the next breath that he *had not* loved her. He then blackwashes himself, not quite believing what he himself is saying. He accuses himself of sins which are not properly his, but nevertheless are unsuspected qualities in himself. These qualities express more of the psychology of the Ghost. Hamlet now has a double personality. His ego complex and the ghost complex have become one. He probably does not quite believe that he has such dark qualities ("I am very proud, revengeful, ambitious"). He uses them for a purpose. He hopes that Ophelia can give him up more easily if she knows him as a bad character. He gives her vehement advice:

> Get thee to a nunnery! (III.i.145)

Five times in this long conversation he repeats the same admonition, each time of course in a different tone, conveying different meanings. I am inclined to believe that Shakespeare meant the word "nunnery" as a *convent* and not, as J. Dover Wilson thinks, a "house of ill fame." Hamlet's main purpose is to get Ophelia out of the atmosphere of the court with its intrigues and loose sexual morals.

Hamlet ends this aggressive scene by testing Ophelia's honesty once again:

> Where's your father? (III.i.135)

When she says, "At home, my lord," Hamlet knows for sure that she lies and is up to something. Deeply hurt, he sees all evil as originating from women:

> . . . if thou wilt needs marry, marry a fool, (III.i.146)
> for wise men know well enough what monsters
> you make of them. To a nunnery, go; and quickly too.

At the same time he has pity for her, knowing that she is more a victim of her father's intrigue than a plotting enemy. In spite of his hurt, his love is still there and he wishes to protect her from being further involved in the sinister plans of her father and the King. Therefore, he repeats his advice: "To a nunnery, go." It is good advice but presented with so much aggressive bitterness and affect that it must seem to Ophelia to be out of context. She cannot understand it, much less accept it. She is quite bewildered. She does not in the least see what she herself is doing. Instead of contact, the rift between them seems unbridgeable. They evidently talk at cross purposes. She cannot help but take all of his speeches and advice as the ramblings of a disturbed mind. It is certainly true that Hamlet is profoundly changed, that he is "blasted" with something. We, the spectators, know it is the Ghost and the terrible secret of the hidden murder. Furthermore, we have to consider that whenever something is unknown we involuntarily project our own condition into the other person and into an outside situation. The deep disturbance in the psychic structure of Ophelia, caused by her enforced rejection of her love for Hamlet, is projected on Hamlet. Her utter lack of understanding breaks her relationship with the only person with whom she has had a meaningful contact. She becomes completely isolated. This isolation in the course of time will also activate her unconscious, as it did with Hamlet, but her consciousness is weak and brittle and cannot stand the activation of the unconscious. It is *her own mind* which is here overthrown by Hamlet's harsh and aggressive words. Her consciousness must break as a result of the withdrawal of her libido from Hamlet.

The King has received a very different impression from overhearing the encounter between Hamlet and Ophelia. He knows that:

> . . . what he spake, though it lacked form a little, (III.i.170)
> Was not like madness.

He realizes that it is some content that is occupying Hamlet's consciousness completely:

> There's something in his soul (III.i.172)
> O'er which his melancholy sits on brood.

But now of course the King has a strong suspicion that perhaps, in some way unknown to him, Hamlet might have found out the truth about the old King's death:

> And I do doubt the hatch and the disclose (III.i.174)
> Will be some danger.

His unspoken conclusion is that Hamlet's continued presence at the court will be dangerous for him. He decides, "in quick determination," to send Hamlet to England, and veils his suspicion in a thick cloud of hope:

> Haply the seas and countries different (III.i.180)
> With variable objects shall expel
> This something-settled matter in his heart.

Polonius, of course, still thinks that Hamlet's love affair with Ophelia is somehow at the bottom of the whole matter, and he proposes a repetition of the experiment. He wants to listen in again on Hamlet, only this time the conversation should be with

his mother. Maybe *she* will find out and, if not, there is still time
to send him to England or

> . . . confine him where (III.i.194)
> Your wisdom best shall think.

The King agrees to this, ending the scene with the famous line:

> Madness in great ones must not unwatch'd go. (III.i.196)

ii

Now begins the great scene of the play-within-a-play which
shows Hamlet at his best, as the artist with full understanding of
the theater. It is a scene of highest symbolism. I find Goddard's
comments on it most rewarding and would refer the reader to his
book.

Our main interest is in Hamlet's psychology. When Polonius,
Rosencrantz and Guildenstern enter, Hamlet's only question is:

> . . . will the king hear this piece of work? (III.ii.52)

After they leave, and while Hamlet is waiting for the Players to
perform, Horatio enters. It is an opportunity for Hamlet to express his gratitude and love for his only friend and confidant at
court. He feels the unique quality of this relationship; it was his
soul that made this choice and their friendship can never be
broken:

> Since my dear soul was mistress of her choice (III.ii.68)
> And could of men distinguish, her election
> Hath seal'd thee for herself.

He also gives the reasons for this extraordinary friendship. He
attributes to his friend a steadiness and a detachment:

> For thou hast been (III.ii.70)
> As one, in suffering all, that suffers nothing.

Horatio's behavior throughout the play indicates that this is truly Horatio's character. In spite of having seen the Ghost himself, the experience has not changed him. But Hamlet is profoundly changed by his encounter with the Ghost. He has lost his steadiness and has been deeply involved in the world around him. The following lines:

> . . . and bless'd are those　　　　　　　　　　(III.ii.73)
> Whose blood and judgment are so well commingled,
> That they are not a pipe for fortune's finger
> To sound what stop she pleases. Give me that man
> That is not passion's slave, and I will wear him
> In my heart's core, ay, in my heart of heart,
> As I do thee.

though addressed to Horatio, express Hamlet's own psychology. They emphasize even more clearly what Hamlet has lost and what he has become. He is now "a pipe for fortune's finger to sound what stop she pleases." He is now "passion's slave," but he does not realize that in truth he is speaking about himself. He hopes that Horatio's presence might help him to be steady, but, alas, circumstances will put him in critical situations without his dearly beloved Horatio. Turning from expressions of love for his friend, he asks for his practical help. He implores Horatio to watch the King most carefully during the play. He needs this in order to decide once and for all whether the King is guilty or whether he, Hamlet, is plagued by foul fantasies, whether

> . . . my imaginations are as foul　　　　　　　(III.ii.88)
> As Vulcan's stithy.

Later they will compare notes, as it were,

> In censure of his seeming,　　　　　　　　　　(III.ii.91)

in order to arrive at an objective opinion on what the King's behavior has revealed.

It is important to note here that Hamlet's purpose in using the play as a form of projective technique is limited to a psychological test. He wants to know the truth about his uncle's guilt, and clarification about the nature of the Ghost. He does not hope for a confession of guilt, as he had earlier:

> That guilty creatures sitting at a play   (II.ii.626)
> Have by the very cunning of the scene
> Been struck so to the soul that presently
> They have proclaimed their malefactions.

Horatio, of course, cooperates and promises to give his unreserved attention to the King during the play. Hamlet's closing remark, "I must be idle," I take to mean "inactive"—in full agreement with Grebanier. It is another expression of Hamlet's attitude of dissembling and hiding his secret.

Now the King enters. Upon seeing him, Hamlet, who just a few minutes before had praised his good friend Horatio for his steadiness, now reacts in a totally different way. He loses his control. Emotions well up which carry images with them, images which although they have profound meaning for him must be utterly puzzling for the King.

The King asks, in a rather conventional way:

> How fares our cousin Hamlet?   (III.ii.97)

He expects a conventional answer, of course. But Hamlet, under the influence of his emotions, quickly takes the other meaning of the word "fare"—in the sense of feeding. In rapid succession, he introduces the image of the chameleon, which was supposed to feed on light and air, taking it also in the symbolic meaning of mind and spirit, then adds "promise-crammed," and further, "You cannot feed capons so."

The King is suddenly confronted with images which his mind cannot fathom quickly, if at all; he can only sense that there is an attack in them. What Hamlet is telling him is: I change my appearances according to the changing situation (chameleons);

you have been feeding me with unsubstantial food, have made all sorts of promises which you certainly do not intend to fulfill. You try to castrate me (capons), but not even a castrate can live on such promises. Although, and because, he is disturbed in his depths, the King defends himself by rejecting the stream of images:

> I have nothing with this answer, Hamlet;   (III.ii.101)
> these words are not mine.

To which Hamlet responds with a parting thrust:

> No, nor mine now.

This is also true. A conscious Hamlet, who would have wanted to remain an objective observer of the King, would have acted in the same conventional, polite manner—but the unconscious complex has the upper hand. His "dagger was in his mouth." He is completely gripped by this aggressive mood, which is also fed by a need to show off his superior intelligence. Turning to Polonius, he asks:

> My lord, you played once i' the university, you say?   (III.ii.105)

This sounds like the beginning of a friendly conversation. Polonius falls for it and, in the manner of small talk, answers with some pride:

> That did I, my lord, and was accounted a good actor.
>   (III.ii.106)
> . . .
> I did enact Julius Caesar; I was killed i' the
> Capitol; Brutus killed me.

Again Hamlet's verbal dagger is plunged into Polonius:

> It was a brute part of him to kill so   (III.ii.111)
> capital a calf there.

At this time, Hamlet's "prophetic soul" does not anticipate that this verbal act will become a factual deed very shortly afterward —and with the same unconcern about killing such a "capital calf." This statement also shows Hamlet's unconscious condemnation of the act ("it was a brute part of him"), but again Hamlet does not listen to himself. He abruptly turns away from Polonius and gives his attention to the Players.

The Queen asks Hamlet to sit by her but, speaking of Ophelia as a stronger magnet, he responds:

No, good mother, here's metal more attractive. (III.ii.117)

Polonius takes this remark as a confirmation of his fixed idea concerning the cause of Hamlet's so-called madness. Hamlet, who in his previous talk with Ophelia had aggressively advised her not to marry, to go to a nunnery, now speaks to her with slightly veiled sexual allusions, implying that sex is uppermost in her mind (as he is convinced is true of his mother). This short conversation between Hamlet and Ophelia has given rise to many commentaries, especially in regard to Elizabethan mores. It certainly indicates that a great intimacy had existed at one time between Hamlet and Ophelia, although it does not prove whether or not a sexual relationship had existed. It is, however, dramatically important, as it indicates the same aggressive mood and tension which was descriptive of Hamlet before the play started. He attacks everyone in his most sensitive spot. He hits everyone's "complex." He also reveals that he is deeply hurt by his mother's behavior and taunts her with his conviction that the reason for her marriage to Claudius was nothing more than sensuality.

Like Polonius, Ophelia falls for Hamlet's pretense—that his father died within two hours:

Nay, 'tis twice two months, my lord. (III.ii.137)

With bitterness, Hamlet speaks of his disappointment in his mother's faithfulness and purity and, quoting from an old bal-

lad, implies that his dear father was nothing more to his mother
than a "hobby-horse," a figure of something quickly forgotten
and probably also alluding once again to sexuality, and thus expressing his low opinion of her.[8]

Now the dumb-show occurs which acts out the crime exactly
as the Ghost had told it to Hamlet. Evidently it goes very fast;
there seems to be no reaction from the Queen or the King. Only
Ophelia asks, "What means this?" In his reply, Hamlet uses a
Spanish expression:

> Marry, this is miching mallecho; it means mischief.
>
> (III.ii.149)

Again, Hamlet tells too much. Under pressure of the knowledge
he is trying to suppress, something spills over. Fortunately,
Ophelia does not understand, but his remark reveals that some
of the unconscious impulse has affected his purpose. At this
point his motive is no longer pure. No longer is he interested in
bringing out the truth. He has forgotten his promise to Horatio
("mine eyes will rivet to his face"); his purpose is dark, *mis-
chievous.*

While the Prologue enters, Hamlet cannot help throwing poisoned remarks at Ophelia. They are also a projection, however,
because he tells too much:

> The players cannot keep counsel; *they'll tell all.*   (III.ii.152)

Ophelia reacts like any decent girl:

---

[8] Kittredge, p. 222: "The hobby-horse was a very ancient character in
May games and morris dances. In Shakespeare's time, however, he was
frequently omitted, partly because the Puritan's regarded him as a remnant of heathen superstition."—J. Dover Wilson, p. 200: "To be remembered nowadays, says Hamlet, one must be a pious benefactor, for the
pious are becoming the only power in the land and are sweeping away
the harmless old pleasures. 'For O . . . forgot' was a line from a popular
ballad, as frequently quoted and jested upon as the refrain of a music-hall
song to-day, partly no doubt because of the equivocal meaning of 'hobby-
horse.' "

You are naught, you are naught; I'll mark the play.

(III.ii.158)

The play begins and the Player King and Player Queen now act out the play, speaking in rather stilted language. As the play progresses, Hamlet's tension increases and causes him to shoot off more poisoned remarks like:

. . . Wormwood, wormwood! (III.ii.193)

—certainly expressing the bitterness of his feeling, but also punning, indicating that the Player Queen, representing his mother, is like wood eaten by worms. When the Player Queen leaves the stage, there is an opportunity for a short conversation between Hamlet and the Queen. Hamlet asks:

Madam, how like you this play? (III.ii.241)

The Queen, quite innocently indicating how utterly unaware she is that this play within a play is intended by Hamlet to test her, replies with the now famous lines which show how great a psychologist Shakespeare was. Any psychological complex necessitates compensatory reaction by consciousness, especially those associated with guilt. The Queen is guilty but represses the guilt and yet is naïvely able to perceive the compensatory attitude in the Player Queen:

The lady doth protest too much, methinks. (III.ii.242)

Hamlet, continuing his attack, says:

O, but she'll keep her word. (III.ii.244)

—(meaning: "not like you"). The Queen does not realize at all that the situation in the play-scene is exactly the same situation she was in only four months before. It may seem incredible that people can forget or repress such important matters in such a very short time, but the psychotherapist observes even stranger things. I saw a woman once who had completely forgotten an extramarital sexual experience she had had a week before. Such people have a psychology like a drop of oil on water: like the oil, which never mixes with water, their consciousness has no communication with the unconscious.

For the Queen, this play is entertainment, a killing-of-time. In no way does she identify with the Player Queen. Hamlet, in his aggressive attitude, directs his words principally at Claudius. Claudius' guilt is much more active; he cannot repress it. Hamlet's words disturb him. He becomes alarmed and, with the increasing tension, cannot help but ask:

> Is there no offence in't? (III.ii.245)

Hamlet answers, "No, no," but means "Yes, yes":

> . . . they do but jest, poison in jest; (III.ii.246)

implying: but *you* did it in full earnest.

Only now the King asks:

> What do *you* call the play? (III.ii.249)

—a very interesting slip. It indicates first how utterly unaware of Hamlet's purposes the King was when he came to see the play; and second, how he is now so unconsciously sure that the play has been acted out in the pursuit of Hamlet's purpose that he does not ask: *what* is the play called? or what is the name of the play?—but what do *you* call the play?

Hamlet has become like a hunter pursuing his prey, the King so much a victim of his own guilt that Hamlet can answer with "The Mouse-Trap," not the true title of this play but certainly the true title of Hamlet's plot. To an extent which Hamlet does not realize himself, this play has become a projective test for him, too, at least to the same degree that it is for the King. There is no question any more of merely finding out the truth about his father's death, nor even the hope that, under the impact of the play, murder will speak with "miraculous tongue"; Hamlet is now the pursuer who wants to kill his victim. Without a moment's hesitation, without reflecting what this would do to his cause, the unconscious supplies him with the image of the mousetrap. Punning further, he uses the word "tropically," which sounds almost like *trap*ically.

Under the pressure of this hunter attitude (an inferior part of his personality), Hamlet bursts out with a stream of images:

> This play is the image of a murder done   (III.ii.251)
> in Vienna. (*Not here in Denmark.*)
> . . .
> 'tis a knavish piece of work; but what o'that?
> your majesty, and we that have free souls, it
> touches us not.

Of course Hamlet knows that the King has no "free soul," cannot look at the play with detachment. On the contrary, the King's soul is, like Cain's, possessed by terrible guilt. What Hamlet does not notice is that *his* soul is not free either. He is possessed by the Ghost and the fires of hell which are inevitably associated with the Ghost. Hamlet amplifies with a bitter image:

> . . . let the galled jade wince, our withers   (III.ii.254)
> are unwrung.

That is, let the vicious horse, which is somehow possessed by something like an evil spirit, *flinch*—but we with our "free souls" are not hit in the back, in the unconscious.

Lucianus enters and, in stating who this player is, Hamlet catches himself for a moment. Ophelia responds half-admiringly and half-ironically:

> You are a chorus, my lord.   (III.ii.259)

Somewhat impatiently Hamlet orders the actor to begin, expressing again his own unconscious psychology:

> Begin, murderer . . .   (III.ii.267)
> . . . the croaking raven doth bellow for revenge.

Hamlet, the "courtier, scholar, soldier" (III.i.159), has now become a "croaking raven." The raven in medieval psychology was a symbol of the devil. These comments with which Hamlet accompanies the dumb-show in the play make him into a rat-catcher; he croaks and bellows for revenge, but does not yet know himself how much he has changed.

When the player finally pours poison into the sleeper's ear, Hamlet again speaks like a Chorus, announcing the further course of the play. The King, seeing his own crime duplicated on the stage, cannot stand the reenactment. The terrible tension in him forces him to move. To this extent he has given himself away; he now knows for certain that Hamlet is cognizant of his secret. But to the same extent, Hamlet has given *himself* away. However, murder has not spoken with "miraculous tongue." The King has *not* proclaimed his crime. This was made absolutely impossible by Hamlet's attitude of rat-catcher, by his only slightly disguised desire for revenge. The King, fighting for his life, has become an enemy of Hamlet, and knows that if he wants to retain his kingship he must kill the Prince. So when the King rises and leaves in a very upset state, Hamlet, again dissembling, exclaims:

> What, frighted with false fire!   (III.ii.282)

Hamlet knows very well the reason for the King's flight, yet it is also true that it was a "false fire," that it was not the genuine fire in him that had made all the punning and aggressive remarks in the play, but the *false* fire of his hellish desire for revenge.

Grebanier remarks on the peculiar involvement of Polonius in this scene. It is he who stops the play. This action, together with certain remarks which show how indulgent the King is toward this dotard, suggests that Polonius possibly knew or possibly even helped the King in the murder. Psychologically, this is perhaps the darkest moment in the whole play—dark in the sense that

the light of consciousness which was present in Hamlet's monologue (III.i.83: "Conscience does make cowards of us all") is
dimmed by Hamlet's affect and now seems extinguished by his
murderous desire for revenge. As we see later, the King is suffering deeply from his guilt and is aware that his crime has placed
darkness in his soul. Concretely confronted with his crime in a
stage play, he needs light to comprehend his terrible psychological situation. Therefore, it is deeply symbolic when the King
gasps, "Give me some light," and the audience shouts, "Lights,
lights, lights!"

Now that Hamlet knows of the crime and all its details, the
King is also confronted with a new situation which he cannot
comprehend. Hamlet is in a heightened mood, over-elated; forgotten is his early intention of just finding the truth. Now he
speaks as the hunter whose arrow has hit the deer, whose aggressive intention has found its mark in the King, and he is sure
that inevitably the deer (the King) will die of it. He feels that
this is the way of the world ("For some must watch, while some
must sleep"). He has done such a good job of it that even if
everything else went wrong in his life he would still find a place
as an actor. Horatio's more balanced opinion is rejected. Hamlet
is convinced of the Ghost's veracity and only now do he and
Horatio discuss their observations and compare notes, as it
were.

Hamlet is in such a gay and gleeful state of mind that he asks
for music: he thinks he has won a victory over the King. It does
not matter any more whether the King likes the comedy. Quoting and singing from an old ballad, Hamlet makes it clear that
Denmark is not ruled by a true king, but by a "pajock." Although its exact meaning is not known, this is obviously a derog-
atory term.

At this moment, Rosencrantz and Guildenstern enter. These
former friends are by now treated by Hamlet as enemies—and
their own behavior, their entrance as messengers of the King,
confirms Hamlet's opinion of them. Again Hamlet constantly
puns on two meanings of a word. He does not allow Rosencrantz and Guildenstern to deliver their message in one whole

sequence. He showers his contempt upon the King and the two gentlemen. He interprets their words in a disrespectful manner. For example, Guildenstern uses the word "choler" which has the meaning of bilious disorder, as well as anger—since from olden times the liver had been considered as the seat of affects. Hamlet tells them they should rather inform the doctor about it because:

> for me to put him to his purgation would   (III.ii.323)
> perhaps plunge him into far more choler.

—the obvious meaning being simply medical and in full agreement with medieval and Elizabethan ideas about liver diseases and their treatment. But of course for Hamlet, in his intense desire for revenge, the other meaning is predominant: that is, the King would have to clear himself from the accusation or suspicion of guilt—or openly proclaim his guilt. This sort of treatment would certainly arouse the King's anger. Beyond that the purgation which Hamlet has in mind could be *killing the King*.

As mentioned before,[8a] terms of illness, contagion, boils, etc., occur with great frequency throughout *Hamlet*. Here the use of medical terms indicates Hamlet's change of attitude. In the last lines of Act I he had said in his monologue:

> The time is out of joint; O cursed spite,   (I.v.188)
> That ever I was born to set it right!

There he felt like a physician whose task it was to set time right, like a surgeon who has to set a joint right. But now, months later, the complex has worked in him to such an extent that the physician's attitude has been vastly contaminated with and poisoned by hatred and contempt. The terms "choler, doctor and purgation" assume quite a sinister quality. Certainly Guildenstern does not understand the double meaning in Hamlet's words, but he reacts to the bitterness and hostility in his affect. He wants Hamlet to control himself and be rational:

[8a] Caroline Spurgeon, *op. cit.*

Good my lord, put your discourse into some   (III.ii.325)
frame, and start not so wildly from my affair.

Guildenstern, of course, means "wildly" in the sense of emotionally upset, but Hamlet takes it in the sense of "wild animal,"
so he replies:

I am tame, sir.   (III.ii.328)

Guildenstern, out of his depths, finds it very difficult to relate to
this strange affect and implores Hamlet to make a "wholesome
answer." Hamlet denies that he can do so because:

. . . my wit's diseased.   (III.ii.340)

This reply certainly comes out of his annoyance with these two
fellows who used to be his friends but who now behave as me-
nial servants and act as go-betweens for the King and himself.
Nevertheless, it is true that this sort of punning is a disease, not
insanity but a condition of consciousness in which images which
stream from the unconscious offer two or three meanings. The
obvious meaning is usually more or less harmless, the other implied meanings betray Hamlet's unconscious intentions. The interpretations of these puns and images by the other characters
are usually based on the obvious meaning and are more rational
and concrete. The unconscious of his antagonist perceives Hamlet's implied intention, of course, and immediately reacts to it.
This is the case here with Rosencrantz and Guildenstern; although they do not fathom in the least what is going on, it is just
this punning and the accompanying affect which puts them on
their guard. The worst thing, however, is that these images cloud
Hamlet's own consciousness. This easy and uncontrolled access
to the unconscious and its imagery at the same time opens him
up to sudden impulses. In his psychological condition it is only
one step from verbal aggression to impulsive action. Hamlet
does not realize that his elatedness (*Übermut*) is actually very
dangerous to his purpose.
    At last Rosencrantz can deliver his message:

> She desires to speak with you in her closet   (III.ii.350)
> ere you go to bed.

Hamlet instantly replies:

> We shall obey, were she ten times our mother.   (III.ii.351)

Again the key word "obey" occurs. Using the royal "we," Hamlet exaggerates and thereby adds irony. Then treating his former friends like salesmen, Hamlet asks:

> Have you any further trade with us?   (III.ii.352)

Rosencrantz collects his courage and attempts to reestablish the basis of their relationship:

> My lord, you once did love me.   (III.ii.355)

—a very necessary statement from his and Guildenstern's point of view, because Hamlet has given them enough hints for doubting the existence of their old relationship. They still feel themselves to be friends of Hamlet. Although obeying the King's commands, they believe that by doing so they are helping to cure Hamlet of his so-called madness. They are utterly unaware of the dark struggle between Hamlet and the King. The situation is completely perplexing and bewildering for them. If Hamlet could have responded to their search for a reestablishment of the old friendly relationship, he might have been able to bring them back to his side; he could have done this without giving away the secret. But for Hamlet they were undoubtedly in the enemy's camp; making themselves the messengers of the Queen is enough evidence for Hamlet to dismiss them as friends. So he assures them of his love, but by adding, "by these pickers and stealers," he tells them he considers them traitors. Rosencrantz hears only: I love you, and asks directly as a friend:

> Good my lord, what is your cause of distemper?   (III.ii.357)

Hamlet fears that whatever he says will be reported back to the King, so again he leads them astray by claiming:

Sir, I lack advancement. (III.ii.361)

Some commentators have thought this to be the true and basic cause for Hamlet's depression and his, in many ways, inexplicable behavior. It seems, however, that the term "imperial jointress" (I.ii.9)[9] indicates that at the death of King Hamlet, Gertrude would immediately inherit the kingship, that whoever she married would become king, and that these two would then jointly rule the kingdom, so that Hamlet could not have expected to become king himself on his father's death; therefore Rosencrantz quite rightly asks:

How can that be . . . ? (III.ii.362)

To which Hamlet again answers with the proverb, "While the grass grows . . . (the steed starves)," thus indicating that this waiting period is intolerable for him. While we, the spectators, know the cause of Hamlet's "distemper," we can admit that his lack of "advancement" is one of the minor motives for his condition.

Human motivation is always a bundle of many factors. The principal factors in Hamlet's case are without doubt his concern with the murder, the opening up of vistas into the unconscious and fundamental questions of human existence. We cannot deny, however, that his expectations of becoming king of Denmark were well grounded and that through the Queen's marriage to Claudius the fulfillment of these expectations has been further

[9] Grebanier on Wilson, p. 192: "We feel in Shakespeare's play . . . that Hamlet's uncle is more than consort to the Queen, that he is very much the king, and that the rule is as much his as hers. It appears that Shakespeare thought of this throne as shared jointly by King and Queen— that the death of Hamlet's father left Gertrude still monarch, and that Claudius' marriage to her rendered him half-sharer of the crown. Is not this the true meaning of Claudius' words in his opening speech when he refers to his wife as 'the imperial jointress of this warlike state'? "

delayed. Comparing this natural ambition in Hamlet, for which training and higher education have prepared him well, with the depths of his experience with the Ghost, we must consider the "lack of advancement" a valid though more superficial reason for his disturbance. The proverb quoted by Hamlet is meant to mislead the interrogator—yet it gives another facet of the truth. It emphasizes the patience necessary in waiting for some great step. As we know from Hamlet's monologue, "To be or not to be . . .", his patience—or his tension capacity—is tested to the extreme, not only by waiting to become king himself but by allowing time and circumstances to bring about a condition in which Claudius can be brought to justice. At this point, just after the play, Hamlet's elation over his success in discovering psychological proof of the King's guilt has overwhelmed his patience and clarity of reasoning. Applied to his inner situation, this proverb, "While the grass grows—," reveals the truth about his psychic condition.

Hamlet is still stirred by the problem of his relationship with his two former friends, so he asks them again: Why do you treat me, as it were, like an animal to be hunted? Guildenstern again emphasizes his love for Hamlet. Although this is honestly meant, it is part of the tragedy that Hamlet, preoccupied with all the questions aroused in him by the King's murder, is unable to make due allowance for the unconsciousness of Rosencrantz and Guildenstern and for their ensuing behavior. With the best of intentions (pleasing the King and Queen and helping Hamlet) they do not realize the situation in which they are now involved.

When the Players reenter with recorders, Hamlet uses one of these instruments to demonstrate to Guildenstern that he, Guildenstern, cannot play on Hamlet any more than he, Hamlet, can play the recorder. Again he uses a word with double meaning when he tells Guildenstern:

> Call me what instrument you will, though you   (III.ii.395)
> can fret me, you cannot play upon me.

He uses the term "fret" in the sense of using the fingers to play the recorder and also in the sense of teasing and vexing him; though they can do all that, they are not able to bring out the melody. Were Guildenstern a little more imaginative, he could understand Hamlet and give up being an intercessor between the King and Hamlet. But somehow Hamlet's well-meant advice does not reach Guildenstern. Too, Hamlet again does not see that in using this simile of the recorder he is also speaking about himself, that the change in himself has gone so far that he himself cannot play upon himself as an instrument, that the relationship between his consciousness and his unconscious has deteriorated to such an extent that when he plays his instrument, his soul, it does not produce music any more, but discordant noise.

Polonius enters. For once, Hamlet greets him in a friendly and gentlemanly way: "God bless you, sir!" Polonius manages to deliver directly the same message brought by Rosencrantz and Guildenstern. If Hamlet could still play his instrument well, he would have answered simply and gone to his mother's "closet," but Polonius is to Hamlet like a stimulus to a complex. As before, he subjects Polonius to a series of questions which obviously have no connection with Polonius' message. They are a verbal attack on the unhappy man. Hamlet wants to prove that Polonius cannot hold an opinion for the briefest time:

HAMLET: Do you see yonder cloud that's almost in shape of a camel? (III.ii.405)

POLONIUS: By the mass, and 'tis like a camel, indeed.

HAMLET: Methinks it is like a weasel.

POLONIUS: It is backed like a weasel.

HAMLET: Or like a whale?

POLONIUS: Very like a whale.

Surely Polonius is utterly suggestible, but Hamlet does not see how suggestible he himself is. Goddard has shown how the

choice of animals—the camel, the weasel and the whale—corresponds to qualities in Hamlet himself.[10]

It is interesting to realize that the modern Rorschach test developed out of looking at clouds. Justinus Koerner was the first
to substitute an unstructured ink blot for clouds. Shakespeare, in
his wonderful imagination, uses this cloud test as a projective
technique, just as the play within the play was a projective technique. I believe the cloud test serves an important dramatic purpose in this play to demonstrate that although Hamlet was a
genius and an excellent psychologist, he projected many important features of his own psychology on figures of his environment, and therefore did not truly know himself.

Hamlet promises to visit his mother at once and remarks in an
aside, "They fool me to the top of my bent," indicating that
these inferior people test his tension capacity to the utmost and
that he is at a point where the unconscious content and its accompanying emotion has reached a degree where his capacity
might break down. A short monologue follows which more
clearly reveals these images and emotions. The images now are
not only *one* grave that opens, *one* ghost that appears—but:

> . . . the very witching time of night   (III.ii.413)
> When churchyards yawn, and hell itself breathes out
> Contagion to this world.

Nothing of heaven, no "ministering angels" are present. There is
nothing left of the horror and fear from his first meeting with the
Ghost:

> . . . we fools of nature   (I.iv.54)
> So horridly to shake our disposition
> With thoughts beyond the reaches of our souls?

[10] *Op. cit.,* p. 357: "A camel, a weasel, and a whale! A camel—the
beast that bears burdens. A weasel—an animal noted for its combined
wiliness and ferocity and for the fact that it can capture and kill snakes
(remember the royal serpent!). A whale—a mammal that *returned to a
lower element* and so still has to come to the surface of it occasionally for
air, not a land creature, to be sure, nor yet quite a sea creature. What an
astonishing essay on Hamlet in three words! (It is things like these that
tempt one at moments to think that Shakespeare *was* omniscient.)"

On the contrary, there is pleasure and lust in his whole being. Now he could meet hell itself and its "contagion," and do the "bitter business" (murder). In psychological language, the darkest and most primitive affects—revenge, the lust for murder—contaminate him and no defense against them is attempted. His consciousness does not even try to struggle against it any more. Only a slight memory remains of the former Hamlet, a "day" (consciousness) would probably tremble at seeing his intoxication with murder:

> . . . now could I drink hot blood,   (III.ii.415)
> And do such business as the bitter day
> Would quake to look on.

In this terrible condition he wants to go to his mother. He reminds his innermost, true, loving self:

> O heart, lose not thy nature; let not ever   (III.ii.418)
> The soul of Nero enter this firm bosom.

But, in fact, he is already psychologically a Nero. Nero procured the assassination of his mother, Agrippina. Hamlet is afraid that in his present mood he might kill the Queen. A conscious ego, filled with such powerful drives, can admonish itself, can express a kind intention, but this "top of his bent" is a thin crust on a bursting volcano:

> I will speak daggers to her, but use none.   (III.ii.421)

His words may be well-meaning, benevolent in their intention, but his soul is vastly contaminated with hell's affects. He may beg his soul

> To give them seals never, my soul, constant!   (III.ii.424)

but the slightest irritation at this "witching time of night" may sweep away these good intentions.

iii

Now we are shown the King and his reaction to the events at the play. He is talking with Rosencrantz and Guildenstern. He can speak quite freely to them of Hamlet's madness, since they are now also fully convinced of Hamlet's wild state of mind. He commissions them to accompany Hamlet to England. "Madness in great ones must not unwatched go" has become a specific danger for the King:

> The terms of our estate may not endure   (III.iii.5)
> Hazard so near us as doth hourly grow
> Out of his lunacies.

What he does not tell them is that he also plans to have Hamlet executed on his arrival in England.

Both Rosencrantz and Guildenstern feel it is their religious duty to act on the King's behalf, agreeing with him that the collective well-being as symbolized by the King requires the elimination or removal from Denmark of such an individual as Hamlet:

> Most holy and religious fear it is   (III.iii.8)
> To keep those many many bodies safe
> That live and feed upon your majesty.

It is the old idea that the well-being of a country is identical with the well-being of the King. This attitude on the part of Rosencrantz and Guildenstern indicates that Claudius is a real king and is accepted by Denmark as such. It shows how vastly isolated Hamlet has become by seeing the King as a "pajock" (probably a defeathered peacock).

When they leave, Polonius enters to inform the King that Hamlet is now going to his mother's "closet" and that it might be best for Polonius to hide and overhear their conversation. As usual, he finds good reasons for his spying, and promises the King that he will report to him before he goes to bed.

With Claudius left alone, we are permitted to see the conflict raging within him. The King speaks a monologue which is something like a meditation, a dialogue with himself, and which serves as a preparation for silent prayer:

> O! my offence is rank, it smells to heaven;   (III.iii.36)
> It hath the primal eldest curse upon't;
> A brother's murder!

He is fully aware that the "primal eldest curse" is on his act: "a brother's murder!" He knows that he is forever cut off from contact with heaven:

> Pray can I not.   (III.iii.38)

Nevertheless, he tries to reach God and to receive an answer. Yet his attempts fail:

> My stronger guilt defeats my strong intent.   (III.iii.40)

He is a deeply divided personality; his conflict is irreconcilable since he wants to retain all the advantages of his crime:

> . . . what form of prayer   (III.iii.51)
> Can serve my turn? 'Forgive me my foul murder'?
> That cannot be; since I am still possess'd
> Of those effects for which I did the murder.

Recognizing his own terrible condition, his wretched state, his "limed soul," which is cut off from all healing, he still dares to hope. He still believes all may be well. Grebanier calls him a strong man because in spite of this horrible condition he can put up a strong front and take up the fight against Hamlet to secure his ill-gained possessions ("my crown, mine own ambition, and my queen"). One could certainly describe as strong an ego which is determined to fight though it feels cut off from divine help, but on the whole one could not call Claudius a strong personality. Real strength can only issue from a united personality. Comparing Claudius with Hamlet, one could say that there is more strength in Claudius because he is not subject to affects and because he can suppress his feelings of guilt. His evil deeds are planned. They are executed only in the measure that he finds it necessary for his goal and to secure his possessions.

Hamlet enters. The King is at his mercy. Hamlet could easily kill him:

> Now might I do it pat, now he is a-praying.　　　(III.iii.73)
> And now I'll do't.

One could speak of ego-strength in Hamlet since he resists his impulse for immediate revenge.

Hamlet's monologue as he watches Claudius pray has been widely and variously commented upon. Grebanier, in his study, quotes a number of interpretations and adds one of his own:[11]

> His words are not at all a pretext, an excuse for delay—but rather addressed to his inner violence. Be patient, be patient, he is telling his blood: the time will come when it will be right to strike, and when the time comes I shall choose the moment—not one like this, when the villain is making his peace with heaven, but
> *When he is drunk asleep, or in his rage,*
> *Or in the incestuous pleasure of his bed,*
> *At gaming, swearing, or about some act*
> *That has no relish of salvation in 't—*
> *Then trip him, that his heels may kick at heaven.*

Goddard, not quoted by Grebanier, says:[12]

> At bottom what deters (Hamlet) . . . is the fact that in his heart Hamlet does not believe in blood revenge in any circumstances. The excuse he offers for not seizing the present perfect opportunity proves this as nearly as anything of the kind can be proved. He says he would not send his enemy to heaven. He

[11] *Op. cit.*, p. 182.
[12] *Op. cit.*, p. 370.

will wait until he can send him to hell. Dr. Johnson declared these words of Hamlet too terrible to be read or uttered. And all will agree to the extent of feeling that it was not the Hamlet we love and admire who uttered them. How then did Hamlet come to utter words that no one can believe Hamlet meant? How did his lips come to utter them? Who at one time or another has not assigned a worldly motive to a noble impulse? Then why not, in an extreme case, an infernal motive to a celestial impulse? The celestial impulse here is to save. Hence the expressed will to damn. Hamlet has a conscious belief that he ought to kill the King. He has an unconscious conviction that he ought not to. To hold the latter powerful conviction under the threshold, consciousness must invent a correspondingly powerful pretext for suppressing it.

I sympathize with Dr. Johnson when he finds Hamlet's words "too terrible to be read or uttered." However, I admire Shakespeare for his courage to pierce through our sentiments and to present to us the horrible truth about Hamlet's condition. He is now fully in the grip of his lust for revenge. There is nothing left of the noble Hamlet, the scholar, the philosopher, the courtier. To kill Claudius at this time would just not be revenge:

> Why, this is hire and salary, not revenge.   (III.iii.79)
> . . .
> But in our circumstance and course of thought
> 'Tis heavy with him.

> (He is a terrible criminal and I have to pay him accordingly.)

Hamlet has descended here to the lowest level of a bitter, hating villain himself. What he wants to do is blackest murder, and he wants to kill not only the man but also his soul. Any consideration that even King Claudius, the murderer, is still a human being and that he is attempting reconciliation with heaven is thrust aside. Here Hamlet's ego is strong enough to suppress and control all his murderous impulses, both for practical reasons and to enjoy his revenge more fully.

The King rises from his prayer with the remark, "Words without thoughts never to heaven go," not realizing that his prayer has saved his life. He does not find psychological relief from his terrible conflict and his prayer does not change him. The following acts reveal that in safeguarding his ambition he will not hesitate to pursue vicious, murderous plans—but his life *is* saved and undoubtedly his prayer has had real effect. The deep irony in the play is that this prayer, which to the King seemed not to have reached heaven, has brought out the worst in his enemy and in doing so has prolonged his "sickly days."

iv

At the opening of Scene 4, in the Queen's closet, there is a short conversation between Polonius and the Queen, in which Polonius advises treating Hamlet as a young boy whose "pranks have been too broad to bear with." Then, with the Queen's consent, he hides behind an arras (curtain).

With this scene we reach the climax of the play: the only occasion on which Hamlet and his mother meet alone. It is a confrontation between two who by the laws of nature should be very close to each other. It was his mother's speedy marriage so shortly after her husband's death which had given Hamlet his first inkling that something was wrong in the "state of Denmark" and which had started a depression in him. As the preceding monologue and his observation of Claudius have shown, Hamlet is in the full grip of the unconscious; he is desirous for revenge and his tension capacity is strained to the utmost.

As far as Hamlet knows, he is meeting only his mother, whom he wants to confront with the terrible truth of her situation. She of course knows that Polonius is listening in. Hamlet and his mother meet as enemies, and both go straight to the point. Hamlet repeats his mother's words, with slight but significant changes which turn them into daggers, and then at last he can confront her with his most penetrating reproach; he says:

You are the queen, your husband's brother's wife.   (III.iv.15)

adding:

And—would it were not so!—you are my mother.

He thus reveals his deepest conflict: that she is a most despicable woman and at the same time she is his mother; that he—who could express the divinity of man:

> What a piece of work is a man! how noble in   (II.ii.323)
> reason! how infinite in faculty! in form, in
> moving, how express and admirable! in action how
> like an angel! in apprehension how like a god!

—that he should have originated from such a pool of wickedness. That she is his mother is quite unacceptable to him, and yet an unchangeable reality ("would it were not so!"). Such a rejection is the worst thing that can happen to a mother, so she wants to end the conversation immediately. But Hamlet is determined to make her see the true situation:

> You go not till I set you up a glass   (III.iv.19)
> Where you may see the inmost part of you.

Goddard and other commentators consider the looking-glass a key image in *Hamlet*. Although every character in this play is unconscious of his essential motives, each tries to a certain extent to understand the other person. This is particularly true of Hamlet, who has an amazing intuitive grasp of others and to a limited extent of himself. But he has missed the essential point about himself and therefore projects a good deal of himself upon others. He demonstrated this earlier in his bitter relationship with Polonius. He not only projects, but feels it as a curse, or holy task, to make others aware of what they do not know about themselves. This motivation now compels him to "set you up a glass" by telling his mother what she really is. Seeing herself as she is must tear away the veil of illusion and self-deception ("seems!"—I.ii.76). But it is difficult for the Queen to see herself because Hamlet is under the overwhelming influence of his own affect. In this highly emotional situation, the mother does not willingly expose herself to this mirror, and obviously wishes to leave the room. But Hamlet uses physical force to "sit (her) down." His words are daggers. His mother feels them as a threat to her life:

> What wilt thou do? thou wilt not murder me?   (III.iv.21)
> Help, help, ho!

Polonius responds to her cries and calls for help too, and in this sudden, unexpected, highly-charged situation the affects in Hamlet take over completely. Shouting, "How now! a rat? Dead, for a ducat, dead!" he makes a pass through the curtain, killing Polonius. The Queen cries out:

> O me! what hast thou done?   (III.iv.25)

Hamlet revealingly says:

> Nay, I know not.   (III.iv.26)

The primitive lust for murder—"hell itself breathes out contagion to this world; now could I drink hot blood"—has taken Hamlet over completely. At this moment, when he tries to kill his mother with words, it does not matter *who* is hidden behind the curtain; to him it is a "rat," that is, an animal that usually lives in dark hidden places. It is symbolic for the sinister content in his unconscious, namely the ghost complex. During the swearing-of-the-oath scene, Hamlet had addressed the Ghost with the term for a kindred animal, the mole:

> Well said, old mole! canst work i' th' earth so fast?   (I.v.162)

When Hamlet says, "Is it the King?" he rationalizes his action. If it had been the King he would have been justified in his own mind in killing him and he would have killed him in "some act that has no relish of salvation in 't." But Hamlet had just left the King a few moments before. Had he given himself a moment's reflection, he would have known that it could not have been the King behind the curtain. The mother's exclamation, "O, what a rash and bloody deed is this!" characterizes the deed completely. Hamlet is so much engulfed in his murderous lust that *no* consideration, moral or otherwise, can enter his mind. On the contrary, he continues in the same vein, turning his mother's words into daggers to use against her:

> A bloody deed! almost as bad, good mother,   (III.iv.28)
> As kill a king, and marry with his brother.

At last he can blurt out his knowledge of King Hamlet's murder, but his statement shows that he has now descended almost to the same level as Claudius, a fact he again does not notice about himself and *can*not. It is only now that he addresses the dead Polonius and treats the killing as an accident, as a natural outcome of Polonius having been a "wretched, rash, intruding fool." Hamlet is quite sure in his own mind that he wanted to kill the King. He turns to the Queen, not using the image of the mirror this time but trying again to make her conscious and to arouse her feelings:

> . . . let me wring your heart.   (III.iv.35)

—*if* her heart is not completely hardened against any insight. Hamlet himself has just demonstrated that *his* heart is not "penetrable." Not even the sight of the dead Polonius can arouse gentler feelings in him. They are buried under his lust for revenge. Now he speaks to the Queen of "such a deed as from the body of contraction plucks the very soul." The Queen, being so unconscious, asks innocently:

> Ay me, what act,   (III.iv.52)
> That roars so loud, and thunders in the index?

Hamlet compares his father with Claudius, describing his father in terms which are certainly highly exaggerated. It is clear that Hamlet projects a god into his father:

> Hyperion's curls, the front of Jove himself,   (III.iv.56)
> An eye like Mars . . .
> Where every god did seem to set his seal.

Setting this god-like image which he has formed against that of
Claudius, Hamlet can see Claudius only in dark colors, in a
most disastrous or negative way. Claudius is "like a mildewed
ear," while King Hamlet is "wholesome." Claudius is a "moor"
while King Hamlet is a "fair mountain." This description of
Claudius clashes with that given by the Ghost, who spoke of the
"witchcraft of his wit," his "traitorous gifts" (I.v.43), although
he also called Claudius "a wretch whose natural gifts were poor
to those of mine."

What upsets Hamlet most and seems utterly incomprehensible
to him is the psychology of his mother. How could she "step
from this to this"? It must be something worse than "madness,"
her sense must be "apoplexed." The only explanation Hamlet
feels fits the situation is that a devil has taken possession of her
and made her unconscious by bringing about a dissociation of
sight from feeling, hearing from action, and isolating the sense
of smell completely. Again Hamlet projects his own inner situation upon the Queen. All of Hamlet's statements are certainly
true of the Queen, but it is a matter of seeing the "mote" in the
Queen's eye while overlooking the "beam" in his own. In these
images Hamlet actually describes the effect of the ghost complex
upon himself; some sense is left in him but is shocked (apoplexed); he is possessed by the devil and his vision (his eyes)
are separated from his feeling (as in his lack of feeling-reaction
to his murder of Polonius). His hearing, that is, his understanding, is separated from his hands (his action) and from his vision. His action (the killing of Polonius) occurred without any
consciousness (eyes or understanding).

Both Freud and Ernest Jones use this particular scene to but-
tress their opinion that the essential complex is the so-called
Oedipus complex: that Hamlet hated Claudius because Claudius
did what Hamlet unconsciously wanted to do. Grebanier, writing on Freud, says:[13]

[13] *Op. cit.,* p. 95.

Hamlet, he says, can do almost anything except kill the man "who did away with his father and has taken his father's place with his mother." Instead of loathing Claudius, he feels self-reproach because he knows himself in wish to be "no better than the murderer" he is supposed to punish. Hamlet has long felt the incestuous urge towards his mother and his feelings are "hysterical" because Claudius has done what he himself has always wished to do, killed Hamlet's father and mated with Gertrude.

It is certainly true that every work of art, like a Chinese painting, only hints at much of its meaning. Shakespeare's *Hamlet* is a case in point. As I wrote in the introduction, the whole play is a symbolon, but it is improbable that Shakespeare would not give the proper motivation for Hamlet's actions or lack of action. The text gives no inkling of childhood fantasies nor of the so-called Oedipus complex as Freud has described it. The interpretation of *Hamlet* as sketched by Freud, and fully painted by Ernest Jones, induced Laurence Olivier in his *Hamlet* film production to present this scene in a most licentious way. The same thing occurred during a performance of the play by the Old Vic Theatre in Los Angeles, California. Certainly Hamlet uses force and keeps his mother physically pinned to her seat, and it is also true that the sexual relationship of his mother with Claudius fills him with loathing and contempt, exasperates him to such an extent that he must assume something worse than madness has brought about this marriage. But the text itself does not hint that Hamlet has any such ardor toward his mother. Hamlet is completely possessed by his affects. His ego has been drawn into the unconscious. Both he and his mother are in identical psychological conditions; both are possessed by an unconscious complex, a devil. For both of them hell has opened and spread "contagion" in them. In the case of the Queen the effect of her complex has been a tremendous sexualization, in the case of Hamlet a thirst for blood. These dark chthonian emotions have driven the mother to marry Claudius and Hamlet to kill Polonius impulsively. At this climactic point in the drama, both are equally unconscious.

For the first time Hamlet's speech has some effect upon the Queen. His words enter into her ears like "daggers" and she can hardly tolerate hearing any more. But Hamlet, with his beam in his eye, is driven to go further. Speaking passionately, he completes the dark picture of Claudius, calling him, among other things, a pickpocket:

> . . . a vice of kings; (III.iv.98)
> A cut purse of the empire and the rule.

Hamlet is so much involved in his affects, his libido has regressed into the unconscious to such an extent, that the ghost complex becomes activated. His father now becomes objectified and visible to him. While in the first act, the phantom appeared to both Hamlet and his friends, here he is seen by Hamlet *only* and is not visible to the Queen. This type of ghost phenomenon is something that I have occasionally observed in some of my patients. In an emotional, powerfully-charged situation in which consciousness is in close contact with the unconscious, any complex can be activated, function autonomously, and be perceived as an objective event by the individual. In Hamlet's case it is the father complex which, in the tense confrontation with his mother, assumes objective form. While in the first act the Ghost appeared to Hamlet in full armor, here in this intimate situation with the mother the phantom also assumes an intimate character —therefore Hamlet sees the Ghost in his *nightgown.* (I accept the stage direction of the Hamlet Quarto of 1603, p. G2R: "Enter the ghost in his night gowne.")

In the first meeting with the Ghost, Hamlet had experienced the phantom as a threat, and had appealed to the "angels and ministers of grace" to defend him. This happens here again and therefore he instinctively reacts to the numinosum with the prayer:

> Save me, and hover o'er me with your wings, (III.iv.102)
> You heavenly guards!

He addresses the Ghost with terms of respect:

What would your gracious figure? (III.iv.103)

It reminds us again of *The Tibetan Book of the Dead,* in which the advice given by the priest is also to address the dead with terms of respect, for example: "O nobly-born (so-and-so by name) . . ." This approach was recommended in order to evoke a benevolent attitude from the dead. In Tibet the proper handling of the unconscious is considered of utmost importance for the welfare of the living.

Hamlet's feeling of guilt over his failure to execute his father's command rises immediately to the surface:

> Do you not come your tardy son to chide, (III.iv.106)
> That, lapsed in time and passion, lets go by
> The important acting of your dread command?

It is this line which has supported the idea that Hamlet delayed the execution of his revenge. As I believe I have demonstrated, the principal problem for Hamlet was the conflict between his higher personality and the Ghost's demand for revenge. It needed a certain time for the gradual transformation from a noble man into a killer. As the previous monologue (III.iii.73-96) and the slaying of Polonius have demonstrated, the inferior part of Hamlet's personality, contaminated by the Ghost, has at last taken over and he is only now ready to satisfy his lust for revenge and to kill the King. From the Ghost's point of view, that is, from that part in Hamlet's personality which knew of his father's murder, Hamlet was ready to kill the King immediately, upon hearing of the vicious murder:

> Haste me to know it. (I.v.29)

The Ghost does not directly refer to this self-reproach but gives the only reason for the second visitation:

> . . . to whet thy almost blunted purpose. (III.iv.110)

As Grebanier convincingly demonstrates, the image here is of a knife which is blunted by too much use, not too little. The

Ghost refers to the killing of Polonius, which was unnecessary and represented too much use of the rapier. But beyond that, the inference is that by slaying Polonius, Hamlet's blood lust has been satisfied and he might not be willing any more to obey his father's "dread command" and kill another time. Grebanier gives an excellent analysis of this encounter between Hamlet and the Ghost, presenting two reasons for Hamlet's failure to carry out the command:[14]

> 1. Circumstance ("time") has made it difficult to bring Claudius to justice, the conditions with which he has had to cope having impeded honorable vengeance; 2. His having allowed *passion* to take his reason prisoner, when he rashly killed Polonius, has thwarted his cause and canceled all the gains made on this very night.

According to Grebanier, the Ghost's answer ("this visitation is but to whet thy almost blunted purpose") is

> words which, if read carelessly, would seem (and are so construed) to reprove Hamlet for causeless delay. But viewing them —as commentators have never viewed them—with an eye to the image the poet had in mind, they mean exactly the opposite of the accepted notion. Hamlet's purpose has become "almost blunted." The figure is of a sword or blade. How do our knives become blunted? From too little or too much use? Certainly, as every housewife could tell, from overuse. The Ghost accuses Hamlet not of having done too little but of having done far too much. He is referring not to his son's mental attitude, but specifically to the murder of Polonius—an act which, by excessive use of his sword, has blunted the edge of Hamlet's revenge.

Grebanier successfully refutes the procrastination theory that the Ghost's purpose is to spur Hamlet out of his hesitation. His understanding is that:

> At the apex of Hamlet's fury, as we have said, the Ghost intervenes to warn Hamlet and to calm him.

[14] *Ibid.*, pp. 232, 233.

The words of the Ghost immediately following also indicate that Hamlet has not fulfilled his father's earlier admonition:

> But, howsoever thou pursuest this act,   (I.v.84)
> *Taint not thy mind,* nor let thy soul contrive
> Against thy mother aught.

As demonstrated before, this is impossible for Hamlet—or for any human being—once he has accepted the Ghost's command. The very effect of the ghost complex has been to change Hamlet into a murderer. Although he does not physically attack his mother, his words become like daggers in her ears:

HAMLET: I will speak daggers to her, but use none.
                                                        (III.ii.421)
GERTRUDE: These words like daggers enter in mine ears.
                                                        (III.iv.96)

This overflow of aggression in words also blunts Hamlet's purpose, and the Ghost points out that his harsh words have had a damaging effect on the Queen. A dissociation between consciousness and the unconscious is taking place in her:

> O, step between her and her fighting soul.   (III.iv.112)

The Queen, who up to the moment of the Ghost's entrance had at last begun to show some insight into her own nature and to feel deep contrition for the terrible situation which has resulted from her marrying Claudius, *now* suddenly is convinced that Hamlet is insane. Seeing him talk to a figment of his imagination, she can let go of the moral confrontation, thus rationalizing all the talk of Hamlet as being an expression of insanity.

Many commentators have accepted the phenomenon of Hamlet seeing a ghost visible only to him as a symptom of his insanity. While it is true that in insanity contents of the unconscious assume autonomy, take possession of consciousness and are seen as part of objective reality, the essential criterion for determining whether insanity is present is always the actual condition of consciousness. In the case of Hamlet, as he himself points out:

> My pulse, as yours, doth temperately keep time,   (III.iv.140)
> . . . It is not madness.

He can remember every word the Ghost has said. The contents from the unconscious rise but do not overwhelm or break the ego. On the contrary, they *confront* the ego—an unusual although not an infrequent occurrence. The result of such a direct encounter of the ego with an unconscious content can be insanity or some violent disturbance—for example, a state of confusion. Or it can be a religious experience which leads to an enrichment of consciousness. It all depends on the ego's reaction to the numinous content. Our hospitals are certainly filled with people in whom consciousness has been shattered by the power of the unconscious content.

In Hamlet's case there is a genuine confrontation between the ego and the ghost complex; the ego remains firm and coherent, relates properly to the "ghostly" phenomenon, and remains a strong vessel for this content. That this encounter is a powerful, numinous experience for Hamlet can be seen by the Queen's description of Hamlet's *appearance* during this experience:

> Forth at your eyes your spirits wildly peep;   (III.iv.118)
> And, as the sleeping soldiers in the alarm,
> Your bedded hair, like life in excrements,
> Starts up and stands an end.

But to call this state of mind "distemper" (a deranged condition of mind), as the Queen does here, again goes too far. It is a natural misunderstanding that any layman might make. Hamlet proves his ego strength and sanity: his attention is fully concentrated on the Ghost, yet he is able to turn immediately to his mother and discuss his own condition and hers.

I cannot find in modern psychiatric terminology a suitable term for characterizing Hamlet's mental condition. It is not insanity, yet it is not the normal condition of consciousness; it is not a neurosis, in the usual meaning of this term, that is, a condition brought about by an unconscious conflict. Although there is conflict present, this is actually a mental condition in which a clarification of the inner situation takes place. It is probably best not to apply any psychiatric term to Hamlet's condition but to describe it as an *Ausnahmezustand des Bewusstseins* (an extraordinary state of consciousness).

Hamlet points to the Ghost, trying to make his mother see it. She of course does not. To Hamlet, the Ghost is quite real; this return of someone from the world of the dead is absolutely convincing to him. Invasions by archetypes are always convincing to the subject:

QUEEN: Whereon do you look?   (III.iv.123)

HAMLET: On him, on him! Look you, how pale he glares!
His form and cause conjoin'd, preaching to stones,
Would make them capable.

J. Dover Wilson thinks that "Hamlet's words suggest that he sees some strange agitation in the Ghost's face and action." He also reminds us of Luke 19:40: "I tell you that, if these should hold their peace, the stones would immediately cry out."

C. T. Onions' *Glossary*[15] mentions among the different meanings of *cause:*

(1) matter in dispute.
(2) charge, accusation.
(3) matter of concern, affair, business.

In this context, *cause probably means all three.*

Hamlet fears that his mother, being more concerned with him and his frightening appearance, might influence him and prevent him from executing his "stern" resolution. This again, although

---

[15] *A Shakespeare Glossary* (Oxford Univ. Press, London, second edition, 1953), p. 31.

also real, is a projection. His conflict has here returned; human feeling, pity, speaks again—but is feared and resisted, and the desire for blood is stronger in him. What a tragic condition in this great man that he prefers "blood" to "tears."

The Queen asks Hamlet, "To whom do you speak this?" Her questioning clearly establishes that only Hamlet sees the Ghost. To the Queen this is "the very coinage of your brain," in modern terms, nothing but a fantasy, and as such has of course no reality whatsoever. Furthermore, it is considered a sure sign of insanity that an unconscious content is perceived as having objective reality. The contrasting attitude between these two is of supreme dramatic value: Hamlet, in the full grip of his experience—the Queen remaining a complete outsider. Her further remark:

> This bodiless creation ecstasy   (III.iv.137)
> Is very cunning in.

has a great deal of truth. Certain psychotics, especially paranoiacs, who are possessed by an archetype, can make ingeniously wrought conclusions and perform dangerously clever actions. This is due to the identity between ego and archetype. In such a condition the ego receives the extraordinary intelligence of the archetype. The question of whether such a state of mind can be considered psychotic or not has been discussed before. With some historical personalities like Hitler, who was certainly possessed by some such "coinage" of the brain, it is difficult to decide where insanity begins. As shown very clearly in this scene, there is here not an undifferentiated identity but a confrontation and discussion between the ego and the Ghost. Therefore Hamlet's mental state is not that of insanity—but must be called, as mentioned before, an *Ausnahmezustand*. For Hamlet it is important that his mother see her sins and not use his so-called madness as an excuse for avoiding the truth:

> Lay not that flattering unction to your soul,   (III.iv.145)
> That not your trespass but my madness speaks.

He refers again to illness, to the "ulcerous place," an image that so frequently occurs throughout the play. In primitive psychology the medicine-man treats spirits as if they were germs which infect the soul. He uses his magical procedures to disinfect the person of such spirits. Modern psychology has shown that complexes (*gefühlsbetonter Komplex*) radiate into consciousness and contaminate consciousness with their emotions and drives.[16] As long as they remain unconscious they act like germs which infect large areas of the conscious personality. As Hamlet has shown before, he sees in his mother's psyche "the ulcerous place," the "rank corruption, mining all within" (her moral deterioration due to her incestuous marriage), but does not see himself, does not realize how the ghost complex (which only a few minutes before had personified and activated his *own* "rank corruption") is gradually destroying *him*. The advice he gives his mother is excellent:

> Confess yourself to heaven;   (III.iv.149)
> Repent what's past; avoid what is to come;
> And do not spread the compost on the weeds
> To make them ranker.

Confession is also the first step in modern psychotherapy.[17] The difference is that in psychotherapy confession is made to a human being and the existence of heaven is usually denied (but not by Jung).

Penitence would certainly be the second step. The third step, "Avoid what is to come," however, is easier said than done. No wonder Hamlet feels rather self-conscious. Only a short time before he had killed a man. He has neither confessed nor shown any feeling of guilt. He does not apply his advice to himself. He

[16] See Jung, "The Psychological Foundations of Belief in Spirits," *The Structure and Dynamics of the Psyche,* Vol. 8 of the Collected Works (Pantheon Books [Bollingen Series XX], New York, 1960), p. 301.

[17] See Jung's description of the four stages, "Problems of Modern Psychotherapy," *The Practice of Psychotherapy,* Vol. 16 of the Collected Works (Pantheon Books [Bollingen Series XX], New York, 1954), p. 55ff.

is not at this point dishonest but very unconscious of his true state.

The Queen however is deeply troubled. This encourages Hamlet to continue with his excellent advice on how she should behave with her husband. To Hamlet, the devil is the sexual contact between Gertrude and her husband. Again the advice is good but more easily said than done:

> Refrain to-night . . .   (III.iv.165)
> . . . either curb the devil, or throw him out.

Whatever the devil is in a human being, psychologically speaking it is a powerful complex, closely associated with numinous archetypal contents. The energy contained in such a content is derived from the most powerful instincts in man. If we try to curb the devil or throw him out, he will reappear in a new form.[18] Still, the Queen now has a somewhat better chance than Hamlet because she has moral insight into the nature of *her* devil. Hamlet at this point has not even recognized that the Ghost is *his* devil and therefore cannot even make an attempt at curbing him or throwing him out. Now at last Hamlet refers to Polonius:

> For this same lord,   (III.iv.172)
> I do repent.

His feeling of penitence is still very weak. He expresses the belief that "heaven hath pleased it so." In other words, Polonius' death was the decision of higher powers and he, Hamlet, had nothing to do with it, or was only their instrument. He has completely forgotten that it was hell itself which "breathed out contagion to this world," that it was the ghost complex which made him act so rashly, and that it was *he* after all who killed Polonius. He is right when he says that he is punished "with this, and this with me." By his rash act he has changed the situation com-

---

[18] *Faust*: "Mephistopheles: In changed form I exert terrible influence. (*Im veräanderter Gestalt übe 'ich grimmige Gewalt.*)"

pletely in favor of Claudius. After the play he had the King, as it were, "running." Now, after killing Polonius, *he* is in the power of the King.

Just as Hamlet talks to his mother in a self-righteous way ("Forgive me my virtue," and, earlier, "O cursed spite, that ever I was born to set it right"—I.v.189), and tells her how to behave, so does he also rationalize his function in regard to the general conditions:

> That I must be their scourge and minister. (III.iv.175)
> . . . and will answer well
> The death I gave him.

He also believes that he will be exonerated for the killing of Polonius and be pronounced "not guilty." How far his confusion in feeling has gone can be seen from his statement: "I must be cruel, only to be kind."

The Queen, speaking to Hamlet as if he were her father confessor, asks him what she should do. Hamlet gives vent to his poisonous feelings and his contemptuous opinion of the King. Meaning the same thing, he says the opposite of what he has told her before:

> Not this, by no means, that I bid you do. (III.iv.181)
> Let the bloat king tempt you again to bed;
> Pinch wanton on your cheek; call you his mouse; etc.

After calling the King a "paddock, a bat, a gib," he ends with the story of a famous ape, of which J. Dover Wilson says:[19]

> The story is lost, but Hamlet makes the outline clear; the ape carries a cage of birds to the top of a house, releases them by accident, and, surprised at their flight, imagines he can also fly by first creeping into the cage and then leaping out. The point for the Queen is the publicity of the proceeding ("on the house's top"—in full view of everyone), and that letting the cat out of the bag will involve her own destruction.

[19] *Hamlet*, p. 216.

The Queen fully understands and can therefore assure Hamlet that she will not betray to Claudius anything of what has gone on between them.

Hamlet's loathing description of sexual intimacy is startling. Although he speaks about his mother's sexual ardor, it is obvious that these fantasies are born out of himself. There is no doubt that he has an incest complex and that he is quite unconscious of it. We owe to Freud and Jones our awareness of Hamlet's incestuous relationship with his mother. But does this represent a so-called Oedipus complex? Or could there be another reason for Hamlet's incestuous fantasies, and for the fact that they make their appearance just at this moment in the play? Freud and Jones are of the opinion that Hamlet's present feelings are due to childhood fantasies and that they are revived in the adult Prince Hamlet by Claudius. The text of the play gives no support for such an assumption; we could make such a decision only if we had Prince Hamlet in analysis. If we follow the heuristic rule that things which occur at the same time belong together psychologically, then we must infer that this incestuous sexuality in Hamlet is due to the influence of the Ghost, for Hamlet expresses these sexual fantasies immediately after the apparent materialization of the Ghost. This fully agrees with clinical experience. One can observe quite frequently that when the death of a close relative results in a ghost complex, the personality affected shows an intensive sexualization. This intensification of sexuality occurs more often when a close relationship between son and mother, or between father and daughter, had existed when the deceased was still alive. It does not necessarily mean that childhood fantasies are revived, but rather that it belongs to the intense and frequently perverse psychology of the ghost. In primitive society, for example on Malekula, the belief is that a dead person can return in one of four forms: as a sexual, emotional or spiritual soul, or finally, as a religious teacher. The form in which he returns depends on the stage of development the individual had attained at death. The sexual ghost is naturally the most frequent one, the religious leader the rarest. Since in our western psychology we are so little concerned with taking care of the dead, our psychotherapists observe the return of the sexual soul quite often, even more frequently than the Tibetans. We have only a few therapeutic rituals concerned with the protection of the living from the dead. There is a Roman Catholic mass for the dead and some prayers for the dead in the Synagogue, but we have nothing to compare with the psychological depths described in the Tibetan *Book of the Dead*. Thus we are more subject to the invasion of ghost complexes in their lower forms than are the Tibetans.

Other commentators have noticed Hamlet's peculiar behavior in his talk with his mother. Charlotte Ehrl,[20] for example, speaks of Hamlet's *starrer Ichbefangenheit* (rigid ego-centeredness) and emphasizes that he does not take in and integrate his mother's answers but stubbornly pursues his own thoughts. This ingenious observation characterizes very well Hamlet's psychological state of possession by the ghost complex. Hamlet is outraged by his mother's blindness and moral obtuseness, by the intense passion in a woman her age, and by Claudius' crime which was the direct result of the illicit affair:

> What devil was't   (III.iv.75)
> That thus hath cozened you at hoodman-blind?
> . . .
> You cannot call it love, for at your age
> The hey-day in the blood is tame.
> . . .
> O shame! where is thy blush? Rebellious hell,
> If thou canst mutine in a matron's bones.

This theme—that reason or sense was overwhelmed by compulsive sexuality—occurs frequently in Shakespeare's poems and plays. Here it is expressed in Hamlet's fury:

> . . . proclaim no shame   (III.iv.85)
> When the compulsive ardour gives the charge,

[20] *Sprachstil und Charakter bei Shakespeare* (Quelle & Meyer, Heidelberg, 1957), p. 96.

> Since frost itself as actively doth burn,
> And reason panders will.

The basis of this incestuous intensity in Hamlet is the archetype of the coniunctio (union of opposites).[21] In "Answer to Job"[22] Jung calls the coniunctio an "archetype of the greatest universality."

Throughout his life Shakespeare was concerned with the problem of the union of the male and female opposites. It was a subject quite frequently expressed in contemporary alchemy. It is the theme of his earliest poem, "The Rape of Lucrece," and many of his plays, for example *Romeo and Juliet* and *Othello,* deal with this archetype—with the creative as well as with the destructive activity of this eternal subject. In the poem, "The Phoenix and the Turtle," written at approximately the same time as *Hamlet,* Shakespeare expresses in a positive way the mystery of the coniunctio in the symbol of two birds:

> So they lov'd, as love in twain
> Had the essence but in one;
> Two distincts, division none:
> Number there in love was slain.

In his later plays, especially *Cymbeline* and *The Tempest,* the emphasis is on the life-giving aspect of the union and on the protection of this union by preventing unlawful sexuality. In the fourth act of *The Tempest,* Scene 1, Prospero tells Ferdinand:

> Take my daughter: But
> If thou doest break her virgin knot before
> All sanctimonious ceremonies may
> With full and holy rite be minister'd,
> No sweet aspersion shall the heavens let fall
> To make this contract grow: but barren hate,

21 See Jung, "Psychology of the Transference" in *Practice of Psychothearpy;* also his *Mysterium Coniunctionis.*
22 In *Psychology and Religion: West and East,* Vol. 11 of the Collected Works (Pantheon Books [Bollingen Series XX], New York, 1958), p. 355.

> Sour-eyed disdain, and discord, shall bestrew
> The union of your bed with weeds so loathly,
> That you shall hate it both: therefore, take heed,
> As Hyman's lamps shall light you.

To which Ferdinand responds:

> The strong'st suggestion
> Our worser Genius can, shall never melt
> Mine honour into lust.

Here, in *Hamlet,* the very opposite situation is represented. The archetype of the coniunctio projects and incarnates itself in the Queen and the King's brother. Because it is projected and lived out by Claudius and Gertrude, it is negative and destructive. It materializes in the form of unlawful sexuality. It overwhelms the two partners with its numinosity and deteriorates into "compulsive ardour," which in its train forces crime and guilt on the two protagonists in whom the archetype is predominantly embodied. Since an archetype always tends to express itself in a situation, it also involves other people and the collective as well in its destructiveness.

The result of this great and tragic scene is the reestablishment of a close contact between Hamlet and his mother. The air is clear between them again. He now knows definitely that his mother was not aware of the murder of her husband. She is now completely on his side. Out of this reestablished trust they discuss the future. Hamlet says:

> I must to England; you know that?   (III.iv.199)

J. Dover Wilson comments:[23]

> Some critics have boggled at Hamlet's knowledge of the mission to England. But the King had decided upon it, for the sake of Hamlet's health, before the play scene; and, though we are not told so, it is natural to suppose that Hamlet would be informed

[23] *What Happens in Hamlet,* p. 258.

of the royal pleasure in order that due preparations might be made.

Hamlet tells his mother that his two "schoolfellows," whom he does not trust at all and by now considers his enemies, have been ordered to accompany him. He is quite sure they are plotting against his life, and the manner in which he speaks about them is extremely cunning and vicious. Using his high intelligence to outwit and destroy these two men, whom he imagines to be willing and knowing instruments of the King's murderous plans against him, he talks now like a hunted criminal who in despair may use every means at his disposal to save himself. Turning to Polonius' corpse, he speaks in the same unfeeling way:

> This man shall set me packing (III.iv.211)

("packing" meaning at the same time "loading," "preparing for a journey," "plotting" and "running away"). He indicates by this that he fully realizes that his killing of Polonius has turned the odds against him and that he must make new plans to execute his revenge on Claudius. The crudeness of his feeling shows up when he says:

> I'll lug the guts into the neighbor room. (III.iv.212)

He remarks that Polonius was a "counsellor . . . who in life was a foolish prating knave," a statement which though true of Polonius again refers equally to himself. He foolishly talked too much during the play scene; he has just said the two gentlemen, Rosencrantz and Guildenstern, would "marshal me to knavery."

Act Four

Although the following scene is considered by Rowes and most other editors as the beginning of the fourth act, the action follows the preceding scene almost immediately and might well be part of Act III.

The King, entering with Rosencrantz and Guildenstern, finds his wife emotionally upset. The King refers to "sighs" and "profound heaves." J. Dover Wilson claims that the King finds the Queen "sobbing upon the couch." This seems highly imaginative. In order to explain herself to the King, she asks for privacy, so Rosencrantz and Guildenstern leave the room. The Queen tells the King that Hamlet, driven by tremendous affects ("mad as the sea and wind, when both contend which is the mightier"), upon hearing something stirring behind the curtain, killed "the unseen good old man." She is now on Hamlet's side so she does not tell the King any more of the long dramatic scene between Hamlet and herself. She tries in every way to protect her son. She speaks of Hamlet's "madness" but does not whisper a word about the Ghost. She actually exonerates Hamlet from premeditated murder by blaming the deed solely on his psychological condition ("brainish apprehension"). The King receives this terrible news with great distress. Had he been in Polonius' place, a possibility he has probably considered, he himself would have been killed. He can now properly demonstrate that Hamlet's liberty is a threat to everyone. He can claim that he should have taken measures against Hamlet before, but was prevented from doing so by much love—without explaining for *whom*. He probably means his love for the Queen, and we believe that his love, although adulterous and incestuous, is genuine. He has probably tried to do the best he could in relating to Hamlet but his feelings for the Prince were never those of love.

Now that Hamlet's so-called madness demonstrably presents a public danger, the King can speak of him—or of his madness —as a "foul disease" which, not being made public, has been allowed to "feed even on the pith of life." It is significant that the King projects on Hamlet and uses the situation to make it apparent to everyone else that the "foul disease" is located in the Prince, although as his monologue (III.iii) proved he was fully aware of his own guilt and even referred to his crime as "my foul murder." He spoke of his "wretched state," his "limed soul, that struggling to be free, art more engaged." But even now—or particularly now—he does not consider his undivulged crime the "foul disease."

The Queen, hiding from the King her knowledge of the murder, emphasizes Hamlet's so-called madness even more, thus doing exactly what Hamlet had bid her do. The image the Queen uses for describing Hamlet's madness—pure precious metal among baser ones—contrasts most sharply with the King's description of it as a "foul disease." Although she calls it madness, it is at the same time "pure" and most valuable, and by saying that Hamlet "weeps for what is done" she lies in order to protect him. In any case, the King now has excellent reason to "ship" Hamlet to England. At the same time he does not wish the public to know too much about Polonius' death, fearing that an investigation might also bring his own crime to public notice. What he tells the Queen, however, is something different:

> . . . this vile deed   (IV.i.30)
> We must, with all our majesty and skill,
> Both countenance and excuse.

thus pretending that he takes these measures for Hamlet's protection only. In this way he can make it appear that his principal motive is his love for the Queen, while in fact he can thus put away the one man who has accurate knowledge of his crime.

The gentlemen, Rosencrantz and Guildenstern, reenter. The King gives them a short report on the slaying of Polonius, done by Hamlet in "madness." He asks them to bring Polonius' body to the chapel. The scene ends with a short discourse by the King to the Queen, in which he expresses his hope of avoiding the "poison'd" rumors.

ii

Hamlet's first words in the second scene of Act IV, "Safely stowed," indicate very clearly that he has hidden the body of Polonius. I have never found any explanation for this strange action. To the King and all the others it must appear as a clear sign of Hamlet's derangement. I would assume that the reason in Hamlet's mind was the same as the one for presenting the Gonzago play to the King—to remind the King most strongly of his own secret murder. It might also be an act of despair since Hamlet now fully realizes that the tables are turned against him. At any rate, when Rosencrantz and Guildenstern call Hamlet, he fully expects them. They come straight to the point, but Hamlet answers in "one of his riddling quibbles" (Wilson) which upset them:

ROSENCRANTZ: What have you done, my lord, with the dead body? (IV.ii.5)

HAMLET: Compounded it with dust, whereto 'tis kin.

Hamlet is using this opportunity to declare and more strongly than ever that he now considers Rosencrantz and Guildenstern, his former friends, to be his enemies. Using the symbol of the sponge, a commonplace of the time, derived from Suetonius,[1] he ridicules them as "soaking up the King's countenance, his rewards, his authorities." They are "officers" whom the King "keeps, like an apple, in the corner of his jaw; first mouthed, to be last swallowed" (IV.ii.18; "apple" instead of "ape"—Wilson, p. 219).

Rosencrantz does not understand, and again Hamlet unconsciously betrays that he has become a knave when he says:

I am glad of it; a knavish speech (IV.ii.25)
sleeps in a foolish ear.

Now Rosencrantz and Guildenstern insist more strongly:

You must tell us where the body is, and (IV.ii.28)
go with us to the king.

The tone is certainly insolent, clearly indicating that they speak as the King's representative with full power over Hamlet. This

---

[1] Wilson, *Hamlet*, p. 219: "The notion of sycophants and extortioners as a monarch's sponges."

talk is like a fencing match in which the superior power is with the two gentlemen, but the superior intelligence with Hamlet. He does not give away this smaller secret of his. He shoots a riddle at them when he says:

> The body is with the king, but the king is   (IV.ii.29)
> not with the body. The king is a thing—

meaning that Polonius' body is with Hamlet's father's body in the next world. Quoting from Psalm 144:4—"Man is like to vanity: his days are as a shadow that passeth away."—Hamlet points out that the King will soon join King Hamlet and Polonius in the other world. Playing a child's game, like hide-and-seek, Hamlet runs off, forcing the two gentlemen to run after him.

iii

Meanwhile, the King, sitting with two or three of his counselors, tells them that he has "sent to seek" Hamlet and "to find the body." Again he states how dangerous it is to allow Hamlet full liberty, not divulging his secret plan but giving Hamlet's popularity with the Danish people as reason for not applying the full strength of the law to him, and ending with the famous lines:

> . . . diseases desperate grown   (IV.iii.9)
> By desperate appliance are relieved,
> Or not at all.

Again the King is indefinite as to what he means by the disease. Is it Hamlet himself? Or his so-called madness? The King knows that he is now fighting for his life and can justify to his counselors the use of his royal power to remove Hamlet from the court. He also avoids specifying the nature of the "desperate appliance."

At this moment Rosencrantz and Guildenstern return to the King, informing him briefly that they cannot find out from Hamlet where he has hidden the body of Polonius, but that they have the Prince under guard, so that he is unable to do any further damage.

Hamlet is brought in and interrogated by the King. In his bitterness, Hamlet continues his quibbling, referring to the ultimate fate of the human body, anticipating the desperate dialogue over Yorick's skull:

> Your worm is your only emperor for diet; (IV.iii.22)
> we fat all creatures else to fat us, and we
> fat ourselves for maggots.

He is here expressing the mood of the play—that man, the crown of creation:

> What a piece of work is a man! how noble in (II.ii.323)
> reason! how infinite in faculty!

ends up as a dish for worms, and that ultimately there is no difference between a king and a beggar. The King sticks to the point, wants desperately to know where the body is. Again taking the King's question literally, Hamlet says, "In heaven"—if you do not find him there then you might find him in hell—and at last tells them where he has hidden the corpse. The King, pretending to speak in sorrow, tells Hamlet directly that he must send him to England with "fiery quickness" and that everything is ready for his departure, if Hamlet knows "his purposes." Hamlet, knowing the King, guesses his murderous purposes: "I see a cherub that sees them." The King exceeds his own two-faced nature in saying farewell to Hamlet as "thy loving father." Hamlet addresses him as "My mother." To the King this must have appeared as a further sign of Hamlet's madness. Hamlet continues with:

> father and mother is man and wife, (IV.iii.54)
> man and wife is one flesh, and so, my mother.

—expressing again the coniunctio, which is essentially that "Two distincts, division none: Number there in love was slain."

Thus he says as clearly as he can that the royal incest is the cause of his irritation.

When Hamlet leaves with his guards, the King turns to Rosencrantz and Guildenstern, imploring them to make haste in transporting Hamlet to England. Left alone, the King reveals in a short monologue his hope that England, as a true friend, will immediately execute his intention and kill Hamlet:

> Our sovereign process, which imports at full,   (IV.iii.66)
> By letters conjuring to that effect,
> The present death of Hamlet.

He believes that Hamlet's death will "cure" him:

> Do it, England;   (IV.iii.68)
> For like the hectic in my blood he rages,
> And thou must cure me.

iv

In the next scene, we see Hamlet on a plain near the port. Fortinbras appears with his army, which has been permitted to pass through Denmark on its way to Poland, and Hamlet has an opportunity to talk with one of the Captains. This meeting with active, uninhibited young men who are willing to give their lives in battle for "a little patch of ground that hath in it no profit but the name," acts as a stimulus for Hamlet to meditate on his own situation. He finds that all occasions do "inform against" him. Compared with their martial conduct, his revenge is "dull." Onion's Glossary[2] quotes the word "dull" here as meaning "slow, inert," and it reminds us of the Ghost's appeal to Hamlet: "to whet thy blunted purpose."

Hamlet asks himself what greatness is:

> Rightly to be great   (IV.iv.53)
> Is not to stir without great argument,
> But greatly to find quarrel in a straw
> When honour's at the stake.

2 *Op. cit.*, p. 65.

A rather questionable state of human greatness! His own greatness by this time is somewhat lost, drowned in his desires for
revenge. He, the great scholar, courtier, philosopher, endowed
with all the gifts of an Elizabethan gentleman, now believes he
can find his greatness in revenge, that the argument he has is a
great one:

> . . . a father killed, a mother stained. (IV.iv.57)

Although he knows that the killing of Polonius has changed
his favorable situation into its opposite, he does not realize that
it has also destroyed his integrity and with it his chance for real
greatness. The sight of the 20,000 soldiers (which we would call
"cannon-fodder") ready "to go to their graves like beds" only
increases his murderous inclination, and strengthens the smaller
man in him. He has really wiped away from the "table of (his)
memory"

> All saws of books, all forms, all pressures past, (I.v.100)
> That youth and observation copied there;
> And thy commandment all alone shall live
> Within the book and volume of my brain,

or, as he now says much more simply:

> My thoughts be bloody, or be nothing worth! (IV.iv.65)

v

The following scene, which is said to be "some time later," takes
place once more in the Castle of Elsinore. Ophelia's mind has
broken down after her father's death and Hamlet's departure.
The Queen has strong resistances against meeting with Ophelia
because she feels involved and guilty in the events which have
brought about Ophelia's mental collapse, but the principal reason is her own guilt, the incestuous marriage, of which she is
now fully conscious. Shakespeare expresses here in beautiful
words the psychological truth that an unredeemed guilt complex

can burst into the open when confronted with a similar condition in another person:

> To my sick soul, as sin's true nature is,   (IV.v.17)
> Each toy seems prologue to some great amiss;
> So full of artless jealousy is guilt,
> It spills itself in fearing to be spilt.

The Gentleman gives a very clear description of Ophelia's condition: her behavior is somewhat erratic, her speech is not coherent but comes out in fragments—the hearer may guess that there "might be thought," but since the associative process has broken down, it is impossible to understand it properly and to relate meaningfully to her. It is *Horatio* (I accept the distribution of the speeches as given in the New Cambridge and Craig editions) who, in order to protect Hamlet, urgently recommends that the Queen receive Ophelia:

> T'were good she were spoken with;   (IV.v.14)
> for she may strew dangerous conjectures
> in ill-breeding minds.

There follows one of the most beautiful scenes in this play—so rich in drama and depth of understanding—presenting as it does the tragedy of human existence in such a poignant way. I can only agree with Grebanier's statement:[3]

> Shakespeare's genius enabled him to reveal the mysterious workings of the unconscious mind in the "mad scenes," centuries before the Freudian theories, and not in the dangerous clinical manner of the psychoanalysts, but, like the true artist, as an imitation of life as it is lived.

As pointed out before, Ophelia's attachment to her father and her attitude of unquestioned obedience to him revealed an exceedingly weak and undifferentiated ego. Her only chance for a development of her personality and for finding a way into life

[3] *Op. cit.,* p. 282.

and health lay in her love for Hamlet. Feeling rejected by him, or at least terribly unsure of his love, she has been thrown back upon herself and is now more than ever at the mercy of her father. Her plot to win Hamlet back had unforeseen consequences. Her feeling of guilt at her involvement in this tragic event was intolerable. Now that Hamlet has killed her father, an unsoluble conflict between her attachment to her father and her love for Hamlet has exploded, but has not been allowed to come to the surface of her consciousness. Her brittle mind has lost its last hold on any hopeful creative image and has quite literally broken into pieces. These pieces, fragments of her unconscious, now emerge into consciousness in an incoherent manner. Her relatedness to people and to the environment is clouded and uncertain. Her unconscious complexes flow out in the form of ditties, some of which in an indirect way refer to her father's death ("White his shroud as the mountain snow") and some of which are extremely bawdy, something unexpected in such a "nice" young girl but in fact common in young schizophrenics. She speaks in short sentences which do not seem to relate to the present situation, yet characterize her own condition, and symbolically could be taken as referring to the whole play.

Grebanier discusses this scene with particular attention to the meaning of the flowers which Ophelia distributes. I would like to refer the reader to his reflections for a detailed understanding of the flower symbolism. He raises the "most interesting question of all":[4]

> How does it happen that Ophelia knows all these things—Claudius' treachery, his and Gertrude's adultery, and the murder itself? . . . Ophelia's references to the past of Gertrude and Claudius seem to come from the darkest recesses within her, as from a hidden knowledge that she has never dared allow to pass her lips. . . . As for Ophelia, what a glimpse we now have of the frustrated life of the poor girl—of all that she had heard and was not supposed to know—of all the terror and misery of her thoughts that she could never express! If we were

[4] *Ibid.*, pp. 236-238.

impatient with her earlier, we can only have the greatest pity for her now.

There are two possible answers to Grebanier's question. One is that Ophelia was aware of all these things but did not dare to reflect upon them. In other words she repressed them. Now that the control of consciousness has broken down, they necessarily return to the surface. There is, of course, the second possibility that she was never consciously aware of them but that the unconscious knew them. There is ample evidence for this possibility in modern psychiatric literature. I have had, for instance, a patient whose husband tried to conceal from her a relationship he had with another woman, but she had dozens of dreams in which the situation was clearly represented. The relationship between parents and children, especially between mother and child, is so close that Jung conceives of the first three to five years of life as one of psychic identity between them. The repressed conflicts of parents appear quite regularly in the dreams of children beyond the age of five. These conflicts are usually charged with more libido than those the individual represses. I am therefore more inclined to believe that, given the atmosphere of insincerity and make-believe that existed in the household of Polonius, the second hypothesis is more probable. The text supports this assumption in that Ophelia does not speak in direct statements but that these complexes express themselves in meaningful imagery.

When the King asks Ophelia, "How do you, pretty lady?" she answers with such an image:

. . . They say the owl was a baker's daughter.   (IV.v.41)

This refers to an old story in which a baker's daughter denied bread to Jesus and was changed into an owl. Symbolically speaking, Ophelia's trouble was that she was her father's daughter and nothing else, and rejected the redeeming possibility in her life when she rejected her love for Hamlet. If we understand her in this way, we see that as a result of this rejection she was changed into an owl—that is, she was changed into the "night" side of her unconscious. The previously repressed content, sexuality in its most collective form, is predominant and has replaced her love for Hamlet. As I have shown before, this change of the personality also occurs in Hamlet, not as a sudden break but as a gradual undermining of the original personality—courtier, scholar, philosopher—if we accept Ophelia's description. Hamlet also rejects *his* luminous personality in favor of the "night" (the ghost returning from the grave!) and is changed into a man of "bloody thoughts," into his dark personality.

Ophelia follows this image of the "owl as a baker's daughter" with:

> Lord! we know what we are, but know not what we may be.
> (IV.v.43)

Of course, we always assume that we know what we are, as long as we believe that our consciousness represents our personality and do not take the unconscious into account. But Ophelia has just experienced the way in which the breakthrough of unconscious contents into her consciousness has changed her. This is always a dangerous event and can only be successful when God is present. Therefore she concludes with, "God be at your table!" Of course the King cannot understand what goes on in Ophelia, so his comprehension of her condition is limited to: "Conceit upon her father." She rightly objects to this misunderstanding:

> Pray you, let's have no words of this; but   (IV.v.47)
> when they ask you what it means, say you this:

—and then she sings a ditty. There is of course the obvious sexual meaning in the ditty (it must have been shocking to the King and Queen, as well as to the attending Ladies and Gentlemen) but it is certainly also meant as a symbol, as she has so clearly said: "When they ask you what it *means,* say you this." She describes here her helplessness vis-à-vis an unconscious content, the penetration by it and the subsequent change of her personality:

> . . . before you tumbled me,   (IV.v.63)
> You promis'd me to wed.

Here too the meaning of her words has to be understood on both levels, the sexual as well as the symbolic. The choice of the word "tumbled" also describes beautifully the *bouleversement* of her mind. After singing her ditties, Ophelia says, "I hope all will be well. We must be patient." But of course we know that the relentless powers of the unconscious, the "foul disease," will inescapably lead to tragedy and everyone affected by the contagion will perish.

When Ophelia leaves, the King again refers to her illness, giving a rich description of the whole situation, but as usual carefully avoiding mention of his own part in the disease. In his opinion, Ophelia's illness "springs all from her father's death," and Hamlet is the "most violent author of his own just remove." Claudius reveals how general and widespread the disease already is when he refers to:

> . . . the people muddied,   (IV.v.81)
> Thick and unwholesome in their thoughts and whispers,
> For good Polonius' death; and we have done but greenly,
> In hugger-mugger (in haste and secrecy) to inter him.

He sees "poor Ophelia divided from herself and her fair judgment." His speech also carries the dramatic plot further; he informs us that Laertes has secretly returned from France. Laertes naturally is full of suspicions about the furtive burial of his father—the highest official at the court and the intimate of the King. Again the King uses an image of illness to describe Laertes' condition:

> . . . wants not buzzers to infect his ear   (IV.v.90)
> With pestilent speeches of his father's death.

Claudius acts as if he were the innocent victim of "sorrows come in battalions." The strongly suppressed guilt about the murder comes out involuntarily in his use of the words "murd'ring piece." By that is meant a piece of artillery, the French *meurtrière,* a kind of mortar loaded with a variety of missiles and intended to scatter its shot.[5] It is a typical "Freudian slip" in which the unconscious reveals the murder. We do not know whether Queen Gertrude notices this slip of the tongue but, since Hamlet has told her, she does now know that the King murdered his brother.

There is a sudden noise. The apparently quiet atmosphere is suddenly disturbed. How chaotic, in fact, the whole situation has become is revealed by the dramatic entrance of a messenger who prefaces his message with a fitting image to describe the matter at hand:

> The ocean, overpeering of his list,   (IV.v.100)
> Eats not the flats with more impetuous haste.

It is true within as well as without. The poetic image of the ocean, "overpeering of his list," describes the collective situation at court, as well as the psychological condition of the principal characters, especially Hamlet, Ophelia and the King. They are all overwhelmed by the unconscious. Their consciousness is "eaten away" with different affects according to the state of their consciousness. Ophelia, representing the anima in this play, is already mentally destroyed by the invasion of the unconscious and, in her own state, anticipates symbolically the tragedy of all. Without, the image describes the political situation in which an aroused population threatens the King and his government.

The messenger delivers the specific message that Laertes, "in a riotous head," is invading the castle. The crowd accompanying him is called a "rabble," and they call Laertes "Lord," and cry:

> Choose we; Laertes shall be king!   (IV.v.106)

[5] Kittredge, p. 260.

The King, with a firm voice, exclaims, "The doors are broke."
The statement too is symbolic and clearly pronounces that the
barrier between consciousness and unconscious is broken, and
the unconscious can enter unimpeded. In Ophelia, the "rabble"
(the unconscious) has rushed in, broken the doors of her mind
and fatally confused her. It is fascinating to observe how cleverly the King handles this seemingly hopeless situation. Laertes,
with others, rushes in, exclaiming in a voice full of contempt and
rage: "Where is the King?" He has persuaded his followers to
remain outside, thus giving the King a great advantage. Claudius
allows Laertes to release his anger. To call the exchange which
takes place between Laertes and the royal couple a "conversation," however, is a very mild term for this encounter. Laertes
demands:

> . . . thou vile king,   (IV.v.115)
> Give me my father!

The discussion between these two men has often been commented on, with Laertes' character compared with that of Hamlet, and I do not believe I can add anything meaningful to the
comments given by Grebanier and Goddard, for example.

Laertes speaks in pompous terms, his feelings are not genuine, his desire for revenge is not born out of his own need, rather
out of that which is expected of him. He is now in the same
position as Hamlet, having lost a dear father by violent death
and feeling impelled to take revenge:

> Let come what comes; only I'll be revenged   (IV.v.134)
> Most throughly for my father.

Excitedly, he shouts:

> How came he dead? I'll not be juggled with.   (IV.v.129)

But that's exactly what the King does with him. He succeeds in
changing the target of Laertes' lust for revenge from himself to

Hamlet. Just at this moment, when the King has successfully turned this tense and dangerous situation to an advantage for himself, Ophelia enters. It is the first time that Laertes has seen his sister mentally deranged and this unexpected sight has a profound effect upon him. He has forgotten, of course, how with his so-called good, brotherly advice he had undermined Ophelia's trust in Hamlet's love. Now he addresses her:

> O rose of May! (IV.v.156)
> Dear maid, kind sister, sweet Ophelia!

He cannot see that he has had anything to do with her madness, lays the blame again upon Hamlet, and strongly intensifies his desire for revenge in a bombastic speech:

> By heaven, thy madness shall be paid by weight, (IV.v.155)
> Till our scale turn the beam.

Ophelia behaves as she did earlier. She sings some ditties which refer to her father's death and possibly to Laertes as the "false steward," who with his false advice has stolen her reason. But as it is throughout this play, the fault is always seen in the other person and Laertes of course makes Hamlet solely responsible for Ophelia's breakdown. Now she distributes flowers; they are probably not real, existing only in her imagination. Her surprising entrance is skilfully used by the King to give him finally the upper hand in his dealings with Laertes. He can convince Laertes that he, the King, is without fault and that even Laertes' friends would agree with this. Weakly, Laertes refers to the hasty and secret burial of Polonius, which must have been by the King's order, but even in this respect the King promises Laertes full satisfaction:

> So you shall; (IV.v.217)
> And where the offence is let the great axe fall.
> I pray you, go with me.

vi

In the next scene we see Horatio receiving some sailors who bring him a letter from Hamlet. In it Hamlet tells Horatio of an attack by pirates on his ship and its consequences for him. He was the only one aboard who was taken prisoner by the pirates. Once on board their ship, he persuaded them to take him back to Denmark in return for doing them a favor. So Hamlet is back in Denmark.

vii

In another room, the conversation between the King and Laertes continues. Laertes asks the King quite specifically:

> . . . tell me   (IV.vii.5)
> Why you proceeded not against these feats,
> So crimeful and so capital in nature.

The King then gives the promised satisfaction, enumerating two special reasons. One:

> The queen his mother   (IV.vii.11)
> Lives almost by his looks;

and *he* lives by her:

> She is so conjunctive to my life and soul.

In this respect he is certainly sincere. The second reason he gives is Hamlet's popularity with the people, which is so great that it would "Convert his gyves to graces."

Sadly, Laertes accepts his great loss:

> And so have I a noble father lost;   (IV.vii.25)
> A sister driven into desperate terms,

and again proclaims his desire for revenge. Just when the King is assuring him that he takes all this very seriously and will act

on it, to his great surprise a messenger comes in with the letters
from Hamlet, one for the King, one for the Queen. The letter
to the King tells of Hamlet's surprising return to Denmark and
his wish to see the King. Both Claudius and Laertes are non-
plussed but, from his point of view, the King makes the best
use of this opportunity by asking Laertes, "Will you be ruled
by me?" Laertes willingly agrees if it would at once serve his
revenge. The King devises a plot in which Hamlet's death
would appear as an unfortunate accident, so that not even the
Queen could blame anyone. He speaks in tortuous terms:

> That we would do,   (IV.vii.118)
> We should do when we would; for this "would" changes,
> And hath abatements and delays as many
> As there are tongues, are hands, are accidents;
> And then this "should" is like a spendthrift sigh,
> That hurts by easing.

These lines have been taken by some commentators to represent the basic theme of the play. In their view Shakespeare
here formulates the idea of delay and explains Hamlet's inability to make decisions and take revenge. Grebanier has, I
believe, decisively demonstrated that delay does not occur in
this play. This tortuous speech of the King appears as a rationalization of his own motive for the actions he plans to take. In
the past he has never delayed; he has always acted when he
wanted to act: for example, when he killed King Hamlet. After
he knew that Hamlet had knowledge of his secret murder, he
also took immediate action and sent Hamlet to England with
orders for his execution. Here the main purpose of these words
is to keep Laertes' desire for revenge as hot as possible. Using
again a term of disease, he tries to find out how far Laertes
would go in his thirst for revenge:

> But, to the quick o' the ulcer: (IV.vii.123)
> . . . what would you undertake
> To show yourself your father's son in deed
> More than in words?

Laertes quick answer, "To cut his throat i' the church," satisfies
the King. It also clearly shows Laertes' utterly base character.
It contrasts most tellingly with Hamlet's behavior when he
found the King at prayer. This unlimited desire for revenge
which would even violate a sanctuary goes too far even for
Claudius, the vile murderer:

> No place, indeed, should murder sanctuarize.   (IV.vii.127)

But, on the other hand, he wants to keep Laertes in this mood
and use him for killing Hamlet. The King also fears that if
Hamlet and Laertes should meet, Hamlet would be able to
convince Laertes that Polonius' killing was only accidental,
and possibly would inform him of Claudius' murder of old
King Hamlet. It is in Claudius' interest to keep the two young
men apart. Laertes is now wax in the King's hands. He can be
molded and used in any way Claudius likes. Claudius therefore asks Laertes to keep "close within (his) chamber"; he proposes a fencing match in which Laertes would use "a sword
unbated" and in a "pass of practice requite him for your father." "Pass of practice" is again a pun on the two meanings of practice—as a bout for exercise, and as a treacherous
thrust. Laertes tops the King's proposal when he says that he
will "anoint (his) sword" with an "unction . . . so mortal"
that nothing "can save the thing from death that is but
scratched withal." He calls this mortal unction "contagion,"
using a term of illness expressing the basic idea of the play:
that an infection pervades and ultimately kills everyone. As
shown before, the hidden source of the infection is the unnamed crimes of old King Hamlet.

It is most natural and fitting that the idea of poison occurs
to both the King and Laertes. Up to this point the poison, or
the infection, has been psychic. It has brought about a moral
deterioration of the principal personalities and the actual psychotic breakdown of Ophelia. Now it is translated into a concrete substance, into actual poison. Laertes speaks of his intention to *anoint* his sword and uses the word *unction* (which

he "bought . . . of a mountebank"). This is great irony because these words are mostly used in connection with a sacred rite, especially a consecration, or possibly a coronation. The King gladly takes up the subject of poison; he wants to be doubly sure that the poison will work and tells Laertes that "for the nonce" he will have a "venomed" drink ready—just in case. It is in keeping with Claudius' subtle cunning that he uses Hamlet's noble qualities to destroy him:

> . . . he, being remiss,   (IV.vii.136)
> Most generous and free from all contriving,
> Will not peruse the foils.

Just when these two vile characters have worked out the details of their murderous plot, an interruption occurs. The Queen brings the terrible news of Ophelia's drowning. She gives a beautiful description of the girl's death, speaking of the "glassy stream" and the "fantastic garlands" of flowers which, made of willow, symbolize Ophelia's disconsolate love. It is significant that the image of water, first used by Horatio ("What if it tempt you toward the flood, my lord"—I.v.69) and then by the messenger ("the ocean, overpeering of his list"—IV.v.100), is now repeated. The Queen relates that her "weedy trophies and herself fell in the weeping brook." She was "mermaid-like" and "chanted snatches of old lauds." [6] She was like a "creature native and indued unto that element."

> Her garments, heavy with their drink,   (IV.vii.183)
> Pulled the poor wretch from her melodious lay
> To muddy death.

These beautiful images clearly indicate that Ophelia is seen here not just as a real woman but as an anima figure, as a content of the psyche, "native and indued" (endowed with qualities fitting her for living in water). In this way the greatest kinship between the anima and the water, that is, the un-

---

[6] From O.2, Wilson, p. 230: *"laude* or vernacular hymns of praise."

conscious, is clearly expressed. It is a return of the anima to the element from which she sprang. In a way it is a return, or perhaps better a regression, to its original state, and she is pulled to a "muddy death." Symbolically, the contents of her unconscious which have already broken her mind have pulled her completely into the unconscious. Her psychotic condition in Scene 5 of this act was already a state of mental drowning. Now it has become physical death. The means and methods suicides use for killing themselves are usually symbolic, expressing in a concrete way the psychological processes that brought about the mental condition which compels them to destroy themselves.

As is so often the case in suicide, one wonders whether Ophelia's death could properly be called "suicide," a murder of self. This will be discussed later on in the grave-diggers scene. We can only state that her mind was certainly not capable of formulating and executing a clear intention. After her father's death, the unconscious overwhelmed her, or one could say her consciousness was pulled into the unconscious. Both expressions mean the same thing, a state of consciousness which would not clearly be described as either conscious or unconscious. In any case there was a mutual attraction between the two. One cannot decide whether she half-willingly fell into the glassy stream or whether the unconscious, with its fascination, powerfully attracted her. Laertes is psychologically right when he says:

> Too much of water hast thou, poor Ophelia,   (IV.vii.186)

thus indicating how important it was to Shakespeare to emphasize the image of water. Laertes can reflect on this but very obviously has no capacity for reflecting on himself. It is firmly established in his mind that Hamlet is the sole cause of Ophelia's doubly tragic death. The event makes him only the more unconscious and he decides "the woman will be out," that is, he will now completely repress all his feelings, his emotions, all attempts at insight, all considerations of the soul. To him they are now nothing but a reprehensible feminine weakness. He is terribly angry:

> I have a speech of fire, that fain would blaze,   (IV.vii.191)
> But that this folly douts it.

The real fact, however, is that the "woman" is *not* out. On the contrary, he is even more in the power of his anima. She actually destroys the last shreds of reason in him.

The King, however, notices Laertes' condition. He fears Laertes' rage (a state in which a man is possessed by the anima). In such a state of mind he might act rashly and undo the carefully laid plan for the fencing match.

Act Five

i

The fifth act begins with the rightly famous graveyard scene. Instead of repeating what other commentators have said, and said very well, I would like to limit myself to the melancholy question of Ophelia's death. Did she intentionally drown herself, or did the fascination of the unconscious pull her down to her own death?—a question we have already briefly touched upon. The First Clown's speech evidently expresses Shakespeare's opinion that it was not *really* suicide, not really "murder" of self. This death was brought about by something else, by a condition in which the ego had very little choice. In the words of the Clown:

> . . . if the man go to this water and drown himself   (V.i.17)
> . . . but if the water come to him and drown him,
> he drowns not himself.

An article by Edwin S. Shneidman[1] distinguishes between many kinds of suicide. Although I cannot accept all of his differentia-

---

[1] "Orientations toward Death: A Vital Aspect of the Study of Lives," in *The Study of Lives,* edited by Robert W. White (Atherton Press, New York, 1963).

tions, it is certainly worth our while to look at suicide in the light of modern research and I would refer the interested reader to his study. It is obvious to me from the discussion of the two Clowns that Ophelia's death was not a clear-cut case of suicide, but rather the natural result of being drowned by the unconscious.

Hamlet and Horatio enter and hear the latter part of the Clown's song. Hamlet is startled by the callousness of the gravediggers:

> Has this fellow no feeling of his business,   (V.i.72)
> that he sings at grave-making?

While this is true of the Clowns, it characterizes Hamlet as well. Has he forgotten that he killed Polonius and is a gravemaker himself? He does not yet know what has happened to Ophelia, but the audience feels that, with respect to her too, he is a gravedigger. He comments on the dire end in mud and decay of all human hopes and intentions. Horatio only answers in short monosyllables like "It might, my lord," "Aye, my lord." The mood expressed in Hamlet's Act III monologue ("the very witching time of night, when churchyards yawn"— III.ii.406) has now become a reality. He is in a churchyard, some of the graves are open and he can contemplate the physical remains, especially the skulls, of once proud people. The gravediggers continue to sing while they perform their grisly task, and from time to time they toss up a skull.

Hamlet decides to talk to the Clown and some rapid punning between them is the result, with Hamlet here finding his master in the Clown. It is here also that we find out from the First Clown how old Hamlet is: thirty ("I have been sexton here, man and boy, thirty years"—V.i.177). We also discover that the rumor of Hamlet's madness has reached the ordinary people. The meditations about death first begun in Hamlet after the meeting with the Ghost ("the country from which no traveller returns") are continued here in a rather macabre way, with a description of everything that may happen to the human body after death. Of course the soul is not mentioned. Death, here, is a physical phenomenon only. In an unexpected way, the water symbolism returns when Hamlet's question, "How long will a man lie i' the earth ere he rot?" is answered by the Clown who says that a tanner will last longer because "his hide is so tanned with his trade that he will keep out water a great while," meaning that the more water there is in the body, the faster the disintegration. Symbolically, it means that the more a man is filled with the unconscious, or the more unconscious he is, the sooner he will deteriorate, the shorter the time he will exist after death. Laertes had said of Ophelia that there was too much water in her, so that in his opinion Ophelia's immortality would not last very long, would also deteriorate completely and nothing would be left of her.

Among the skulls that are unearthed by the gravediggers is that of Yorick, a man whom Hamlet remembers well:

> . . . a fellow of infinite jest,   (V.i.202)
> of most excellent fancy.

Hamlet is shocked by the fate of this most noble human being. His thoughts wander to Alexander and the possible use his remains may have served:

> . . . may not imagination trace the noble   (V.i.223)
> dust of Alexander, till he find it
> stopping a bung-hole?

This mood is carried on in a little song about "imperious Caesar":

> O, that that earth which kept the world in awe   (V.i.237)
> Should patch a wall t' expel the winter's flaw!

A mood far removed from that with which Hamlet had met the Ghost:

> . . . O, answer me!   (I.iv.46)
> Let me not burst in ignorance; but tell

> Why thy canonized bones, hearsed in death,
> Have burst their cerements . . .
> What may this mean,
> That thou, dead corse, again, in complete steel,
> Revisits thus the glimpses of the moon,
> . . . and we fools of nature
> So horridly to shake our disposition
> With thoughts beyond the reaches of our souls?
> Why, why is this? wherefore? what should we do?

And a mood most outspoken in his "To be or not to be . . ." monologue:

> To sleep! perchance to dream! aye, there's the rub;   (III.i.65)
> For in that sleep of death what dreams may come,
> . . .
> But that the dread of something after death,
> The undiscovered country from whose bourn
> No traveller returns.

Now that the graveyard is open, these thoughts concerning the possibility of a continued existence after death are gone. No consideration is given to a non-temporal, non-physical existence—only to the body and its demonstrable and complete destruction by time. Although Hamlet speaks with the intelligence he has always shown, something is missing. His soul is missing; he has become completely rational and factual. It is in this moment of utter despair over the meaning of human existence that the procession enters the graveyard: the corpse of Ophelia in an open coffin, a few mourners, Laertes, the King, the Queen and a Doctor of Divinity.

Hamlet watches from a distance and draws the conclusion that:

> The corse they follow did with desperate hand   (V.i.242)
> Fordo its own life.

The Doctor of Divinity expresses rather cruelly why, according to the laws of the Church, no more can be done for the dead.

Laertes, in an analogy to the story of Lazarus in the Bible
(Luke 16), exclaims:

> I tell thee, churlish priest,   (V.i.262)
> A ministering angel shall my sister be,
> When thou liest howling.

It is natural that man thinks and expresses only the best of a
close relative whom he has lost. Laertes has so recently been
exposed to such terrible shocks—his father dead suddenly and
buried under mysterious circumstances; his sister gone mad
and drowned—that any doubts he might have had about her
chastity are forgotten. Remembering perhaps his own liber-
tine life in Paris, he must express his feelings about her in
celestial terms, especially when he meets the stony heart of the
official representative of heaven on earth. In the context of the
problem, "What comes after death?" his words strongly affirm
a hope for full resurrection. They remind us of Hamlet's appeal to the "angels and ministers of heavenly grace" when he
first met the Ghost. It is a theme which Goethe took up in
Faust: the figure of Gretchen is modeled very much after
Ophelia. Gretchen dies a suicide also but returns as one of the
"penitent women" (*Una Poenitentium*) in the last scene of
Faust II, which takes place in the beyond.

Hamlet is shocked when he learns it is Opehlia who lies in
the coffin. The Queen, deeply moved by the tragic death, scat-
ters flowers and addresses Ophelia as if her words might follow
the dead girl into the beyond:

> I hop'd thou shouldst have been my Hamlet's wife.   (V.i.265)

Without calling him by name, Laertes curses Hamlet furiously.
In Laertes' undoubted opinion, it is Hamlet and Hamlet alone
who was responsible for Ophelia's insanity. The scene now becomes intensely dramatic. Laertes leaps into the grave and
Hamlet, deeply disturbed by Ophelia's death and Laertes'
speeches, suddenly runs out of hiding and leaps into the grave
as well.

Much has been written about this scene: the contrast between Laertes' pompous and showy expression of sorrow and
the deeply-felt grief of Hamlet; the leaping into the grave; the
fight. What Claudius had tried to prevent—the meeting of
these two before the fencing match has taken place—has now
occurred in an unexpected way. Under the pressure of this extraordinary situation, both are overwhelmed by their affects
and lose themselves in far-fetched images.

Hamlet can see that Laertes has some reason to believe him
to be the cause of Ophelia's unfortunate death, but any understanding is impossible, although he assures Laertes:

> I loved you ever.   (V.i.312)

Hamlet tries to present *his* side of the matter, but it seems that,
under these circumstances and in the face of Laertes' fury, it is
hopeless to talk to him. Both men are in the grip of their ani-
mas and each tries to establish that he loved Ophelia more,
and more truly. We cannot doubt that Laertes loved his sister
in a kind of brotherly manner. There was probably even an
undercurrent of incestuous feeling, but by slandering Hamlet
and Hamlet's love for Ophelia he undermined the only element which could have preserved his sister's sanity. Hamlet's
love for Ophelia was deep and genuine, but he did not grasp
how desperate she really was when she allowed herself to be
used by her father for his spying. Now when both men are
faced with the final and irreversible outcome of their mistakes
in fathoming the subtlety of a naïve woman, the excited anima
drives them into a heated duel, a verbal fencing-match:

> 'Swounds, show me what thou'lt do;   (V.i.296)
> Woo't weep? woo't fight? woo't fast? woo't tear thyself?
> Woo't drink up eisel? eat a crocodile?
> I'll do't. [2]

2 Wilson, p. 240: "What will you do for her (i.e., to show your grief)?
will you weep? fight (as you have just been doing)? fast (a ceremonial
sign of grief)? tear yourself (i.e. rend your clothing)? drink vinegar
(eisel) to induce melancholy? or eat a crocodile to catch his trick of
hypocritical tears?—a crescendo of sarcasm."

Heaping up more of these comparisons, Hamlet ends with:

> Nay, an thou'lt mouth,
> I'll rant as well as thou.

—indicating to what a low level of fish-wifery both have descended, each violating the majesty of death. Wilson points out that in Elizabethan days graves were shallow and wide and that the dead were uncovered. This scene, perhaps more than anything else, shows the tragic transformation of Hamlet.

As for Laertes, had he not been involved in the tragic events of the Danish court, he would probably have turned out to be a so-called normal average man, but under the circumstances the worst side of him has taken over and he has become possibly the lowest of all the characters in the play, outdoing even Claudius in his baseness. The "average" man is the man who manages to keep his dark side unconscious and inactive. A significant parallel to this type of psychology is that of many Nazi leaders like Eichmann, Himmler, etc., who led quite inconspicuous, even virtuous lives, until the Nazi regime permitted, encouraged and sanctified living out their darkest, most sadistic impulses. Some of these men continued to live an apparently blameless family life while their official duties permitted them to commit nameless crimes without punishment.

The fight between Hamlet and Laertes, and the accompanying altercation, is a dramatic scene of the highest intensity, but beyond that it is also of the highest symbolic meaning. The picture of two antagonists, standing on either side of the woman both loved, speaks to us as an image transcending the action situation and indicates the real tragedy in *Hamlet*. As the Germans say, *Hamlet* is a *Seelendrama*. Hamlet's soul dies by drowning in the unconscious.

Naturally, the King and Queen are deeply affected by this violent verbal match in the grave. Since the Queen now knows the real reason for Hamlet's extraordinary behavior, she tries to protect him. She dissimulates and hides her knowledge from her husband. Therefore she speaks of Hamlet's "mere madness" (he is sick; it is just an emotional fit, otherwise he is gentle):

> And thus awhile the fit will work on him;   (V.i.307)
> Anon, as patient as the female dove,
> When that her golden couplets are disclosed,
> His silence will sit drooping.

Hamlet leaves furiously. The King, however, has only one thought in mind: to preserve Laertes for the fencing match as originally planned, and he naturally keeps his murderous plans to himself.

ii

The last and final scene of the dark tragedy begins. Hamlet and Horatio meet; Hamlet reports to his friend what occurred on board ship. On his trip the unconscious was understandably quite active and did not let him sleep:

> . . . in my heart there was a kind of fighting   (V.ii.4)
> That would not let me sleep.

For once his rashness was of good use to him:

> Rashly,—   (V.ii.7)
> And praised be rashness for it, let us know,
> Our indiscretion sometimes serves us well,
> When our deep plots do pall; and that should learn us
> There's a divinity that shapes our ends,
> Rough-hew them how we will.

Grebanier comments:[3]

> This rashness of his is, of course, allied to his best qualities—his strength, his courage, as made demonstrable on the many occasions when he leaps into action. It is allied, too, to his indifference to the esteem of the court, his willingness to let them think what they please of his sanity. It is a by-product, as are

[3] *Op. cit.*, p. 263.

his wit, irony, and toying with words, of his excessive good health, his strong animal spirits. But, as in life our defects are usually on the other side of our best qualities, it is also allied to his worst faults. . . . The same quickness of temper which makes his discourse scintillate, prompts him to rapid decisions that can be grossly unfair.

When Grebanier mentions Hamlet's "excessive good health," I must agree in regard to physical health. His psychic health, however, is a very different matter. I would also question his "strong animal spirits." The fact, as has been stated several times, is that Hamlet is in the continually increasing power of the ghost complex. He tends more and more to explode with affects. His "rashness," his impulsive actions, are the result of the venom which has slowly infiltrated his whole psychic system. I would therefore modify Grebanier's conception of *rashness*. It is no part of Hamlet's character, but rather the effect of the ghost complex now being fully allied to Hamlet's worst qualities, as well as to the best. But Grebanier is right when he says further:

> But as he speaks we tremble for the issue: what can be hoped for a man who is glad to be rash? He is, as usual, too ready "to take arms against a sea of troubles."

This is one of the few places in the play where Hamlet refers to divinity ("There's a divinity that shapes our ends"). But as is so often the case, Hamlet forgets to take proper account of his own part in this matter. His story to Horatio—that he was the only man who got on the pirate ship and that he then induced the pirates to take him back to Denmark—has always appeared to me as a strange tale. Did he perhaps arrange all this with the pirates before leaving Denmark? If not, it was an extraordinary coincidence that the pirate ship tried to fight the ship on which Hamlet was traveling to England under guard. I am inclined however to believe in such an accident. When archetypes are activated (as they certainly are throughout the entire play) extraordinary coincidences are bound to happen.

At least, every psychotherapist can tell of such unusual occurrences.[4]

Hamlet now tells Horatio of his discovery in the "packets" of Rosencrantz and Guildenstern of the King's commission to have him executed upon arrival in England. Even Horatio, who knows of Claudius' secret murder, is shocked. Hamlet continues his story, relating how he devised a new commission in which he earnestly besought England, the "faithful tributary," to have the two "bearers put to sudden death." Hamlet of course could only assume that his former friends, now tools of the King, were fully aware of the King's commission. We know that this was not the case. Actually, it would have been quite enough to have these two men out of harm's way in England, but the murderous drives in Hamlet now have full possession of him and he acts in the same base manner as Claudius. How far Hamlet has already moved from his former self! He even kills his conscience:

> Why, man, they did make love to this employment;   (V.ii.57)
> They are not near my conscience.

Hamlet has even less regret for the deaths of Rosencrantz and Guildenstern than for the death of Polonius:

> 'Tis dangerous when the baser nature comes   (V.ii.60)
> Between the pass and fell incensed points
> Of mighty opposites.

For Polonius he had said:

> . . . take thy fortune;   (III.iv.32)
> Thou find'st to be too busy is some danger.

At that time he could still say:

[4] See Schopenhauer on "The Role of Coincidence in the Life of Individuals"; also Jung on "Synchronicity: An Acausal Connecting Principle" in *The Structure and Dynamics of the Psyche*, p. 417.

> I do repent; but heaven hath pleased it so,   (III.iv.173)
> To punish me with this, and this with me.

Horatio no longer questions Hamlet's motives, but sees King Claudius as the cause of all the trouble:

> Why, what a king is this!   (V.ii.62)

Hamlet then justifies his own actions by describing briefly this vile king's actions:

> He that hath kill'd my king and whor'd my mother,   (V.ii.64)

together with a line that has puzzled commentators:

> Popped in between the election and my hopes.

Grebanier remarks:[5]

> Claudius plainly rules with the consent of those he governs, and has been legally accorded the "election" of the nobles. From this point of view, Claudius cannot be said to have deprived Hamlet of the throne by either force or chicanery.

The term "imperial jointress" which Claudius had used in his address from the throne (I.ii.9) implied that on the King's death Gertrude would become queen and Hamlet would naturally have been *elected* to rule jointly with her, had Claudius not married her so quickly. Grebanier continues:

> To insist with Professor Wilson that the question of the succession is a major issue with Hamlet and therefore fundamental to the plot, is to tamper with the very premises of the story. It is also hard to see how anyone can read the play with an open mind and conclude that Hamlet is bitter because *he* has not been made king, however bitter he is to see the man he loathes on the throne; his mind dwells on wider perspectives than per-

[5] *Op. cit..* p. 193.

sonal ambition. He is agitated by far nobler and far more tragic
concerns than an impatience to rule Denmark.

This line then ("Popped in between the election and my
hopes") is important for a proper understanding of the play.
True, it appears in the midst of lines which concisely enumer-
ate Claudius' crimes: "hath kill'd my king and whor'd my
mother." It is therefore termed by Hamlet in his intimate talk
with his only friend as an important crime. That this theme—
Hamlet's own natural ambition to be king—is mentioned so
late in the play would indicate either that it is not very important to Hamlet, that it is an afterthought, just another little
crime in the covey of crimes which Claudius has perpetrated,
or that it is of equal weight with the other crimes but has been
unconscious in Hamlet. I am inclined to believe that the latter
is true. The use of the word "popped" would imply that it is a
fact which Hamlet has kept unconscious and which he tries to
repress in all his thinking. In this connection it is significant
that Shakespeare called this play, "Hamlet, *Prince* of Denmark." It certainly calls to mind the potential of a future king.
The most decisive argument, however, is the Ghost, in its psychological significance. As stated before, the Ghost is a psychological phenomenon composed of two elements: one, the personal father, and, two, the archetype of the Self. Throughout
history, especially in ancient Egypt and in the Middle Ages,
the king had such a powerful numinous quality because the
Self was projected on him, and all his insignia were symbols of
the Self (orb, crown, scepter, etc.). Old King Hamlet became a
"ghost" not only because he was murdered under mysterious
circumstances but because Hamlet, with his strong philosophical trend, had kept himself unconscious of his own royal nature. He is unconscious of his own Self, represses it and
throughout the play gives it no attention whatever. It is only
toward the end of the play that for a moment it "pops" out of
his unconscious, but even here he does not take it too seriously.
Therefore, the ghost complex continues to work as a canker in
his psychic structure. As usual with Hamlet, he does not see it

in himself but projects it upon Claudius. At this late point in the play, having killed Polonius and signed the secret order for the execution of Rosencrantz and Guildenstern, there is of course no chance for him to meditate on his own royal nature or to accept it. More than ever, he prefers to deal with this disturbing complex on the outside. Therefore he continues:

> . . . is't not perfect conscience (V.ii.67)
> To quit him with this arm? and is't not to be damn'd
> To let this canker of our nature come
> In further evil?

He immediately proves how unconscious he is, how unaware of the real situation, when he tells Horatio:

> But I am very sorry, good Horatio, (V.ii.75)
> That to Laertes I forgot myself;
> For, by the image of my cause, I see
> The portraiture of his.

Although Laertes had the same cause as Hamlet, that is, to take revenge for a murdered father, Hamlet does not see that Laertes' reactions would be different. By now Hamlet should also understand that he gave Claudius ample reason for removing him from the scene. It seems natural that a man who killed his brother secretly would use all sorts of trickery to kill *him*. He now has sufficient evidence of the King's need to kill him, as well as of his base and treacherous ways.

The apparent similarity of their motivations seduces Hamlet into assuming a further-reaching identity between himself and Laertes. His "towering passion" at the graveside, undignified though it was, has a great deal of truth in it; it is a violent reaction against the showiness and pompousness of Laertes' affected love for Ophelia. Now, regretting his "towering passion," Hamlet assumes Laertes' integrity to be the same as his. It never enters his mind, even as a distant possibility, that Laertes, who after all was Polonius' son, could also be a tool of the King. Hamlet feels a sense of kinship with Laertes since each of them loved Ophelia, although each in a different way.

Now young Osric, a courtier, enters. Speaking in the stilted manner of an Elizabethan gentleman, he attempts to convey the King's invitation for a fencing-match. He gives Hamlet an opportunity to ridicule him and to treat him in a manner similar to the way Hamlet once treated Polonius. Osric is forced to say at one moment: "it is very hot"; in the next moment: "indifferent cold"; and again: "very sultry and hot for my complexion," thus proving to Hamlet that he has no conviction of his own, and making him uncertain as to whether he should have his hat in his hand or keep it on his head as was the custom in Elizabethan days. When Osric speaks of Laertes and his excellence as a gentleman, Hamlet—outdoing him in the use of unusual words—prevents Osric from actually delivering his message in full. But in the midst of this, Hamlet speaks truthfully about knowing oneself. In reply to Osric's statement, "You are not ignorant of what excellence Laertes is," Hamlet again takes up Polonius' statement, "To thine own self be true":

> I dare not confess that, lest I should compare   (V.ii.145)
> with him in excellence; *but to know a man*
> *well were to know himself.*

This line proves that Hamlet is at least aware that he does not know himself.

Evidently so many words have been exchanged between Hamlet and Osric that the King is not sure whether Hamlet has accepted the fencing bout or not. Another Lord is sent who can deliver the message simply and can also receive a simple answer from Hamlet. This Lord also informs Hamlet that the King and Queen are coming down and that the Queen wishes him to

> . . . use some gentle entertainment to   (V.ii.215)
> Laertes before you fall to play.

When the Lord is gone, Hamlet and Horatio are alone again. Horatio senses something strange about this fencing match, although he certainly does not guess the vicious plot in the so-called "play":

> You will lose this wager, my lord.   (V.ii.218)

Hamlet knows he is well trained for the match because he has been in "continual practice," but his unconscious warns him of dangers present:

> I shall win at the odds. But thou wouldst not   (V.ii.222)
> think how ill all's here about my heart.

He rejects these dark premonitions, however:

> . . . it is no matter . . . it is but foolery . . .   (V.ii.224)
> it is such kind of gaingiving as would
> perhaps trouble a woman.

Again his friend Horatio speaks with the voice of reason, begging Hamlet to listen to the unconscious:

> If your mind dislike any thing, obey it;   (V.ii.229)
> I will forstall their repair hither,
> and say you are not fit.

But Hamlet rejects Horatio's proposal, going so far as to take a stand against these inner warnings:

> Not a whit; we defy augury.   (V.ii.232)

He continues now with a paraphrase from Matthew:[6]

> . . . there's a special providence in the fall of   (V.ii.232)
> a sparrow. If it be now, 'tis not to come;
> if it be not to come, it will be now; if it be

---

[6] 10:28-29: "And fear not them which kill the body, but are not able to kill the soul: but rather fear him which is able to destroy both soul and body in hell. Are not two sparrows sold for a farthing? and one of them shall not fall on the ground without your Father."

not now, yet it will come: the readiness is all.
Since no man has aught of what he leaves, what
is't to leave betimes? Let be.

It is a religious attitude: it is as if he were saying, "Whatever is
to come is the will of God. It might be now or any time, but it
will happen." He speaks as if he had no choice in the matter,
but the fact is that this discussion with Horatio offers him
a choice. The unconscious warns him. Actually it is the anima
which communicates this message to him in the form of a
mood, but just because it comes from the feminine in him he
rejects it: "But it is such a kind of gaingiving (misgiving) as
would perhaps trouble a woman."

In Hamlet's words, which paraphrase Matthew, there is a
definite hint that what was hidden (the secret murder and all
the events resulting from it) must be uncovered in the course
of time. What happened in darkness must emerge into the full
light of day. But the idea which refers most strongly to him
personally is not to fear those who kill the body but those who
are able to kill the soul. Something in him says: Laertes, and
certainly the King, will be able to kill my body; the King has
tried hard enough; but they cannot kill my soul. The tragedy,
however, is that Hamlet's soul is already killed, and this last defiance of augury only confirms that this is the case. Ophelia's
death already represented this as an irreversible fact. Hamlet
follows this thought with a rationalization:

> If it be now, 'tis not to come.   (V.ii.233)

which, as Brandes notes, is a distillation of Montaigne: "That
to Philosophie is to learne how to die."

Hamlet ends with the famous words:

> . . . the readiness is all.

which, in this context, is Hamlet's consent to die. Since his soul
has already died, unconsciously he now agrees at last that his
body be killed as well.

What follows translates these inner events into action. Obeying the Queen's command "to use some gentle entertainment to Laertes," Hamlet speaks frankly and from the depths of his heart:

> Give me your pardon, sir. (V.ii.240)

and continues:

> And you must needs have heard, (V.ii.243)
> How I am punished with a sore distraction.

The term "distraction" means mental derangement—which we have traced in detail throughout the play. Hoping to move his adversary by frank admission, Hamlet says:

> What I have done, (V.ii.244)
> . . . I here proclaim was madness.

I do not think we can take this term "madness" in the modern sense as a clinical term, but, generally, as a mental condition in which consciousness is profoundly affected by an unconscious content. The following lines make it very clear that what Hamlet means here by madness is the state of consciousness which we call possession. Hamlet was not himself, but in the power of the ghost complex:

> If Hamlet from himself be ta'en away, (V.ii.248)
> And when he's not himself, does wrong Laertes,
> Then Hamlet does it not; Hamlet denies it.
> Who does it then? His madness.

Hamlet describes his psychological condition with great honesty and amazing insight, but before the bar of life and fate no distinction is made whether man acts as himself or under the influence of a strong complex. Actually, the human being is very rarely himself but is for the most part influenced by more or less unconscious complexes, that is, he is usually possessed. The question of freedom of will is here discussed under particular and dramatic circumstances, and it is not often that a frank admission of one's psychological "distraction" also brings a relief from the consequences of such a condition. Hamlet makes a moving appeal to his antagonist and at last frankly states:

> If't be so,   (V.ii.252)
> Hamlet is of the faction that is wronged;
> His madness is poor Hamlet's enemy.

It is true insight. It comes late but even now it would not be *too* late if in these last moments Hamlet could give up the idea of revenge, and his supposed duty to act as executioner. He acknowledges that he has wronged Laertes. He has not done it on purpose:

> Free me so far in your most generous thoughts,   (V.ii.256)
> That I have shot mine arrow o'er the house,
> And hurt my brother.

To the three points that Hamlet enumerates:

> What I have done,   (V.ii.244)
> That might your nature, honour, and exception
> Roughly awake,

Laertes responds by saying, "In my terms of honour I stand aloof," and adding:

> But till that time   (V.ii.265)
> I do receive your offered love like love,
> And will not wrong it.

—a most treacherous remark by a man preparing to use an "unbated poisoned" sword, and who wants to use a gentleman's match of skill for murder, thus violating all the rules of knighthood. Set against his true intentions, his insistence on "terms of honour" appear doubly base. Hamlet is influenced by the image he has of Laertes, that Laertes is his brother and has the same cause as he. His own integrity, the trust in his opponent as an honorable man, returns at a most unfortunate moment. He completely overlooks the fact that the King, the man of whose murderous intentions he is fully aware, is the arranger of this match. Hamlet pays no attention to the manner in which it was arranged, the urgency revealed by the King having sent two messengers in a row. Hamlet's complete ignorance and his noble nature at the start of the match are revealed in his *double-entendre:*

I'll be your foil, Laertes.   (V.ii.269)

The obvious meaning of "foil" is that of a fencing weapon. It also means, however, defeat, a stain, the cause of failure. The meaning, beyond that of weapon, which Hamlet evidently has uppermost in his mind, is something that serves by contrast or quality to adorn or set off another thing to advantage, since he continues:

. . . in mine ignorance   (V.ii.270)
Your skill shall, like a star i' the darkest night,
Stick fiery off indeed.

In a deeper sense, here at this point, these two men are a foil to each other. By contrast of character each brings out the most outstanding qualities of the other. Although each loved the same woman, and although each enters the fencing match to revenge the death of his father, they are opposites, as different from each other as possible. Hamlet, in spite of the psychological changes (his so-called madness) is a noble man, "the observed of all observers" (III.i.163), and truly "like a star i' the darkest night" sticks "fiery off indeed." Laertes, however, is very dark, has no trace of decency, actually acknowledges no code of honor—while at the same time pretending to obey the gentlemen's code to the finest point. In spite of his premonitions, Hamlet does not realize that the darkest night is approaching so quickly. The strong antagonism which had first broken out in Ophelia's grave has now become a reality. Instead of gentle words, hot words. But the sharp edge of the foils and the poison carry fate for both of them.

Hamlet's unconsciousness causes him to omit inspection of the foils. After two bouts with no result, and after the Queen has taken the poisoned drink, Laertes dares to wound Hamlet. Laertes' remark, "And yet 'tis almost against my conscience," is a complete giveaway of this weak, despicable character.

When Hamlet is wounded, he suddenly realizes Laertes' evil intention and, in scuffling, takes the "unbated foil" from him and wounds Laertes. The King's belated attempt to separate the two is in vain. The dying Queen has a chance to tell Hamlet that the drink is poisoned. Laertes confesses, "I'm justly killed with mine own treachery," and in his dying moments repents and reveals to Hamlet the extent and nature of the whole plot:

> The treacherous instrument is in thy hand,   (V.ii.330)
> Unbated and envenomed.
> . . . The king, the king's to blame.

When Hamlet hears this, the full truth bursts on him, a tremendous affect grips him, overruns all conflicts and doubts which have beset him. Exclaiming:

> The point envenomed too!—   (V.ii.335)
> Then, venom, to thy work.

he stabs the king. Hamlet was "envenomed" physically and psychically. Not satisfied with the stabbing, he wants to make doubly sure that the King dies and so forces him to take the poisoned drink:

> Drink off this potion! Is thy union here?   (V.ii.340)
> Follow my mother!

This refers back to the King's long declamation just before the match:

> The king shall drink to Hamlet's better breath;   (V.ii.285)
> And in the cup an union shall he throw.

Of course "union" meant a pearl, a unique pearl that would dissolve in the wine. Hamlet remembers this term in his dying moments, because he realizes now that this pearl, this union, was the poison in the drink; but more than that, it was the poison from the very beginning—Claudius' illicit union with the Queen—which started the whole series of tragic events, the hasty union only two months after King Hamlet's death—and now:

> Is thy union here?
> Follow my mother.

And so Hamlet forces the King to unite with his mother in death. The killing is committed in a rage. It is questionable whether it really represents revenge. Surely it is something other than Hamlet anticipated. His own "madness" has heaped tragedy upon all the important figures in the play. He could not have anticipated this bloody, envenomed end when he demanded of the Ghost:

> Haste me to know't, that I, with wings as swift   (I.v.29)
> As meditation or the thoughts of love,
> May sweep to my revenge.

Nevertheless, fate has meted out justice to everyone according to his or her deserts. This statement is not meant as a moral judgment but as poetic justice which responds to everyone's unconsciousness and tragic ignorance about himself.

In regard to the King, Laertes properly remarks:

> He is justly served;   (V.ii.342)
> It is a poison tempered by himself.

At last Laertes asks to "exchange forgiveness" with "noble Hamlet." Hamlet still has time to ask Horatio to "report me and my cause aright to the unsatisfied."

Horatio is so identified with Hamlet that he wants to die by suicide like an antique Roman, but is prevented by Hamlet from taking the poisoned liquor also. Hamlet saves his friend's life and in moving words asks him to "absent (himself) from felicity awhile" and to tell Hamlet's "story." He is fully aware that to the court (and to the audience) many things are enigmatic and will need a good deal of explanation, that he has not fulfilled his royal nature: [7]

> O God, Horatio, what a wounded name,   (V.ii.358)
> Things standing thus unknown, shall live behind me!

The tragedy of noble Prince Hamlet is expressed in his dying words:

> The potent poison quite o'er-crows my spirit.   (V.ii.367)

This poison began to work in him when he was called back to Claudius' coronation, so strangely coupled with the hasty marriage of his mother to the King. This incestuous union aroused emotions and thoughts which like a poison filtered into his mind. They were intensified beyond tolerance by the Ghost's appearance and his call for revenge of the foul murder. Envenomed as Hamlet was, and denying his royal self, the archetype of the Self returned in its most destructive aspect— as Ghost. It became the "potent poison." The Ghost, together with the adulterous union of his mother, "o'er-crowed" (triumphed over) Hamlet's spirit. He could not "live to hear the news from England," nor many other things. As Fortinbras says at the end:

> For he was likely, had he been put on,   (V.ii.411)
> To have proved most royally.

A royal soul, born for greatness, was poisoned and destroyed.

[7] I accept the 2nd Quarto reading.

He was a soldier in the noblest sense but never able to fight an open battle of deed or thought. Fortinbras' last line characterizes this situation:

> . . . such a sight as this   (V.ii.415)
> Becomes the field, but here shows much amiss.
> Go, bid the soldiers shoot.

Conclusion

Since we know so little about Shakespeare, it might appear altogether superfluous to consider what the herculean writing of this tragedy may have meant to Shakespeare himself. It was written during his so-called tragic period. Although there is very little to go by, *Hamlet* seems to represent the expression of a particular stage in Shakespeare's own life. It was the same period in which he also wrote the poem, "The Phoenix and the Turtle," which celebrated the union of male and female in sublime verses. Tragedies like *Romeo and Juliet,* many of the comedies such as *A Midsummer Night's Dream*, also *Cymbeline*, *The Tempest* and *King Lear,* have the *union of the opposites* as a central theme. Goddard, in commenting on *Hamlet,* writes that Hamlet is a character molded in such a way that it could be Shakespeare himself if he had been compelled by circumstances and inner necessities to commit murder. This is a possible theory, but it appears to me of equal or even greater significance that the play's emotional center is the question of adulterous union—incest. Murder, revenge, Hamlet's love for Ophelia and its destruction, Polonius' and Laertes' deeds, are all part and parcel of this ulcer. Horatio and Fortinbras are the healthy tissue which can continue to live. We can dare the hypothesis that by writing this play Shakespeare may have freed himself from an illness and was thus able to continue more than ever to be himself. In *Lear* he struck the same note. At one point, Lear recognizes the action of his daughters as his own illness ("But yet thou art my flesh, my daughter; or rather

a disease that's in my flesh, which I must needs call mine"
—II.iv.225).

It appears to me very doubtful that Hamlet reacts out of an
Oedipus complex, in the sense in which Freudian theory
speaks of it. Nothing in the play supports the theory that the
mainspring for Hamlet's actions is the resurgence of infantile
incestuous desires for the unfortunate Queen. The underlying
motive in the play is the archetype of the coniunctio which is
always experienced as incest, and therefore sinful. As Jung
states, the coniunctio is regularly the stage immediately preceding the realization of the Self. Jung says: "As a totality, the
self is by definition always a *complexio oppositorium.*" [8] In
"The Phoenix and the Turtle," which was published in 1601,
the mysterium of the coniunctio speaks loudly:

> So they lov'd, as love in twain
> Had the essence but in one.

But it also says that union brings death to the two-in-one:

> Whereupon it made this threne
> To the phoenix and the dove,
> Co-supreme and stars of love;
> As chorus to their tragic scene.
> . . .
> Death is now the phoenix' nest;
> And the turtle's loyal breast
> To eternity doth rest.

It is the poet's gift to translate the mystical experience of his
own soul into human relationships. Shakespeare could do this
in a way that was truer than life. What Iachimo in *Cymbeline*
says of the piece of work done by the sculptor is even truer of
Shakespeare himself:

> . . . the cutter (the sculptor)   (II.iv.82)
> Was as another nature, dumb; outwent her,
> Motion and breath left out.

[8] *Psychology and Religion,* p. 443.

In *Hamlet,* Shakespeare "outwent" nature. The mysterium of the coniunctio, an innermost mystery of the soul, was projected and materialized in the sexual union of Claudius and Gertrude, and thus violated its true nature. The coniunctio—so beautifully expressed in Shakespeare's poem: "co-supreme and stars of love"—set up a tragic course of events. Projected, materialized, it became a poison which destroyed Ophelia, Hamlet's soul, and ultimately killed him. In *King Lear,* which was written somewhat later, another solution is found. There terrible events occur as well. All the principal characters die. But at the moment of death, King Lear has an innerworldly experience of eternal union. In Shakespeare's later plays, for example *Cymbeline* and *The Winter's Tale,* the inner experience of union no longer results in tragedy and death. In an even greater and more mysterious way, the union of Ferdinand and Miranda in *The Tempest* proclaims peace and immortality.

King Lear

A PLAY OF REDEMPTION

Introduction

In the vast literature of man, there are probably no two greater works which, though separated by 2,000 years, belong more together than the Biblical poem *Job* and Shakespeare's poetic drama, *King Lear*. The theme of both is man's suffering, but each treats the problem in a different manner.

In *Job,* the suffering issues from God through his son, Satan. Job was a righteous man, "perfect and upright, and one that eschewed evil," so his suffering is God's doing—the conflict is between man and God and occurs in Job's soul. Once the situation of extreme suffering is established, there are no external dramatic events. The external unity is established by Job's metaphysical discussions with his friends. The final resolution is an act of God, speaking out of the whirlwind.

The situation in *Lear* is very different. Lear is a king, in full possession of power and wealth, and the dramatic events occur as a result of his own actions. Suffering is brought about by human beings but is *interpreted* as the action of gods or of God. The structure of the play is far more complex than that of *Job,* with all of the events relating to the meaning of man's suffering; insight into the riddle of man's existence develops out of Lear's reactions to these events. The source of suffering is not God, but man himself. So, while in *Job* God redeems Job, in *Lear* it is Lear's changing attitude toward God which redeems him.

Despite their differences in focus, then, *Lear* and *Job* are parallel in that they both explore the meaning of man's suffering. In both works, the main character is forced by fate to reestablish a vital relationship to the numinous factors of the unconscious. In *Job,* all that is necessary to bring this about is a direct revelation of God. But Lear has to undergo a long and complicated process in order to reestablish a living relationship with God.

In several respects *Lear* is a much more tragic and complicated play than *Job.* God returns to Job all his former riches; Lear dies. The meaning of Lear's death has often been misinterpreted, possibly because of the complexity of Shakespeare's vision. It is my purpose in this analysis to trace through the play the growth of Lear's consciousness toward insight and harmony in order to shed light on the meaning of his death, and on the meaning of Shakespeare's view of the universe.

Act One

i

Although Shakespeare's theme in *King Lear* is the meaning of man's suffering, the opening scene does not immediately pose the question of suffering. Instead, it introduces problems which later on will be discussed in meaningful association with suffering. The first words spoken announce one of these problems:

KENT: I thought the king had more affected   (I.i.1)
                  the Duke of Albany than Cornwall.

GLOUCESTER: It did always seem so to us; but now, in
the division of the kingdom, it appears not
which of the dukes he values most; for
equalities are so weighed that curiosity
in neither can make choice of either's moiety.

From these words, we can deduce that the drama is going to deal
with values, and throughout the play we will have to pay attention to terms of measure (nothing, all, half, a hundred knights,
fifty, twenty-five), which in turn are confronted with values that
cannot be expressed by measure; fair and equal division of the
kingdom is associated with love and with the relationship between father and children.

After this short discussion between Kent and Gloucester concerning the division of the kingdom, Gloucester introduces a
second problem, his son Edmund, and reveals to Kent that Edmund is a bastard, a "whoreson (who) must be acknowledged."
It is significant that this admission by Gloucester about Edmund
(later one of the principal carriers of evil) should be mentioned
so soon and in such close connection with the distribution of the
land. Gloucester describes Edmund's siring with great pleasure:

> . . . yet was his mother fair; there was good   (I.i.23)
> sport at his making.

Thus the motif of the coniunctio[1]—the union of opposites, specifically those of male and female—is emphasized, but in its
most collective and purely biological form. Edmund, the fruit of
this illegitimate relationship, is a source of constant embarrassment to his father, who wants to send him abroad. In the words,
"Do you smell a fault?" Gloucester admits a feeling of guilt, but
he glosses over it (he is "brazed to it"). He obviously has a
conflict about having a bastard son but he avoids reflecting upon
it. Though his relationship with Edmund is full of ambiguous
feelings, he is not critical of his own psychology at all. Having
an illegitimate son has not developed consciousness in him. His

[1] See Jung. "Psychology of the Transference," *The Practice of Psychotherapy,* p. 163; *Mysterium Coniunctionis.*

light tone indicates how little he is aware of the possible consequences of having ignored his son for so long. Therefore, fate
must bring consciousness home to him.

It is significant that Shakespeare does not introduce Lear and
his problem at once, but precedes him with Gloucester and his
bastard son. Here the opening chord is struck, in a minor key,
as it were, of a theme which is sounded throughout the whole
play. The plot of Gloucester and his sons runs parallel to that of
Lear and his daughters. Therefore, at the play's end, Gloucester's
death will give us hints for the understanding of Lear's death.

This first part of the first scene then has briefly stated four
interrelated subjects: (1) the problem of values, (2) the division of the kingdom, (3) the relationship between fathers and
children, and (4) the motif of the coniunctio.

The dramatic interest in this first scene lies in Gloucester and
his glib talk about his bastard son. We are impressed by his lack
of awareness. The question arises: Why does Shakespeare present Gloucester's unconsciousness right at the beginning of the
play? It is perhaps not too early to assume that suffering will
serve the purpose of developing consciousness. Full consciousness would include an understanding of the fate-producing superhuman factors, the gods or God. Both principal carriers of
the theme, Lear and Gloucester, are unaware of their own real
condition at the beginning. Following the misguided assumptions of their egos, the opposite of what they expect occurs and
at the end of the play they achieve a state of consciousness corresponding to their potential. The values they hold at the beginning have to be given up. A differentiation of consciousness occurs. The new values are found by a union of opposites. This is
achieved by a change in the relationship to their children.
Through this scheme, the ending of the play ties up all the problems introduced in the first scene, creating a level of philosophical insight and harmony which reinforces the union of opposites
in the minds of men.

When Lear himself enters for the first time (together with his
three daughters, the husbands of the two older daughters, and

attendants), he proclaims what Kent has already told Gloucester in the first few lines of the play. He has decided to divide his
kingdom into three parts and wants to give the "largest bounty"
to the daughter who loves him most. Now "eighty or more
years," he has decided to "shake all cares and business from
(his) age" and "unburdened crawl toward death." He wishes to
invest his three daughters with the privileges of royalty, but since
the division is unequal, rivalries must be expected, and he believes that by publicly announcing his will at this time, "future
strife may be prevented." We hear later (I.i.125) that the reason for this unequal portion is that Lear loves Cordelia, his
youngest daughter, the most, and wishes to live with her, with a
retinue of one hundred knights. It appeared from Kent's discussion with Gloucester that the idea of a three-fold division had
been known at the court for some time before this official pronouncement. What is evidently unexpected is that the division
will depend on a condition imposed by Lear; and what Lear
does not realize is that the condition he attaches must inevitably
incite conflict, which no pronouncement can prevent.

Since the development of the tragedy is the result of the questions he asks and the answers he receives, it is important to clarify the meaning of the basic question. Because Lear obviously
knows that Cordelia loves him most, it is astounding that he
demands a public expression of this love and seeks justification
for his unfair partition. The motif of a father with three daughters, in which the youngest is distinguished, is an old fairy-tale
motif which Shakespeare has used here for the particular purpose of making Lear appear childish when he asks, "Which of
you shall we say doth love us most?" To combine this question
with the promise of material advantage reveals an immature
concept of love and of the essence of human relationships. The
parallel is drawn here very closely with Gloucester's attitude toward love. Gloucester's relationship to Edmund's mother was
evidently childish, dictated by opportunity and the pleasure
principle ("this knave came somewhat saucily into the world").
His responsibility toward Edmund has been only reluctantly accepted. Both men's understanding of love has a childish, quan-

titative aspect. Lear imposes conditions on love, rather than knowing that his daughters love him.

Indeed, many people associate love with quantity. Our language favors such assumptions by phrases like "loving someone more than someone else," or "loving somebody very much." Freud's understanding of libido is also associated with quantity, because libido and love (or sexual energy, in the universal sense that Freud has given to it) are more or less the same for him.[2] For Freud, therefore, love can be expressed in terms of quantity. But it should be stated quite clearly that although, psychologically, entities like affection, attention, fondness, and similar feelings *can* be expressed by quantity, it is the nature of love *not* to tolerate quantity. Love always involves the whole human being and therefore transcends anything which can be expressed by rational definitions. This is certainly Shakespeare's view of love in Sonnet cxvi:

> Let me not to the marriage of true minds
> Admit impediments. Love is not love
> Which alters when it alteration finds,
> Or bends with the remover to remove;
> O no; it is an ever-fixed mark,
> That looks on tempests, and is never shaken;
> It is the star to every wandering bark,
> Whose worth's unknown, although his height be taken.
> Love's not Time's fool, though rosy lips and cheeks
> Within his bending sickle's compass come!
> Love alters not with his brief hours and weeks,
> But bears it out even to the edge of doom.
>   If this be error, and upon me prov'd,
>   I never writ, nor no man ever lov'd.

Lear's mental condition has been characterized by two illusions: (1) that he, a king, bearing all the mana of a king, could,

---

[2] Jung does not identify love and libido. For his discussion of the possibilites of measuring libido, see *The Structure and Dynamics of the Psyche*, p. 6; also his *Symbols of Transformation*, Vol. 5 of the Collected Works (Pantheon Books [Bollingen Series XX], New York, 1956), p. 190ff.

like any ordinary human being, retire and put away the burden of kingship; (2) that in love there is a "more" or a "less," or even a "most." ("Which of you shall we say doth love us *most?*") If love, as Lear believes, is quantitative and divisible, it could be exchanged materially and whoever loves him "most" should receive the most opulent portion of land. The two daughters, Goneril and Regan, respond easily to this concept of quantity in love when they say:

GONERIL: I love you *more* than words can wield the matter;
(I.i.57)

Dearer than eye-sight, space, and liberty;
Beyond what can be valu'd, rich or rare;
No less than life . . .
As much as child e'er lov'd . . .
Beyond all manner of *so much* I love you.

REGAN: Prize me at her *worth* . . . she comes too short.
(I.i.73)

Lear, in giving them their land, emphasizes quantity again when he speaks of "champaigns riched, with plenteous rivers" and "an ample third, no less in space." When he addresses himself to the third daughter, he uses the same quantitative language:

What can you say to draw   (I.i.87)
A third *more opulent* than your sisters?

Cordelia has three difficulties in answering this question. One is her inability to express and formulate love, as one can see from her aside:

. . . Now I am sure my love's   (I.i.79)
More richer than my tongue.

Secondly, it is contrary to her nature to think of love in quantitative terms. Thirdly, she is unable to draw material advantage from her love. One could meditate whether she might have compromised, out of her love for and understanding of her father, and found a way to express her love in simple terms, but that would not have been possible without compromising the essence of her being. Diplomacy was farthest from her at this moment, so her answer is simply: "Nothing."

Lear is astonished. The word "nothing" is used in various shades of meaning throughout the play. Cordelia, of course, means that there is "nothing" she can say, while Lear takes the word in its quantitative sense, and possibly in the sense of non-existence. He therefore says, "Nothing will come of nothing." The opposite of course is true. Everything comes of nothing once it is taken in a non-rational, non-quantitative sense ("nothing" being identical with the unconscious in its modern sense).[3]

Lear at this point is the gracious king, in full possession of everything, and so he gives Cordelia a second chance: "Speak again." Under this pressure she simply says aloud what she previously had said only to herself:

> Unhappy that I am, I cannot heave   (I.i.93)
> My heart into my mouth.

She is unable to express adequately, in words, the quality of love she feels for Lear. She attempts to express it in a measureable way, limiting it to:

> . . . I love your majesty   (I.i.94)
> According to my bond; nor more nor less.

She circumscribes her love by "according to my bond"; this bond by its true nature cannot, of course, be measured. The statement then can mean very much or very little and, just by its soberness and in contrast with her sisters' verbosity, could have alerted Lear.

Lear's amazement increases. He gives her a third chance, ask-

---

[3] Cf. the Cabbalistic concept of *Ein Sof;* "the origin of everything" in S. Friedlaender, *Schöpferische Indifferenz* (Ernst Reinhardt Verlag, Munich, 1926); Hegel's "the quality of utter indistinguishableness."

ing for some diplomacy: "Mend your speech a little." It would need just a word. But Lear again connects his request with material advantages. One feels his rising anger and the implied threat: ". . . lest you mar your fortunes." Cordelia, pushed into a corner, repeats her previous statement, in more detail but in the same laconic fashion. She speaks of "duties," but one can feel the rising affect which, in her, characteristically takes the form of a sharp-pointed attack upon her sisters. Under the pressure of the affect, she then also uses quantitative logic: "Why have my sisters husbands if they say they love you *all?*" She hopes that the clear logic of her statement will pierce the fog which surrounds her father's consciousness. She continues the measuring of love, and one can feel the pride when she says, "Haply, when I shall wed . . . I shall never marry like my sisters, to love my father all."

Lear is very disappointed because he evidently expected words from Cordelia which would promise him all her love, and anything less than total love means no love at all to him. Therefore, his question: "But goes thy heart with this?" He hears only the rejection of love and reacts with: "So young, and so untender?" Cordelia answers: "So young, my lord, and true." The conflict between father and daughter has now broken into the open. What Lear demands is tenderness, affection and a one-hundred-percent love—love that finds ready verbal expression. He is quite stubborn in his demand, but Cordelia is stubborn too; she cannot compromise in the least in her fanaticism for truth. Two human beings who, by the bonds of blood and kinship, are very much alike, are nevertheless opposed to each other. In both, a powerful ego comes to the fore and insists on totality: Lear on total love, Cordelia on absolute truth. Each sees the other's weakness, without being able to see his own. Lear claims something that is feminine in nature—love; Cordelia something masculine—logos.

Lear reveals himself here as a very unconscious man. He is "eighty and more," but obviously psychological maturation did not go hand in hand with the progress of years; it stopped somewhere in the first part of life. Up to now, the unconscious evidently has had no chance to participate in Lear's life and consciousness. Because the flow of the unconscious has been arrested for a long time, a great deal of libido has piled up there, while the ego has become highly inflated and power-drunk; therefore, Lear has no conscious relationship with his feelings. The unconscious has been waiting for the right occasion to find its way into consciousness, and this is evidently the right occasion: Lear's desire for total love and his wish to be relieved of all royal duties in order to wait for death have hit upon the rock of Cordelia's stubborn insistence on truth. It must now explode into consciousness through the means of hot affectivity. Lear's anger wells powerfully up and bursts like a flood. Words stream from him which, in their intensity and power, can only be compared with the words of Moses in Deuteronomy.[4]

The reason for the terrible curse in Deuteronomy is disobedience to the Lord. In *King Lear* it is Cordelia's disobedience to her father's command to speak what he wanted to hear her say. Lear acts like a god who can give and take away as he pleases. The position of a king, and especially of Lear as he is presented in this first scene, *is* similar to that of a god. Such a psychology is only possible, however, if the conscious ego is identified with the archetype of the Self.[5] This possibility exists very strongly of course in an archaic king who, under primitive conditions, is considered the source of fertility and of all the blessings of the country.[6] If the carrier of so much mana does not realize his humanity—in other words, if he does not differentiate between himself as a human being and his great office—he must necessarily feel omnipotent, a god.

The paradoxical thing is that Lear behaves most like a god at that moment when he considers his mortality ("Unburdened

---

[4] "The LORD shall smite thee with madness, and blindness, and astonishment of heart: And thou shalt grope at noonday, as the blind gropeth in darkness, and thou shalt not prosper in thy ways: And thou shall be only oppressed and spoiled evermore, and no man shall save thee."—Deuteronomy 28 : 28-29.

[5] See Jung, "Rex and Regina," *Mysterium Coniunctionis,* p. 258ff; also *Aion,* p. 23.

[6] See *Die Gekrönten* by Philipp Wolff-Windegg (Ernst Klett Verlag, Stuttgart, 1958).

crawl toward death"). It is the moment in his life when, speaking from a political point of view, he can give all, a portion, or nothing to his daughters. In Cordelia he finds a human being who challenges him by pointing to something more important than his majestic will. She is a woman who has her own will. She is an individual in her own right and will not sacrifice her independence, her truth, for a few words. By being more than a creature who only wishes to please her master, she creates a doubt in his power. In his affect, Lear calls on the sacred gods of his pagan psychology and cuts all bonds between himself and his previously beloved daughter.

It is now that Kent tries to speak up, but the flow of powerful affect in Lear cannot be interrupted:

> Come not between the dragon and his wrath.   (I.i.124)

The use of this image is most significant. The "dragon" is really *wrath*. In symbolic language, Lear is saying that he is totally identified with his affect. He fears anything that would intervene between his ego and his affectivity, that would force him to step aside from his wrath, that is, anything that would break up the identity of his ego with the wrath. In this case, he would have to reverse his action of disowning Cordelia. He explains that he loves Cordelia most and that is why she can hurt him most:

> . . . and thought to set my rest on her kind nursery.
>
> (I.i.124)

A pun is contained in "to set my rest." It is a phrase taken from a game of cards called Primero, meaning "to stake one's all"—but in Lear's remark meaning also "to find his peace." It means then that Lear is trying to find his peace by staking his all on Cordelia's love. "On her kind nursery" is a dead giveaway for Lear's desire to return to the Mother. The love he is seeking in Cordelia is really the total love that a mother gives to her child. If he cannot have Cordelia as mother, he does not want her at all. It is a frequent occurrence that older men, realizing their

increasing weakness and failing capacities, strongly wish for a
return into the all-embracing care of a mother and therefore arrange conditions in which all their needs are taken care of by a
nursing woman.

Without further reflection, Lear now divides his kingdom in
two parts only and makes it clear that, although he has given up
all the cares and business of kingship, he wants to retain for
himself the name and all the additions to a king. In other words,
he has not really given up anything of psychological value. He
again mentions Cordelia's pride:

> Let pride, which she calls plainness, marry her. (I.i.131)

This strengthens the impression that it is her pride which has
hurt him so much. He speaks of it with irony: in his opinion her
pride should remain her only possession.

Kent speaks up again. To Kent, Lear is everything—king,
father, great patron, but particularly "master." It is a term
which Kent uses throughout the play when talking to Lear, or *of*
Lear. Kent is the "faithful servant" who maintains his loyalty to
the King whatever happens. He attempts to restore the relationship between Lear and Cordelia. He speaks up for reason, common sense and royal dignity. His loyalty is not weakened in the
least by the King's rage. The difference between Kent and Cordelia is due quite naturally to position and also to their vastly
different psychologies. For Kent the King is a numinous figure
and, as his master, symbolizes the center of Kent's life. For Cordelia the father is only part of her life and belongs essentially to
her past. The center of her life lies in the future and is concerned
with her husband, whoever he may be.

Kent breaks the courtly conventions in order to protect the
King against the terrible results of his affect; in spite of Lear's
threat ("the bow is bent and drawn"), Kent is able to say:

> Let it fall rather, though the fork invade (I.i.146)
> The region of my heart: be Kent unmannerly
> When Lear is mad.

So Lear shoots the arrow of his anger against Kent: "Out of my sight!" To which Kent answers: "See better, Lear; and let me still remain the true blank of thine eye."

The repeated emphasis on sight in this play is quite remarkable. We commented before on Gloucester's unconsciousness. Here the theme of consciousness is announced in a positive manner. Seeing is consciousness. Since olden times, the image of vision has been used in many languages to characterize consciousness. This is particularly so in English, where the words "I see" are popularly used to convey "I understand." In his *Structure and Dynamics of the Psyche,*[7] Jung states: "Consciousness has always been described in terms derived from the behavior of light." In his *Mysterium Coniunctionis,*[8] he says: "By reason of its solar nature, the eye is a symbol of consciousness." The sun and moon have been considered God's eyes.[9]

Harold C. Goddard [10] has already pointed out that images referring to eyes, vision and sight occur with great frequency in *King Lear,* and I would like to quote some of them.

In Act IV, Edgar says:

> I'll *look* no more,   (IV.vi.23)
> Lest my brain turn, and the deficient *sight*
> Topple down headlong.

Gloucester, in his prayer to the gods, says:

> O you mighty gods!   (IV.vi.35)
> This world I do renounce, and, in your *sights,*
> Shake patiently my great affliction off.

Later, Edgar, on seeing Lear, exclaims:

> O thou side-piercing *sight!*   (IV.vi.86)

[7] P. 199.
[8] P. 207.
[9] Zechariah 4:10—"They (seven lamps) are the eyes of the LORD, which run to and fro through the whole earth."
[10] *The Meaning of Shakespeare,* p. 143ff.

Again, a Gentleman speaking of the King, remarks:

> A *sight* most pitiful in the meanest wretch,   (IV.vi.208)
> Past speaking of in a king!

Lear himself:

> Does Lear walk thus? speak thus? Where are his *eyes*? (I.iv.229)

> Old fond *eyes*,   (I.iv.305)
> Beweep this cause again, I'll pluck ye out.

Kent, in the stocks:

> Take vantage, heavy *eyes*, not to *behold*   (II.ii.178)
> This shameful lodging.

Later, Lear's exclamation becomes a dreadful reality for Gloucester. In a talk with Cornwall, Regan, Goneril and Edmund, Goneril proposes:

> Pluck out his *eyes*.   (III.vii.5)

Gloucester, before knowing what harsh fate Cornwall has decided to inflict on him, says:

> Because I would not *see* thy cruel nails   (III.vii.56)
> Pluck out his poor old *eyes*.

Cornwall, before doing the terrible deed:

> Upon these *eyes* of thine I'll set my foot.   (III.vii.68)

The servant then says:

> My lord, you have *one eye* left   (III.vii.80)
> To *see* some mischief on him.

And Cornwall again:

Lest it *see* more, prevent it. Out, vile jelly!   (III.vii.82)
Where is thy lustre now?

Gloucester, blinded:

I have no way, and therefore want no *eyes;*   (IV.i.18)
I stumbled when I *saw.*

The Gentleman describing Cordelia's reaction when she
learns about Lear's misfortune:

There she shook   (IV.iii.31)
The holy water from her heavenly *eyes,*
And clamor-moistened.

Edgar, describing to Gloucester the poor, unfortunate beggar:

As I stood here below, methought his *eyes*   (IV.vi.70)
Were two full moons.

And Lear, close to the end, states:

Who are you?   (V.iii.279)
Mine *eyes* are not o' the best, I'll tell you straight.

Lear's last words at the moment of death are:

Do you *see* this? *Look* on her! *look!* her lips!   (V.iii.312)
Look there, *look* there!

The frequent use of the imagery of vision is clear evidence
that the gaining of consciousness is the main dramatic intention
of Shakespeare in this play.

Scene 1 of Act I has introduced Lear as a rather unconscious
man. He can see, but his sight is certainly not sharp. It is the
outbursts of affect which make him *completely* blind. These
affects take over and prevent him from seeing the proper implications of Goneril's and Regan's "so much" statements, or of

Cordelia's true feelings. Nothing can penetrate the blinding fire of his rage, neither Cordelia's remarks about her sisters nor Kent's "unmannerly" approach. Kent's reference to Lear as "mad" should not be understood in the modern clinical sense as a "psychosis," but as a reference to Lear's psychological state of possession. His consciousness is overwhelmed by an immense affect. Kent takes it upon himself to carry Lear's consciousness:

> Let me still remain the true blank of thine eye.   (I.i.160)

We can therefore expect that Kent, in the further course of the play, and on to the end, will behave as the "true blank" of Lear's eye, that he will attempt to see situations in their proper perspective, situations which Lear on account of his mental blindness cannot see. Kent's "reasonableness," however, will also be his limitation. The reality which Shakespeare explores in this play by far transcends Kent's ability to see.

In his rage, Lear calls Kent a "miscreant." The word is probably used here in the original sense of "misbeliever." [11] In this context, it clearly points to the religious implications of the play. To Lear, Kent is now almost a heretic. When Kent again speaks the naked truth, "I tell thee thou doest evil," Lear calls him "recreant." [12] It is part of Lear's unconsciousness to misjudge Kent's loyalty.

France and Burgundy are ushered in and Lear's mocking words, "Let pride which she calls plainness marry her," come to the test. (Although it is true that Cordelia's insistence on truth unavoidably also reflects pride, it is actually Lear's immense pride which he projects on her.) Burgundy values her only together with her possessions, and so refuses her. France responds to her true essence and clearly states:

> Love is not love   (I.i.234)
> When it is mingled with regards that stand
> Aloof from the entire point.

[11] The Arden edition of *King Lear,* ed. by Kenneth Muir (Harvard Univ. Press, Cambridge, 1952), p. 14.
[12] *Ibid.,* p. 14: "one who proves false to his allegiance."

He knows that she herself is the dowry; he totally rejects the association of love with quantity. Cordelia can truly let Burgundy go:

> Since that respects of fortune are his love,   (I.i.251)
> I shall not be his wife.

France says:

> Most choice, forsaken; and most lov'd, despis'd!   (I.i.254)
> . . .
> Is queen of us, of ours, and our fair France.

For France Cordelia represents a value which cannot be bought for any amount:

> Not all the dukes of waterish Burgundy   (I.i.259)
> Shall buy this unpriz'd precious maid of me.

The remarks of both Cordelia and France serve to emphasize again the contrast between values which can be measured and exchanged, and those whose nature transcends quantity.

Lear repeats his utter rejection of Cordelia—"For we have no such daughter"—and predicts, "nor shall ever see that face of hers again." The irony of course is that in the end he does see her again, under the most trying of circumstances, and that the meaning of life for him is then concentrated in her love.

And so the subject of genuine values in human life and of what truly represents them is clearly drawn. On one side we have "love" associated with material values which can be measured and therefore divided, on the other hand true love and the indescribable value of human individuality; easy verbalization as opposed to the indefinable yet meaningful quality of the human being; a power-drunk ego against a man who prizes the truthful human being as the highest value. And yet there is a loyal servant—Kent—who is not fooled. He recognizes even in the power-drunk king the hidden potential of higher values, the unmistakable quality of royalty which will make itself felt in new, yet unforeseen ways.

This scene of great tension is followed by a farewell speech between Cordelia and her two sisters, and ends with a discussion between Regan and Goneril. Cordelia knows her sisters and their dark nature well. She gives expression to her forebodings, begging her sisters to treat their father with kindness. Regan and Goneril reject her pleas and Regan even scolds Cordelia, declaring that she very well deserves the awful fate they see coming for her. After Cordelia and France depart, the two sisters talk with each other and very coldly discuss the new situation. In their dark hearts, there is no expression of gratitude for receiving such an unexpectedly large bounty, nor any feeling of love for Lear. What they are concerned with are practical matters.

They realize that their father's action has its origin in his weakness, and they bring up a topic that in one way or another we find in all of Shakespeare's plays: *self knowledge.* C. G. Jung has introduced the term *individuation* for the process by which man achieves adequate knowledge of himself. It is Regan's remark:

> 'Tis the infirmity of his age; yet he   (I.i.296)
> hath ever but slenderly known himself.

which definitely states that Lear has known himself very little. His initial situation is then characterized by a very small amount of self-knowledge and by a desire to turn to the Mother,[13] without wanting to sacrifice anything. This is the opposite of individuation. Lear understands his approaching death as a regression into the womb of the Mother. The function of Cordelia is to reject this regression, that of the two evil sisters to initiate a process in Lear which will force individuation upon him. My understanding of *King Lear* as a process of individuation is psychological and more specific but agrees with D. G. James's

[13] Jung, *Symbols of Transformation,* p. 402n: "Separation and differentiation from the mother, 'individuation,' produces that confrontation of subject and object which is the foundation of consciousness."

more general conception[14] that Shakespeare's tragedies, and some of his other plays like *The Tempest,* represent his experiment with knowledge. Lear's very last speech will enable us to understand this point fully.

In a cold, matter-of-fact way, Goneril agrees with her sisters that at all times Lear has been subject to affects ("the imperfections of long-engraffed condition"), and that old age has only brought them out more clearly. As evidence, Regan mentions Kent's banishment and France's leavetaking. They decide to counsel and act together because they fear their father's faults (his "rashness" and "unruly waywardness") might be a nuisance to them.[15]

At the end of Act I, Scene 1, the conflict is drawn between Lear's godlike ego and the two daughters anxious to maintain their power and privileges. They do not yet have a plan to do any evil against their father, but their words betray a cold, egotistic attempt to protect what they have received. Though they are sisters, it is not their mutual love, but their common interest, which holds them together. This attitude bodes ill for Lear's future, but it does not yet indicate the terrible things to which his daughters will eventually resort.

Since the first scene has introduced, or at least named, all the essential characters, it may be useful to visualize the symmetrical structure of protagonists and antagonists in the play.

On the "good" side we have:

Lear
Kent
The Fool
Cordelia
Edgar

On the "evil" side:

Edmund
Cornwall

[14] *The Dream of Learning* (Oxford Univ. Press, London, 1951).
[15] Kenneth Muir's explanation of "offend us."—Arden, p. 23.

Goneril
Regan

Albany is not decidedly on one side or the other. He becomes
gradually involved in the plot, assuming the role of a chorus,
especially toward the end, and then is decidedly on Lear's side.
Gloucester takes an intermediate, changing position between the
two sides. The Doctor who appears in one later scene is not
involved in the plot as such.

ii

In the second scene of the first act we meet the principal masculine protagonist of evil—Edmund, who at the very beginning of
the play was introduced as Gloucester's bastard son. He is engaged in a monologue, a classical device of the Elizabethan theater and especially of Shakespeare to reveal the psychology of a
character and, less often, to develop the action of the play.

Edmund declares here his personal religion. (By "religion" I
mean an individual's relationship to the numina, the fate-
producing factors of the objective psyche.) Edmund's religion
does not change essentially during the entire play. Though he is
certainly a principal figure, no transformation occurs in him. (In
general, it can be said that the representatives of evil in the play
do not change. Instead, their evil natures are progressively revealed through their speeches and actions.) This failure to
change is in outspoken contrast to the psychologies of Lear,
Gloucester and Edgar, which in each case is significantly expressed in their changing relations to gods and to God. Nature is
Edmund's goddess, the one and only goddess who has bestowed
her gifts on him and whom alone he wants to serve. His concept
of Nature (which Shakespeare uses in many shades of meaning)
can best be understood through his negative description of those
things he finds opposed to Nature. For Edmund, Nature is the
opposite of civilization, of culture and social conventions
("Plague of custom" and "curiosity of nations").[16] It is true that

---

[16] Mason, quoted in Variorum edition of *King Lear,* ed. by Horace
Howard Furness (J. B. Lippincott, Philadelphia, 1908), p. 43: "By 'curiosity,' Edmund means the *nicety,* the *strictness,* of civil institutions."

as a bastard he is an outcast in his own society and therefore deprived of all the advantages and privileges which the laws of society would otherwise have bestowed on him. True to Elizabethan etymology, "bastard" for Edmund is derived from "base," so that in addition to being a social outcast, he realizes that society also considers him to be of inferior nature. He suffers greatly from feelings of inferiority and compensates for it by claiming that nature is far superior to society and that he has greater gifts than other mortals. The fact of his illegitimacy has created a "complex" in him; in modern terms, one would say an "inferiority complex." Edmund feels deprived of power and position. He is filled with a tremendous greed to acquire them:

Legitimate Edgar, I must have your land.　　　　　(I.ii.16)

He appeals to Nature as his goddess, and the gods in general, to help him gain these ends. His imagination ("my invention") is directed toward these external goals. In trying to rectify *by all means* the injury society has inflicted upon him, he overlooks the fact that such profound inferiority feelings always indicate the existence of a real psychological inferiority, and that by disregarding social customs he also disregards morality and conscience per se. He overlooks the fact that a fundament of human nature is the necessity to live with other human beings, and that whatever the social conventions are, there is also a natural law working in human society, regulating human relationships. Edmund's conclusion that because he is a bastard and an outcast he is entitled by nature to gain all his ends by force or by stealth actually collides with other laws of nature, which require respect for fellow beings and justice and love in all dealings with others. It is as much a human instinct to accept and develop all the gifts Mother Nature has given as to give proper consideration to the fellow human being. In regard to Edmund's monologue and his religion, we must say that he worships Nature one-sidedly as the giver of bounteous gifts, but actually disregards the other side of Nature which expresses herself in human relationships. Worshipping Nature, he also violates Nature. Psychologically speaking, it is obvious that in Edmund's psychology the mother image receives the highest value. This mother image is definitely not the personal mother, but by calling her "Nature," "Goddess," it is obvious that the archetypal image of the Mother is meant, while "custom," "curiosity of nations," "legitimacy," point to the father image, toward which Edmund has most negative feelings. We know from Gloucester's first remarks to Kent about his son that he also has negative feelings about Edmund, that he has completely rejected him in the past and intends to do so in the future:

> He hath been out nine years,   (I.i.34)
> and away he shall again.

Progressing further into the second scene, we are made aware of the beginning of Edmund's plot to remedy his position as a bastard son. With infinite cunning, he uses a forged letter supposedly written by his half-brother, Edgar, to convince Gloucester that Edgar is plotting to murder him, and succeeds in convincing him. There is again a replay on the word "nothing." When Edmund tries to attract Gloucester's attention by hastily hiding the forged letter, Gloucester asks, "What paper were you reading?" to which Edmund replies, "Nothing, my lord." Gloucester then says:

> . . . What needed then that terrible dispatch . . .   (I.ii.33)
> The quality of nothing hath not such need to
> hide itself. Let's see. Come, if it be nothing,
> I shall not need spectacles.

"Nothing" is used here in the sense of being of no importance. It is used to hide, and by hiding, emphasizing the importance of the letter. "Nothing" here is a term not so much of quantity, but of size. At the same time it reflects a motif frequently occurring in Shakespeare. It is the contrast of *appearance* of actual being against reality (*Schein* and *Sein*).[17]

17 Wolfgang Clemen, *Schein und Sein bei Shakespeare* (Bayerische Akademie der Wissenschaften, Munich, 1959).

Edmund's pretending that it is nothing in order to emphasize the letter's importance is thus particularly effective in deceiving his father. Gloucester easily falls for this trick. He becomes completely convinced of Edgar's treachery when he accepts Edmund's assertion that the letter is really written in his brother's handwriting ("character").[18] Gloucester is as rash as Lear. He does not stop to hear about the other side or to check further. He dismisses his beloved son from his affections as quickly as Lear did Cordelia. Instead of reflecting on the situation at hand, he immediately blames objective factors expressed in astrological terms. These "late eclipses" have caused breakups and divisions, and he is quickly convinced that his son ("this villain of mine comes under the prediction") is guilty. This belief that far distant events in the cosmos *cause* certain changes in human relationships points to a weak ego. Such assumptions are a magic belief and relieve man of the effort to think through a situation, and help him to escape from his own responsibility. The similarity between Lear and Gloucester lies in the weakness of their egos. In Lear's case it is the powerful affect that overwhelms him and deprives him of the royal privilege of man, of consciousness ("sovereignty of reason").[19] In Gloucester, it is credulity. One could call it a laziness of thinking, a pat willingness to accept, unreflectingly, far distant factors like astrological constellations as causes of human behavior. This weakness of the ego makes him particularly suggestible. In his favor one can say that he attempts to see recent events in a larger context, but even this view is distorted because he does not accept man's active part in it.

When Gloucester leaves, Edmund in a monologue quite rightly criticizes Gloucester's stupidity, which he calls "the excellent foppery of this world," and of which he has made such clever use. Edmund distinctly recognizes his father's weak point,

---

[18] Cf. *Hamlet,* IV.vii.52: 'Tis Hamlet's character.
[19] Cf. *Hamlet,* I.iv.72: And there assume some other horrible form,
   Which might deprive your sovereignty of reason
   And draw you into madness.

his use of astrology for avoiding personal responsibility, when he says:

> An admirable evasion of whoremaster man, to   (I.ii.142)
> lay his goatish disposition to the charge
> of a star!

To Edmund, it is nothing but stupidity to believe that the reasons for our psychological qualities and behavior are due to remote, objective and seemingly inaccessible factors. Or to put it more simply, it is of no avail to project our darkness, the cause of our vices, into the planets—or, as Edmund says, "And all that we are evil in, by a divine thrusting on." Edmund, however, is certainly wrong when he denies all significance to objective factors. He says:

> I should have been that I am, had the   (I.ii.147)
> maidenliest star in the firmament
> twinkled on my bastardizing.

This would put all the emphasis on the ego and makes it clear that Edmund's appeal to Nature as his goddess is not only one-sided but also insincere, revealing him as a naked egotist. He believes that all the power needed to determine one's own fate lies in the ego alone. He does not see that he is also ruled by objective factors. The unconscious dominates him in the shape of greed for power. In this he is similar to Gloucester. Edmund, however, is driven by lust for power; actually, he is as superstitious as Gloucester in his unlimited belief in the power of the human ego.

Edmund immediately sets his plot in motion, employing an almost feminine cunning, and he does not hesitate to use astrological terms for his machinations, terms which only a moment before he had declared "excellent foppery." He succeeds brilliantly in maneuvering his brother Edgar into a defenseless position.

The short soliloquy ending this scene indicates how conscious

Edmund is in using the weaknesses of others for his own purposes. With Gloucester, it is his suggestibility. With Edgar it is
the nobility of his character. This latter point is a frequently repeated feature in Shakespeare's drama—that is, a noble or good
quality is weakness in a particular situation and becomes the
cause for downfall:

> A credulous father, and a brother noble,   (I.ii.201)
> . . . on whose foolish honesty
> My practices ride easy.

iii

The third scene makes it clear that Lear has been residing with
Goneril, and that the tensions that were only to be expected
have come into the open. In spite of the strong dislike that we
must surely feel for Goneril already, we can believe her when
she says that Lear and his Knights have been behaving in a disturbing manner. Her complaints about her father reveal that
Lear still feels and acts like a king; he has not changed at all.
She is irked by his continual assumption of authority and we
sympathize with her when she charges: "Himself upbraids us on
every trifle"—though she probably exaggerates.

The basic difficulty between Goneril and her father is their
common egocentricity. She has no feeling for him and he acts
with the full authority of a sovereign. As personalities, however,
they are far apart. Since she is his daughter, one would expect
some similarity in character and general outlook. The fact, however, is that he lives in a world utterly different from hers.

It was Goneril who in her first talk with Regan remarked on
Lear's bad moods and his rashness ("unruly waywardness").
Now she is irritated by his behavior. She has no understanding
for the essentially royal quality in Lear. Without this grasp of
Lear's personality, love simply cannot develop. She can accept
him only as an obligation imposed on her, as if he were an utter
stranger—while Lear continues to live as a king, expecting everyone to obey his commands. Regan's earlier remark that Lear
has "always slenderly known himself" is still very true. Lear has

not in the least realized how much the situation has changed since he voluntarily gave up his crown. Goneril's cold eye perceives his weakness. From her rational, practical and greedy point of view, it is quite logical for her to call him "Idle old man, that still would manage those authorities that he hath given away!" And right then and there she decides to rid herself of him. She immediately develops a plan. Her first step is to instruct Oswald, her steward, to be negligent in his service to the King. She intends to make the abdication of the King a reality and she is certain of agreement with her sister, Regan, on this point. The course she takes is meant to bring home to Lear the fact that he has given up the crown and that now he is no more than any other subject of the realm. In so doing, she is only executing what Lear himself wanted to do, though he did not realize its implications. Although she is a daughter of King Lear, and is herself now Queen, there is no indication in the play that her personality has the royal imprint. Though she has power, she has no authority. For her to have received one-third of the realm is simply an acquisition of wealth and power. It accentuates the ego but otherwise does not change the personality. Oswald, whom we meet here for the first time, simply accepts her commands, without comment. In the further course of the play he behaves like an obedient servant with no personality of his own, as an extension of Goneril's will. Thus we can understand him as a "function" of Goneril's.[20]

iv

The fourth scene brings Kent in disguise.[21] It is a favorite device of Shakespeare's to make characters appear in his plays as something other than they are. He uses disguise for many differ-

[20] We find quite frequently in close relationships, for instance in marriage, or in the boss-secretary or similar relationships, that one person develops one psychological function and keeps another function undeveloped, and that the partner compensatorily develops the unlived function of the other. Throughout the play we find that Goneril and Oswald belong very closely together, that Oswald appears functionally as nothing more than an extension of Goneril's personality.

[21] See V. O. Freeburg, *Disguise Plots in Elizabethan Drama* (Columbia University Press, New York, 1915).

ent purposes. In this play it is used twice with great effect. There is Kent, the "nobleman" who voluntarily puts on the humble weeds of the servant in order to perform his noble task. And there is Edgar, the character with the sanest mind, who puts on the dress of a madman.

In spite of being banished, Kent has decided he must stay with the King for he foresees great difficulties for Lear as a result of his abdication. He is also the one who sees Lear's behavior as an illness ("Kill thy physician, and the fee bestow upon the foul disease"). To appear not to be himself is Kent's trick of being most himself. Loyalty and honesty are his outstanding traits. Paradoxically, they force him to put on a dishonest front. It is of particular significance that Kent, in referring to the King directly, always calls him "Master." In the moving conversation between Lear and Kent in disguise, Kent emphasizes that the only reason for offering his services to Lear is that Lear obviously has a distinguished quality, something which enables him to be an individual:

L E A R: Dost thou know me, fellow? (I.iv.28)

K E N T: No, sir, but you have that in your countenance which I would fain call master.

L E A R: What's that?

K E N T: Authority.

"Authority" had a wider meaning in Elizabethan English than it does today, since the strong influence of the New Testament associated the word with power over man and demons. (For instance in Luke 9:1, "the authority over all devils, and to cure diseases," and in John 5:27, "authority to execute judgment.")

Goneril's orders are obeyed at once. The negligence she has commanded Oswald to show the King is still slight, but it is noticed by the Knight and by Lear. (Cf. I.iii.13: "Put on what weary negligence you please.") Several times Lear asks for his Fool. He needs him and becomes slightly irritated when the Knight, in his inoffensive way, says:

Since my young lady's going into   (I.iv.79)
France, sire, the fool hath much pined him away.

When Oswald re-enters, Lear asks him: "Who am I, sir?" In
the immediate context of the scene, Lear simply demands of
course to be acknowledged as king, and uses this question to
assert his authority, that authority which Kent had voluntarily
recognized just a few moments before. But beyond this immediate dramatic situation is the psychological question. The circumstances into which Lear has placed himself willy-nilly are now
forcing him to find self knowledge. As stated before, this is a
keynote of the play and substantiates my conception of the
tragedy—that it deals with the process of individuation, that is,
with the question of knowing and fulfilling oneself. The question, "Who am I?"—or, in more general terms, "What is man?"
—cannot be answered in intellectual terms, but requires a
knowledge which must be *experienced* and lived out. The best
method of finding out about it is active imagination, which dramatically presents all the problems and possibilities that the intellect alone cannot formulate and decide.[22] It was Shakespeare's
way of finding himself and exploring the limits of human knowledge. In knowing himself, man invariably discovers his creator.[23]
It cannot be otherwise and therefore Lear, in finding himself,
experiences God, though not in a form that is concordant with
the conventions of his time.

Since, as mentioned before, we have three groups in the play
—the Lear, the Gloucester and the Edmund groups—we will
have to accept three different answers[24] to the question, "What is

[22] See p. 6. Active imagination differs from *passive* imagination in
that the ego actually produces the fantasy and participates in it. A drama
like *King Lear* ideally represents active imagination in the highest form
of art. Lear represents an important part in Shakespeare's own process of
individuation. It is an exact parallel to the much humbler products of
modern man. (Cf. my article, "Journey to the Moon," in *Studien zur
Analytischen Psychologie,* Jung Festschrift I (Rascher Verlag, Zurich,
1955), where I also quote bibliography on Jung's writing re active imagination.)
[23] Jung, "The Undiscovered Self," *Civilization in Transition,* p. 293ff.
[24] Answers, not in an intellectual form, but as expressed in their lives.

man?" But it is undoubtedly Lear who, because he is King and because he experiences and suffers the most, is also the one who will be representative of man in his fullest capacities. Once asked by Lear, the question will have to be fully answered.[25]

In the dramatic context, Oswald's reply is brief and to the point: "My lady's father." Lear's pride is deeply wounded because Oswald's statement negates Lear's royalty, declares him a has-been, and clearly places him at least one step below Goneril. Lear can only react with foul curses, and so forgets himself that he strikes Oswald. The affect, however, is a clear indication that something in Lear's depths has been aroused, that his own question, "Who am I?" has not been adequately answered by Lear himself.[26] Kent is similar to Lear in being easily aroused, but his language is not quite as foul as Lear's when he talks to Oswald.

The Fool enters. He is a typical *familiaris*. Like Kent, he tries to help the King but by a very different method. He speaks in parables and symbolic actions, in songs and proverbs which speak directly to the unconscious in Lear. Lear himself, as we noted in the first scene, is inclined to use abstractions sparingly. His language is more that of images. In the opening scene his images tended to be vast, though somewhat hollow ("sacred radiance of the sun . . . by all the operation of the orbs . . ."). The Fool's images are simple and direct. Instead of saying to Lear, "You are a fool," he tells him: "You were best take my coxcomb." It is his way of conveying truth to Lear. Naturally, Lear's ego is hurt. He threatens the Fool with a whip. Again, the Fool uses a plain image:

[25] We find, in analytical work, that once a human being has asked himself, "Who am I?" the unconscious will by necessity be activated and will respond by imagery in dreams, and by life situations; the human being—to his peril or to his benefit—must also respond.

[26] *Affect* always indicates a maladjustment between ego and unconscious. A great deal of libido is piled up in the unconscious. It activates many images. These images, now having a larger charge of energy, are ready to pass over the threshold into consciousness. At this point, Lear is not yet ready to receive them. The ego still lives under the illusion of great power.

> Truth's a dog must to kennel; he must   (I.iv.124)
> be whipped out when Lady the brach may stand
> by the fire and stink.

In his "Shakespeare's Significances," Edmund Blunden[27] states that the "brache" was a 'mannerly' Elizabethan term referring to she-hounds, both canine and human, and that here also is a reference to Goneril.

Herman Melville marked this passage in his own copy of *King Lear*.[28] In an essay on Hawthorne in *The Literary World* (August 17 and 24, 1850), Melville writes of the "blackness of darkness beyond." In his opinion, it is this blackness that

> furnishes the infinite obscure of his background,—that background, against which Shakespeare plays his grandest conceits, the things that have made for Shakespeare his loftiest but most circumscribed renown, as the profoundest of thinkers. For by philosophers Shakespeare is not adored as the great man of tragedy and comedy. . . . But it is those deep far-away things in him; those occasional flashings-forth of the intuitive Truth in him; those short, quick probings at the very axis of reality;— these are the things that make Shakespeare, Shakespeare. . . . For in this world of lies, Truth is forced to fly like a scared white doe in the woodlands; and only by cunning glimpses will she reveal herself, as in Shakespeare and other masters of the great Art of Telling the Truth,—even though it be covertly and by snatches.[29]

This is understood by Lawrance Thompson[30] to mean that Melville saw in the Fool's phrase the final truth—as one of those "occasional flashings-forth of the intuitive Truth in him." But it appears to me that this statement by the Fool is only an initial though important step in bringing truth home to Lear. Answer-

[27] *Shakespeare Criticism, 1919-1935* (Oxford Univ. Press, London, 1936).
[28] Now in Harvard College Library.
[29] *Herman Melville, Representative Selections,* ed. by Willard Thorp (American Book Co., 1938), pp. 333-334.
[30] *Melville's Quarrel with God* (Princeton Univ. Press, Princeton, 1952).

ing the question, "Who am I?"—finding oneself—means also
finding truth as oneself. In his *Aion*,[31] Jung speaks of Gerhard
Dorn, a philosophical alchemist who lived in the second half of
the sixteenth century. In Dorn, Jung finds the "crucial importance of self-knowledge for the alchemical process of transformation expressed most clearly." Dorn said:

> No one can know himself unless he knows *what*, and not *who*,
> he is, on what he depends, or whose he is and for what end he
> was made.

For Dorn, certainly, the Self is *veritas*, that truth which is the
"medicine, improving and transforming that which *is no longer*
into that which it *was before* its corruption, and that which *is
not* into that which it *ought to be.*"

As there are many levels of truth, so correspondingly there
are many stages in this play in which Lear discovers truth about
himself. Together, they point to a knowledge of truth which, in
its fullness, will be revealed only at the final moment of Lear's
life. What the Fool tries to do here is to point out to Lear his
external situation which is a result of his abdication. Lear has
difficulties in seeing the effects of his own act, the "stupidity" of
it, and therefore to accept himself as a "fool." He can only draw
the obvious conclusion from the Fool's little song:

> That lord that counsell'd thee   (I.iv.155)
>   To give away thy land,
> Come place him here by me,
>   Do thou for him stand:
> The sweet and bitter fool
>   Will presently appear;
> The one in motley here,
>   The other found out there.

Lear asks: "Dost thou call me fool, boy?" The Fool answers:

> All thy other titles thou hast given away;   (I.iv.164)
> that thou wast born with.

[31] Pp. 161, 164, 166.

But even Kent has to agree: "This is not altogether fool, my lord."

Now, for the third time in the play one of the key words, "nothing," occurs. When Kent throws the word "nothing" to the Fool ("This is nothing, fool"), using it in the sense that this little song of practical wisdom has no meaning, the Fool then turns to Lear and asks, "Can you make no use of nothing, nuncle?" Using the proverbial *ex nihilo nihil fit,* Lear answers, "Nothing can be made out of nothing." But he suddenly understands and says, "A bitter fool!"

The Fool also brings up a point touched upon in our discussion of Goneril's understanding of Lear, when he says:

I marvel what kin thou and thy daughters are.   (I.iv.200)

The Fool mentions this in relation to being whipped for speaking truth, or for lying. But there is a deeper level: though Lear and his daughters are related to each other by the strongest ties of nature, they are far apart in spiritual nature.

In the course of the play the "good" find their way to Lear and in the hovel scene they are all together—Kent, the Fool, Edgar and Gloucester—while the "bad" gather around Edmund. Nevertheless, Lear has a quality of his own which separates him from, and raises him above even his "good" companions. This extraordinary quality is reflected in Kent's acceptance of Lear as master, of Lear's having authority, but also by the concentrated friendly attacks of the Fool on Lear's unconsciousness and naïveté. In spite of the auxiliary plots in the play, it is Lear who again and again represents the center of the drama. All events and speeches are radii that run toward this center. All have some reference to Lear's fate and developing consciousness. The more conscious, the more human he also becomes. Though a king, he is the protagonist of man and it is this potential of realizing humanity to the fullest which sets him radically apart from the Edmund group and negates any kinship between him and his evil daughters. True kinship is based rather on likeness of mind than likeness of blood. Kent, Edgar, Gloucester, and especially Cordelia, are his true family. It needs, however, all the tragic events of the play to bring this truth home to Lear. Even within his own circle, he is set apart by the depth and extent which his human development achieves. The more Lear falls externally into misfortune, the more he grows inwardly into full humanity. He reaches depths and a totality which even Kent can only partially comprehend.

Goneril enters and the two worlds of Lear and Goneril clash immediately. While in the first scene Lear was in full possession of all his power and privileges, it is now Goneril who is in full power and therefore also commands the situation.

Goneril speaks in the cold reasonable way of a practical housekeeper on whom a wayward, foster-child has been imposed. The Fool perceives the utter discrepancy between Lear's and Goneril's worlds. In one of his little images he harps on the theme of lacking kinship between father and daughter:

> The hedge-sparrow fed the cuckoo so long,   (I.iv.238)
> That it had it head bit off by it young.

This couplet may have been proverbial, but it fits the situation precisely.

Goneril reminds Lear to "put away these dispositions which of late transform you from what you rightly are." Thus she confronts Lear with an image *she* has of what he is, or what she would like him to be. His own image of himself is certainly very different from hers. Therefore, he must ask the question again:

> Does any here know me? This is not Lear;   (I.iv.247)
> Does Lear walk thus? speak thus? Where are his eyes?

He certainly does not yet know who he is. He still lives in the illusion of being king. So once more he asks, "Who am I?"— much more extensively, with more seriousness, but not yet grasping to the full extent the significance this question has for *him*. When Lear asked the question the first time, Oswald responded simply with an answer designating Lear's changed social position. Now, the Fool's answer is more comprehensive and also includes an important aspect of Lear's psychology; his biting retort is: "Lear's shadow." [32]

In this context, the term "shadow" shows that Lear is now a bleak, two-dimensional remnant of his former self, a weak, dependent man who is in no sense his own master. But we may take "shadow" even in the sense in which analytical psychology uses it (though Shakespeare did not use it this way). Then it would mean that Lear has become identified with the archetype of the shadow; that is, a change of personality has taken place in Lear, in which the ego is no longer the ruler of the personality. Instead of ruler, Lear becomes subject to, even victim of his own unconscious. Up to this point, Lear had been walled off against the unconscious and any true knowledge of himself. Now that his ego has no longer the support of his royal position, the walls which he had erected against the unconscious break down. The Fool acts as a typical *spiritus familiaris,* the objective spokesman for Lear's unconscious. Like a battering ram, the Fool breaks down these walls by telling Lear that he is a counterpart of his former self. He means that Lear is now close to the unconscious and has to assimilate all those contents which he has walled off in the past.

Lear "would learn that" (would learn to be his shadow) for:

> . . . by the marks of sovereignty, (I.iv.254)
> knowledge and reason, I should be false
> persuaded I had daughters.

In Elizabethan times, these three things—sovereignty, knowledge and reason—[33] represented the most valuable points of con-

[32] For a discussion of the meaning of "shadow" in Shakespeare, compare *Das Schattenmotiv bei Shakespeare* by Maria Wickert, *Anglia,* Vol. 71 (1952-53), particularly p. 300, where Miss Wickert quotes these two lines from *Lear.* In her analysis, "dream and truth are nothing else than 'shadow and substance' on a different plane of pictorial expression." See also Arden edition of *Alls Well that Ends Well,* edited by G. K. Hunter, fn. 301.

[33] Cf. Max Deutschbein's discussion of "Reason" in *Der Hamletmonolog, Shakespeare-Jahrbuch,* Vol. 80-81, 1946, p. 56, fn., especially his statement about "sovereign reason, so called because according to Platonic conception, Reason is the leader among the powers of the soul."

sciousness. If these three outstanding qualities of the proud Elizabethan broke down, a new orientation had to be sought. This new orientation is contained in the unconscious and will gradually be brought to Lear's attention. Furthermore, Lear becomes aware for the first time that although he is the natural father of daughters, there is no real kinship and that actually no bonds exist between him and them.

In Goneril's following speech we find two terms of importance. One is her request, which is also a threat and a command: ". . . to *disquantity* your train." "Disquantity" (to reduce in size) is an unusual word. It is used by Shakespeare to emphasize Goneril's quantitative thinking. It continues the discussion of the problem of values. Can they be measured in quantity or not? The second term is found in Goneril's requirement of the Knights: she will allow to her father "such men as may besort your age, which *know themselves* and you." In her mouth, "know themselves and you" means knowing their proper position and behaving accordingly as obedient subjects. Lear naturally feels challenged in his royal privileges. Again he answers with strong affect. His language is full of oaths, though a shade less foul than before: "Degenerate bastard!" "Detested kite."

Goneril's description of Lear's Knights as "riotous" and their behavior as appropriate to a "brothel," is exaggerated and distorted. Lear resents her description because it reveals her ingratitude:

> Ingratitude, thou marble-hearted fiend. (I.iv.283)
> More hideous when thou show'st thee in a child
> Than the sea-monster!

When Albany, Goneril's husband, enters, it is apparent that he is amazingly ignorant of what is going on between Lear and his wife. It is important for Shakespeare's dramatic purposes that Albany is kept unconscious of the real situation and of the real character of his wife, and that only later does he learn the stark reality. When he speaks in the latter part of the play, he fulfills, as Miss Ingeborg Gurland [34] states, the role of a "chorus."

At this point, Albany's love for Goneril is so strong that he does not dare to think evil of his wife. Goneril's shocking, icy behavior reminds Lear of Cordelia and gives him a first insight into his own condition at the time he clashed with her and she could not say what he wanted her to say. It was a "most small fault" in Cordelia which appeared to him quite ugly. Her refusal to speak according to his expectations upset his psychic stability. He describes precisely how Cordelia's speech had the effect of breaking his ego away from the rigidly established concepts of his consciousness:

> . . . like an engine, wrenched my frame of nature (I.iv.292)
> From the fix'd place; drew from my heart all love
> And added to the gall.

We can now see in retrospect that he had projected his anima image onto Cordelia. According to the image he had of her, she should have spoken words of love and flattery. She acted, however, as a woman of independent will and thought. The realization of the vast difference between his anima and the real Cordelia plunged him into a deep abyss because the anima projection instantly broke down. His "frame of nature" (his ego with the customary contents of his consciousness) was "wrenched" from its "fix'd" (and projected) place. A new relationship of the ego to meaningful contents, which so far had been projected onto Cordelia, had to be established. (His "frame of nature" had to relate to a new "place.") All of his libido, or what he called love, was then naturally drawn inwards. It was this sudden loss of the anima projection which had such a tremendous impact. It was a real trauma, and unleashed Lear's affectivity.

The first step in the withdrawal of the projection of the anima image is its symbolization as Nature. Lear now addresses Nature as his "goddess"—just as Edmund had done. While Edmund's

---

[34] *Das Gestaltungsgesetz von Shakespeares* "König Lear." (Druckerei u. Verlag wissenschaftlicher Werke Konrad Triltsch, Würzburg, 1938).

appeal was cool, reflective, born out of his inferiority, and was contrasted with the social order of man, Lear's appeal is passionate. He asks Nature to withhold her outstanding quality, that of giving life bountifully. If she has to create, because she cannot help but create, she should create only monstrous forms! Lear's violent reaction is the result of being hurt in his vital spot, in his illusion that he was a good father when he gave away his lands, and that he could expect gratitude from his daughters:

> How sharper than a serpent's tooth it is   (I.iv.312)
> To have a thankless child!

Like every egocentric individual, he has made the assumption that if he *gives* something he must also get an equivalent back in return; that by giving, he has a power over the other human being. As it is, he gave too much away and therefore lost all power. His anger is due to the destruction of this illusion. He has not yet learned that love can only grow where a gift is not accompanied by an expectation of receiving something in return, not even by an *unconscious* expectation. Lear also shows that he is still thinking in terms of quantity. When he realizes that Goneril has the power to take away *half* of his Knights, his affects pour out in violent language: "Blasts and fogs upon thee!" and he gives vent to his wounded feelings as a father. His rage anticipates an action which, ironically, becomes true in a very different way than he expects:

> Old fond eyes,   (I.iv.325)
> Beweep this cause again, I'll pluck ye out,
> And cast you, with the waters that you lose,
> To temper clay.

He anticipates revenge:

> When she shall hear this of thee, with her nails   (I.iv.331)
> She'll flay thy wolfish visage. Thou shalt find
> That I'll resume the shape which thou dost think
> I have cast off for ever.

This comforts him and restores the illusion in him that the wheel of destiny could be turned back, that he will be again what he has been before. He still believes that his other daughter will be what he wishes her to be. He has not yet understood the course his destiny irrevocably must take.

Shakespeare's supreme artistry is clearly revealed when he allows Lear to use the image of plucking-out-the-eyes. Here it wells up out of Lear's unconscious and tellingly symbolizes his despair. He could not anticipate that this image will later become a stark reality with Gloucester ("I'll pluck ye out"). It demonstrates that Shakespeare wanted Gloucester to be understood as a part-personality (*Teilpersönlichkeit*) of Lear. For Lear the idea of getting rid of these eyes is not so much to get rid of sight as to get rid of suffering—because they are also the fountain of tears. This, of course, is a paraphrase of Matthew 18:9:

> If thine eye offend thee, pluck it out, and cast it from thee.

It is also evidence that *King Lear* was meant as a paraphrase of Christ's own Passion.

In our daily psychological work we can observe that a person confronted with an unpleasant problem, or with an incompatible quality of his personality, will try to cut it out or to behave as if it did not exist. We cannot deny our sympathy to such a reaction. It is understandable and very human. Very frequently the human ego is too weak to face some of the dark aspects of its psyche. Sometimes it is necessary for the analyst to convey as much as possible of this unacceptable content to the sufferer, but more often it is the course of destiny that compels the individual to face the undesirable problems of human existence. In *King Lear,* Shakespeare presents this universal human problem: a man, for non-rational reasons, as a result of his own actions, loses his habitual standpoint ("wrenched . . . from the fix'd place") and fate consequently forces him to learn simultaneously all about his personal psychology and the eternal aspects of human life. For a time he holds on to his customary viewpoints and attitudes, tries to rid himself of the hellish darkness to which he is exposed, and cherishes the illusion of reestablishing the former status quo. But once the wheel of destiny has begun its course, it must irrevocably arrive at its destination. Shakespeare knew this very well. Therefore, he puts into Lear's mouth the words: "Old fond eyes . . . I'll pluck ye out . . . I'll resume the shape which thou dost think I have cast off for ever."

As noted before, sight symbolizes consciousness and Lear's first instinctive reaction is to rid himself of consciousness and, with that, of suffering—because it is always human consciousness that suffers.

Lear leaves. Kent and the attendants leave. Goneril drives the Fool away. A short discussion takes place between her and Albany, in which she explains her cruel behavior to her husband. She fears that Lear, with his one hundred Knights, represents too much power and might endanger their lives:

> He may enguard his dotage with their powers   (I.iv.351)
> And hold our lives in mercy.

It is ridiculous to attribute so much power to Lear. She misrepresents the whole situation. Nevertheless, there is a kernel of truth in her fear. Her ego is very insecure. She is cut off from her instincts and is thereby forced to compensate by rationalizations and distortions. Albany's weak rejoinder, "Well, you may fear too far," is answered by the characteristic answer of the shaky ego which has no relationship to its own self:

> Safer than trust too far.   (I.iv.354)
> Let me still take away the harms I fear,
> Not fear still to be taken.

Kenneth Muir explains this as meaning: "rather than continue in the fear of being overtaken by harm."

Goneril immediately sets her plot to work and dispatches Oswald with a letter to Regan, in order to deprive Lear of those remnants of power he still has. Something in her, of course, tells her that she has taken the wrong, guilty course against her husband. She must repress the natural feelings she once had for her father and therefore, compensatorily, she attacks her husband by calling his humane and respectful attitude "milky gentleness" and "harmful mildness." Like every "realist," she believes that cruelty is practical wisdom. Albany's answer again is weak, expressing not much more than a doubt in the wisdom of her "course."

v

In the last scene of Act I Lear is executing his plan to take up residence with his other daughter, Regan. The Fool continues with his pointed ribbing, but it is not strong enough to pierce Lear's illusion that he will be well received by Regan. Though the Fool does not mention Cordelia, something stirs in Lear and, seemingly out of context, the insight strikes him: "I did her wrong." Lear begins to suffer. He feels wronged, maltreated by two of his daughters, and he severely complains of ingratitude. This suffering opens his eyes to the wrong he has done to Cordelia. He feels the impending effect which his rising affects might have on him. He recognizes the truth in the Fool's sharp statement:

> Thou shouldst not have been old till thou   (I.v.49)
> hadst been wise.

Lear retorts:

> O, let me not be mad, not mad, sweet heaven!   (I.v.51)
> Keep me in temper; I would not be mad!

This is no longer directed to the Fool. Lear is addressing God or a power in himself. It has the quality of a monologue. In fact, it is a short prayer. It demonstrates that the insight which began with his realization that he has wronged Cordelia is reaching deeper levels in him. While we could see in Scene 1 that the affects overran him, he is now aware that they can harm his mind, and that he needs divine help to face them and deal with them. From now on, his principal struggle will be to maintain sanity.

Thus the first act ends. All the principal figures have been introduced and fully described, and the problems clearly stated: quantity confronted with love—appearance contrasted with truth—Lear's unconsciousness versus insight—sanity against uncontrolled affect.

Act Two

i

The second act opens with a development in the Edmund-Gloucester plot. Edmund's trickery and base libel works well on credulous Gloucester, now convinced that Edgar is a disloyal son who is even planning to murder his father. Gloucester's fate (just as Lear's) is set in motion by the disloyalty of one of his children and (just as with Lear) he mistakes the good child for the bad. Edmund uses Gloucester's weakness very skillfully. Ruthlessly, he tells extreme lies. They have the expected effect: Gloucester immediately plans to arrest Edgar and to gain the assistance of the Duke of Cornwall. In his spiritual blindness, Gloucester calls Edmund his "loyal and natural boy":

> . . . I'll work the means　　　　　　　　(II.i.86)
> To make thee capable. (. . . able to inherit.)

It is important to realize that these disturbances going on within the Gloucester and Lear families are accompanied by vague and unsettling rumors that a war between the Dukes of Cornwall and Albany is in the making. Actually, at no point in the play do we ever hear that such is the case, but Curran's mention of such a rumor serves the purpose of showing that the conflicts are not limited to the principal groups of characters, but that the developing chaos is also felt in the collective.[1]

Cornwall and Regan arrive at Gloucester's castle. They believe Edmund's story and Regan even tries to connect Edgar's assumed misbehavior with the so-called "riotous" behavior of Lear's knights. The Duke and Regan accept Edmund as one of them:

> For you, Edmund, (II.i.115)
> Whose virtue and obedience doth this instant
> So much commend itself, you shall be ours.

Their conclusion is the irony of thieves:

> Natures of such deep truth we shall much need. (II.i.117)

Both Edmund and Gloucester agree to serve these two:

EDMUND: I shall serve you sir, (II.i.118)
               Truly, however else.

GLOUCESTER: I serve you, madam. (II.i.129)
               Your Graces are right welcome.

ii

The second scene brings a meeting of Kent and Oswald before Gloucester's castle. Oswald of course does not recognize Kent in his disguise, while Kent knows at once who Oswald is. He knows his vicious character very well and makes no bones about his low opinion of him. Kent's affects are as little controlled as Lear's; a stream of invective pours out of him. He threatens Oswald with his sword, eventually even besting him. It might have ended badly for Oswald had not Edmund, Cornwall, Regan, Gloucester and servants entered at this moment. Edmund separates the two, but Kent continues his insulting de-

---

[1] Cf. Jung's "Contribution to the Psychology of Rumour," *Freud and Psychoanalysis*, p. 35.

scription of Oswald. With his master at his side, Oswald lies
when he says:

> This ancient ruffian, sir, whose life I have   (II.ii.66)
> spar'd at suit of his grey beard—

The Duke, disturbed by this unexpected unmannerly behavior,
calls Kent "beastly knave," and has difficulty in quieting him.
Kent, of course, has no tangible evidence for his unflattering
description of Oswald. Driven into a corner, he has to admit:
"His countenance likes me not." In his defense, Kent can only
state:

> Sir, 'tis my occupation to be plain: (II.ii.98)
> I have seen better faces in my time
> Than stands on any shoulder that I see
> Before me at this instant.

In other words, Kent thinks that he must express the truth no
matter what the circumstances. He is incapable of reflecting
properly on his situation. He is so deeply convinced of the truth
of what he is saying that he makes no attempt to control his
affects; his unimpeded stream of abuse (which, nevertheless,
contains truth) must be constrained by external means. Cornwall decides to put Kent in the stocks.

This scene is an ironic parallel to an important incident in the
first scene of Act I, in which Lear, responding to Cordelia's *truth-*
ful statement, later says, "Let pride, which she calls plainness,
marry her" (I.i.131). Here, in the present scene, there is a considerable play on the word "plain," as expressing frank, unveiled
truth. Psychologically, this free flow of images represents the
state of mind in which the anima dominates consciousness with
her images, irrespective of the particular circumstances or the
possible consequences of such behavior. For Cornwall, however,
who just a short while before had commended Edmund as a
"nature of deep trust," this plainness appears to hide particular
cunning:

> These kind of knaves I know which in this *plainness*
>
> > (II.ii.108)
>
> Harbor more craft and more corrupter ends
> Than twenty silly-duckling observants
> That stretch their duties nicely.

Subsequent events show that Kent has not understood the situation well because he considers himself inviolate as the King's messenger:

> You shall do small respect, show too bold malice   (II.ii.137)
> Against the grace and person of my master,
> Stocking his messenger.

Regan turns out to be even more cruel than her sister. Unburdened by any scruples (Goneril had to fight some doubts; cf. p. 224), she demands an even longer time for Kent to be "stocked" than Goneril had proposed. If one compares Kent with the Fool, one realizes that although Kent was the first to perceive Lear's mistake, and although he assumed the attitude of a physician toward Lear, it is the Fool alone who from the very beginning has a deep understanding of the *whole* situation.

It is just this irascible quality in Kent (which he has in common with Lear) that limits his understanding. He must therefore share Lear's fate to some degree. He is the first to suffer directly from the cruelty of Lear's daughters and he is specifically punished as a messenger of Lear. In putting Kent into the stocks, Cornwall, and Regan in particular, mean to punish the King.

Gloucester has been present during this shocking incident. It awakens him to the reality of the situation, and as a result he takes a first step away from the group of Edmund and the daughters. The "stocking" has a much profounder effect on Kent. The physical limitation imposed on him forces him to contain his affect. His irascibility disappears completely. He resigns himself to the situation very quickly. In a short talk with Gloucester, he accepts his position as one of the blows of fortune. Left alone, he expresses his inner condition in a short monologue. He comforts himself with the realization that he is standing here in the place of the King, and with the knowledge of a letter he has received from Cordelia. In it she writes that she has been informed of Kent's "obscured course." Kent knows that such abnormal conditions ("this enormous state") will release forces which will alter the situation. Such extreme misery must bring about miracles, he believes, and, finally, the image of Fortuna standing by a wheel presents itself to Kent's mind:

> Fortune, good night, smile once more; turn thy wheel!
>
> (II.ii.180)

In discussing Hamlet's monologue, "To be or not to be," Max Deutschbein[2] speaks of the three powers to which, in Shakespeare's conviction, man is subject and which determine his life: *Fortune, Nature* and *Time*. These are the factors which defile man's dignity and against which the outstanding individual must fight. He is helped in this struggle by a divine factor which shapes man's end:

> There's a divinity that shapes our ends,
> Rough-hew them how we will.[3]

Here in *Lear* we find these three powers described in a new variation. Kent's position in the stocks certainly exemplifies man's humiliation by superior powers. Fortune here is associated with the image of a wheel. As Jung's studies on the mandala prove, the image of the circle, in its various forms, is an archetypal symbol. In the form of a *Rota,* it has been used to describe the horoscope, expressing the idea that the cause of human life is inescapably determined by the Moirai. In Shakespeare's time, Fortune's wheel was current in two forms, as Kittredge mentions in commenting on *Hamlet* II.ii.517:

> The allegory of Fortune's wheel is current under two forms, both known to Shakespeare. In the strictly classical form, For-

[2] *Shakespeare Jahrbuch,* Vol. 80-81, p. 66.
[3] *Hamlet,* V. ii. 10.

tune is represented as riding on her wheel, which turns constantly. . . . The second form, popular in the Middle Ages and
later, represents Fortune as sitting by a wheel which she turns
by means of a crank. On this wheel are mortals, who are therefore sometimes at the summit, and sometimes declining or at
the very bottom of their fate.

Kent here uses the symbol of the wheel in the second sense, he
being the one who rides on it, and who is now at the "very bottom." The use of the wheel is akin to some oriental concepts,
although there was no oriental influence on Shakespeare. The
symbol of the Rota naturally arises from the archetypal depths.
Kent's appeal to Fortuna to "smile once more" and "turn thy
wheel" is almost a prayer. The wheel occurs in *Lear* four times,
each time at a significant moment. (Cf. p. 283ff.)

iii

In Scene 3 of Act II Edgar is in a wood, having "escaped
the hunt" by "the happy hollow of a tree." This image suggests
that Edgar, in order to escape, has almost become a part of a
tree and represents a descent into primeval life. It is as if he had
become a tree-spirit.[4] For primitive man, every tree was
haunted by a tree-spirit. While Kent has had to disguise his true
appearance and accept a socially inferior position, the disguise
which is imposed on Edgar goes much further. In order to survive at all he has had to lose the cast of human dignity, to assume a shape as near the beast as possible, and to veil reason,[5]
that quality which in the opinion of the Renaissance raised man
above the animal. Now he remains only

[4] Cf. Jung, "The 'Arbor philosophica,'" *Von den Wurzeln des Bewusstseins* (Rascher Verlag, Zurich, 1954), p. 351.
[5] In *Hamlet* (III.i.159), Ophelia says of Hamlet:
  O! what a noble mind is here o'erthrown:
  The courtier's, soldier's, scholar's, eye, tongue, sword;

  . . .

  And I, of ladies most deject and wretched,
  That suck'd the honey of his music vows,
  Now see that noble and most sovereign *reason*,
  Like sweet bells jangled, out of tune and harsh.

Poor Turlygood! poor Tom!   (II.iii.20)
That's something yet: Edgar I nothing am.

According to Roland M. Smith[6] "Turlygood" might mean "stammering Turley" or possibly "mad Turley."

iv

Lear again appears on the scene and is suddenly confronted with Kent in the stocks. He is shocked and has the greatest difficulty in believing it:

They durst not do't;   (II.iv.23)
They could not, would not do't; 'tis worse than murder.

Kent informs Lear of what has happened, admitting that in his clash with Oswald, Regan and Cornwall, he had "more man than wit about (him)." "Wit" in Shakespeare's use, very similar to "mind," represents man's highest faculty—consciousness and orientation to higher moral principles.[7]

The Fool, in his usual manner, accompanies Lear's and Kent's conversation with pregnant songs. Lear, realizing that the affront against Kent in fact is directed against himself, becomes angry. He feels affect rising in him, describes it in physical terms, as if it were ascending from the abdominal area:

O! how this mother swells up toward my heart;   (II.iv.56)
Hysterica passio! down, thou climbing sorrow.
Thy element's below.

Edward Jordan, quoted in the Arden edition,[8] describes the "hysterico passion":

This disease is called by diverse names. . . . *Passio Hysterica, Suffocatio, Priefocatio,* and *Strangulatus uteri, Caducus Matricis,* i.e., in English, the Mother or the Suffocation of the

---

[6] *Modern Language Quarterly,* 1946, p. 168.
[7] See Deutschbein, *op. cit.*
[8] P. 85.

Mother, because, most commonly, it takes them with choking in the throat; and it is an affect of the mother or womb, wherein the principal parts of the body by consent suffer diversely according to the diversity of the causes and diseases wherewith the matrix is offended.

Lear wants to talk with his daughter, alone. He leaves the stage and Kent, having noticed that Lear arrived with only a few knights, has a chance to ask the Fool how this has come about. In his answer, the Fool uses the symbol of the wheel again:

> Let go thy hold when a great wheel runs   (II.iv.72)
> down a hill, lest it break thy neck with
> following it; but the great one that goes
> up the hill, let him draw thee after.

The symbol refers to Lear himself, and there is certainly an association with Fortuna. However, the wheel, and not Fortuna in the Renaissance sense, represents Fate. The Fool advises man not to hold on to the wheel when it goes down because it will destroy him, but to stay with it when it goes upwards. Through this image of a great wheel which runs down a hill, he conveys the idea that, like gravity, a natural force is functioning in Lear's destiny, and that its power is great just because Lear is a great man. This effective simile is the Fool's way of warning Kent to leave Lear but, of course, in his loyalty Kent is inevitably bound to Lear and Lear's fate. Contrary to Kent's belief—expressed in his prayer: "Thou out of heaven's benediction comest to the warm sun!"—the Fool understands that Lear's fate has not yet reached its nadir; there are much worse calamities ahead for Lear and his friends.

This dialogue between Kent and the Fool serves to describe the dark background of what is going on and prepares us well for what happens to Lear next. Regan and Cornwall have simply refused to speak with Lear. Lear bursts with affects:

> Vengeance! plague! death! confusion!   (II.iv.95)

He cannot accept the disloyal behavior of his daughters. He ends his angry speech with:

> . . . bid them come forth and hear me,   (II.iv.118)
> Or at their chamber-door I'll beat the drum
> Till it cry sleep to death.[9]

Gloucester succeeds in bringing Cornwall and Regan back, and Kent is immediately set free. Lear still addresses his daughter as "beloved Regan," and still speaks to her as if she were his loving child. He complains to her of Goneril, but Regan very quickly reveals that she is no different from her sister. She coldly informs him that Goneril is right. She treats him as an unruly child:

> You should be rul'd, and led   (II.iv.150)
> By some discretion that discerns your state
> Better than yourself.

She even urges him to ask Goneril's forgiveness. Lear naturally resents this very much. Righteous ire takes hold of him and he pronounces his terrible curse:

> You nimble lightnings, dart your blinding flames   (II.iv.168)
> Into her scornful eyes! Infect her beauty
> You fen-suck'd fogs, drawn by the powerful sun,
> To fall and blast her pride!

Nevertheless, he makes himself believe in Regan's kindness. Goneril enters (as her letter had indicated, she would soon arrive). Regan refuses to accept Lear in her home, recommending that he return to Goneril:

> I am now from home, and out of that provision   (II.iv.208)
> Which shall be needful for your entertainment.

---

[9] Sleep as a healing factor has great meaning for Shakespeare. This line in particular reminds us of *Macbeth* II.ii.37:
> 'Macbeth does murther Sleep,' the innocent Sleep,
> Sleep that knits up the ravell'd sleave of care.

Lear realizes he cannot return to Goneril and cuts himself off from her, just as he did with Cordelia—but under very different circumstances. He has become far gentler. The affect does not overwhelm him, because he is now aware how dangerous the affect is to his mental condition. Therefore, he prays:

> I prithee, daughter, do not make me mad. (II.iv.221)

He declares this separation in a few monosyllabic words:

> We'll no more meet, no more see one another. (II.iv.223)

The decrease in affect corresponds to an increase in insight. Although he separates from his daughter, he realizes that she is inescapably part of his own nature, even a disease:

> But yet thou art my flesh, my blood, my daughter; (II.iv.224)
> Or rather a disease that's in my flesh.

There is no word here of how he could cure himself of this disease, and perhaps it is only a passing moment, but this insight that Goneril represents a "disease" in his flesh deflates his ego, makes it impossible for him to blame anyone else for his condition. He will no more identify with the "thunder-bearer" (Cf. p. 194, "the dragon and his wrath") and he will leave Goneril to her own fate:

> I do not bid the thunder-bearer shoot, (II.iv.229)
> Nor tell tales of thee to high-judging Jove.
> Mend when thou canst; be better at thy leisure.

The unpleasant discussion between Lear and his two daughters continues. Regan will let Lear have only twenty-five attendants. And so, believing that Goneril was in earnest about the "fifty" attendants, he suddenly turns to her, saying that he will go with her, although just a few moments before he had said, "I will not trouble thee, my child . . . we'll no more see one another." He reasons for human dignity, for the minimum amount that man needs beyond what nature needs. He points out to her:

Thou art a lady: (II.iv.270)
If only to go warm were gorgeous,
Why, nature needs not what thou gorgeous wear'st,
Which scarcely keeps thee warm.

It has dawned upon him how weak he is in this situation.

We have already noted Lear's inclination to think in terms of
quantity, and to measure love in quantitative terms. Having just
rejected Goneril, he now accepts her again, being once more
impressed by quantity. He says:

I'll go with thee.   (II.iv.262)
Thy fifty yet doth double five-and-twenty,
And thou art twice her love.

Here Lear clearly reveals how similar his psychology is to
that of his two daughters. He is willing to accept Goneril's love
because she grants him twice as many knights as Regan. It
means to him that she loves him twice as much as her sister.
Lear has changed very little. He still needs to be confronted with
the negative aspects of his own "quantitative" psychology. He
has to learn that his two daughters give him nothing, even when
they grant him a certain number of knights, be it fifty or twenty-
five. The irony is that now they reduce the number of knights to
"nothing" in a numerical sense. When Regan asks, "What need
one?" he realizes that their love is "nothing" when the non-
existence of love has been translated into the number "zero."
The only thing these two daughters consider now is need, and
human need is extremely variable, though it is something that
can be expressed in quantitative terms. Lear quite rightly resents
their bringing up the question of need. He is still very far from
realizing what real love is. It certainly includes taking care of the
needs of others. It does not ask what the upper or lower limits of
need are. To have reduced their filial duty to taking care of
Lear's minimal needs makes Goneril and Regan utterly inhuman.

Deeply wounded, Lear reacts with great affect, but this time
the affect inspires his speech:

> O! reason not the need; our basest beggars   (II.iv.267)
> Are in the poorest thing superfluous:
> Allow not nature more than nature needs,
> Man's life is cheap as beast's. Thou art a lady;
> If only to go warm were gorgeous,
> Why, nature needs not what thou gorgeous wear'st,
> Which scarcely keeps thee warm.

His words ring with truth but of course they have no effect on these icy daughters. Their hearts are like stone. Lear's anger rises and, as before, he is aware of the danger which threatens him from his wrath, holy as it may be. He must control it. Since he can compel neither material help nor love, he realizes that his greatest need then is patience:

> You heavens, give me that patience, patience I need! (II.iv.274)

He feels quite alone now, "a poor old man, as full of grief as age." Deserted by his daughters, he realizes that only the gods can help him. And yet, his rage takes hold of him again. In his old manner, being the thunder-god himself, he exclaims.

> *No, you unnatural hags!*   (II.iv.281)

and feels that the affects might overrun him again, this time in the form of tears. But this release of affect will not give him comfort, will not release him of his burden, but will destroy his consciousness. Therefore he says:

> I have full cause of weeping, but this heart   (II.iv.287)
> Shall break into a hundred thousand flaws
> Or ere I'll weep. O fool, I shall go mad!

Lear exits, together with Gloucester, Kent and the Fool, and the Folio here has "Storm and tempest" as stage directions.

The storm of affect rising in King Lear's breast is synchronistically accompanied by a storm in nature. It is as if the laws of nature, of love between father and child, once violated would call up all the elements in nature in order to heal the unnatural breach. This participation of nature in Lear's conflict gives universal greatness to the drama. Simultaneously with Lear's great suffering, the affects move Lear's mind into areas of experience which are usually closed to man. Here, at this point, the play extends far into nature and, at the same time, far into the nature of the human soul. This move beyond the limits of ordinary consciousness, this direct experience of the uncharted depths of the unconscious, has usually been understood as madness. I believe that Lear's state of mind and Shakespeare's poetical intention need a great deal of clarification, since Shakespeare's use of the words "mad" and "madness" is vastly different from our clinical use of these words. I will try to clarify this later. Here, at the end of the second act, and during the third act, the "tempest" occurs in nature and—in both the internal and the exterior worlds—it brings extreme suffering to Lear.

Goneril and Regan discuss what to do with Lear under the threat of the approaching storm. Regan would like to give him shelter, but not to any of his followers. Goneril, in the iciest, coldest manner, rejects all responsibility. Speaking like a goddess of fate, she says:

> 'Tis his own blame; hath put himself from rest, (II.iv.293)
> And must needs taste his folly.

Gloucester, who had accompanied Lear and his train outside, returns to report that Lear "is in high rage" and has left, but he does not know where the King has gone. Both sisters refuse help and Regan, also refusing all responsibility, now assumes the same icy attitude as her sister:

> O, sir, to wilful men (II.iv.305)
> The injuries that they themselves procure,
> Must be their schoolmasters.

Like Goneril (in Scene 4 of Act I: "Safer than trust too far"),
Regan proclaims it wisdom to be afraid of Lear's attendants.

The second act ends with Cornwall approving his wife's counsel. Thus he proves a worthy companion of Regan. He is equally
as evil as Edmund, although not driven by the same ambition.

Act Three

i

As the second act ended, with a painful discussion, sounding a
shrill tone of evil in the world of man, the rage of the King and
the approaching storm have prepared us for a participation of
nature in the conflict. The rift between Lear and his daughters
has, as it were, aroused the anger of the gods. Now, at the beginning of the third act, this storm dominates the stage. We hear
about it in a discussion between Kent and a Gentleman. We are
told that Lear's fury closely parallels the storm in nature. In the
Gentleman's words, it competes strongly with the "impetuous
blasts" and the "eyeless rage" [1] of the storm. Lear "strives in
his little world of man to outscorn the to-and-fro conflicting
wind and rain." There is some measure of hope in all this—for
there may be conflict between the two dukes, and Cordelia is
preparing to land in England with an army to help the King in
his "unnatural and bemadding sorrow."

ii

What was only pointed out and described by friendly observers in Scene 1, we see fully developed in Scene 2. The heavens
are raging, and Lear, in the company of the Fool, is fully exposed to the inclement storm. In rejecting Regan's proposal for

---

[1] Kenneth Muir (Arden edition) explains "eyeless" as blind, sightless. H. H. Furness (Variorum edition) does not comment on the word
at all. As stated before, this play abounds in images of sight. It is significant that the rage of the storm is characterized as "eyeless." It indicates that the fury of the storm has no consciousness at all. It blasts
right out of the unconscious.

him to return to Goneril with "fifty men dismissed," he had exclaimed:

> No, rather I abjure all roofs, and choose   (II.iv.211)
> To wage against the enmity o' the air,
> To be a comrade with the wolf and owl.

Now the image is a fact. He has no roof and is a comrade to the wolf and owl. It is Shakespeare's deep understanding of human nature and human destiny that his characters first use poetic images which later manifest themselves in a reality situation. It is Shakespeare's way of indicating that it is the individual himself who arranges his own fate. The behavior of Lear's viper daughters is then an acting-out of Lear's unconscious. We do not need to go as far as Melville who, in Chapter 19 of *Moby Dick*—titled "The Prophet"—, has Elijah, the "beggar-like stranger," say:

> Ye've shipped, have ye? Names down in the papers? Well, well, what's signed, is signed; and what's to be, will be; and then again, perhaps it won't be, after all. Anyhow, it's all fixed and arranged a'ready.

—and then everything happens in this novel as Elijah had prophesied.

In such parallel phenomena the action occurs on two planes: first, on the psychic plane, then later as an external event. My viewpoint is not causalistic. I do not contend that these images *cause* the objective event, but rather that they arrange events. Analytical psychology uses the term "constellate" to describe the relationship between images arising from the unconscious (psychic factors) and events which correspond to these images. In our psychological work we frequently see that certain images occur in dreams, or in fantasies, or in a figure of speech, and later become objectively real.[2] To use Melville again, a clas-

---

[2] I knew, for instance, a certain English student who was particularly fond of his pair of glasses. In teasing him about it, a friend remarked, "You would give your life for that pair of glasses!" A few months

sic example of such a situation is this passage about the customs officer in *Redburn*,[3] written in 1849:

> And weary days they must have been to this friendless custom-house officer; trying to kill time in the cabin with a newspaper; and rapping on the transom with his knuckles. He was kept on board to prevent smuggling; but he used to smuggle himself ashore very often, when, according to law, he should have been at his post on board ship. But no wonder; he seemed to be a man of fine feelings, altogether above his situation, a most inglorious one, indeed; worse than driving geese to water.

Since the books that followed *Moby Dick* were financial failures and since no other source of income was available to him, Melville was finally forced to accept a position as customs inspector in New York on December 6, 1866. The image of the customs inspector as he appeared in *Redburn* became a reality seventeen years later. At $4.00 a day, it was an office Melville unwillingly held for nineteen years and which he left on the day he received a small inheritance.

In his discussion with the Gentleman (Act III, Scene 1), Kent had described Lear's condition as an attempt to "outstorm the storm." Now we see it directly. On the heath, Lear addresses the storm in majestic images. Although the Fool is present and even interrupts the King, asking him to return to his daughters, Lear pays no attention to him. He is no longer communicating with man, but with Nature herself. A true *Auseinandersetzung* with the gods, a true confrontation with his affects, takes place. The storm raging in nature is paralleled by an equally violent tempest in his own breast. The images emerging in his address to the elements apply simultaneously to the storm on the heath and to the fury of his affects:

> Blow, winds, and crack your cheeks! rage! blow!　　(III.ii.1)
> You cataracts and hurricanoes, spout

---

later, the young man went mountaineering with friends. Standing on a high cliff, the glasses slipped from his nose. Instinctively, he bent down to pick them up, and fell several hundred feet to his death.

[3] Doubleday & Co., New York, 1957, p. 130.

Till you have drench'd our steeples, drown'd the cocks!
You sulphurous and thought-executing fires.

The term "thought-executing" has been variously explained.[4] I
take it literally to mean "the fires execute thoughts," that is, the
fury ("fires") of his affects create thoughts that he has never
allowed himself before. He discriminates clearly between the elements, his affects, and his children, and at last admits the weakness of the human ego when the individual encounters the gods:

> . . . Then let fall   (III.ii.18)
> Your horrible pleasure. Here I stand your slave,
> A poor, infirm, weak, and despised old man.

He accuses the elements of joining their "high-engendered battles" with his daughters. The Fool, as usual, accompanies Lear's
speech with a song which, in spite of its vulgar images, expresses
common sense and clarifies Lear's extreme condition from a
practical viewpoint:

> The cod-piece that will house   (III.ii.27)
>   Before the head has any,
> The head and he shall louse;
>   So beggars marry many.
> The man that makes his toe
>   What he his heart should make,
> Shall of a corn cry woe,
>   And turn his sleep to wake.

Lear again pays no attention. His introversion has proceeded
very intensely since the break with his two daughters. The
strength of his affect has forced his consciousness to give sole
attention to the inner process. He is inside a circle of affects, his
libido has been withdrawn to a considerable degree from the
external objects and is concerned only with the inner event.

---

[4] Arden edition, p. 106 (4): Barret points out that Johnson's explanation, "doing execution with rapidity equal to thought," is supported by the
parallel passage in *The Tempest*. Moberly, however, explains "executing
the thought of him who casts you."

It is no wonder, therefore, that when Kent enters Lear continues his great monologue, a dialogue with the elements in himself. He finally admonishes himself to be patient; patience is obviously the best means to maintain the strength of his ego, and
therewith maintain his sanity. Kent gives a vivid description of
the storm, asserting that "Man's nature cannot carry the affliction or the fear." A condition is reached here in which normal
man's ability to tolerate the onslaught of nature has been surpassed. In spite of that, Lear's introversion is so intense that he
cannot relate to another human being, and so he continues his
inner discussion. Now the elements are to him the gods, holding
court on guilty man. All the hidden guilt is brought up in Lear.
He does not see that the gods are sitting in judgment on *him;* he
projects the guilt on other men and ends with:

> I am a man   (III.ii.59)
> More sinn'd against than sinning.

There is great resistance in him to accepting his own guilt and to
seeing that the Self has staged the storm of affects and the course
of his destiny. Not seeing his own guilt is a serious obstacle. No
man can arrive at full consciousness if he cannot accept the hidden guilt in himself. The terribly aroused unconscious (his
"god") is now ready to reveal the long-repressed guilt. Without
this acceptance of himself as a fallible and guilty human being,
the danger will persist and the affects may overrun his consciousness and destroy it. He is aware of this when, in speaking
to the Fool, he says, "My wits begin to turn."

Nevertheless, an important change has taken place in Lear.
Suffering himself, he is aware of his fellow being's misery:

> Come on, my boy. How dost, my boy? Art cold?   (III.ii.68)
> I am cold myself . . .
> . . . I have one part in my heart
> That's sorry yet for thee.

Lear now listens to Kent and accepts his proposal to enter a
hovel nearby.

iii

The storm scene is momentarily interrupted to give us a short but important development in the Gloucester plot. Gloucester, trusting Edmund completely, confides to his bastard son that he has been forbidden to give any help to Lear and further that he is in possession of a letter informing him that an army has landed which has come to aid Lear. For Edmund, this is the God-sent opportunity. He immediately decides to betray his father and to tell the Duke about the letter. Thus Gloucester, in his own blindness, prepares his own horrible fate.

iv

After this brief interruption, we are again with Lear. He is in front of the hovel. Kent, of course, gives all his attention to the storm in nature, but to Lear the storm in his inner nature has more reality:

> . . . where the greater malady is fixed,   (III.iv.8)
> The lesser is scarcely felt . . .
> . . . The tempest in my mind
> Doth from my senses take all feeling else
> Save what beats there. Filial ingratitude!

Again he seeks the cause of his troubles outside himself, that is, in his daughters' ingratitude, and he swears to "punish home!" But then he decides to "endure." He now knows that if he allows his resentment to thunder against his daughters, he will lose his mind:

> O, that way madness lies; let me shun that!   (III.iv.21)
> No more of that.

Again and again, throughout the central part of the play, Lear fights against madness. It is a running battle between himself and his affects. Most of the time, as it is here, he is able to contain the affects, to gain new insight, to maintain enough ego strength (patience) to avoid a breaking of his mind. In this battle the libido is withdrawn to a large extent from external reality. This libido is urgently needed to give uninterrupted attention to the inner process, and thereby save his mind. To his companions, this withdrawal of libido must already appear as madness. The vital question, however, is whether in this intense introversion, even though it means at times losing outside contact, Lear can maintain cohesion and continuity of his consciousness. We will pay close attention to this question as we continue this analysis, but I might state my thesis now: the most that happens is a complete withdrawal of the libido from outer reality (a loss of reality sense), but the cohesion of Lear's consciousness is preserved at all times. Clinically speaking, we might diagnose his mental condition as a traumatic psychosis.[5] From an inner point of view, this intense introversion is actually a healing process, a process that will lead to increasing consciousness in Lear.

Lear's awareness here of man's poverty and his consequent lack of protection against nature is a step in his development. His capacity to commiserate now extends beyond himself and his immediate companions to all mankind. In modern terms, we would say that his social consciousness awakens:

> Poor naked wretches, whereso'er you are,   (III.iv.28)
> That bide the pelting of this pitiless storm,
> How shall your houseless heads and unfed sides,
> Your loop'd and window'd raggedness, defend you
> From seasons such as these?

He, the King, accepts himself as just one of all human beings who suffer the tragedy of existence. Old wrathful Lear has changed indeed! He who could so easily reject or banish another human being, now accepts every human being and acknowledges that we are all subject to a common fate.

A further expression of Lear's need for introversion is his desire to go into the hovel and *sleep*. It is only natural that his

---

[5] This viewpoint agrees with Dr. Hans Laehr's diagnosis. In describing Lear's clinical condition, he uses the old term *akute Verwirrtheit* (acute state of confusion). See *Die Darstellung Krankhafter Geisteszustände in Shakespeares Dramen* (Stuttgart, 1898).

exposure to the storm has tired the old man. At the same time his mind has been very active, so his need for sleep is understandable. Psychologically, sleep represents a return of the ego into the unconscious and is the most natural form of introversion. A good sleep, that is, a deep immersion in the unconscious, is a periodical necessity for man to restore the strength of consciousness. Seeing the hovel, Lear hopes to find the health-restoring sleep but this is not granted him. The Fool, who has entered the hovel first, comes running out, strangely frightened and trembling and announcing that there is a spirit in the hovel:

> A spirit, a spirit! He says his name's poor Tom.   (III.iv.41)

The spirit who frightens the Fool so much is actually Edgar, now disguised as a madman.

And so we now find everyone belonging to Lear's party concentrated in this hovel—centered around and participating in his great suffering.

Edgar is here described in the typical tattered-and-torn dress of a madman just escaped from Bedlam. Lear's newly acquired affinity with all human beings makes him accept Edgar at once. It is enough for him that Edgar is one of those "poor naked wretches." He immediately notices Edgar's subhuman—or perhaps nonhuman—condition, but he is still so possessed by his daughter complex that he can only assume that the cause for Edgar's deteriorated appearance must be *his* daughters. Three times Lear asks:

> Didst thou give all to thy two daughters?   (III.iv.47)

> What! have his daughters brought   (III.iv.63)
> him to this pass?

> . . . nothing could have subdu'd nature   (III.iv.69)
> To such a lowness, but his unkind daughters.

He does not relate to Edgar as to a person and does not try to discover the reason for his condition. The bridge for his under-

standing is the projection of his own daughter complex upon
Edgar.

Edgar pretends to be insane yet his speeches, though wild, are
quite coherent and rational, and have no sign of true madness.
The images that he uses actually represent again a choric ac-
companiment to the events. Again and again he insists that the
"foul fiend" has pursued him and led him into some form of
hell.

Lear asks Edgar:

> What hast thou been?   (III.iv.83)

Edgar answers in a long speech, which at first appears somewhat
incoherent and wild, and serves his intention of appearing mad.
Looked at quite closely, all the outlandish statements he makes
about his supposedly sinful life are lies. These statements are as
much a spiritual disguise of his true identity as his tattered
clothes are of his physical identity. The psychological implication is that Edgar, in portraying himself, brings out all the dark
possibilities that are in him. The sudden change in his life has
just as quickly brought out his own darkness, has made him conscious of the questionable possibilities in his own nature. Edgar
has experienced a *bouleversement,*[6] while for Lear his misfortune releases a process in which the unconscious, step by step,
comes gradually to consciousness.

The shock of seeing Edgar in the tattered clothes of a typical
madman renews Lear's question: "Who am I?" (I.iv.86) He
asks it here as the existential question:

> Is man no more than this? . . .   (III.iv.105)
> Thou art the thing itself:
> unaccommodated man is no more but such
> a poor, bare, forked animal as thou art.

---

[6] This represents a *sudden* psychological change from one condition
of consciousness into another. In Edgar's case, he has, as it were,
suddenly fallen into his own shadow. This evidently characterizes
Edgar's psychology—that like an actor he can at will change from
one role into another, not only in regard to dress, but also in regard
to language and behavior.

Lear's answer comes as a vivid image. He identifies with the "poor, bare, forked animal" to such an extent that he begins to tear off his clothes:

> Off, off, you lendings!   (III.iv.112)
> Come; unbutton here.

This need to be naked is a familiar occurrence with psychotic patients, and from an observer's viewpoint this picture of Lear tearing off his clothes is certainly convincing evidence of his "madness." It proves that Lear at this point has lost all contact with reality and that the inner images have full possession of his consciousness. However, it strongly serves the poet's concern with the question, "What is man?" and his exploration of the fundamentals of human existence. In his confrontation with Edgar, Lear discovers man's kinship, or even identity, with the animal. This image is charged with tremendous affect and Lear's struggle to contain his affects and gain insight into his own condition seems to be lost. When he said, "I am a man more sinn'd against than sinning," he projected and therefore lacked insight into his own condition. Necessarily then, the daughter complex had to take hold of his consciousness. In meeting Edgar, the image of his horrible daughters persisted and the image of "unaccommodated man," rising from the unconscious, took possession of his consciousness to such an extent that he felt constrained to act it out.

The storm has brought all of Lear's party to the limit of their endurance. The Fool exclaims:

> This cold night will turn us all to fools and madmen.
>
> (III.iv.77)

Lear's consciousness has reached the breaking point. It is only natural that in this blackness of despair, the Fool wishes that a "little fire" would come, a fire that would keep life going and bring new light to all of them, especially to Lear.

The Fool's wish immediately materializes: Gloucester arrives with a torch. The Fool calls it a "walking fire." Gloucester's appearance brings new hope, yet Edgar, in his continued pretense of madness, calls him the "foul fiend"; he sees the "prince of darkness" in him. Actually, Gloucester comes to give some relief to their extreme situation, disobeying the daughters' "hard commands." He proposes to take Lear and his company where "both fire and food is ready." Lear however, even now, is more concerned with his inner problem:

> First let me talk with this philosopher.   (III.iv.158)
> What is the cause of thunder?

Lear wants to know what causes his affects, the wrath that he feels comes from the gods. Kent has a difficult time convincing Lear of the necessity of seeking better shelter. Lear still thinks that he can receive the answer to his question from "this same learned Theban."

In the midst of this chaotic disorder, Gloucester informs Kent of his own misfortune. He fears that he is going mad himself:

> I am almost mad myself. I had a son,   (III.iv.170)
> Now outlawed from my blood: he sought my life,
> But lately, very late, I loved him, friend,
> No father his son dearer. True to tell thee,
> The grief hath crazed my wits.

The irony is extreme because he does not realize that "poor Tom" is his son Edgar.

This dark scene ends with a line from a lost ballad:

> Child Rowland to the dark tower came,   (III.iv.187)
> His word was still, Fie, foh, and fum,
> I smell the blood of a British man.

—symbolically indicating that it is only now that the King will come to the *darkest* experience.

v

There is again a short interruption during which the Gloucester plot moves forward. In a scene between Cornwall and Edmund,

Edmund delivers the damaging letter which "approves (Edgar) an intelligent party to the advantages of France." Edmund simply pretends to have a conflict between loyalty and nature—but in fact he is really following the course which promises him the greatest practical advantage. His character has not changed. He uses opportunities as they come his way. He proves to be a skillful, ingenious egotist without the slightest admixture of feeling. He is a villain in the true Machiavellian style. Cornwall, whom we met before when he clashed with Kent and put him into the stocks, immediately makes Edmund Earl of Gloucester, declaring his trust in him and promising him to be "a dearer father in (his) love." Edmund's star is rising, while the fates of Lear, Edgar and Gloucester are approaching their nadir.

vi

In the meantime, Gloucester has taken Lear and his group into a farmhouse. Kent thanks him and describes Lear's state of mind:

> All the power of his wits has given way (III.vi.5)
> to his impatience.

Edgar enters and talks again in the fashion of his assumed madness, warning of the "foul fiend." Just as his last remark in the hovel was a reference to the darkness ("Child Rowland to the dark tower came"), he begins here with:

> . . . Nero is an angler in the lake of darkness. (III.vi.7)

All of these scenes on the heath seem to be a paraphrase of hell.[7] Edgar has the voice of a chorus which, in symbolic speeches, characterizes the psychic condition of Lear. He is really in hell!—a fact which Kent states in more psychological terms ("All the power of his wits has given way to his impatience"). Both statements are saying the same thing: that with the release of Lear's affects, the unconscious, with its imagery, has completely taken over Lear's consciousness. Nero is a sym-

---

[7] Cf., for details, Arden edition, p. 130.

bol of Lear as a former autocrat. Paradoxically, he is now trying to fish ("angle") for the contents in his unconscious. This image of an autocratic ego fishing in the "lake of darkness" is a perfect symbol for Lear's introversion. To an outsider his condition would appear to be insanity but the fact is that the imagery comes to Lear in an orderly fashion. The images which present themselves to Lear describe his intense affects as an army with "red burning spits," that come "hizzing[8] in upon 'em."

Lear has no defense against this onrush of images which now pour upon him. The first is that of a court trial in which Goneril and Regan are imaginary defendants. Of the group accompanying Lear in this sorrowful setting, Edgar and the Fool enter completely into his vivid imagination and participate in the fantastic trial. This is the only way in which Lear can abreact the affects caused by his daughters. Kent does not take part in this fantasy; he sees in Lear's behavior only the breakdown of his impatience (that is, his inability to contain the affects):

> O pity! Sir, where is the patience now,   (III.vi.61)
> That you so oft have boasted to retain?

Lear pays no attention to Kent's remarks—and cannot. Actually, Edgar and the Fool, by allowing the images to assume reality for Lear, help him much more to work through his problem. Edgar suffers through this participation, so much in fact that he fears for a breakdown of his pretense to be insane:

> My tears begin to take his part so much,   (III.vi.63)
> They'll mar my counterfeiting.

It requires a great deal of libido, of ego strength, to maintain this counterfeit insanity.

---

[8] "Hizzing" as explained in the Arden edition is a form of *hissing*. It suggests the whizzing sound of the red-hot weapons as they are brandished by the thousand assailants. Cf. Phineas Fletcher, *The Purple Island*, v. 70:
> See Phlegon, drenched in the hizzing main,
> Allayes his thirst, and cools the flaming carre.

Lear's affects have a certain autonomy; they personify as "little dogs," and therefore he sees them as "barking at him." Edgar takes up the theme of dogs:

> Mastiff, greyhound, mongrel grim,   (III.vi.71)
> Hound or spaniel, brach or lym,
> Bobtail tyke or trundle-tail—
> Tom will make them weep and wail;
> For, with throwing thus my head,
> Dogs leap the hatch, and all are fled.

This elaboration on the dogs helps Lear to integrate his affects so that their contents can now reach him. They contain the burning question of Regan's and Goneril's behavior:

> Then let them anatomize Regan. See what breeds   (III.vi.80)
> about her heart. Is there any cause in nature
> that makes these hard hearts?

There cannot be an answer to this question because Lear still seeks the cause outside himself.

This living-out of his images has given Lear enough release of tension to realize his physical needs, and at last he feels his extreme tiredness: he wants to go to sleep. Therefore, he says he will "go to supper i' the morning." Whereupon the Fool, exaggerating, says, "I will go to bed at noon." He means also, of course, that the grave will be his bed. Blunden[9] sees seven different meanings in these last words. This may be the case, but it appears to me important that these are the last words the Fool speaks! As mentioned before, he is a typical *familiaris,* a companion with whom one can converse and who always speaks the truth. Like a knife, he has opened Lear's unconscious—with his direct statements as well as with his images and songs. Now that Lear has been directly confronted with his affects ("red burning spits," "the little dogs . . . bark at me"), the Fool's function is taken over by the affects. The Fool can disappear or die like a "scarlet pimpernel" (as Blunden thinks).

[9] *Shakespeare Criticism,* p. 336.

Kent cannot communicate with his master. He does not understand the power the inner images have over Lear. Being an outsider to Lear's tremendous experience, his conclusion is:

His wits are gone. (III.vi.95)

He tells this to Gloucester, who has just returned with a dark report. The two daughters are plotting Lear's death. The cottage will have to be abandoned in a hurry if Lear's life is to be saved. Gloucester urges Kent to take Lear "in his arms" and carry him out to "drive to Dover." Kent realizes how healing sleep might have been for Lear. It is characteristic for Shakespeare that in this play he brings out the extremes in human nature. For this reason he exposes his characters, especially Lear, to the extreme of suffering without any let-up. Now, just when healing appeared to be possible, Lear is not allowed to sleep.

Oppressed nature sleeps. (III.vi.106)
This rest might yet have balmed thy broken sinews,
Which, if convenience will now allow,
Stand in hard cure.

Why must Lear suffer so much? The reason, as stated before, is that his attitude still seeks the cause for his misfortune outside himself, that is, in his daughters. It appears that for individuals who are intended to know themselves, the Self creates extraordinary situations in order to force the individual to experience himself to the utmost.

Edgar, again speaking as a chorus, comments on Lear's suffering and, in comparing it with his own suffering, draws some comfort for himself:

How light and portable my pain seems now, (III.vi.117)
When that which makes me bend makes the King bow.

Russell Fraser, in *Shakespeare's Poetics*,[10] says:

[10] Routledge & Kegan Paul, London, 1962, p. 74.

Lear is culpable, not because he abdicates, in any case not in that alone, but because of the manner in which he gives over. It is so fatuous and irresponsible, so patently self-indulgent, blind pride going before the inevitable fall. Lear's abdication is a kind of mean charade: "Unburdened (to) crawl toward death." (I.i.42) In that sense abdication is felt as 'sloth and want of courage.'

This is certainly true but Lear is not only a king by being the head of a country; the essence of his being is royal. In spite of his abdication, he remains a king. His royalty must assert itself as an inner truth. Therefore, his own Self constellates this extreme of suffering in order to fulfill his humanity to the utmost. From an outer point of view, his abdication might be felt as "sloth and want of courage," as Fraser says—but from an inner point of view his stupid action served just to bring out the royal quintessence of humanity in him.

vii

The seventh and last scene of Act III gives us another aspect of hell. Cornwall, Regan, Goneril, Edmund and servants assemble. Cornwall tells Goneril of Gloucester's traitorous letter, which reveals that "the army of France is landed." The reactions come in brief, hacked lines:

REGAN: Hang him instantly.   (III.vii.4)
GONERIL: Pluck out his eyes.

There is only a slight redeeming feature: Edmund is sent away, so as not to observe his father's punishment. Cornwall does not want to execute Gloucester "without the form of justice." Even this action does not derive from kindness of heart but from a pretense at propriety.

What follows has been called the most horrible incident in Shakespeare's plays, and some producers have omitted it from their productions. Cornwall and Regan insult and villify Gloucester, exposing him to rough interrogation. Regan is so mannish that to insult him she plucks his beard. Gloucester honorably protests but cannot talk himself out of this treatment. Shakespeare wrote this scene, in all its fierce cruelty, to emphasize the wolfish nature of Regan and her husband, and to demonstrate the extremes of suffering to which Gloucester, like all "good" characters, is exposed. It is the retribution due him for his unconscious, pleasure-loving attitude of the past. That his punishment is the plucking-out of his eyes brings glaringly into relief that the central theme of the play is consciousness, for which the essential symbol is sight. It was Goneril who had said in the first scene of Act I:

> Sir, I love you more than words can wield the matter; (57)
> Dearer than eyesight, space and liberty.

It was Lear who said:

> Old fond eyes, (I.iv.305)
> Beweep this cause again, I'll pluck ye out.

Gloucester finally knows that he cannot escape:

> I am tied to th' stake (III.vii.54)
> and I must stand the course.

It is an event which in its symbolization is a close parallel to Christ on the cross. It portrays the Christian character of the play: the process of individuation. The way to know oneself is a parallel to Christ's passion.

In the course of his close questioning, Gloucester is asked why he sent Lear to Dover. He answers:

> Because I would not see thy cruel nails (III.vii.56)
> Pluck out his poor old eyes, nor thy fierce sister
> In his anointed flesh stick boarish fangs.

The image which Gloucester had used for characterizing the fiendish nature of Regan now becomes a horrible reality. Cornwall actually plucks out Gloucester's eyes. It is Regan who, not satisfied with one eye plucked out, insists that the other must be plucked out too. This barbaric behavior is too much for one of the servants. Common humanity revolts. Called a "dog," he attacks Cornwall. In the ensuing fight, the servant is slain and Cornwall mortally wounded.

In the new Variorum edition,[11] Furness quotes Capell:

> The barbarity exercis'd upon Gloucester is indeed a part of the story that was the source of this episode, for that 'Paphlagonian king's' eyes were put out by a son; but the putting-out of poor Gloucester's seems to be more immediately copy'd from *Selimus.*

And Steevens:

> In *Selimus, Emperor of the Turks,* one of the sons of Bajazet *pulls out the eyes* of an Aga on the stage, and says: "Yes, thou shalt live, but never see the day, wanting the tapers that should give thee light. (*Pulls out his eyes.*)"

Furness:

> I have introduced this passage to show that Shakespeare's drama was not more sanguinary than that of his contemporaries.

I also wonder whether Shakespeare, who knew the Bible very well, did not think of Zedekiah, King of Israel, the putting-out of whose eyes is mentioned in the Old Testament no less than five times:

> II Kings 25:7—And they slew the sons of Zedekiah before his eyes, and put out the eyes of Zedekiah, and bound him with fetters of brass, and carried him to Babylon. (Also Jeremiah 39:6-7, 52:10-11.)

[11] P. 224.

While Lear's suffering brings him deep understanding and pity for all mankind, the characters of the "bad" party become obviously more and more bloodthirsty and cruel. Simultaneously, their contempt for ordinary man increases. For Regan, the servant is no more than "a dog, a peasant," and it is she who kills him. In his despicable contempt for man, Cornwall says of man's eye, his most precious organ:

> Out, vile jelly!   (III.vii.83)

—and with these words, he crushes Gloucester's second eye. Darkness descends on Gloucester. For comfort he calls for Edmund. But just here, in the midst of tragedy, after Gloucester has lost his eyes, he is at last told the truth—ironically, by Regan. Cornwall and Regan, believing that Gloucester, bleeding and blind, is finished anyhow, have no hesitation in revealing to him:

> Thou callest on him that hates thee. It was he   (III.vii.88)
> That made the overture of thy treasons to us,
> Who is too good to pity thee.

At last Gloucester is "seeing":

> O my follies! Then Edgar was abused.   (III.vii.91)
> Kind gods, forgive me that, and prosper him!

Regan heaps contempt upon Gloucester's injury:

> Go thrust him out at gates, and let him smell   (III.vii.93)
> His way to Dover.

Only the servants have pity on Gloucester, applying some "flax and whites of eggs" to his bleeding face. Like a chorus, they express simple faith in the justice of Providence, saying that if these two people—Cornwall and Regan—can find a natural death, then mankind will have surrendered to every beastliness.

Both Lear and Gloucester have experienced their hells in this third act. Lear is overtaken by his unconscious, has lost a great deal of contact with reality, yet has also made giant steps in integrating his experience. Gloucester, having lost his eyes, has in a flash *seen* his true situation.

The time of tribulation is not over for either of them however. In an external sense, their conditions become worse from now on, but both are now profoundly aware of the true feelings and intentions of their children. At last they see. Furthermore, both have found reliable companions to help them in their misery. Both have paid a terrible price, but there is no illusion any more about their real situation. We are deeply concerned how both will deal with the reality as it is.

Act Four

i

The fourth act returns to the heath or, as some editors think, the open country. It begins with a monologue by Edgar, about which there has been some controversy. The best interpretation is probably that it is better to know the true state of things, even though man will be despised and exposed to ill fortune if he does, than not to know the truth and live in a world of flattery. Here again Edgar has the function of chorus, stating the essence of the psychological stage at which both Lear and Gloucester have arrived. Still, when he is directly confronted with eyeless Gloucester, it shakes him and makes him "hate" the consequences which often follow when the world, acting as the hand of fate, executes fate's will.

The old man who accompanies Gloucester is a parallel figure to Lear (he is also "four-score years" old) but without Lear's royal temperament. Gloucester, now aware of the reality of his situation, is in utter despair and cannot see any possible meaning in his living on:

> I have no way, and therefore want no eyes; (IV.i.18)
> I stumbled when I saw.

Although he cannot see any goal in his life, he has yet one wish: to "see" his son Edgar:

> Might I but live to see thee in my touch. (IV.i.23)

It is at this moment that Edgar, still disguised as "Mad Tom," comes upon his blind father and realizes that there is no point at which man can say: "This is the worst." The meeting between them is most touching. For once Gloucester is more perceptive. He listens carefully and concludes correctly from "Mad Tom's" speech that he could not be completely insane:

> He has some reason, else he could not beg. (IV.i.31)

Gloucester remembers that the night before, on the heath, he had seen this "fellow" and had been reminded of his son. At that time he still had eyes, yet he could not allow his intuitive perception to come to full consciousness. Then he sums up his faith, the result of his experience up to this moment:

> As flies to wanton boys are we to the gods; (IV.i.36)
> They kill us for their sport.

These lines have been taken to sum up Shakespeare's fundamental idea about the play. Actually, from the beginning of the first act, the attitude of different characters to the gods constantly changes as a result of their experiences. For instance, Edgar, in the monologue preceding the meeting with his father, was still much more optimistic:

> The lowest and most dejected thing of fortune, (IV.i.3)
> Stands still in esperance, lives not in fear;
> The lamentable change is from the best;
> The worst returns to laughter.

Gloucester, who has lost his eyes, seen his "follies," and is now fully aware of his tragic predicament, still does not accept his own attitude and actions as the real cause. By expressing the relationship between man and the fate-producing gods as "flies to wanton boys," he reduces the ego to a mere object of the gods. I do not think that Shakespeare wanted to express his own philosophy in these lines but rather that he wanted to character-ize as briefly as possible Gloucester's own attitude immediately after the loss of his eyes. He did not want to leave Gloucester in this perfectly passive condition, however, and so later on he de-votes a whole scene (IV.vi) to Gloucester's depression, suicidal ideas and change of heart, a scene in which Edgar succeeds in curing Gloucester of this fatalistic belief. These lines ("as flies to wanton boys . . . they kill us for their sport")[1] characterize Gloucester at the nadir of his life and certainly do not express Shakespeare's fundamental philosophy.

Describing the ego as a plaything for the gods means that Gloucester does not attribute any strength to the ego in relation to the gods; he denies dignity to man in intercourse with God. Such an attitude necessarily deprives man of hope and actually has a destructive effect on the fate-producing factors. Left alone with this attitude, Gloucester would necessarily perish. As it happens, his "good" son is present. This fact alone contradicts his despairing attitude. Although Edgar puts on a mad disguise, it is he who can teach his father a different attitude. He does not do it by discussion, but by letting Gloucester experience to the fullest the result of his despair. That Gloucester is still psycho-logically blind is obvious when he remarks:

'Tis the time's plague, when madmen (IV.i.46)
lead the blind.

Now Gloucester asks Edgar whether he knows the way to Do-ver.[2] Edgar answers Gloucester's question in rich imagery. He

---

[1] Cf. Ernst Th. Sehrt's discussion of the motif of sport in *King Lear* in *Wandlungen der Shakespeareschen Komödie* (Vandenhoeck & Ru-precht, Göttingen, 1961), pp. 41-42.

[2] Dover is one of the few places which is mentioned in *King Lear*.

does know the way to Dover, and adds the names of all sorts of evil spirits to maintain his mask of madness. It is apparently at this point that he decides to bring about a different attitude in his father. For this purpose it is necessary for him to continue the disguise and to let his father act out his suicidal fantasy.

Now reconnected with mankind through having found a friend and guide in the "madman," Gloucester's attitude is already changing. In his speech, he addresses "heavens." His attitude is truly devout. In describing his follies as something more than acts committed, he shows some psychological understanding. He recognizes that the cause of all those follies was that he had been a "superfluous and lust-dieted man." [3] Furthermore, he now knows that his attitude of indulgence toward his own sexual affects is acting against the statutes of divine law:

> . . . heavens, deal so still!   (IV.i.67)
> Let the superfluous and lust-dieted man,
> That slaves your ordinance,[4] that will not see
> Because he does not feel, feel your power quickly;
> So distribution should undo excess,
> And each man have enough.

Edgar, of course, agrees to lead Gloucester to the cliffs of Dover.

ii

For the time being we leave Edgar and Gloucester. Shakespeare now takes us to a place before the Duke of Albany's palace where Goneril and Edmund meet. She welcomes him. It appears rather tactless of her to speak critically of her "mild" husband to Edmund. Oswald immediately enters and informs them of the

---

Although it is certainly meant as the real Dover, the vagueness in geographical definitions makes it a symbolic place as well. It serves as the place to which all the "good" characters flee, and in which the final conflicts are acted out.

[3] Arden, p. 151: a "pampered" man "whose desires are fed to the full, feeding gluttonously."

[4] I take the words "slaves your ordinance" to mean "tears away, or rends," from O. E. *slaefan,* following J. Sledd, *Modern Language Notes,* 1940, p. 595.

change which has taken place in Albany. Albany's reactions to everything that Oswald had told him had evidently been brief and just the opposite of what Goneril, Edmund and Oswald had expected. It is at this point that we get the first indication that Albany, who at first appearance had seemed so unconscious, so neutral, now because of the shock of Gloucester's punishment has suddenly realized the terrible character of his wife and of the people she trusts and uses. The change in Goneril has widened the breach between her and her husband. What at first had appeared as tactlessness now reveals its true character. In her opinion, Albany's reaction to the terrible events betrays his *cowardice*. She prefers Edmund, who has a strong physical appeal for her. Using the prerogative of a queen, she gives him a "favor," which in medieval fashion makes him her Knight. Her language is equivocal and amounts to a promise of sexual surrender:

> . . . this kiss, if it durst speak, (IV.ii.22)
> Would stretch thy spirits up into the air.
> Conceive . . .

To top this ruthless betrayal of her husband, she transfers the command of the army from him to Edmund.

Both Oswald and Edmund leave. Albany arrives and a confrontation between husband and wife occurs which, in its directness, poetic diction and humanity, belongs among the greatest things Shakespeare wrote. Albany has awakened fully to the true nature, to the abyss of cruelty in Goneril, although he does not know that she has personally betrayed and deserted him. In his speech to her, he goes straight to the root of her fiendish psychology. He refers to the fact that she rejects her origin ("that nature which contemns its origin"),[5] has cut herself off from the

---

[5] Russell A. Fraser, *Shakespeare's Poetics*, p. 34: "The image, expressive almost of the physiological imperatives of kind, is central to *Lear* and, beyond the play, to other work of the playwright, and further, to the Renaissance itself. Its function is to assert an organic relation between conduct and the consequences of conduct. Necessarily it defines nature: not a tissue of precepts but a fund of possibili-

natural ties of kinship. Shakespeare evidently considers it most important that the individual remain related to and conscious of his ancestry. Only by remaining in a living relationship with ancestors and tradition can he be contained. Through the mouth of Albany, Shakespeare here emphasizes a natural law, in contrast to the social law.[6] The relationship between the individual and his kin certainly, in a natural and cultural sense, is that of a branch to a tree. Shakespeare also considered it necessary for the individual to have limitations, to be contained: "be bordered certain in itself." Goneril, by having actually rejected her father and all that naturally connects her with him, has, as it were, "disbranched" herself from her "material sap," and must necessarily destroy herself:

> . . . perforce must wither   (IV.ii.35)
> And come to deadly use.

These lines are further evidence that Shakespeare attempts to describe the course of human fate as a result of conscious attitudes and actions. A comparison of these lines with those in which Shakespeare's characters speak about the "wheel of fortune" allows certain conclusions. The maturity and state of consciousness of an individual expresses itself by the manner in which the individual accepts responsibility, not only for what he does but also for what happens to him. In Lear himself, as stated repeatedly, the acceptance of full responsibility for his fate occurs in definite stages. Albany, confronted with all the facts, states this law very clearly and fully. For this reason, he functions from this point on like a Greek chorus, which expresses an objective opinion on the present event.

Goneril, of course, cannot accept Albany's contention—that man, to live and prosper, has to remain in vital connection with

---

ties whose character and limitation are susceptible of testing. Shakespeare's play is such a testing. A tree cut away from its roots, which are the condition of its being, cannot survive. Neither can a man survive who repudiates his conditon."

[6] Cf. discussion on Edmund's monologue, p. 204.

his origin. Actually, she has already gone too far in "disbranching" herself to see Albany's point. In her the destructive powers of the unconscious have taken over. She has become completely blinded to any human value ("Wisdom and goodness to the vile seem vile"). A cold, tiger-like ferocity possesses her whole being. In this condition, she has no access to Albany's wisdom, must disregard his terrible warning. This total rejection of Albany's faith in the avenging power of the gods makes her eventual suicide inevitable.

Kenneth Muir in the Arden edition, commenting on the line, "must come to deadly use," refers to Hebrews 6:4, 8, where St. Paul speaks of those "who have tasted the good word of God, the heavenly gift, and were partakers of the Holy Ghost. . . . But that which beareth thorns and briers is rejected, and is nigh unto cursing; whose *end is to be burned.*"

If we take the lines spoken by Albany as a paraphrase of St. Paul's words, we must then accept the probability that this chapter was in Shakespeare's mind when writing these lines and that the context has to be considered as well. What Shakespeare then calls "origin" would refer to the Holy Ghost. It would be Shakespeare's religious conviction that the Holy Ghost is the origin of man's nature. In Shakespeare's opinion then, Goneril, by rejecting her father, ultimately rejects the Holy Spirit. It seems to me that Shakespeare is deeply moved in these lines and tries to express his conception of man and his heavenly roots. Albany's continuing speech compares Lear's daughters with "tigers" and carries this idea further. If we assume that by "heavens" Shakespeare meant the Holy Ghost, or used this term as a simile of God, then the lines:

> If that the heavens do not their visible spirits   (IV.ii.46)
> Send quickly down to tame these vild offences,
> It will come,
> Humanity must perforce prey on itself,
> Like monsters of the deep.

express Shakespeare's conviction that man is only human if he is connected with the heavens like a branch with a tree. Furthermore, if man cuts himself off from the living God, then Heaven must send down its "visible spirits" to "tame these vile offenses," and man sinks lower than the animal and becomes more destructive.

The question that naturally arises from Albany's statement is whether Shakespeare wanted, among other things, to explore the fate of man when he cuts himself off from his heavenly roots. Such a spiritual displacement exists in our time, with its vastly preponderant materialistic prejudices. In Shakespeare's opinion, this "disbranchment" changes men into monsters. The Nazi concentration camps attest to this truth!

Goneril's mind is of course completely closed to Albany's profound statements about man's true nature. "Heavens" is no reality to her. All she can see is that Albany is a "milk-livered" man who does not recognize the practical and real threat to his country. She points out another reality, that is, that Lear is in league with France, that France has landed an army in England and plans to fight Albany. To her, Albany is a "moral fool." [7]

Husband and wife now stand absolutely on opposite sides, he defending humanity, she her country. They address each other in the strongest terms. He calls her "devil":

> Proper deformity shows not in the fiend (IV.ii.60)
> So horrid as in woman.

Woman as mother of children and giver of life would naturally support the bonds between parents and children, would love her origin. We have seen before that it was a powerfully masculine character (the so-called animus) which has taken control of her consciousness. To Goneril, of course, Albany is a eunuch:

[7] A similar problem arose during the last war in Germany, where there were Germans fully aware of the depravity and crimes of the Nazi government, knowing that humanity was on the side of the Allies. After the war, I had a talk with such a German. To my question: "Why didn't you help the Allies then?" he answered: "That would have meant death for 5,000 Germans." Certainly a difficult moral problem! Albany, in spite of his clear insights, does not go over to the Lear party—yet.

Marry, your manhood—mew! (IV.ii.68)

No reconciliation between these two points of view is possible.

A Gentleman enters with news for Albany that the Duke of Cornwall is dead and recounts how Gloucester lost his eyes. Albany sees Cornwall's death as a sure sign that, as always, the "justices" are at work, a confirmation that the heavens *do* send their "visible spirits down." To Goneril, however, Cornwall's death means a much more intimate threat. She rightly fears that her plot to marry Edmund might come to nothing because now her sister, whom she knows has the same nature as her own, will have the same desires and a better chance of obtaining them as a widow. Albany is grateful to Gloucester for the "love (he) show'dst the King."

iii

In Scene 3 we move to the French camp near Dover. Kent and a Gentleman converse and we hear briefly what has happened since Cordelia and her husband landed on English soil in order to rescue Lear from his tiger daughters. We are amazed that so soon after having landed in England, the King of France has returned to his own country. The Gentleman says that urgent business in France was the reason. Gregg[8] suggests that the real reason was "that Cordelia succeeded in persuading her husband to abandon his purpose of wresting a portion of the kingdom for himself and retire to his own land, thus leaving her free to use his army in defense of her father, should the occasion arise." Cordelia, by employing a foreign army to rescue her father from his evil daughters, exposes herself to a serious conflict. Such an invasion could only be understood as treason and it follows from this that for the purposes of the play the British Army has to be victorious. Shakespeare does everything possible to minimize the treasonable aspect of Cordelia's invasion, and to concentrate the drama on its human aspects.

Kent's further questioning of the Gentleman reveals Shakespeare's concern in this play with the relationship of man to his

[8] *The Modern Language Review,* 1940, p. 445.

affects. When the Gentleman relates the Queen's—Cordelia's—reaction to the recent terrible events, Kent asks:

> Did your letters pierce the Queen to any   (IV.iii.11)
> demonstration of grief?

The Gentleman answers:

> *It seemed she was a queen*   (IV.iii.15)
> *Over her passion,* who, most rebel-like
> Sought to be king over her.

The affects here are not defined. Shakespeare uses the general term "passion." It is interesting however to note that the affect in Cordelia's case is described as a "king." This fully agrees with Jung's discoveries that the affective side, the emotions in a woman, have a masculine character. We see Cordelia not only as a "good" daughter, but as a woman who is well-contained, well related to the "material sap." Her actions therefore appear well reflected on and appropriate to the situation. The effect of this well-rounded personality is almost that of a saint:

> There she shook   (IV.iii.31)
> The holy water from her heavenly eyes,
> And clamor-moistened.

The contrast between the hellish sisters and this heavenly daughter is brought out very strongly, so that Kent who has only once before made reference to the powers that govern man's fate ("A good man's fortune may grow out at heels . . . Fortune . . . turn thy wheel") now exclaims:

> It is the stars,   (IV.iii.34)
> The stars above us, govern our conditions.

Kent acknowledges that superpersonal factors, projected by him into "stars," govern our fate. To "govern" in the sense of to direct and control the actions and affairs of people is now quite as absolute as the verb "determine." In the verb "govern" the possibility of a personal will, however slight, is assumed. In using the term "to govern," Kent acknowledges the overwhelming power of the superpersonal to direct and arrange human situations. Now he speaks of Lear's great change and his suffering from shame:

> A sovereign shame so elbows him; his own unkindness,
>
> (IV.iii.43)
>
> That stripped her from his benediction, turned her
> To foreign casualties, gave her dear rights
> To his dog-hearted daughters—these things sting
> His mind so venomously that burning shame
> Detains him from Cordelia.

Therefore, Lear strongly resists meeting Cordelia.

Kent's report on Lear's condition is further evidence that Lear is not insane in the modern sense of the word. In insanity there is either a complete flattening-out of all affects, or such an exaggerated intensity of affect that any communication with the outside is impossible. In such a case, the affect is as a rule determined by inner images. In Lear's case, however, it is determined by a psychologically understandable cause ("his own unkindness, that stripped her from his benediction. . . . gave her dear rights to his dog-hearted daughters"). The affects are appropriate and proportionate to the cause, and certainly reveal *insight* into his own condition. Modern psychiatry considers insight a prime criterion for distinguishing between sanity and insanity.

iv

The next scene takes us into Cordelia's camp, where she and the Doctor are discussing Lear, seemingly in contrast to Kent's description of him. Cordelia reports that

> . . . he was met even now   (IV.iv.1)
> As mad as the vexed sea, singing aloud,
> Crowned with rank fumiter and furrow-weeds,
> With hardocks, hemlock, etc.

When we last saw Lear on the heath, we saw that the images of the unconscious had taken hold of him and had to be acted out, and that at one point he had tried to tear his clothes off since he wanted to be nothing but "unaccommodated man." Now, in parallel with Christ, he wears a crown, not of thorns but one woven with different common flowers that grow in England. Blunden, in *Shakespeare Criticism,*[9] writes:

> I have not at the moment the means to explore fully the association of 'all the idle weeds' that Cordelia names as making up Lear's 'crown'—already we see that they carry a meaning beyond that of mere picturesque detail of madness. They are his crown of thorns. But among them the *nettle* that throngs about graves, the *hemlock* with its fame for poison and narcotic, the sickly and usurping *darnel,* can quickly be perceived as speaking to the imagination of the spectator on the elements of Lear's affliction.

Blunden also quotes John Clare's *Shepherd's Calendar:*

RED AND PURPLE
Fumitory too—a name
That superstition holds to fame.

("Rank fumiter" is the first of the items in Lear's mockery crown that Cordelia distinguishes.)

These plants must have had for Shakespeare a symbolic meaning which we cannot fathom today. The common denominator seems to be that they are all common flowers of the English countryside. Their togetherness indicates that Lear descends to the common man and finds his "crown" his supreme fulfillment, by being an ordinary man in closest association and identity with all life.

Speaking more in detail of these weeds and flowers, it might be of significance to note Farren:[10]

---

[9] P. 334.
[10] *Essays on Mania* (1833), p. 73.

Its leaves (fumiter) are of a bitter taste, and the juice was formerly employed in the cases of hypochondrism and black jaundice.

Farren also says that hemlock is used as a poison and as a narcotic, and that nettles throng about graves, that cuckoo-flowers refer to the Bedlam Cowslip and so might indicate madness.

In speaking of Lear's plight, Cordelia avoids the word "mad." She asks the Doctor what "man's wisdom (can do) in the restoring his bereaved sense?" Lear is here described in the worst possible condition and no doubt, from a practical point of view, he has lost his contact with reality to such an extent that it seems fitting to call him mad. However, one should not identify Shakespeare's term "mad" with our modern clinical terms. One should rather see in its use the poet's intention: to describe Lear's state as one which goes far beyond the limits of ordinary human experience, a condition in which the images and the tempestuous emotions of the unconscious have taken complete possession of him.

There exists a threshold between consciousness and the unconscious. Only contents which are powerfully charged with libido can pass over the threshold and enter consciousness. In Lear's case the threshold is considerably lowered, which makes it possible for contents of the unconscious to pass easily into consciousness. The images of the unconscious are so intensely charged that Lear's consciousness is fully possessed by them and he is compelled to act them out. The crown of common weeds and flowers is such an image. He *must* wear it. It makes him into a king again, but it is very different from the crown he used to wear as monarch. This crown is a meaningful symbol of the ordinary human-being-become-king. It represents a reversal of all social values. It makes Lear part and parcel of nature. He is "unaccommodated man," who suffers nature as a cross, and achieves a higher stature by becoming part of nature. Lear at this point has broken through the limits which usually contain human consciousness. From the observer's point of view, he has become mad—but from the inner point of view, he is a new

man. As we will see later, this is by no means the last stage in
Lear's development.

Shakespeare's physicians are usually very wise and represent
the most objective opinion in his plays. This Doctor knows that
Lear suffers from a powerful inner conflict ("anguish"), and
Cordelia also realizes that his "mad" state (his "bereaved
sense") is caused by powerful affects (his "ungoverned rage"),
and that even his life is endangered. Like a modern psychiatrist,
the Doctor recognizes that Lear needs rest more than anything,
and he is well acquainted with efficacious medicinal plants
which can calm Lear's wild emotions. Rest would allow consciousness to become strong again and to contain the unconscious. In other words, a sedative, together with adequate sleep,
would restore Lear's sanity.

It seems most difficult to provide this rest for Lear. A messenger enters, bringing the news, "The British powers are marching
hitherward." The approach of violent conflict provides an opportunity for a short monologue which illustrates how Cordelia
deals with her own conflicts—which are the result of having
brought a foreign army to England in order to rescue her father.
By so doing, she is undobutedly guilty of treason against her
own country, but it is the highest motive which compels this
action. She exclaims:

> O dear father,   (IV.iv.23)
> It is thy business that I go about.

It is a significant paraphrase of Luke 2:49:

> Wist ye not that I must be about my Father's business?

It is further evidence that Shakespeare intended this play as a
parallel to Christ's life. The passion occurs, however, on a human level. One important difference is that Christ, seen as a
human being, was a perfect man, free from any guilt. Lear, in
contrast, is decidedly described as a guilty, unconscious man, for
whom Shakespeare likes to use the term "fool." Seen in a histo-

rical context, *King Lear* would represent a further step in consciousness.[11] It is also perhaps significant that it is a daughter, and not a son, who shares the father's suffering and undergoes a similar death for the rescue of the father. Not having a son would emphasize that a renewal of the King ("consciousness") is not intended. The daughter's participation in Lear's suffering puts the emphasis on the anima, the inner process, and indicates that Shakespeare intended to stress the transformation of the individual human being, that is, Lear.

v

Scene 5 presents a brief yet revealing view of the emotional conflicts in the camp of Lear's opponents. Oswald has arrived at Gloucester's castle, bringing with him a letter from Edmund to Goneril. Regan learns from Oswald that Albany, after much hesitation, has decided to fight on the English side. She, knowing her sister well, is jealous of her and afraid that an illicit relationship might already have developed between her and Edmund. She tries to persuade Oswald to unseal the letter, flattering him and making a suggestive remark:

> I know you are of her bosom. (IV.v.26)

Whereupon Oswald asks, "I, madam?" This short remark gives us an insight into Oswald's own conviction of his lack of masculinity. His cowardice, his lying and his pretence at being strong and manly, was first observed when he met Kent alone. We have mentioned that Oswald somehow represents an extension of Goneril's personality—but nothing more than a *function* of hers. He obviously has the right idea about himself as a man.

Regan does not succeed in winning Oswald over to her side but she does use him in her attempt to dissuade Goneril from pursuing Edmund amorously:

---

[11] These ideas have been stimulated by Jung's "Answer to Job," (*Psychology and Religion*), in which he sets forth the development of consciousness from the time of Job to modern times, as determined by the changing image of God.

> And when your mistress hears thus much from you,   (IV.v.34)
> I pray desire her call her wisdom to her.

In her customary bloodthirsty way she ends her infamous speech by telling Oswald to "cut off the blind traitor." She realizes that by blinding Gloucester all sympathies will turn against the perpetrators of such a crime:

> It was great ignorance, Gloucester's eyes being out,   (IV.v.9)
> To let him live. Where he arrives he moves
> All hearts against us.

vi

Scene 6 is one of the playwright's most moving scenes. Edgar, no more disguised as "mad Tom," but in the dress of a peasant, has led blind Gloucester to some fields near Dover. Gloucester feels that the ground is level, but Edgar, in describing it as a cliff with birds flying:

> The crows and choughs that wing the midway air   (IV.vi.14)
> Show scarce so gross as beetles,

with ships in the distance and the "murmuring surge of the sea," succeeds in convincing Gloucester that he is really standing at the edge of the Dover cliffs. Edgar's language no longer has a wild, seemingly incoherent quality. Now it is clear, direct, and certainly poetic. There is no more talk of the "foul fiend." Gloucester notices the change in Edgar's language. Edgar of course denies it. In an aside, he gives us his reason for using Gloucester's blindness to deceive him and create this realistic fantasy:

> Why I do trifle thus with his despair   (IV.vi.36)
> Is done to cure it.

Gloucester, kneeling, prays to the gods. He intends to commit suicide because he cannot bear life any longer and, again, as several times before, he sees the will of the gods as "opposeless" (irresistible). This utter despair is due to Gloucester's deepseated conviction of man's impotence. He, the "superfluous and lust-dieted man," has been unable to control his concupiscence. The only way for him to deal with it is suicide:

> My snuff [12] and loathed part of nature should   (IV.vi.40)
> Burn itself out.

Jung states that a depression is frequently due to the repression of powerful unconscious desires.[13]

Gloucester ends his short prayer with a blessing for Edgar. Thinking that he stands on the edge of a cliff and will fall far, possibly into the sea, he throws himself forward.

In allowing his father to go through the experience of suicide, Edgar has undertaken a dangerous experiment. He has of course arranged it in such a way that not the slightest physical harm will come to Gloucester. Yet the possibility of death was present. There are cases known in medical history of men dying from their own imagination, by psychic shock—and even the most diligent postmortem cannot discover any physical cause of sudden death. In Gloucester, we have to reckon with his advanced age, the physical and psychic shock which the traumatic loss of his eyes has brought, and the tremendous suffering after this terrible experience. So the possibility exists that Gloucester might die from a conviction that he has dropped from a considerable height. But Edgar is foremost concerned with Gloucester's psychic condition, with the weakness of his ego and the complete surrender to his depression, to the "opposeless" will of the gods. He must cure his father of his depression. Edgar's intention is to effect a transformation in Gloucester by the simulated suicide, experienced as real. Fortunately, Gloucester does not die, but sustains a shock of some severity; he evidently falls

---

[12] "Snuff" is explained in the Arden edition as "smouldering wick."
[13] See *Two Essays on Analytical Psychology*, p. 212; also *Symbols of Transformation*, p. 404.

into a deep faint of some duration. Edgar has to call his father
several times before he can arouse him, and even then Gloucester believes he is dying. Edgar is certainly aware that in Gloucester's condition this very realistically imaginative suicide might
have actually led to his death. Edgar continues with his curative
deception by persuading Gloucester that he has fallen down
from a terrific altitude:

> From the dread summit of this chalky bourn.   (IV.vi.58)

Edgar now assumes still another role—that of a passerby at the
bottom of the cliff. Thus he can convey to his father the idea
that a miracle has happened, and that it was the gods themselves
who saved him, the same gods whom Gloucester, before his suicide attempt, had looked upon as enemies.

> . . . therefore, thou happy father,   (IV.vi.73)
> Think that the clearest gods, who make them honors
> Of men's impossibilities, have preserved thee.

I am inclined to accept Reyher's statement about the *"clearest
gods"*:[14]

> This word, which expresses the pure and luminous essence of
> the divinity, reflects the clear, and profound nature of the man
> who utters it.

Kittredge connects it with the Latin word *clarissimi.*

Gloucester is now a changed man. He has learned patience;
he now has the will to tolerate whatever fate may bring, and he
will not again attempt suicide:

> . . . henceforth I'll bear   (IV.vi.76)
> Affliction till it do cry out itself
> "Enough, enough," and die.

This is approximately the highest psychological development
that Gloucester can achieve before his death.

14 *Essai sur les Idees* . . . *de Shakespeare,* quoted in Arden, p. 173.

At this moment Lear appears. The Folio stage direction reads: "Enter Lear," while the Quarto reads: "Enter Lear, mad." Most modern editors add stage directions, such as: "Fantastically dressed with wild flowers" (Arden), or "Fantastically dressed with weeds" (Kittredge).

Edgar is deeply shocked and naturally convinced from Lear's appearance and behavior that he is mad. Lear does not relate to the reality situation. His consciousness is concerned only with what goes on before his inner eyes. Images arise which deal with his inner problems. Kenneth Muir admits that Lear's "mad speeches have an undertone of meaning and although he leaps from one subject to another, it is often possible to see that there is a *sub*conscious[15] connection between them." Blunden comments fully on this "maddest and wildest" of Lear's speeches:[16]

> His talk then leaps from one subject to another with wilder haste; and still there is a contexture in it. He has now the additional confusion of the rumored war with France among his principal motives. And so, when he has made his escape at Dover, and comes with his crown of weeds to the side of Gloucester and Edgar, he begins: 'No, they cannot touch me for coining'; the metaphor echoes, and he changes it into actuality, 'There's your press-money.' He is 'the King himself,' preparing his army for the quarrel with France, inspecting recruits. 'That fellow handles his bow like a crow-keeper.' Again we must see not only the fantasy of Lear, but the bird-boy passing over the farm. 'Look, look! a mouse'; apparently a reminiscence of the classical proverb, certainly a Falstaffian comment on a supposed recruit's usefulness, and clearly a remark, brought on by his spying a field-mouse in the corn. 'O! well flown, bird,' by no great extension of this, is his enthusiasm for falconry bursting forth as he sees the hawk drop on that mouse. We have from him a picture both of the country circumstances and his life

[15] It is a western prejudice that the unconscious is "beneath" consciousness. In India, the unconscious is perceived as being above consciousness; therefore they call it superconsciousness. With Jung, I prefer not to localize what is beyond consciousness. I therefore call the field outside of consciousness the unconscious. Our language however supports the conception of a subconscious, for example, "images *arise*."

[16] *Shakespeare Criticism*, pp. 332-333.

and his times. 'Give the word,' he finishes, like a sentry. 'Sweet marjoram,' says Edgar. It sounds 'aloof from the entire point;' yet Lear says 'Pass.' And with good secret reason. Sweet marjoram was accounted, according to Culpeper, a blessed remedy for diseases of the brain. Edgar was clearly a friend.

Actually, in itself, each image and idea formulated here by Lear is logical and coherent. However, the connection between the different images is *not* logical. They follow more the law of free association. The connection between these ideas has something of the quality of "flight of ideas" (defined as "repeated changes in the line or type of thought"). The images and the connections between them are not fragmented. In the line, "Peace, peace; this piece of toasted cheese . . ." there is probably an indication of "clang association" (the uttering of words or syllables having superficial tonal resemblances). Kenneth Muir[17] explains in detail this type of free association.

The principal problem for Lear still appears to be his difficulty in giving up his kingship, and in all these "mad thoughts" he functions as a king. He imagines himself as a king, executing varied regal powers. The underlying complex is obviously his loss of kingship and all of his "free associations" are conditioned by this "kingship complex." Lear is dimly aware of his abnormal psychic state. Edgar's giving the password "Marjoram" (Cf. Blunden) also indicates that Lear is aware of possible healing.

Now "mad" Lear and blind Gloucester meet. Lear, possessed by his images, cannot relate to the situation. The inner images now become contaminated [18] with reality. He sees Gloucester fused with Goneril:

[17] Arden, p. 174.

[18] "Contamination" is a technical psychiatric term indicating that two different images are fused into one. Contaminations as they occur in schizophrenia are characterized by the fusion of images which are incompatible with each other. For example, "grassbear." Grass and bear are incompatible, but in schizophrenic thinking they contaminate. Therefore, such contaminations are called "bizarre."

In contrast to this, Gloucester and Cupid represent a contamination of compatible contents. Both have in common blindness and lust. One calls

Ha! Goneril with a white beard! (IV.vi.98)

Later he sees Gloucester contaminated with the sign of a brothel, as "blind Cupid."

Such contaminations of images can only occur when the threshold between consciousness and the unconscious is extremely lowered or non-existent. The succeeding part of the speech reveals a constant stream of unconscious images entering consciousness. They force a great deal of helpful insight upon Lear. He now knows that he was flattered into believing that he was wise, a kind of god—but his experience in the rain has utterly convinced him that he was not wise, that he was not a god. He has learned that he is a human being and not "ague-proof."

Gloucester recognizes Lear by his voice and his simple question, "Is't not the king?" touches on Lear's complex of lost kingship. He speaks in the same excited manner, but now his thoughts no longer consist of loosely connected associations. On the contrary, the images are quite coherent, and his insight grows. As King, he was certainly also a "judge." He feels deep guilt about having judged, according to the law, human beings who simply followed the commands of nature. The problem of human law against nature, which was previously discussed by Edmund, is taken up by Lear. In the following speech, sexuality is to him simply a compelling drive which nature manifests in the animal kingdom:

> The wren goes to it, and the small gilded fly (IV.vi.115)
> Does lecher in my sight.

It is quite ironic that he believes that Gloucester's "bastard son"

---

such a contamination "odd" in contrast to bizarre. Goneril and Gloucester have in common being humans. The white beard emphasizes Goneril's lack of femininity and places the emphasis on her mannishness. It happens under normal conditions that certain people, especially those of the introvert-intuitive type, see a particular symbolic image together with the real person—but they do not contaminate. Such images then symbolically express the true charatcer of this person or his essential thought.

> Was kinder to his father than my daughters   (IV.vi.118)
> Got 'tween the lawful sheets.

It makes no difference to him whether the child was begot in lawful marriage, or extramaritally, according to the commands of nature. Like any other dictator, he wants to encourage "copulation" because

> I lack soldiers.   (IV.vi.120)

He wants to tear away from women the mask of cold, virtuous appearance. He sees now, in an intensely exaggerated way, their "riotous (sexual) appetite." He sees them as consisting of a pair of opposites, "heavenly above" and "hellish below." He sees them as "Centaurs" from the waist down, that is, women above and of animal nature below the girdle. This union of opposites, however, is not harmonious. Rather, the upper part is inhabited by the gods, the lower part by the devil. What lies underneath this wild speech is Lear's urgent need to understand the behavior of his two daughters. He cannot avoid the natural fact that he is their father, that he has begotten them and, like Gloucester, has brought his present predicament upon himself, due ultimately to his own sexuality. While the first part of his speech proclaims the unavoidable necessity of sex, he now sees also its dark aspects, and a tremendous revulsion grips him against the terrible results of his own sexuality. The unconscious here overwhelms him with a dark and disgusting image. He can hardly tolerate it and therefore sees Gloucester as a "good apothecary," of whom he can ask an "ounce of civet" to sweeten his imagination.

Gloucester, deeply moved, says, "O, let me kiss that hand!" and here Lear at last relates directly to Gloucester:

> Let me wipe it first; it smells of mortality.   (IV.vi.137)

Quite naturally, the images of sexuality also convey the idea of mortality because sexuality is nature's trick to maintain life—at the expense, of course, of the individual. Like every character in the play, Gloucester remains an observer who sees only madness in Lear's wild speeches and behavior. He does not realize that these images are a healing process. He does not see that Lear, directly responding to him, is beginning to gain back the world, is relating to an "object" (his hand) without confusing it with an inner image. Gloucester can only exclaim: "O ruined piece of nature!" Taking Lear to be far removed from reality, he asks, "Dost thou know me?" But as before, when Gloucester was fused with the image of Goneril, Lear has now fused Gloucester's image with that of "Blind Cupid" (see p. 277). The connecting link between the two of course is that both are blind, but it is certainly not too far off psychologically for Lear also to project "Cupid" on Gloucester, especially since a moment before he had been so obsessed with the "riotous appetite" of sex, and Gloucester had referred to himself as a "lust-dieted" man.

Edgar, the only witness to this meeting, is naturally deeply shocked. The conversation between Lear and Gloucester continues. It is now a real dialogue. Lear communicates with Gloucester, although of course he still projects a good deal of his inner images on him—for example, his own madness. Yet he expresses the profound truth that one does not need "eyes" to see how the world goes. He returns to the problem of kingship and its various functions. For instance, the king is "judge," but the fact that we are all guilty means that those who judge might have committed the same or worse crimes. His speech is a strong plea for abolishing the judgment of man:

> None does offend, none, I say none.[19]   (IV.vi.172)

Edgar, in an aside, can only admit that in spite of his apparent madness, Lear is uttering great truth:

> O! matter and impertinency[20] mix'd;   (IV.vi.179)
> Reason in madness!

[19] These lines are further evidence for the Christian attitude of the play: John 8:7—"He that is without sin among you, let him first cast a stone at her."

[20] Arden: Florio's word for "nonsense" is "impertinency."

And now this fusing of images comes to an end. Lear says:

I know thee well enough   (IV.vi.182)
Thy name is Gloucester.

He speaks feelingly of Gloucester's affliction, and his emotions overtake him again. He sees life as nothing but a tragedy. He hates his "sons-in-law" so much that if he could he would kill them.

A Gentleman arrives as messenger from Cordelia. His attempt to reach Lear frightens the old man who cannot help but take him as an enemy. Lear feels himself "the natural fool of fortune," and so he runs away. The Gentleman is moved to great pity and in the ensuing conversation with Edgar we hear that the rescuing army is here on "special cause." Gloucester still craves death but no longer wishes to commit suicide. Edgar has not yet revealed himself to his father and offers to take him to some safe place.

At this moment Oswald enters and perceives an opportunity to kill blind Gloucester, to "raise (his) fortunes." Edgar is dressed as a peasant and, speaking like a peasant, defends Gloucester, mortally wounding Oswald in the fight. In Oswald's dying moments, he begs Edgar to bury him and to transmit the letters he has on him to Edmund. Edgar reads one of the letters, written by Goneril and addressed to Edmund. In it she asks Edmund to kill her husband and promises herself to him. Edgar is deeply shocked by the intense and murderous will of this woman who will stop at nothing to satisfy her sexual desires.

vii

Scene 6 ends with Gloucester being led away by Edgar, and the seventh scene moves once again to the French camp. We find Cordelia, Kent, a Doctor and several Gentlemen. Cordelia expresses her sincerely-felt gratitude to Kent for all he has done and begs him to change his dress—but Kent refuses. He thinks it is not yet time for giving up his disguise. Cordelia turns to the Doctor. We hear for the first time that Lear is sleeping: at last he has found rest.

Gloucester, in the preceding scene, had addressed the gods as "gentle gods." Now Cordelia addresses them as "O you kind gods," and prays for the cure of her father's mind:

> The untun'd and jarring senses, O, wind up   (IV.vii.16)
> Of this child-changed father!

We can assume that—as is so often true in Shakespeare—different meanings are contained in this one term, "child-changed." The first meaning—to be changed to a child—is obvious, but Lear is certainly also a man who has been changed by the experiences he has had with his children.

The Doctor feels certain that Lear has recovered his sanity ("I doubt not of his temperance") and also that he has slept long enough and may now be awakened. Lear is brought in, still sleeping. It is symbolically significant that his garments have been changed:

> Ay, madam. In the heaviness of sleep   (IV.vii.21)
> We put fresh garments on him.

It is a most touching scene, in stark contrast to Lear's meeting with his other two daughters. They were calculating and vicious, hiding their hostility under cold logic. This scene has all the warmth and love of a daughter for her sick father. Cordelia expresses those profound feelings which unite human beings in their struggles against the harsh cruelty of nature and of other human beings turned beasts. Cordelia's saintly love reaches out to all life, even to her enemy's dog:

> . . . Mine enemy's dog,   (IV.vii.36)
> Though he had bit me, should have stood that night
> Against my fire.

—a telling comparison with the Fool's statement concerning truth in I.iv.124: "Truth's a dog must to kennel; he must be whipped out, when Lady the brach may stand by the fire and stink."

Cordelia's short speech, although addressed to the still sleeping Lear, is more like a monologue. She closes with the remark that it is miraculous for such an old man to have survived all those bitter sufferings and not to have completely broken down in mind and body.

Music is very much a part of Shakespeare's plays. There are, for example, two instances of the use of music in *The Merchant of Venice*. Shylock's villainous personality is characterized by his hatred of music:

> Lock up my doors; and when you hear the drum,   (II.v.29)
> And the vile squealing of the wry-neck'd fife,
> Clamber not you up to the casements then.

When Jessica has difficulty with music ("I am never merry when I hear sweet music"), Lorenzo, her lover, understands and restores to her the healing quality of music with these remarkable lines:

> The reason is, your spirits are attentive: (V.i.70)
> For do but note a wild and wanton herd,
> Or race of youthful and unhandled colts.
> Fetching mad bounds, bellowing and neighing loud,
> Which is the hot condition of their blood;
> If they but hear perchance a trumpet sound,
> Or any air of music touch their ears,
> You shall perceive them make a mutual stand,
> Their savage eyes turn'd to a modest gaze
> By the sweet power of music: therefore the poet
> Did feign that Orpheus drew trees, stones, and floods;
> Since nought so stockish, hard, and full of rage,
> But music for the time doth change his nature,
> The man that hath no music in himself,
> Nor is not mov'd with concord of sweet sounds,
> Is fit for treasons, stratagems, and spoils;
> The motions of his spirit are dull as night,
> And his affections dark as Erebus;
> Let no such man be trusted. Mark the music.

In the same way Lorenzo employed music for the healing of Jessica's torn soul, the Doctor employs it for the cure of the much more deeply disturbed Lear. There are modern psychotherapists who use music for the same purpose.[21] The theoretical assumption is that music expresses order, a solution of disharmonies with harmony, without words, which underlies or parallels our conflicts. Music, as it were, tunes man in to a new wholeness and thus assists healing. (Wholeness and healing are the same.)

Lear awakens and Cordelia speaks to him. Coming out of the "heaviness of sleep," he is overtaken by inner images. Just as earlier he had taken Gloucester to be Cupid, so now an inner image fuses with the real Cordelia standing before him. He sees her as "a soul in bliss." The same considerations hold true which we made earlier in regard to the fusion of images—with the difference, of course, that a man awakening from sleep is still under the influence of the unconscious; the dream he has just had still appears as reality. Such a condition could therefore be true of anyone who awakens from a deep sleep. It would be particularly natural in someone who has undergone severe physical and/or psychic traumata. The image which Lear has is obviously that of being in hell, of meeting in Cordelia a spirit who has descended from heaven and is, by some accident, visiting him in hell:

> Thou art a soul in bliss; but I am bound   (IV.vii.46)
> Upon a wheel of fire, that mine own tears
> Do scald like molten lead.

When Lear is reunited with Cordelia, his rage has already been transformed and the intensity of his affectivity now appears as an inner image, as a "wheel of fire." It reminds us of the Lamaistic Vajra-Mandala reproduced in *The Secret of the Golden Flower*,[22] where the outermost circle of the mandala is repre-

[21] See *Der tönende Mensch* by Aleks Pontvik (Rascher Verlag, Zurich, 1961).

[22] A Chinese text, translated by Richard Wilhelm, with a European commentary by C. G. Jung (Wehman Bros., New York, 1955).

sented as a wheel of fire. It also brings to mind the story of Ixion, who was bound to a fiery wheel which whirled him perpetually through the sky. Ixion is chastized for coveting the goddess Hera. Lear's suffering, however, is more similar to the suffering of Christ. Lear's libido is no longer attached to the world; it is almost completely introverted. His affects are now contained. They are all within him and are symbolized as a wheel. "Bound on a wheel of fire" then expresses the psychological status in which his ego is bound on the wheel of his affects.

It is highly meaningful that the image of the wheel appears in significant places in the play. When Kent was in the stocks, he finished his monologue with: "Fortune, good night; smile once more, turn thy wheel" (II.ii.180). Later, the Fool, talking to Kent, said: "Let go thy hold when a great wheel runs down a hill" (II.iv.73). Edmund, fatally wounded in his duel with his brother Edgar, will say: "The wheel is come full circle; I am here" (V.iii.176). But it is only Lear who is directly connected with the wheel and who experiences something like a crucifixion. He is not bound to a cross as Christ was, but to the wheel. This image demonstrates that Lear undergoes an ordeal similar to that of Jesus, but in a different and individual manner. In Christ's case, it is the sinless god-man; in Lear's, it is the sinful man, elevated only by being a king. As a guilty human being, he is bound to the wheel of his own concupiscence.

Kenneth Muir[23] refers to H. W. Crundle, who has pointed out:

> The torment of the wheel of fire, although not scriptural, is traditional in the medieval legends and visions of Hell and Purgatory. They all draw upon the New Testament Apocrypha.

Although I have no doubt that Shakespeare drew this picture from medieval sources, it appears significant to me that it is just at this point in Lear's development, in his first meeting with Cordelia after her rejection in Act I, that this powerful image arises in him.

[23] Arden, p. 190.

The circle is an archetypal image. (Cf. p. 229.) The magic circle (mandala) has been described by Jung in many of his books as possibly the most universal symbol of an archetype. One particular form of the mandala is that of the wheel, of which Jung gives many examples. Here I would like to mention the wheels in Ezekiel's great vision (Ezekiel 1). The particular combination of wheel and fire is a common one in Indian tankas. The nearest scriptural image which mentions wheel and fire in close association is found in the Epistle of James 3:6:

> And the tongue is a fire, a world of iniquity: so is the tongue among our members, that it defileth the whole body, and *setteth on fire the course of nature;* and it is set on fire of hell.

The Latin text says:[24]

> Et lingua ignis est, universitas iniquitas. Lingua constituitur in membris nostris, quae maculat totum corpus, et inflammata a gehenna *et inflammat rotam nativitatis nostrae.*

Therefore, the words "setteth on fire the course of our nature" in the Epistle of James should rather be translated as "setteth on fire the *wheel* of our nature." (Cf. *Aion.*[25])

The image of wheels of fire occurs in the Apocrypha of Peter:[26]

> And there are *wheels of fire,* and men and women
> hung thereon by the strength of the whirling *thereof.*

In *Lear* then, the "wheel of fire" could be understood as Lear's *horoscope,* that is, his fundamental constitution; his Self is set on fire by his wild affects.

[24] I quote the Latin text because it makes it clear that "the *course* of nature" is inaccurate. It is actually "the *wheel* of nature," by which antiquity meant the horoscope.

[25] Pp. 135, 136, where Jung also quotes Meister Eckhart as saying that "on returning to his true self, he enters an abyss 'deeper than hell itself.' "

[26] *The Apocryphal New Testament,* translated by Montague Rhodes James (Oxford Press), p. 517; *The New English Bible* (1961): "keeps the wheel of our existence red hot."

Psychologically then, this image emerging from Lear's unconscious indicates that he is now bound on his highly emotional
Self.

Earlier, in Act IV, Scene 6, his affects were directed to an
outside object:

> . . . Thou hast seen a farmer's dog bark   (160)
> at a beggar? . . .
> And the creature run from the cur? There thou
> mightst behold the great image of authority: a
> dog's obeyed in office.
> Thou rascal beadle, hold thy bloody hand!
> Why dost thou lash that whore? Strip thine own back.
> Thou hotly lusts to use her in that kind
> For which thou whippest her.

Now, in Scene 6, all the fire of these affects is within him and his
ego is irretrievably bound on it. We cannot help but see a cross
within the wheel, or Lear with his outstretched arms forming a
cross within the wheel. This cross would be an equilateral cross,
in contradistinction to the Christian cross. Furthermore, the
emphasis would undoubtedly lie on the wheel rather than on
the cross. As a natural symbol, the cross has of course many
meanings and throughout history has been interpreted in many
different ways. The significance for Lear is that he is now
forcibly connected with his Self. It means tremendous suffering
to be so utterly exposed to his own affects and to the essential
nature of his being. At the same time it is a healing process since
the mandala is essentially a symbol of wholeness. His ego is
attached to the greater man, to the whole man in himself. The
very fact that the perfect wheel appears here as an image from
the unconscious is a strong indication that Lear was never insane in a clinical sense. (In cases of schizophrenia, we see the
symbol of the mandala broken or fragmented.)

Lear is still not fully awake. His consciousness is permeated
by the unconscious. His further question clearly denotes that he
is still in a dreamy state:

> You are a spirit, I know; when did you die? (IV.vii.49)

To Cordelia, this is a sign of madness: "Still, still, far wide."
The physician, understanding better, corrects her opinion:

> He's scarce awake; let him alone awhile. (IV.vii.51)

Lear gradually awakens. It is only natural that first he tries to
orient himself in time and space, and to relate to his own body:

> Where have I been? Where am I? Fair daylight? (IV.vii.52)
> . . .
> I will not swear these are my hands: let's see;
> I feel this pin prick.

Finding his orientation, and having concrete reference to his
body, his ego solidifies. He can now make an important statement about himself:

> I am a very foolish old man, (IV.vii.60)
> Fourscore and upward, not an hour more nor less;
> And, to deal plainly,
> I fear I am not in my perfect mind.

He is aware of the instability of his ego. This insight into his
own psychological and physical condition is of the greatest importance. It is a statement no really insane person could make.
Lear's need for orientation in space, and in regard to his
body, needs further confirmation:

> . . . I am mainly ignorant (IV.vii.65)
> What place this is; and all the skill I have
> Remembers not these garments; nor I know not
> Where I did lodge last night.

When he is fully awake, Lear can clearly discriminate his inner image ("you are a spirit") from the person standing before
him:

> . . . I think this lady   (IV.vii.69)
> To be my child Cordelia.

The description of the step-by-step awakening of Lear is tes-
timony to Shakespeare's wonderful psychological understanding.
Now that Lear is completely conscious, adequately oriented to
the present situation, with a strengthened ego, he can fully relate
to the real Cordelia. He feels deep guilt and has the remarkable
courage to express it to her. He is even willing to die for his
guilt. Loving Cordelia speaks the kindest lie:

> No cause, no cause.   (IV.vii.76)

Again Lear attempts to round out his orientation and asks,
"Am I in France?" Whereupon Kent answers, "In your own
kingdom, sir." This is certainly literally true, but has a far
deeper symbolic meaning, because Lear, by having submitted
fully to the wheel of his own suffering has gained his inner kingdom. Lear, who not long before had to put a crown of weeds
and wild flowers on his head to make himself feel like a king, is
now truly a king and has realized his royal privilege. He is no
more the autocrat, the power-mad father and king. He has become king by accepting his suffering and being bound on the
wheel of fire, just as Christ was nailed to his cross. Also as
Christ, Lear has become king, and his kingdom is also "not of
this world."
Lear himself does not believe he is in his own kingdom, but
the Doctor knows that Lear has now made the decisive step toward healing:

> . . . The great rage,   (IV.vii.79)
> You see, is kill'd in him.

The affects no longer burst out into the open but have become
a healing fire in Lear. The cautious Doctor realizes that this step

in Lear's convalescence must be followed by many more steps. The process needs still "further settling."

Act Five

i

In the first scene of the fifth act, set in the English camp, we see Edmund and Regan, accompanied by a Gentleman and soldiers, drums and colors, all emphasizing the military aspect. Yet there is only a short discussion of military plans. Personal relations seem to be of more importance to Edmund and Regan. They express their fears concerning Oswald's fate, then Regan proceeds with her personal attack. Her greatest fear, as we saw before, is that Edmund might also be in love with her sister. She is most direct; over Edmund's protestation, she goes from the question of whether Edmund loves her sister to the matter in dispute:

> But have you never found my brother's way   (V.i.11)
> To the forefended place?

It is psychologically meaningful that both Goneril and Regan, with their sharp, cold intellect and fiendish cruelty, are characterized by Shakespeare as victims of sexual lust and jealousy. The animal terms so often applied to them throughout the play are also most suitable for expressing the character of their desires in regard to Edmund. Their powerful, beastlike appetites are strongly contrasted with Cordelia's love for France. As stated in our introduction, Shakespeare paints many different aspects of love in this play: the pretended love of Goneril and Regan for Lear, as against Cordelia's true love for her father; the warm and conscious love between Cordelia and France, based on a mutual appreciation of their integrity; the egocentric covetous "love" of the two sisters for the equally base Edmund, who apparently must physically be something of an Adonis.

Albany, Goneril and soldiers now enter. Only the Quarto contains Goneril's remark upon first seeing Edmund and Regan together:

> I had rather lose the battle than that sister   (V.i.18)
> Should loosen him and me.

This double-play on the word "loosen" is significant if we accept Dover Wilson's interpretation of the word as used by Polonius in *Hamlet* (II.ii.162) :[1]

> Polonius's words 'I'll loose my daughter to him' offer the leading clue. The expression 'loose,' notes Dowden, 'reminds the King and Queen that he has restrained Ophelia from communicating with Hamlet'; but it has also another meaning, still connected with the breeding of horses and cattle, which Shakespeare makes use of again in *The Tempest* (2.i.124), when the cynic Sebastian sneers at Alonso because he would not marry his daughter to a European prince, "but rather loose her to an African."

Wilson's glossary also contains his definition for *loose:*

> (a) release (as a dog from a leash), (b) turn loose (in cattle or horse breeding); c.f.M.W.W.2.1.164 'turn her loose to him.'

If we accept this meaning, we see in Goneril's aside that she cares much more about possessing Edmund than about affairs of state, or the war—in fact, that she does not care one bit for the welfare of the country.

[1] *The New Shakespeare,* Introduction, lvii.

The following discussion between Albany, Regan, Edmund
and Goneril shows that Albany has the same conflict as Cordelia. Where Cordelia invades her country for a just cause, Albany must fight the invader knowing that his cause is unjust:

> . . . Where I could not be honest   (V.i.23)
> I never yet was valiant.

Right or wrong, Albany's "country" is certainly not his leading
principle. The following lines are unfortunately somewhat corrupt:

> It toucheth us, as France invades our land,   (V.i.25)
> Not bolds the king, with others, whom, I fear
> Most just and heavy causes make oppose.

Kenneth Muir, in the Arden edition, assumes that Albany says
something like, "We intend to repel the invader, but not to treat
the King and his supporters as enemies."

Goneril and Regan, of course, do not want any discussion of
the conflict. They prefer to see it as nothing but a fight against
the foreign invader. For these two women, the possession of Edmund means more than the impending battle, and, out of jealousy, Goneril decides to go with Regan and Edmund.

Edgar enters, disguised as a peasant. He manages to talk to
Albany and hand him the letter that he had found on Oswald
(IV.vi.268). Anticipating that Lear's army might be defeated,
Edgar suggests a medieval joust as a judgment of God. He promises to "produce a champion" for Albany that "will prove what
is avouched there" (in the letter). Should Albany lose the battle,
then of course there would be no point in such a contest, con-
ducted according to the rules of chivalry.

Edgar steals away before Albany can read the letter. Edmund
enters, urges Albany to display his forces for battle, and this
brief dialogue is followed by a monologue of Edmund's. His first
monologue was delivered in Act I, Scene 2. His psychology is
still the same, although his circumstances have changed considerably:

> To both these sisters have I sworn my love;   (V.i.55)
> Each jealous of the other, as the stung
> Are of the adder.

He obviously does not love either sister, but will decide which of the two he will take simply on the basis of what would be most advantageous for him. He seems to prefer Goneril. Of course Albany is still alive; Edmund decides to use Albany's "countenance for the battle" and afterwards leave it to Goneril to get rid of him quickly. Just as coldly, he decides to do away with Lear and Cordelia, since both of them would be an obstacle to his unlimited ambition. In short, he is a truly Machiavellian devil who wants to use the worst instincts of these women and the war situation to take possession of the woman who would make him king, and have all others killed who could dispute his ambition.

ii

The battle follows but is only mentioned in the stage directions. It proceeds very quickly. Edgar leaves his father under the protection of a tree, but soon returns to take him away because France's army has lost the battle. Lear and Cordelia have both been taken prisoner. Gloucester objects to leaving; he is willing to die right where he is ("A man may rot even here"). Edgar fights Gloucester's depression and suicidal thoughts. I believe his wonderful lines most completely express Shakespeare's intention in this play:

> What! in ill thoughts again? Men must endure   (V.ii.9)
> Their going hence, even as their coming hither;
> Ripeness is all.

We could possibly reword Shakespeare's idea by saying that the goal of life is to reach or bring about the greatest possible maturity of the psyche, or to achieve the highest possible consciousness. The word "ripeness" is taken from plant life. Shakespeare seems to see the development of the personality as a tree whose final goal is a ripe fruit. This consideration is significant in regard to Gloucester's end and especially Lear's death. We must assume then that both die at the moment they have achieved full ripeness. Muir quotes Steevens,[2] who compares Edgar's line with *Hamlet,* V.ii.234:

> There's a special providence in the fall of a sparrow. If it be now, 'tis not to come; if it be not to come, it will be now; if it be not now, yet it will come; *the readiness is all.*

I believe that in *Hamlet,* as well as in *Lear,* Shakespeare discusses the question of what man is and what the goal of life is. I believe, however, that *Hamlet* represents the failure of a man to fulfill himself, even the betrayal of self. Therefore, the most he can achieve is *readiness* to die at any moment, irrespective of whether his psyche has matured. In *Lear,* the meaning of life has assumed a totally different character. Lear is also exposed to overwhelming difficulties. Externally he is defeated, but his personality grows with every blow that he receives, and the unconscious helps him to mature, although at times his relationship with external reality is extenuated.

iii

The final scene, which takes place in the British camp near Dover, is filled with rich and dramatic events. All of the important characters appear, with the exception of the Fool, and we hear about their fates. Many die, each in his or her own way: all three sisters, Gloucester, Edmund, and finally Lear himself.

The victorious British army enters, bringing Lear and Cordelia as prisoners. Cordelia is resigned to her fate and is depressed only for Lear. She had not succeeded in saving her father, but for Lear being a prisoner does not appear a misfortune. He greets it with a surprising serenity, almost happiness, because to him the most wonderful thing has happened: he

[2] Arden edition, p. 198.

has been reunited with Cordelia. His introversion has reached a tremendously high degree. Reality is no more distorted as, for example, in his talk with Gloucester ("blind Cupid"), or in his first talk with Cordelia when awakening from sleep ("Thou art a soul in bliss"), but is evaluated in a manner which contradicts cruel reality. In no way does he reflect on the possible intentions of their captors. Occasionally we find in dreams that "prison" is used as a symbol for complete introversion. This is a condition in which the attention of the ego is totally directed toward the unconscious to the exclusion of reality. Lear's strong sense of guilt sees in imprisonment the possibility for complete redemption:

> We two alone will sing like birds i' the cage.   (V.iii.9)
> When thou dost ask me blessing, I'll kneel down
> And ask of thee forgiveness.

He imagines that in captivity he and Cordelia will be perfect companions. There is now a deeply religious feeling in Lear:

> . . . So we'll live,   (V.iii.11)
> And pray . . .

and in this profound introversion the world will have lost much of its meaning, will present no temptation to act or to be involved:

> . . . and hear poor rogues   (V.iii.13)
> Talk of court news; and we'll talk with them too,
> Who loses and who wins; who's in, who's out;
> And take upon's the mystery of things,
> As if we were God's spies.

Since both the Folio and the Quarto have *gods* here without an apostrophe, Kenneth Muir "follows Perrett in assuming that Shakespeare intended the plural since he was writing of a pagan world." Being thus centered in the gods, and understanding their hidden intention, Lear believes:

. . . we'll wear out, (V.iii.17)
In a walled prison, packs and sects of great ones
That ebb and flow by the moon.

Thus Lear's fantasy runs in almost complete detachment from
the world; his attention is fully concentrated on the inner life
and its mysterious events. Harsh reality, however, breaks upon
them with Edmund's curt words: "Take them away." Lear has
time to conclude:

Upon such sacrifices, my Cordelia, (V.iii.20)
The gods themselves throw incense.

Lear fully realizes that to give up the values of the outer world is
a real sacrifice, and he believes that, necessarily, the gods must
approve such action. Such a sacrificial attitude, expressed here
by Lear, is genuinely Christian in its intent. As a result of such
an offering, this inner world would be, in his imagination, a
blissful state of eternal union with Cordelia. Any separation
from Cordelia would bring fiery revenge from the gods:

The goujeres (goodyears) shall devour 'em, flesh (V.iii.24)
    and fell,
Ere they shall make us weep!

It is possible, according to Golding, that the word "goodyears"
may denote some undefined or malefic power or agency. Muir
suggests that the story of Joseph (Genesis 41) was "vaguely at
the back of Shakespeare's mind," and that "Lear may mean that
Goneril and Regan will be destroyed, not by misfortune, but by
their evil prosperity." I believe that in the term "goodyears" the
concept of time is implied and that Lear expresses here his firm
conviction that time alone will destroy his evil daughters. Being
insolubly united with Cordelia, no suffering could then ever enter their world of inner bliss. Ironically, Lear's hope for Para-
dise, for freedom from tears, is shattered forthwith. Edmund's
command is immediately executed; both Lear and Cordelia are
taken away under guard.

Edmund remains on the stage. By promising "noble fortunes," he persuades a Captain to kill both Lear and Cordelia.

Albany, Goneril, Regan, Officers and Soldiers enter with martial music. Albany praises Edmund for his valiant behavior in battle, and "requires" the captives from Edmund, who replies that for political reasons he thought it "fit"

> To send the old and miserable king   (V.iii.47)
> To some retention, and appointed guard

and to decide their fate later on at a more appropriate time and a "fitter place." Of course he conceals from the two daughters, and especially from Albany, the order for the murder of Lear and Cordelia. This dissembling of his real intention from his close associates serves his uninhibited ambition well. It is difficult to decide which of his evil actions is the worse—the ruthless betrayal of his father or the treacherous murder of Lear and Cordelia. Albany guesses that something is wrong but probably not the full extent of it. He criticizes Edmund's independent act as overstepping his authority. An ugly quarrel develops. Both sisters speak up, claiming that they have conveyed the highest authority on Edmund. Albany admits that this would be true if Edmund were Regan's husband, and a jealous quarrel breaks out between the two sisters. Regan, although she is feeling ill, publicly declares Edmund to be her husband with all the rights accruing to him from this position:

> . . . I create thee here   (V.iii.78)
> My lord and master.

Albany contests this and Regan proposes a tournament:

> Let the drum strike, and prove my title thine.   (V.iii.83)

Now Albany speaks openly and says, "Edmund, I arrest thee on capital treason." With high irony he contests Regan's claim to Edmund:

> For your claim, fair sister,   (V.iii.86)
> I bar it in the interest of my wife.

Edmund accepts the challenge, throws down a glove, and prepares for the joust. Regan's illness becomes more acute and she
is finally led away; we hear later that she had been poisoned by
her sister (V.iii.229).

Edgar enters dramatically to accept the "summons." He does
not reveal his name, but claims to be of as noble descent as
Edmund. He calls his brother a traitor:

> . . . thou art a traitor,   (V.iii.135)
> False to thy gods, thy brother, and thy father;
> Conspirant 'gainst this high illustrious prince;
> . . .
> This sword, this arm, and my best spirits are bent
> To prove upon thy heart, whereto I speak,
> Thou liest.

Edmund accepts the challenge. In the ensuing duel between the
two, Edmund is mortally wounded. When Goneril speaks up for
him, Albany finally shouts his true opinion of his wife:

> Shut your mouth, dame,   (V.iii.156)
> Or with this paper shall I stople it.
> . . .
> Thou worse than any name, read thine own evil.

Goneril answers that by being sovereign and therefore the maker
of laws she is above the law:

> Say if I do—the laws are mine, not thine.   (V.iii.160)
> Who can arraign me for't?

In this respect, she is similar to Edmund. She rejects any inner
law and order. Belief in the validity of man-made laws necessarily leads to the destruction of any humanity in her. Albany is
shocked to the utmost, so that he can only exclaim: "Most mon-

strous! O!" Her words had always been strong, giving the appearance of a supremely self-conscious woman. How brittle this structure really is is instantly demonstrated when Albany surprises her by presenting her with the letter she had written to Edmund. She leaves in great agitation. The irony is complete and Albany must tell an officer to "govern her," the woman who a moment before had said, "The laws are mine, not thine."

The final scene in *King Lear* is crowded with dramatic events and in short order brings one solution after another. Mortally wounded, Edmund finally admits his crimes and is willing to forgive the opponent who has struck the mortal blow. Edgar at last reveals his name. It is one event in this tragedy in which the "good" win. The archetype of the hostile brothers, which underlies one of the patterns of the drama, has fulfilled itself. Generally speaking, one could say that one of the essential themes in *King Lear* is the struggle between good and evil. Just as in *Job* Satan is one of the sons of God and Christ is certainly His son—and the two are therefore brothers—so Edmund and Edgar represent this archetype in *King Lear*. One can only draw the conclusion that since Edgar defeats Edmund, Shakespeare's general idea in the play must be that good wins over evil. Such jousts between two knights were considered as judgments of God. Edgar makes direct reference to the divine:

> The gods are just, and of our pleasant vices   (V.iii.172)
> Make instruments to plague us.

Edgar, in summing up, recounts the events of his life since he was persecuted by his father; how he assumed the "madman's rags," how he became his father's "guide":

> Led him, begg'd for him, sav'd him from despair.   (V.iii.193)

—and gives us the news of his father's death:

> . . . but his flaw'd heart—   (V.iii.198)
> Alack! too weak the conflict to support;

> 'Twixt two extremes of passion, joy and grief,
> Burst smilingly.

Thus the Gloucester story comes to an end and we hear that at the moment of death two strong, opposite emotions—joy and grief—killed him, but that the emotion of joy was stronger because his "flawed heart . . . burst smilingly." His death could not be spoken of as true redemption, or as complete failure, but as an attempt in reconciliation of the opposites. The highest level that Gloucester could reach was to become conscious of a powerful conflict. He achieved the "ripeness" *he* was capable of.

Albany is so deeply moved that he can hardly bear to hear more:

> For I am almost ready to dissolve,   (V.iii.205)
> Hearing of this.

There follow now some twenty lines which are only found in the Quarto. Although they are not essential to the progress of the drama (the spectators have known all along that the Faithful Servant Caius and the banished Kent were identical), nevertheless the dramatis personae did not know it, so the function of these lines is to give this information to the figures in the drama and prepare them for the return of Kent, who now at last, like Edgar, can drop his disguise and reveal his true identity.

Before this happens, however, we hear of the horrible end of the two evil daughters. Regan dies, poisoned by her sister Goneril. Goneril, aware that all her dark plots have been revealed, sees no future in remaining alive, and dies by her own hand. This news evokes a strange though fitting statement by the dying Edmund:

> I was contracted to them both: all three   (V.iii.230)
> Now marry in an instant.

It appears that the archetypal motif of the death wedding made a deep impression on Shakespeare and is therefore used in several of his tragedies. It is certainly most outspoken in *Romeo and Juliet,* where both lovers die in the monument. Othello follows Desdemona in death, while she is still dressed in her wedding gown. Shakespeare's poem, "The Phoenix and the Turtle," describes the death wedding in symbolic form as Shakespeare's own experience. Here, in *Lear,* Edmund and the two sisters die almost simultaneously, and Edmund experiences his death as a wedding with both of them. It is a dark coniunctio, indeed! For Edmund personally, it serves to give a last flattering illusion:

> Yet Edmund was beloved. (V.iii.287)
> The one the other poisoned for my sake,
> And after slew herself.

It is very doubtful that anything either of these two women felt for Edmund was love. What they really felt was intense sexual desire and power. For them Edmund was an object to be possessed, not a human being to be loved. One can admit that he appeared to Goneril as such a valuable possession that she poisoned Regan for his sake, but it must be doubted that she slew herself solely because she could not live without him; his death would have made it impossible for her to attain him. The revelation of all her dark plans, the breakdown of all her plots—in which Edmund certainly figured prominently—and the lack of all inner values were the causes of her suicide. Albany's love for his wife has completely evaporated. As we find throughout this play, Albany is profoundly impressed by the active intervention of God in human fate. He feels the action of the heavens as just:

> This judgment of the heavens, that makes us tremble,
> (V.iii.233)
> Touches us not with pity.

Now Kent enters:

> I am come (V.iii.236)
> To bid my king and master aye good night.

It is amazing, yet quite understandable, that Lear has been completely forgotten. If we reconsider the quick succession of events in this scene—Edmund and Edgar in a joust, Edgar's revelation of his true identity, the death of the two sisters, Edgar's tale of his life and the death of his father—we can easily understand how the dramatic action involving all the other characters of the play has swept Lear from everyone's mind. It is Kent's entrance which, in this hardly tolerable tension, suddenly directs our attention back to Lear. Kittredge writes:[3]

> This amnesia on everybody's part is necessary for the climax that follows, but—though the audience thinks little of it—the reader always feels a shock.

I agree with Kittredge that the sudden reminder of Lear shocks us and prepares us properly for the climax that follows. Although Albany could not know that Lear was in any danger, this line of his ("Great thing of us forgot!") serves to impress us again with the incredible emotional tension that exists here with both daughters dead and Edmund dying. The harvest of this tragic fraternal war should now be brought home.

So Albany, who had started the quarrel with Edmund on account of his disposal of the two royal persons, returns to this question and asks—some 200 lines later:

> Speak, Edmund, where's the King? and where's Cordelia?
>
> (V.iii.239)

—and at last Edmund decides to do something good:

> . . . some good I mean to do   (V.iii.245)
> Despite of mine own nature.

So in utmost haste, an Officer, with Edmund's sword as credential, is sent to Lear and Cordelia, to prevent if possible their execution, previously ordered by Edmund. But alas, it is too

---

[3] *King Lear,* ed. by George Lyman Kittredge (Ginn & Co., New York, 1940), p. 234.

late. Lear enters with the dead Cordelia in his arms, and the high climax of the play begins.

Opinions have differed vastly as to what Shakespeare intended to convey with this final scene. Lear's language has always been majestic, not to say flamboyant. Here the majestic quality is coupled with the greatest simplicity, born of the greatest possible suffering. We can see that Albany's intention was to keep these two prisoners alive and treat them with all dignity due to a king and a queen. Had Albany remembered Lear and Cordelia immediately after asking Edmund of the whereabouts of the prisoners, they might perhaps have been saved. If Shakespeare had written his tragedy with such an ending, all the evil ones (Edmund, Goneril, Regan) and Gloucester (good-and-evil), would have died, while all the good ones would have survived. The history of *King Lear* on the stage[4] indicates that this tragic ending for both Cordelia and Lear has been difficult to tolerate.[4a] Fortunately, *Lear* is now always performed the way Shakespeare wrote it, and we must seek the deeper meaning which he intended in the final scene. It seems impossible that after the death of Goneril, Regan and Edmund (and Gloucester, whose death we only hear about), a further climax could occur. But this is exactly what happens.

Lear is inconsolable over Cordelia's death. Just as earlier in Act III, Scene 2 ("And thou, all-shaking thunder, strike flat the thick rotundity o' the world, crack Nature's molds"), the enormity of his suffering reaches into the Universe:

> Had I your tongues and eyes, I'd use them so   (V.iii.259)
> That heaven's vaults should crack.
>
> . . .
>
> She's dead as earth.

Kent asks:

> Is this the promis'd end?   (V.iii.265)

[4] Described in some detail in the Arden edition, pp. xliii-xlv.

[4a] Arden edition, p. xliv: "Garrick, though he omitted many of Tate's additions, retained the interpolated love scenes between Edgar and Cordelia, and also the happy ending."

Kenneth Muir, in his annotation to this line[5] states that it refers to the Last Judgment. There is no doubt in my mind that this is one meaning, but as so often, Shakespeare uses words and lines with more than one meaning. Therefore, we must agree that on one level Kent's question indicates that seeing Lear with dead Cordelia in his arms is for him the most terrible thing that can happen. It is Doomsday, as predicted by the Prophets. He sees it as the Final Judgment of God, His final and irrevocable judgment on Lear. On another level, I believe that Kent's question also refers to Shakespeare's final solution. What is the meaning of Lear's vast and profound suffering? Edgar's response in the form of a question, "Or image of that horror?" certainly proves that he understands it as the Last Judgment, and Albany's exclamation, "Fall and cease!" indicates that for Albany too this means the end of the universe. I believe, however, that Shakespeare also intended this question to mean: "Is this the final state?"—the ripeness which Lear is intended to achieve?

Lear, however, pays no attention to his friends. His unfathomable anguish sees nothing but dead Cordelia. For a moment he believes that she lives;

> This feather stirs; she lives! If it be so,   (V.iii.267)
> It is a chance which does redeem all sorrows
> That ever I have felt.

Kent attempts to break the magic circle that surrounds Lear and Cordelia. Kneeling before Lear, he addresses him as always: "O my good master!" Lear feels Kent's approach as an intrusion, as an act which destroys his last chance to save Cordelia:

> I might have sav'd her; now she's gone forever!   (V.iii.272)

—and reports:

> I kill'd the slave that was a-hanging thee.   (V.iii.276)

[5] Arden, p. 215.

Now Kent has a chance to reveal his true identity as Lear's servant Caius. He can tell Lear that his two eldest daughters "desperately are dead." It makes no impression on Lear because Cordelia is his whole world now and nothing else matters. Both Albany and Edgar misunderstand Lear's seeming unconcern and consider it as a symptom of his mental derangement. Ironically, Albany reacts to the message of Edmund's death, which is brought in a moment later, with the same indifference:

> That's but a trifle here.   (V.iii.298)

Then he formally acknowledges Lear as King and promises justice to "friends" and "foes." He turns to Lear with the words:

> O, see, see!   (V.iii.306)

Lear then speaks:

> And my poor fool is hanged!   (V.iii.307)

This speech has again very strongly the quality of a monologue, although toward the end of it he addessses somebody. As it turns out, this is Lear's last speech, and it has been the source of much controversy. The majority of commentators believe that the line, "My poor fool is hanged!" refers to Cordelia alone, and that "my poor fool" is a term of endearment. Kenneth Muir quotes the following comments:[6]

> Sir Joshua Reynolds thought Lear was referring to the Fool. Brandl, Quiller-Couch and Edith Sitwell have argued that the two parts of Cordelia and the Fool were taken by the same actor; but Thaler, T.L.S. 13 Feb. 1930, shows that the parts could not have been doubled. Perrett points out that 'when Cordelia is away her place as the representative of utter truthfulness is taken by the Fool. In this respect the two characters are one.' And Empson, while pointing out that the assumption that Lear is referring to the Fool must be wrong because in the

[6] Arden, p. 217.

rest of the speech he is obviously talking about Cordelia, remarks, following Bradley, 'that his mind has wandered so far that he no longer distinguishes the two . . . Lear is now thrown back into something like the storm phase of his madness, the effect of immediate shock, and the Fool seems to him part of it. The only affectionate dependent he had recently has been hanged and the only one he had then was the Fool.'

W. W. Lloyd says:[7]

I have no doubt that Shakespeare intended the Fool should be remembered in Lear's last exclamation, though no more may be meant than that in his wandering state he confuses the image of the Fool with that of his daughter in his arms.

Sir Joshua Reynolds, however, thought the term refers to the Fool alone:[8]

I confess I am one of those who *have thought* that Lear means his Fool, and not Cordelia. If he means Cordelia, then what I have always considered as a beauty, is of the same kind as the accidental stroke of the pencil that produced the form. Lear's affectionate remembrance of the Fool, in this place, I used to think, was one of those strokes of genius, or of nature, which are so often found in Shakespeare, and in him only.

In my opinion, it belongs to the group of fused images such as Goneril with the "white beard." The intense emotion and the weakness due to approaching death would make it quite possible for such a fusion to occur. It would mean then that the image of the Fool and that of Cordelia are united into one: the image of a male figure and that of a female, that is, a pair of opposites have become one. While in the prison fantasy Lear imagined himself eternally united with the anima, that is, the ego with the anima, in this final scene the union of a male with a female occurs as an image in the non-ego. The ego is here an emotionally absorbed

[7] Variorum, p. 347.
[8] Variorum, p. 345.

observer. Thus the coniunctio occurs *within* him. This is followed by his full awareness that what he holds in his arms is
absolutely dead, and life will never return to this body.

At this moment, death approaches and, like a man suffering
from a coronary attack and feeling great difficulty in breathing,
Lear says:

> Pray you, undo this button: thank you, sir.　　　　　(V.iii.311)

The Shakespeare Survey, Vol. 13, 1960,[9] devotes nine essays
to *King Lear,* two of which are directly concerned with Lear's
last speech and thus with the meaning of the whole play. "Lear's
Last Speech" is the title of an essay by J. K. Walton. "The Catharsis of King Lear," J. Stampfer's paper, derives all its existen-
tialist conclusions from the final speech. W. M. T. Nowottny's
article, "Some Aspects of the Style of King Lear," while dealing
only tangentially with this speech, helps in understanding the
particular brilliance of it. Miss Nowottny states as her "final
suggestion":

> . . . a contrast of dimension is a characteristic of the play's
> tragic vision: surely it hardly needs saying that the heartbreak
> of the very last scene is in the contrast between infinite concern
> and the finiteness of its object; put into words, it is all hope and
> all despair divided by the down of a feather: 'This feather stirs:
> she lives! it if be so,/It is a chance which does redeem all sor-
> rows/That ever I have felt.'

Walton compares Lear's last speech with the ending of *Macbeth* and quotes the lines of Albany:

> All friends shall taste　　　　　　　　　　　　(V.iii.302-4)
> The wages of their virtue, and all foes
> The cup of their deserving.

as an ending which might be adequate for a play like *Macbeth.*
In Walton's opinion:

[9] Edited by Allardyce Nicoll (Cambridge University Press, London).

An ending of this kind may be adequate for, say, *Macbeth* . . . but for this play it will not do. It is Lear himself who in his last speech and death demonstrate its inadequacy. . . . If we take it that Lear finally believes that Cordelia is alive, we alter the direction of the whole movement which has been taking place throughout the play, a movement by which he attains to an ever greater consciousness and eventually becomes the agent who brings about an enlargement of the consciousness of others; and we are also guilty of confusing together Lear and the evil characters, for it is especially they who remain incapable of adequately assessing events.

Walton pays great attention to Cordelia's voice and lips:

Cordelia's lips might, by a change in colour, give a sign of death but hardly one of life; and it is appropriate that Lear's attention should be finally concentrated on her organ of speech. At the beginning of the play she says nothing, but this time Lear dies with the effort of realizing to the full the implications of her silence. That, and not merely despair, brings about his death.

I agree with Walton's criticism of Bradley's conception and that of William Empson:

We should remember that Bradley's interpretation of Lear's last speech finds its logical development in the view proposed by William Empson, who regards Lear in the last scene as mad again, and as, finally, the eternal fool and scapegoat who has experienced everything and learned nothing. This is an interpretation which makes it difficult to regard *King Lear* as a tragedy at all.

Walton emphasizes in general terms the principal concern that I have tried to outline in specifics:

Moreover, it is only by bearing in mind the active role of Lear's progress towards knowledge that we can see the later part of the play as having a convincing dramatic form.

The only question is: "Which is the highest knowledge that Lear attains?" Walton does not state it specifically. All he really says is that

> . . . this time Lear dies with the effort of realizing to the full the implications of her silence.

He finds that:

> The extent of his consciousness, as well as of his sufferings, is emphasized in the concluding speech: 'The oldest hath borne most: we that are young/ Shall never see so much, nor live so long.'

Jennens comments that these "two last lines as they stand are silly and false." [10] Although I cannot agree, I do feel that the lines fail to describe in any way the extent of Lear's consciousness, but rather what consciousness has been generated in Edgar (or possibly Albany).

In Ingeborg Gurland's dissertation, referred to earlier, she quotes Gundolf as follows:

> Just as he (Albany) remained Chorus throughout the play, the poet has also used him as Epilogue, who impartially speaks the final word over this field of wreckage, a respectable funeral oration, but far remote from essence and meaning of death.

Miss Gurland says that, in her opinion,

> Albany's lines rather point once again to this life of Lear, who has taken upon himself the mystery of things. It is a deed of such extraordinary dimension as mankind will hardly ever again fulfill in one human life. ('We . . . shall never see so much, nor live so long.')

Miss Gurland's conclusion—that Albany is, as it were, aware of the size of Lear's consciousness—is certainly quite possible, but

---

[10] Variorum, p. 350.

this does not in any way describe its quality or its particular meaning. In order to do this we must study Lear's last speech in context with his whole development.

Stampfer's article goes very thoroughly into this problem. His understanding of the last speech is based on a total view of *King Lear*. I quote here some characteristic lines to indicate the scope of his vision:[11]

> But society, in Shakespeare, is now no longer capable of self-renewal. And so the counter-movement of the play, the re-clothing of Lear, by charity and natural law, with majesty, sanity, family and shelter, after the most terrible of penances, does not close the play. At its close, the completion only of its dramatic 'middle,' Lear is utterly purged of soul, while the hierarchy of society is reduced, as at the end of *Hamlet*, to an equation of 'court news' with 'gilded butterflies' (V.iii.13-14). At this point, if the universe of the play contained a transcendent providence, it should act as in the closing movement of *Hamlet*, mysteriously to redeem a society unable to redeem itself. Shakespeare's pessimism, however, has deepened since *Hamlet*, and the deaths to no purpose of Lear and Cordelia controvert any providential redemption in the play's decisive, closing movement, so that another resolution entirely is called for. Narrowing our problem somewhat, the catharsis of any play lies in the relationship of the denouement to the expectations set up in the play's 'middle.'

He continues, giving a description of the middle movement as he sees it:

> In *King Lear*, this middle movement has to do primarily with Lear's spiritual regeneration after his 'stripping' in the opening movement of the play. These two movements can be subsumed in a single great cycle, from hauteur and spiritual blindness through purgative suffering to humility and spiritual vision, a cycle that reaches its culmination in Lear's address of consolation to Cordelia before they are taken off to prison (V.iii.9-17).

[11] *Shakespeare Survey*, pp. 8-9.

Although consolation is certainly intended by Lear, the imagery he uses points to the truly religious intent of the play.

Stampfer continues:

> *The catharsis of King Lear would seem to lie, then, in the challenge of Lear's subsequent death to the penance and spiritual transcendence that culminates the play's second movement.*

In describing this "challenge," Stampfer gives a long and philosophical description of what he thinks man's fundamental relationship to society is. He overlooks completely that this is his own conception and need not be Shakespeare's understanding of human nature at all. The sentence:

> *The notion of intelligible reward and punishment, whether formulated as a theological doctrine and called retributive justice or as a psychological doctrine and called the reality principle, is as basic to human nature as the passions themselves.*

reveals Stampfer's own psychological type to be that of an extravert, that is, he derives all libido from the external object—in this case, society. This psychological type, as we know from Jung,[12] is inclined to neglect or disregard the inner subjects, the world of eternal images or, as Jung calls them, the archetypes. Shakespeare as a poet was certainly related to the world of inner images, although certainly not exclusively. His plays quite regularly, and to a large extent, use archetypes and archetypal patterns. It is one of the reasons for their universal appeal. *King Lear,* to repeat, uses for example the archetype of the hostile brothers. Lear's three daughters distinctly reveal the characteristic aspects of the archetype of the anima. In speaking of the "notion of intelligible reward and punishment . . ." Stampfer betrays the prejudice of the extravert for whom theological doctrine is only an epiphenomenon, a rationalization. This viewpoint does not accept the psyche and her imagery as a phenome-

---

[12] *Psychological Types* (Routledge & Kegan Paul, Ltd., London, 1923).

non *sui generis*. As I have tried to demonstrate, the essential point in Lear's development is that he moves from certain pagan doctrines through suffering and spiritual regeneration to an inner experience of God—from:

> . . . by the sacred radiance of the sun,   (I.i.111)
> The mysteries of Hecate and the night,
> By all the operation of the orbs
> From whom we do exist and cease to be.

to:

> And take upon's the mystery of things,   (V.iii.16)
> As if we were God's spies.

It is therefore not astonishing to see that Stampfer views Lear's end with utter pessimism. His concluding thesis on the catharsis in *King Lear* is as follows:

By the time he enters prison, he has paid every price and been stripped of everything a man can lose, even his sanity, in payment for folly and pride. He stands beyond the veil of fire, momentarily serene and live. As such he activates an even profounder fear than the fear of failure, and that is the fear that whatever penance a man may pay may not be enough once the machinery of destruction has been let loose, because the partner of his covenant may be neither grace nor the balance of the law, but malignity, intransigence or chaos. The final, penultimate tragedy of Lear, then is not the tragedy of *hubris,* but the tragedy of penance. When *Lear,* the archetype not of a proud but of a penitential man, brutally dies, then the uttermost that can happen to man has happened. One can rationalize a passing pedestrian struck down by a random automobile; there is no blanching from his death. Each audience harbours this anxiety in moments of guilt and in acts of penance. And with Lear's death, each audience, by the ritual of the drama, shares and releases the most private and constricting fear to which mankind is subject, the fear that penance is impossible, that the covenant, once broken, can never be reestablished, because its partner has no charity, resilience, or harmony—the fear, in other words, that we inhabit an imbecile universe. It is by this vision of reality that Lear lays down his life for his folly. Within its bounds lies the catharsis of Shakespeare's profoundest tragedy.

I must therefore part company with Stampfer in his final understanding of the play. I do not believe that the text of Lear's last speech justifies Stampfer's description of the catharsis: that this vision of reality for which Lear lays down his life is a folly and that "within its bounds lies . . . Shakespeare's profoundest tragedy."

D. G. James's analysis of *King Lear* in his valuable book, *The Dream of Learning*,[13] adds some important contributions. He talks at length about the "vagueness of temporal and spatial characteristics in the play." He emphasizes how much of character and plot must be carved away. He does not see this as a weakness of the play but as a necessity to express more strongly Shakespeare's intention. To quote:[14]

> Now if we think so, we shall not put down these things I have spoken of as mere faults; and we shall be no more disposed to shrug our shoulders, to leave them for a mystery, to take a note of them and leave a question-mark after them. They were, we must suppose, integral to Shakespeare's intention when he wrote the play; they must become integral to ours when we read it or see it. Shakespeare will not allow us to imagine Cordelia in the human context of wifehood and queenship; he also will not allow the goodness of Edgar and Kent the comfort they may give and receive in the world's conflict.

All these so-called weaknesses, as he also states, give the play the quality of a fairy-story and help us to understand the main point of his book, which is that many of Shakespeare's plays, and particularly this one, were tools in his quest for knowledge, that *King Lear* represents

[13] Oxford University Press, London, 1951.
[14] *Ibid.,* pp. 108, 121, 124-125.

a candid exploration of our human experience. . . . It exhibits the limits merely of our human experience as they are reached by souls of surpassing excellence and beauty.

His comparison with Bacon's understanding of knowledge is very valuable and sets it up clearly against Shakespeare's method:

Shakespeare turned his mind principally to human nature. . . . each play is a symbol of his vision of life; he is concerned, in the way of a poet, to make manifest the truth of things; and as he goes on, the symbols become more expressive and less translatable; more and more they render their great object as it really is.

But when we come to the idea of the ultimate meaning of *King Lear,* James is strangely disappointing:

I have used *King Lear* to exhibit Shakespeare now dealing boldly and even violently with his material in order that he may thereby see more clearly. And what in *King Lear* does he chiefly see? Evil certainly, from which he promises the world no escape; but also, and principally, the wholly good, suffering indeed, but also altogether proof against all that is brought against it. This suffering he savagely surrounds with all that evil and mischance can bring; but it never declines from its standards of complete disinterestedness. To exhibit this, Shakespeare has dealt hardly with his story; and for my part, I cannot doubt that he has dealt thus hardly with his material in order, at all costs, to communicate beyond doubt the perception of values to which he has now come. *King Lear* is, so far, if you will, didactic. I only add that he is not here letting his emotions rip; we shall be more disposed to say that he is rendering life as it really is; here, we shall say, is the truth and secret of things. It is, indeed, a painful enough secret; we behold it in the hanging of Cordelia by the world's wickedness; or rather, we behold it in the life and death of Cordelia, who could truly say: 'For thee, oppressed King, am I cast down;/Myself could else out-frown false fortune's frown.' The father of whom she speaks is the father of Goneril as well as of herself; and he has stumbled his way through the storm from Goneril to her. This is what Shakespeare finally saw in his greatest play; and this perception is his great bequest to us.

Accepting James's statement that *King Lear* is essentially a fairy-story (the simplicity of the characters, the de-emphasis of plot in favor of psychological development and the transformation of Lear—and particularly in the imagery) we are compelled to see this play as a dramatization of *inner* events, that is, a continuous confrontation of the ego with inner psychological factors, and not a confrontation of man with society. The question Hamlet asked, "What is man?" is answered by Lear in a very different way. *King Lear* is truly a dramatization of Shakespeare's own process of individuation. The ego, attached to the outside world—and ruling it—is step by step deprived of all it possesses, and finally even of the beloved daughter. Then, when life has definitely left Cordelia's body, he sees something:

> Do you see this? Look on her! look! her lips!   (V.iii.312)
> Look there, look there!

We are not told what he sees but it can only be a vision which is projected on her and in which her lips move in some way. It is the same psychological fusion of an inner image with a concrete object as when, awakening from sleep, he had addressed Cordelia: "Thou art a soul in bliss" (IV.vii.46). Since he is completely concentrated on her being dead, the emphasis on her "lips" suggests to me that in this fantasy image of Cordelia-Fool, the lips possibly speak—at any rate, come to life. Please notice that it is the image and not the actual Cordelia he is observing. Considering that, in the prison fantasy, his exaltation was due to an anticipated eternal life with Cordelia, I can only conclude that at this moment the image of the coniunctio has come to life. A vision of transcendental impact lights up and floods him. This is the secret of the play. At the moment of death, the coniunctio occurs and in this vision Lear perceives *ultimate truth,* achieves *full consciousness,* and thus experiences

see p 318 for meaning of the coniunctio.

redemption. This is the fruit of his suffering, this the "ripeness," the end Shakespeare promised us.

It has been emphasized in many comments that the ending of this play is most unsatisfactory and that the speeches of Edgar, Kent and Albany give only half-hearted restitution. This is true, particularly if one compares the ending of this play with those of *Hamlet* and *Macbeth*. Fortinbras will reestablish order, and so will Malcolm, after the death of the tyrant. Albany can only say: "Our present business is general woe," and ask his two friends to sustain the "gored state." Edgar somehow repeats the same tune: "The weight of this sad time we must obey." D. G. James mentions that if Kent's two last lines have any meaning at all, they would indicate that he anticipates an early death.

We can only conclude that Albany and Edgar have not understood what has happened to Lear at the last, and that Shakespeare wanted to express their inadequate comprehension. It did not matter to Shakespeare, as James shows clearly, what happened before the play began, and very little what happened afterwards. It is only Kent who properly understands what happens to Lear at the moment of his death. Kent says:

> Vex not his ghost. O, let him pass! He hates him   (V.iii.316)
> That would upon the rack of this tough world
> Stretch him out longer.

He is the only one who knows that Lear has had a vision of the inner world. He therefore rejects Albany's request to "rule in this realm." He wants no part in the kingdoms of the world. He knows of the Kingdom of God which Lear has seen at the very last. Therefore, he wants to go on this *inner* "journey" which Lear has taken before him:

> I have a journey, sir, shortly to go.   (V.iii.323)
> My master calls me; I must not say no.

Again, D. G. James is certainly correct when he writes:[15]

[15] *Ibid.*, pp. 91-93.

Renaissance drama was, by and large, created and sustained by men whose imaginations, as shown in their writings at least, were free of any religious prepossessions. Drama had in all truth moved out of the Church; it had undertaken its own exploration of human life which owed little, in its spirit, to the Church's teaching. . . . It is true, no doubt, that their moral values could not have been what they were, had they not been reared in a Christian country . . . But however that may be, on the evidence of the plays themselves, and of these only we can speak confidently, these men clearly did not think as Christians. . . . When we look especially at Shakespeare, all this remains, I think, true. . . . What I wish to emphasize is that Shakespeare, in devising his version of the story, carefully declined to give it anything approaching a Christian setting: he puts the story back, where it had always earlier belonged, in a remote Celtic past; and the gods of the play become Apollo and Jupiter. . . . What seems certain is that it was Shakespeare's fully conscious decision not to give to the story any fraction of a Christian context. The play's action is terrible in all conscience; but there is no crumb of Christian comfort in it.

This is true on a superficial level. Shakespeare tried to avoid all Christian context—but I believe the play is essentially Christian in attitude and experience. It parallels Christ's own suffering, despair on the cross, and final resurrection on the level of a human being. This parallel, I feel, is of the greatest importance. It is not an *imitatio Christi*. It is an experience of the cross of an ordinary human being. Lear did not take up Christ's cross, but his own. Shakespeare is not explicit, but gives sufficient hints for us to understand Lear's final redemption.

To a certain extent, Miss Ingeborg Gurland's dissertation helps us to understand these hints. She illustrates the dramatic structure of *King Lear* with a diagram,[16] comparing it with that of *Richard III*. Seeing the structure of both dramas side by side emphasizes her point—that *King Lear* is a *Seelendrama*. The diagram presents the five acts in sequence from left to right. A strong horizontal bar divides the play into an upper and a lower sphere. The upper sphere is called the sphere of the human order

[16] *Op. cit.,* p. 8.

of consciousness, the lower the sphere of "all those powers which are situated beyond consciousness: madness and death." Furthermore, there is an equally strong vertical bar passing between Scene 4 and Scene 5 of Act III. This indicates the climax of the play. Thus a cross is established.

I would prefer to call these two "spheres" of Miss Gurland "Consciousness" and "the Unconscious," using these terms in the sense employed by C. G. Jung.

In her commentary, Miss Gurland writes:

> What is important and decisive for the inner law of the *Lear* drama is that for Shakespeare the limit of human consciousness is not at the same time the limit of dramatic possibilities, that is, the drama does not end after Lear has passed through this first sphere, but there is a transition into the unknown sphere of madness, and the whole second part of the drama puts this second sphere on the stage. The transition from one sphere into the other occurs for Lear in the middle of the third act.

As indicated before, I cannot quite agree with Gurland's interpretation of madness. I believe that unconscious elements arise in Lear much earlier than the third act. I do not find helpful those assumptions that Lear, when holding Cordelia in his arms, becomes temporarily mad—that within a short span of time he walks in and out of insanity.

But I do find Miss Gurland's division very useful. I prefer to call the change in Lear's consciousness a process of continuing and intensifying introversion. It began in the first talks with the Fool. It is true, however, that with the hovel scene in the third act, the introversion is complete. Lear's monologue ("Blow wind. . . .") represents an inner discussion with the gods. At that point the introversion assumes a totally different character than it had in the first two acts.

I would prefer to add to this diagram one line which would represent Lear's development of consciousness. It would begin at the lower left end, indicating a stage of extreme unconsciousness. It would steadily rise during Act II, closely approach the horizontal line in Act II and cross it in the middle of Scene 4 of Act III. It would then rise and reach its highest point (the point of highest consciousness) shortly before the end of Act V (V.iii.312: "Do you see this? Look on her, look. . . ."). Seeing the development of Lear's consciousness in this concise, graphic manner, one is forced to assume that Shakespeare's intention could only be that Lear experience the highest level of consciousness at the very end. A catastrophic drop of consciousness at the end would make no sense. A further advantage of seeing these two lines is that they illustrate the acme of tragedy: the highest point of consciousness is reached at the moment of death.

Conclusion

Looking back, we are now in a position to describe more clearly the difference between the poem of *Job* and the tragedy of *King Lear*. We stated in the beginning that the drama of *Job* occurs in Job's soul and that there are no external dramatic events once the situation of extreme suffering is established. A long series of discussions is suddenly and unaccountably ended by an invasion of the unconscious with a tremendous vision in which God reveals Himself to Job and demonstrates His immeasurable power. Job continues to live and, in recompense for his suffering, "the Lord gave Job twice as much as he had before."

In Lear we have an essentially egocentric man who, by his own mistake, resigning his ego power, is exposed to continuously increasing suffering. While in the beginning the gods were more or less "names," his experiences force him to know himself and therewith the reality of the unconscious and the terrible aspect of the gods. The intensity of the inner process separates him from outer reality to such an extent that to outsiders his condition appears as madness. In his continuing experience, even the gods vanish before the dawn of God-consciousness, and at the moment of greatest suffering a vision of God occurs, the nature of which is mysteriously veiled.

Job's redemption occurs when he can say, "I know that my Redeemer liveth": the direct revelation of God is also the redemption. Lear experiences the power of the gods, or even of God, which brings about a certain amount of healing. His redemption occurs at the moment of death, at the moment of greatest suffering, through an inner vision. His vision evidently goes beyond Job's. Shakespeare gives us only hints of what this vision is: a coming to life of the soul and a union at the moment of death. It is only in later plays that Shakespeare deals more extensively with the questions left unanswered by Lear's vision in death. In *Cymbeline, The Winter's Tale* and *The Tempest,* the archetype of the coniunctio is the central theme.

Macbeth's

DESCENT INTO HELL
AND DAMNATION

Introduction

Macbeth has always been considered one of Shakespeare's greatest plays. In it his questing mind reached a further dimension, revealed mysteries of the soul, touched upon problems of humanity for which man has yet to find a valid answer. Our progressive age, so bent upon achieving universal freedom, has had to discover that it has produced many and monstrous tyrants. The conditions of chaos, conflict, bloodshed and war, which make cruel dictators possible, occur again and again, and free men have to take up arms to rid themselves of such monsters and to reestablish tolerable social conditions. In *Macbeth*, Shakespeare could so describe this sickness of the human soul, and with such great poetry, that mankind, for its own healing, has had to confront itself with this play again and again. It is only natural that *Macbeth* was the first play to be performed on the German stage after the armistice in 1945.

It is just as natural that with the discovery of the unconscious, modern depth psychologists were particularly attracted to *Macbeth*. Freud himself was among the first who made illuminating, though brief, comments on it. More recently Dr. David B. Barron, in an outstanding article,[1] made quite remarkable observations about *Macbeth* and considerably advanced its deeper understanding. Great and helpful as his contribution was, it was limited, especially because he did not differentiate between the personal and the collective unconscious.

In this study I am particularly interested in three interrelated subjects: the relationship between consciousness and the collective unconscious; the effect of the feminine on Macbeth; and Macbeth's development into a tyrant and his subsequent destruction.

The collective unconscious is represented here almost completely by the Three Witches, and to that degree appears to be identical with the feminine. However, in Act IV, Scene 1 (63), we hear that these Witches have "masters," so that the metaphysical realm, or the collective unconscious, is not described as totally feminine. On the other hand, the feminine plays a decisive role on the *human* level in the person of Lady Macbeth. She has strong parallels with the Witches. Macbeth's development into a tyrant is of course intimately connected with the first two themes. For a clear analysis it might be better to discuss each of these three themes separately, going through the play as it were three times, but it would be a cumbersome procedure. I prefer to go through the play once, discussing the themes and the different stages of their development as they appear. I believe that in this way the living tissue of the play will be seen distinctly. After all, emphasizing these three themes is a method of grasping the life in this miraculous play, of becoming conscious of the problems which Shakespeare's imagination has taken up there.

---

[1] "The Babe that Milks: An Organic Study of *Macbeth*," *The American Imago*, Vol. 17, No. 2 (1960).

Act One

i

It is of great significance that the beginning of this play presents a scene in which three witches appear. Thus, like a somber gong, the tone of the whole play is struck. As in a dream, the opening scene announces the theme. This happens in most of Shakespeare's dramas, as for example when the Ghost in *Hamlet,* appearing in the first scene, conveys the essential influence and atmosphere of death and the world of the dead. In *Macbeth,* the characteristic atmosphere of the play is accomplished by the appearance of the Three Witches with thunder and lightning. They have a function similar to the prologue in heaven in the book of *Job.* There the problem originates in heaven, but affects the human realm. Job's suffering and his final redemption are due to his individual response to events in heaven. In *Macbeth* the Witches inform us of what is going on in the superhuman realm. It is they who plan the meeting with Macbeth and the drama and its tragic solution are the consequences of his response to these transcendental powers. The Witches are not a personal feature of Macbeth's psychology. They represent the psychic condition of Scotland. Only after we have learned about the "metaphysical" condition of Scotland do we hear about her physical condition. Scotland has been invaded by a foreign army and is threatened by treason and inner rebellion.

In his *Explorations,*[1] Knights goes further when he declares:

> Each theme of the play is stated in the first act. The first scene, every word of which will bear the closest scrutiny, strikes one dominant chord.

He suggests that

> the word hurly-burly implies more than the tumult of insurrection. Both it and 'When the Battaile's lost, and wonne' sug-

[1] L. C. Knights (Chatto & Windus, London, 1946), p. 18.

gest the kind of metaphysical pitch-and-toss which is about to be played with good and evil.

Meta-physical (literally, that which is beyond the physical) refers to something which is beyond consciousness, that is, unconscious. I therefore prefer to use Jung's term, the *unconscious*. The area of the unconscious in which this "hurly-burly" takes place is that of the *collective unconscious*. Whichever term is used—metaphysical or unconscious—Shakespeare clearly means to say that the drama begins in a non-human realm. This "metaphysical pitch-and-toss" is to be played with good and evil. Evil is to be hurled at a particular human being, and the victim will be an entire country.

The Witches determine the time:

> When the hurlyburly's done,   (I.i.3)
> When the battle's lost and won.
> That will be ere the set of sun.

The place:

> Upon the heath.

And the conditions:

> Fair is foul, and foul is fair;
> Hover through the fog and filthy air.

It is they who decide upon whom they will settle: "there to meet with Macbeth."

In brief, the first scene gives a vivid description of the Scottish psyche at that time. The unconscious is in upheaval. Destructive feminine forces are at work, which choose Macbeth as their victim. This agrees very well with the frequent observation in psychological work that when an archetype, that is, a living content of the collective unconscious, is activated, it appears in the unconscious of many people at the same time, disturbs all of them, but seeks one or a few individuals in whom to make its appearance in consciousness. What happens as a result of this invasion depends on the attitude of the individual. He might become a sayoshant, a prophet, a poet, a neurotic, a psychotic, a tyrant or a criminal. It is this individual victim who then suffers most, who carries the burden of collective guilt or becomes the speaker for new knowledge and new attitudes. Here in *Macbeth,* the Witches are mainly destructive. They seek an individual who is constitutionally most open to their influence. We must therefore expect that unless the victim understands them and knows how to integrate them fate will destroy him in one way or another.

The effect of all this unconscious activity is:

> Fair is foul, and foul is fair; (I.i.11)
> Hover through the fog and filthy air.

All values become indistinct, lose their meaning or even become opposite values. What they produce is not just a reversal of values, as Knights says,[2] but a disturbance and blurring ("fog") of all values and a moral defilement ("filthy air") of the psychological atmosphere.

This brief scene, which presents three witches and no equivalent masculine figures, illuminates like lightning the terrifying psychic condition of Scotland at that time. The feminine is in the ascendancy. The destructive aspect is grimly emphasized. The masculine exists only in diminished and reduced form. The very appearance of the witches blurs the feeling function ("fair is foul . . ."). Where they appear, all moral values will become questionable. It will no longer be possible to distinguish clearly between good and evil. Good might seem to be evil, and evil good. Thus the soil and the climate are made ready to confuse weak man and lead him into temptation.

ii

The second scene brings us down to earth, where we hear what is going on in the human realm. Indeed, a chaotic condition prevails in Scotland. Our expectation that the collective conscious-

---

[2] The Arden edition of *Macbeth,* p. 5.

ness is as much in uproar as the unconscious (as the Witches had led us to believe) is immediately fulfilled. Blood is mentioned in the very first line: "What bloody man is that?" We hear of a "revolt," a battle, a "damned quarrel." Macbeth is mentioned for the first time when the Sergeant tells the King of his "knowledge of the broil":

> For brave Macbeth,—well he deserves that name,—   (I.ii.16)
> Disdaining fortune, with his brandish'd steel,
> Which smok'd with bloody execution,
> Like valour's minion carv'd out his passage
> Till he fac'd the slave;
> Which ne'er shook hands, nor bade farewell to him,
> Till he unseam'd him from the nave to the chaps,
> And fix'd his head upon our battlements.

The style of these lines is so unusual that an outstanding Shakespearean scholar like Cunningham has called it a "corrupt piece of bombast," not wholly Shakespearean. Nosworthy, however, has defended it on literary grounds.[3] From a psychological point of view this somewhat stilted style is exceedingly apt for characterizing the intense state of conflict of collective consciousness, and Macbeth's profound involvement in it. Macbeth's martial conduct and the Witches' conclave belong together. Surely he is brave and successful indeed. Yet the quality of his courage seems strange; it is not cool and superior. Macbeth is drunk with fighting, blood and killing. Although his action was skillful and successful, the Sergeant's story conveys the extraordinary emotion which carries Macbeth and inspires him to commit superhuman deeds of valor. His state of mind reminds us of wars as they are fought in primitive societies. There, warriors are completely possessed by a war mood, a mood which has been induced by a *rite d'entrée,* and which can give way to a more peaceful condition only if an adequate *rite de sortie* is performed. In primitive societies such rites are a necessity because of the weakness of the ego and the lack of differentiation of

3 *Ibid.,* pp. 5-6.

consciousness. In *Macbeth* we never hear of such rites, but war and battle ring throughout the whole play. The lines quoted show that Macbeth is drunk with fighting. He and Banquo are both possessed *by* this tremendous fighting mood ("like valour's minion carv'd out his passage"), rather than being in possession of it.

Some of the images with which the intensity of the battle is characterized are the same as those used in the Witches' scene (the Witches met in "thunder, lightning, or in rain"—I.i.2; the Sergeant speaks of "shipwracking storms and direful thunders" —I.ii.26). There is no let-up. When the rebels seemed to be defeated, a foreign enemy had entered the battle:

> . . . the Norweyan lord surveying vantage, (I.ii.31)
> With furbish'd arms and new supplies of men
> Began a fresh assault.

This new situation did not discourage Macbeth and Banquo. On the contrary, against all expectations, their fighting intensity only increased. The images which the Sergeant uses in his report portray most vividly the growing intensification of Macbeth's and Banquo's activity:

> As cannons overcharg'd with double cracks; (I.ii.37)
> So they
> Doubly redoubled strokes upon the foe;
> Except they meant to bathe in reeking wounds,
> Or memorize another Golgotha.

The first image points to an almost unbelievable explosiveness, the second emphasizes the goriness of the battle, and the last image most unexpectedly calls up a powerful religious associ-ation: Golgotha, "a place of a skull" (Matthew 27:33), the place of Jesus' crucifixion. It is as if the country itself were on the cross, suffering tremendously, bleeding from many wounds. But the last image promises ultimate salvation. Macbeth's and Banquo's superhuman deeds bring victory and save Scotland from further rebellion and foreign occupation. Physically, the two generals are unhurt, but the furious fighting has inflicted deep wounds upon their souls. No *rite de sortie* is ever performed and so the war mood continues to possess them. Can this bloody mood, this intensely activated unconscious, depart from these two men and, if so, with what result?

It is at this point that the Sergeant's wounds make further talk impossible. Ross, a Scottish Nobleman, enters and continues the story where the Sergeant left off. His report adds a new element. Lennox remarks on his appearance: "So should he look that seems to speak strange things." Ross relates how the foreign invader, Norway, was "assisted by that most disloyal traitor, the Thane of Cawdor." But, nevertheless, says Ross, "the victory fell on us." He calls Macbeth "Bellona's bridegroom." Bellona was a Roman goddess of war whose temple was in the Campus Martius, near the altar of Mars. Instinctively Shakespeare chose the term, "Bellona's bridegroom," to describe Macbeth's identity with the anima. If Macbeth is married to Bellona, that is, completely possessed by the war mood, can he possibly divorce himself from her? What significance can Duncan's decision to transfer the Thane of Cawdor's title directly and immediately upon Macbeth have upon such an impressionable man? Duncan's line, with which this scene ends, indicates that what the Thane of Cawdor has lost, noble Macbeth has won. The irony and the double meaning contained in these lines has frequently been commented on. Is it possible that in the wild conditions of medieval Scotland Macbeth has received the treacherous character as well as the title of the Thane of Cawdor? Is it possible that the upheaval in Scotland requires a traitor as well as a king? Can one expect that a man who is "Bellona's bridegroom" will be able to resist involuntary suggestions such as Duncan expresses in this last line? Indeed, the title "Thane of Cawdor" is a dubious gift. It is no wonder that in the wounded state of Scotland some healing should be attempted and that the activated unconscious should try to contact some outstanding individual. Consciousness and the unconscious must meet in someone. The Witches said as much in the first scene.

iii

The Witches appear very soon again and, as in Scene 1, alone. This time the stage directions do not mention thunder, only lightning, yet it is enough to convey once more the uncanny character of the whole scene. It is only somewhat later that Macbeth and Banquo enter and meet the Witches. Only then is communication established between the metaphysical and human realms, with consciousness and the unconscious meeting for the first time.

The Witches' discussion, before the entrance of Macbeth and Banquo, is descriptive of their nature. In general, the feminine principle clearly carries the implication of fertility, creativity. Its positive aspect is that of the giver of life, as expressed for example in the giving of the Hebrew name Chavah, giver of life, to the mother of mankind in the Genesis story (3:20):

> And Adam called his wife's name Eve; because she was the mother of all living.

But, in contrast, in *Macbeth* the negative aspect of the mother—destruction, killing—is clearly expressed.

As in a genuine fairy tale, the Witches are not described as destructive in so many words, but their conversation about their activities tells us of their hostility to life. The Second Witch has just returned from "killing swine." The First Witch had tried to rob a sailor's wife of chestnuts (a symbol of fertility). She also tells how she will drain the sailor "dry as hay" and destroy his sleep, and although she cannot kill him the winds as her servants will drain all his strength: "Shall he dwindle, peak and pine." The stage direction in the Folio calls these three figures "Witches," but they refer to themselves as the "weyward Sisters"—"weyward" being pronounced weird.[4] The word comes

---

[4] Hilda M. Hulme, *Explorations in Shakespeare's Language* (Longmans, London, 1962), p. 236: "The Folio's spelling *weyward Sisters* in the earlier scenes of *Macbeth* (I.iii.32, I.v.8, II.i.20), in conjunction with their words 'faire is foule and foule is faire' (I.i.11), may give

from the Old English *wyrd,* M.E. *werd* (i.e., fate).[5] By calling them "weird Sisters," goddesses of destiny, rather than witches, we gain a different understanding of their function in the play. They are figures which to a large extent correspond in mythology to the Roman Parcae, the Greek Moirai, and the Germanic Norns. It is only natural that as such the Three Sisters soon tended to become negative; their dangerous character is spun out at great length. Therefore, the term "witch" is quite applicable. Yet we should not forget their archetypal and more neutral character, which the term "weird Sisters" preserves. We should also notice that their power is not absolute; they do not kill. The sailor ("master o' the Tiger") will only "dwindle, peak and pine."

> Though his bark cannot be lost, (I.iii.24)
> Yet it shall be tempest-tost.

Evidently the image of the "bark" had particular meaning for Shakespeare. It occurs in his Sonnet cxvi, also in close association with "tempest":

> (Love) is an ever-fixed mark,
> That looks on tempests, and is never shaken;
> It is the star to every wandering bark,
> Whose worth's unknown, although his height be taken.

To the poet, the bark symbolizes man's frail and uncertain consciousness in quest of meaning and wholeness in life. Here in *Macbeth,* it must carry the same significance. The Witches themselves emphasize the fact that in spite of tempests the bark

---

to the 'three Witches' a perverted eye and judgment . . . And if the 'perverted' eye is also 'perverting,' the 'three Witches' are ill-looked women in the Stratford sense."

[5] Holinshed, Arden, p. 178: ". . . these women were either the weird sisters, that is (as ye would say) the *goddesses of destiny,* or else some nymphs or feiries, indued with knowledge of prophesie by their necromanticall science, because euery thing came to passe as they had spoken."

(i.e., consciousness) cannot be lost. The "master o' the Tiger" would then indicate the ego as the representative of consciousness. In the violent upheaval of the unconscious, consciousness with its governing center will brave all dangers and maintain itself. Yet this Witch, who evidently let the "winds loose," possesses a "pilot's thumb," which would probably indicate man's willpower.

The power and strength of the unconscious appear to be very great. The scales are tipped in favor of the destructive forces. Everything will depend on the decision and action of the human being because, even in this dark hour, the individual human has a choice. The meeting of the "master o' the Tiger" with the "weyward Sisters" occurred in the unconscious. It is the prelude of such encounters with destructive feminine forces, describing many possibilities. But now the decisive step occurs; the potential descends into the world of reality; the Three Witches become visible to the two men.

It is Banquo who first notices them. They obviously appear very suddenly, as is characteristic of psychic phenomena. Banquo's startled questions reveal the incredible sight: they are unearthly beings ("look not like th' inhabitants o' the earth") yet they live on the earth; they are women yet they have beards. What are they? And can he communicate with them?

These two men are particularly open to the unconscious. In their psychological structure the threshold between consciousness and the unconscious is considerably lowered. This makes it possible for the unconscious contents to flow easily into consciousness. However, we never hear that Banquo has such psychic experiences again. For him, this vision is an exceptional occurrence. We may conjecture that the particular situation, the loneliness and the eerie atmosphere of the Scottish heath, facilitates this interplay between consciousness and the unconscious. The strongest reason for Banquo's awareness of the Witches is his closeness to Macbeth at the time. In fact, we know from the Sergeant's report (I.ii) that the two men were strongly identified. When such a *participation mystique* (Levy-Bruhl's term for psychological identity) exists, moods and emotions are quite contagious. It is the outstanding gift of Macbeth that throughout the play his fascination with the unconscious perseveres and that, after the first unsought encounter with the Witches, he can contact them almost at will. This fact characterizes him as an introvert-intuitive. Such strong affinity with the unconscious need not have negative results. Many prophets, seers, poets and artists of all kinds have had this psychology, in which there is no wall, or only thin transparent walls, between consciousness and the unconscious. I strongly believe that Shakespeare himself was such a man. In all such cases there always arises the problem of what the individual does with his revelations, how he interprets and integrates them in his life. In writing this play Shakespeare made himself very conscious of the inherent dangers of his own psychic constitution. My hunch is that the "dark woman" of the Sonnets is no real person but Shakespeare's direct experience of the dark aspect of the anima, whereas in writing *Macbeth* he could allow his imagination to run a course in which the anima would produce complete destruction.

Immediately following Banquo's questions, Macbeth addresses the Witches: "Speak, if you can." Like Banquo, he wants to hear something specific. But they do not answer the more important question of what they are. We should notice here that Macbeth's question is not, "Who are you?" but "What are you?"

In his *Aion,*[6] Jung quotes Gerhard Dorn and discusses the distinction between "who" and "what" at length:

> The objective knowledge of the self is what (Dorn) means when he says: "No one can know himself unless he knows *what,* and not *who,* he is (*quid, et non quis ipse sit*), on what he depends, or whose he is [or: to whom or what he belongs] and for what end he was made." The distinction between "quis" and "quid" is crucial: whereas "quis" has an unmistakably personal aspect and refers to the ego, "quid" is neuter, predicating

[6] Pp. 164-165.

nothing except an object which is not endowed even with personality. Not the subjective ego-consciousness of the psyche is meant, but the psyche itself as the unknown, unprejudiced object that still has to be investigated. The difference between knowledge of the ego and knowledge of the self could hardly be formulated more trenchantly than in this distinction between "quis" and "quid." An alchemist of the sixteenth century has here put his finger on something that certain psychologists (or those of them who allow themselves an opinion in psychological matters) still stumble over today. "What" refers to the neutral self, the objective fact of totality, since the ego is on the one hand causally "dependent on" or "belongs to" it, and on the other hand is directed towards it as to a goal.

The same difference between "quis" and "quid" exists here in *Macbeth* in regard to the weird Sisters. In asking, *"What* are you?" instead of *"Who* are you?" Macbeth inquires into the objective nature of the unconscious. To a degree, the audience knows what the Witches are because in preceding scenes they have described themselves to each other by their actions, but at no time in the play do they reveal their intrinsic nature to Macbeth. It should be his conscious task to discover their true nature in order to know and to appreciate their prophecies. The tragedy arises out of his misunderstanding, or perhaps it would be better to say his *limited* understanding, of their nature. In all his dealings with them he will submerge all his doubts and believe in their prophecies. He will reduce and simplify their capacities to nothing more than fortune-telling. This will captivate his mind and kindle his ambition into a darkly glowing fire. His inadequate understanding, his uncritical faith in the prophecies, and his attachment to temporal goods constitute the tragic flaw in his character. It is this weakness which makes him, the valiant hero of a battle, a helpless victim of the Witches' craft.

Let us return to the encounter of Macbeth and Banquo with the weird Sisters. Neither Banquo's question, "What are these, so withered, and so wild in their attire?" nor Macbeth's direct address, "What are you?" is ever answered. Instead the Three

Sisters exultantly shout (in words taken literally from Shakespeare's source, Holinshed):

FIRST WITCH: All hail, Macbeth! Hail to thee, Thane of Glamis! (I.iii.48)

SECOND WITCH: All hail, Macbeth! Hail to thee, Thane of Cawdor!

THIRD WITCH: All hail, Macbeth! that shalt be King hereafter!

For some time, ambition has been smoldering in Macbeth. He desires kingship. For this goal, thoughts of murder have already crossed his mind and have been exposed in intimate talks with his wife. Evil has lain buried in him as a seed, as it does in every human soul. The din of war and battle has nourished this grim ambition, but now that the Witches pronounce a glorious future, with all the temporal goods he has aspired to—evil, as it were, comes to life. Deep emotion almost suffocates him. He cannot utter a word. Only from Banquo's remarks do we know that the Witches' prophecy startles Macbeth and frightens him, although Banquo cannot know the reason for this reaction.

Banquo's approach to the Witches, his attitude and reactions to them, are totally different from Macbeth's. He maintains a royal, independent attitude, manifests an amazing emotional objectivity, even detachment, in the face of a sudden numinous experience. He is much more articulate than Macbeth in inquiring into the nature of the Witches: "Are ye fantastical . . . ?" Are they illusions or reality? He even describes his partner to the Witches:

> My noble partner (I.iii.54)
> You greet with present grace, and great prediction
> Of noble having, and of royal hope
> That he seems *rapt* withal.[7]

[7] Hulme, p. 237: "His word *wrapt* may contain more meaning than the usual modernisation 'rapt' would suggest: as well as having relation to the imagery of 'borrowed Robes' and 'strange Garments' which follows, it may imply also Banquo's later judgment: 'oftentimes, to winne us to our harme, the Instruments of Darknesse tell us Truths . . .' The word can mean 'entangled, caught,' or 'implicated'."

Yet Banquo also wants to know the future:

> If you can look into the seeds of time,   (I.iii.58)
> And say which grain will grow and which will not,
> Speak then to me, who neither beg nor fear
> Your favours nor your hate.

In full harmony with several of the principal themes of the play, *time* and *mother* occur in close association. Time is felt as a fertile womb, the Witches are supposed to know which seed will grow and which will not. Walter Clyde Curry,[8] in quoting Thomas Aquinas, demonstrates that in medieval conception

> . . . the demons know the future development of events conjecturally though not absolutely. They know the causes of things, in the sense that the *rationes seminales* may be called the causal virtues from which all things are created.

Still, it is a great step from these philosophical concepts and definitions to Shakespeare's greater vision of time as a primal mother, and the Witches as other forms of the same mother image—who knows which seed will become a reality, a historical fact, and which will not. The intuitive function of the anima, as symbolized by the Witches, is able to distinguish in the seed-stage which potential will materialize.

Banquo can proudly state that he "neither beg(s) nor fear(s) (their) favours nor (their) hate." He evidences a remarkable strength of ego, a freedom of mind born of guiltless conscience and an absence of boundless ambition. And yet he had been as much involved in the battle as Macbeth—or almost as much. Both were "as cannons overcharged with double cracks," but only Macbeth is especially called "brave" (I.ii.15), only he is called "Bellona's bridegroom." Undoubtedly, Macbeth has the weaker ego of the two and is correspondingly more possessed by the anima. Both have enough in common to be called "partners," their unconscious identity great enough to make such a

---

[8] *Shakespeare's Philosophical Patterns* (Louisiana State University Press, Baton Rouge, 1959), p. 48.

parapsychological experience possible for *both* of them. Actually this is a most astounding thing from our modern point of view. It is nothing unusual to hear in psychological practice that someone has had a parapsychological experience. As long as only one individual is concerned, it can be considered a subjective experience and need not have any objective validity, but whenever more than one person is involved in such a numinous experience, the objectivity of the factors bringing it about can no longer be denied. This, of course, does not mean that such factors are of physical nature. We may call them psychic, a convenient term which in no way describes their true nature nor explains anything. Such experiences, however, support the hypothesis of the existence of an "objective psyche." Jung elucidates a similar situation in reference to the flying saucer rumors:[9]

> The basis for this kind of rumour is an *emotional tension* having its cause in a situation of collective distress or danger, or in a vital psychic need. . . . In the individual, too, such phenomena as abnormal convictions, visions, illusions, etc., only occur when he is suffering from a psychic dissociation, that is, when there is a split between the conscious attitude and the unconscious contents opposed to it. . . . Things can be seen by many people independently of one another, or even simultaneously, which are not physically real. Also, the association-processes of many people often have a parallelism in time and space, with the result that different people, simultaneously and independently of one another, can produce the same new ideas, as has happened numerous times in history.

All those psychological conditions which Jung mentions were present in both Macbeth and Banquo, and produced such psychic dissociation, which in turn opened the unconscious to both of them and made the apparent visualization of the weird Sisters a phenomenon experienced by both of them simultaneously.

Since the categories of time and space become indistinct in

---

[9] *Civilization in Transition,* p. 319. Cf. Jung's experience in Ravenna, *Memories, Dreams, Reflections* (Pantheon Books, New York, 1961), p. 285.

the unconscious, the weird Sisters, as dominant factors of the unconscious, know the future ("look into the seeds of time"). Their prediction naturally has some of the qualities of the unconscious. Therefore, the distinct naming of Macbeth's future titles has its counterpart in the riddle quality of their prophecy for Banquo:

> Lesser than Macbeth, and greater   (I.iii.65)
> Not so happy, yet much happier,
> Thou shalt get kings, though thou be none.

Neither to Banquo nor to Macbeth do the Witches indicate in any way how all these things shall come about. Naturally, their predictions seem unbelievable. Macbeth argues quite reasonably with them and wants to know "whence this strange intelligence" and why they communicate "such prophetic greetings" to him. He orders them to speak, but they disappear as suddenly as they came. His urgent questions never find an answer.

Deeply moved by their strange experience, the two men try to understand and integrate it:

BANQUO: The earth hath bubbles, as the water has,   (I.iii.79)
            And these are of them.

MACBETH: . . . what seem'd corporal melted
            As breath into the wind. Would they had stayed.

Today we call such a phenomenon "psychic." Psychic events do not obey physical laws. They appear, disappear, move in ways impossible for matter. While both men have had the same experience, the effect is quite different in each of them. Macbeth is fascinated with his vision and sighs his wish, "Would they had stayed." In contrast, Banquo is concerned and fears the dangers attending such an invasion of numinous contents:

> Were such things here as we do speak about?   (I.iii.83)
> Or have we eaten on the insane root
> That takes the reason prisoner?

Psychiatric experience informs us that such an invasion of unconscious contents as Macbeth and Banquo suffer on the
"blasted heath" always represents a great challenge to consciousness and, not uncommonly, consciousness breaks down
under the impact. The impact of the strange prediction on Macbeth and Banquo is so strong that they cannot doubt for a moment what they have been told. Each acknowledges that his experience came out of a psychic substratum common to both;
both of them heard the same music, as they assure each other:

MACBETH: Went it not so?   (I.iii.88)

BANQUO: To the selfsame tune and words.

At this moment they take different paths. Macbeth, caught by
his fascination, will fall victim of the Witches' spell. Banquo will
preserve his honor, his royal strength, his proud ego—but he
will never be able to integrate his numinous experience and will
fall victim of a dastardly murder plotted by his partner.

Suddenly both are called back to ordinary reality by the arrival of Ross and Angus who, after praising Macbeth as the
great warrior, immediately inform him that the King has named
him Thane of Cawdor. Naturally, the unexpected verification of
the first of the Witches' predictions shakes Macbeth to the pith
of his being: "Can a devil speak true?" Any doubt that Macbeth
might have had is silenced. Hope is raised. He turns to Banquo,
asking him:

Do you not hope your children shall be kings,   (I.iii.117)
When those that gave the Thane of Cawdor to me
Promised no less to them?

The strength of ego which Banquo had manifested in his direct
dealings with the Witches is demonstrated again. He feels how
Macbeth is captivated by the Witches, how their prophecies
lure him, and how unreservedly he believes in gaining those temporal goods. He also sees that Macbeth cannot allow things just
to happen, that supported by this prophecy he might push his

fortune, *corriger la fortune*. Later we shall see that Macbeth is never satisfied to let events take place but always tries to add something to them or change them in his favor. In other words, he never accepts his fate. Only at the very end Macduff forces him to accept it.

Although the unconscious may convey information concerning future events, the fact that it invades us may also destroy our inner truth. How Macbeth relates to the unconscious, and in particular to its feminine aspect, is, I believe, the principal theme of the play. An ego that is invaded by any numinous content of the unconscious must maintain its inner truth and be able to evaluate the contents in order to survive. Therefore, Banquo warns Macbeth:

> That, trusted home,   (I.iii.120)
> Might yet enkindle you unto the crown,
> Besides the Thane of Cawdor. But 'tis strange!
> And oftentimes, to win us to our harm,
> The instruments of darkness tell us truths,
> Win us with honest trifles, to betray's
> In deepest consequence.

The emphasis here lies on "That, trusted home"—the full and uncritical acceptance of utterances of the unconscious. Banquo clearly sees and realizes that such utterances might have monstrous effects on a human being. To believe anything because it speaks with the numinous voice of the unconscious is as naïve and dangerous as the attitude of twentieth century man who, in his rationalism, often willfully disregards the unconscious, or tries to deprive it of its power by giving it harmless names. For modern man the unconscious will then appear in a projection; sexuality, or society, or entire nations may then be cast in the role of assuming all the marvelous or all the fiendish qualities which properly belong to the unconscious. At the beginning of the seventeenth century, when belief was common in witches, demons, familiars, etc.,[10] it was imperative that Shakespeare,

[10] G. L. Kittredge, *Witchcraft in Old and New England* (Russell & Russell, New York, 1956).

through the medium of Banquo, should proclaim such a warning in regard to the power and knowledge of psychic forces. In our time, we need a dramatist who will declare a different truth, one who would establish the reality of the unconscious and its healing effects. Or we might turn to the so-called romances of Shakespeare, especially *The Winter's Tale* and *The Tempest,* which admirably fulfill this modern need.

In *Macbeth,* an ego is represented which does not put up any resistance against an invasion by unconscious contents, and as a consequence is overwhelmed and destroyed by them. Such a human being is made to desire worldly and ephemeral goods, and to betray that which is of deepest consequence to him, that ineffable truth which Macbeth later calls "mine eternal jewel" (III.i.67).

Banquo's warning words evidently have not made any impression on Macbeth. Shakespeare allows us to "listen in" as we become witnesses to the drama which now commences in Macbeth's soul:

> Two truths are told,   (I.iii.127)
> As happy prologues to the swelling act
> Of the imperial theme . . .
> This supernatural soliciting
> Cannot be ill; cannot be good. If ill,
> Why hath it given me earnest of success,
> Commencing in a truth? I am Thane of Cawdor.
> If good, why do I yield to that suggestion
> Whose horrid image doth unfix my hair
> And make my seated heart knock at my ribs
> Against the use of nature? Present fears
> Are less than horrible imaginings.
> My thought, whose murder is yet but fantastical,
> Shakes so my single state of man that function
> Is smothered in surmise and nothing is
> But what is not.

To Macbeth, the Witches' prophecy and its immediate fulfillment are "two truths." The second prediction, that he will be

king, is of course not yet fulfilled, but both predictions are to
him "the happy prologues to the swelling act." As is so frequently the case with Shakespeare, this line has meaning on
different levels. For one thing, the "swelling act" refers to his
real increase in power and prestige. On another level, it has a
sexual connotation. It indicates his lack of true masculinity and
his hope of becoming masculine at last. On still another level,
"swelling" means "blowing in," [11] indicating Macbeth's in-flation
and his beginning megalomania. Whenever the ego identifies
with an archetype, it becomes inflated and to that extent unconscious. Such is the moment in which the "weird Sisters" take
possession of Macbeth and, with that, his ego trembles and betrays insecurity on many levels. In spite of all appearances, it
tries to convince itself that the Witches intend something good
for it. The "sickening sea-saw rhythm" (Knight's phrase) describes the terrible conflict into which Macbeth has fallen.

This "horrid image" which is accompanied by a wild emotion
("doth unfix my hair, and make my seated heart knock at my
ribs") has a tremendous effect upon him. Prior to battle and its
terrible aftermath, the epiphany of the Witches, there had been
fleeting thoughts of murder in him, but they were of no consequence. Now, after having been exposed to the weird Sisters, all
the power and numinosity of the unconscious are added to these
thoughts. Everything he might fear in reality is as nothing compared with these horrible fantasies which now stream from the
inner world. They frighten and shake him so that they almost
split him.[12] In consequence, his consciousness ("function")
loses its capacity to screen inrushing ideas, images and feelings.
It is smothered by these speculations ("surmise"). Reality and
fantasy interpenetrate. Everything changes its quality, loses its
existential reality ("nothing is but what is not"). Before Macbeth met the Witches, he had felt as one, as an undivided personality. With this invasion by powerful murderous fantasies he
becomes dissociated and totally uncertain about reality. The life-

[11] Oxford English Dictionary, Vol. IX, pt. II.
[12] I follow Grierson (Arden, p. 21), who thinks that "single" means
here "indivisible."

saving fact is that Macbeth at all times also *knows* what is going on in him.

In the midst of the numinous experience, Banquo has had the strength to notice Macbeth's "rapt" condition. Now that they are back in reality, talking with Ross and Angus, Banquo draws the attention of the two noblemen to Macbeth's appearance: "Look how our partner's rapt." His remark indicates how deeply Macbeth is immersed in his fantasy and meditation: outer reality does not penetrate to him. The promise of future glory, "the earnest of success," was the gate through which the weird Sisters had entered. Macbeth knows that he has been taken over by the archetype. His defenses are gone—only weakly can he whisper:

> If chance will have me King, why, chance may crown me,
> Without my stir.   (I.iii.143)

He still hopes that he will be able to avoid guilt, that his goal of kingship may be achieved without his active participation.

Using one of the clothing images which so frequently occur in *Macbeth,* Banquo comments:

> New honours come upon him,   (I.iii.145)
> Like our strange garments, cleave not to their mould,
> But with the aid of use.

—expressing the idea that the new rank given Macbeth might not agree with his personality. We will have an opportunity later to discuss the question of whether Macbeth is a royal personality and therefore fit to be a king, whether he had it in him to fulfill such a great challenge as kingship.

Macbeth's aside, following immediately, has puzzled the commentators a great deal:

> Come what come may,   (I.iii.148)
> Time and the hour runs through the roughest day.

I believe the meaning is as follows: Macbeth is now sure that he will be king but he does not know whether he will be a passive recipient of fate or an active and criminal participant in it. Whichever way it will be, time, the inexorable carrier of fate, will run through it. Fate must take its course and he, Macbeth, must suffer it, even if he has to commit murder.

Called back to reality, Macbeth excuses his "rapt" condition with a lie:

> The interim having weigh'd it, let us speak　　(I.iii.154)
> Our free hearts each to other.

It sounds like a courteous phrase, and Banquo responds in a like manner, but Macbeth is affected by his murderous fantasies. He knows that his heart is free no more.

iv

The next scene brings Duncan, the King, with some attendants. The execution of the former Thane of Cawdor is reported by Duncan's son, Malcolm, and Duncan remarks:

> There's no art　　(I.iv.11)
> To find the mind's construction in the face.

There is bitter irony in this statement by Duncan, who so frequently admits to not having any intuition. His goodness is really an unconsciousness, an innocence unbecoming to a king. He cannot suspect evil in anyone. He has no knowledge of his "shadow" and therefore no contact with the unconscious. In this sense, he is an outspoken antagonist of Macbeth. It is as if his utter unawareness of the unconscious attracts an opponent like Macbeth, who is flooded with the unconscious.

The balance of the scene is filled with expressions of Duncan's deep gratitude to Banquo and Macbeth, and his promises of outstanding rewards to his lieges. The unstable condition of his country prompts him to determine at once the royal succession, naming Malcolm as his heir. Banquo's response to this an-nouncement is free and open, whereas one can sense Macbeth's divided feelings toward his King in the coldness of his response. The Thane is deeply disturbed because the unexpected naming of Malcolm as Duncan's heir removes all chances of his attaining the crown in a normal manner. Consequently, his murderous desires are suddenly rekindled.

Macbeth lives in deep communion with the cosmos. Images of sky, ocean, and nature in general come easily to him. It is perfectly fitting that his conscience is a firmament. The stars are "eyes" which can see everything going on in his soul. In order to live with his black and criminal ambition, the stars must be prevented from seeing. In contrast to Duncan's statement, "Signs of nobleness, like stars, shall shine on all deservers," Macbeth asks the stars to hide their fires. But he cannot extinguish the light of his conscience:

> Stars, hide your fires! (I.iv.51)
> Let not light see my black and deep desires.

The division in his soul is now quite obvious, since functions which ordinarily are united are felt as separated:

> The *eye* wink at the *hand;* yet let that be (I.iv.52)
> Which the eye fears, when it is done, to see.

He has definitely gone a step further. His ego is now on the side of the "hand," that is, action, and he tries to repress his conscience, which Banquo termed "deepest consequence." Duncan is completely blind to Macbeth's emotional state and calls him a "peerless kinsman."

v

Scene 5 introduces Lady Macbeth. She is reading a letter from her husband, in which he informs her of the experience with the Witches, whom he here calls the "weird sisters." Again he emphasizes their superhuman knowledge ("more than mortal knowledge") and the numinous quality of the encounter:

Whiles I stood rapt in the wonder of it.   (I.v.6)

He does not doubt them nor question their intention. He refers to "greatness," in which Lady Macbeth in time will share. In spite of these promises she has some doubts as to whether he is the man to fulfill such expectations:

> Yet do I fear thy nature;   (I.v.17)
> It is too full o' the milk of human kindness[13]
> To catch the nearest way.

She knows that Macbeth has a conscience, that actions like those anticipated in the letter would throw him into a profound conflict. In brief, he is not a reckless man who would give unobstructed sway to his dark nature. He wants power, but only if the stars of his conscience can light the way. Nevertheless, she also knows that he is a weak human being, that he would not mind achieving his goal by evil means if evil came to him indirectly, so long as he himself did not do the wrong.

As mentioned before, the Witches do nothing more than foretell the future. Lady Macbeth is, as it were, a continuation of the Witches into the human realm. She has no moral scruples whatsoever. She intends to become quite active in Macbeth's plans, to stimulate his anima with her criminal intentions. She incarnates his murderous impulses. In this monologue she reveals herself as a one-sidedly dark figure. She is more goddess than human being, and must therefore be understood as a representation of Macbeth's unconscious. There are two layers in Macbeth's psyche: the weird Sisters represent the activated collective unconscious, and Lady Macbeth represents his personified unconscious, nearer the conscious level. She corresponds to Jung's strict definition of the anima:[14]

> . . . this omnipresent and ageless image, which corresponds to the deepest reality in a man . . . she is the great illusionist, the seductress, who draws him into life with her Maya. . . .

[13] "Kind"ness, meaning species, nature, not the modern sense of "friendly."

[14] *Aion*, p. 13.

Because she is his greatest danger, she demands from a man his greatest, and if he has it in him she will receive it.

Considering Lady Macbeth as a product of Shakespeare's imagination, we can see her as a remarkable aspect of the poet's anima. She represents a dramatic personification and differentiation of the "dark lady" of the Sonnets. Here in the play her dark influence on Macbeth is not exerted by love or emotion but by the *word*. It is her "spirits" which she wants to pour (like liquid!) into his ear,[15] it is the "valour of her *tongue*" which she would have sweep away all mental reservations Macbeth might still harbor against committing murder. The fascinating image which hovers before her eye is the "golden round," an archetypal image of universal significance which lends to kingship an immense numinosity:

> Hie thee hither,   (I.v.26)
> That I may pour my spirits in thine ear,
> And chastise with the valour of my tongue
> All that impedes thee from the golden round,
> Which fate and metaphysical aid doth seem
> To have thee crown'd withal.

Her monologue is interrupted by a messenger who informs her of the impending arrival of the King. When she is alone again, she unreservedly surrenders to the "murthering ministers." In the following monologue she calls upon the spirits to fill her with murderous thoughts to such an extent that she will be nothing but a vessel for them. She would not be a woman any longer and, like Macbeth who asked the stars to hide their fire, she asks the spirits:

> Make thick my blood,   (I.v.44)
> Stop up the access and passage to remorse,
> . . .
> Come, thick night,
> And pall thee in the dunnest smoke of hell,

---

[15] Cf. the Ghost's description of his death in *Hamlet* (I.v.60-73).

That my keen knife see not the wound it makes,
Nor heaven peep through the blanket of the dark,
To cry, 'Hold, hold!'

Thus she becomes an incarnation of the murderous anima. She is not only an instrument of hell, she herself becomes "thick night," "the dunnest smoke of hell," "the blanket of the dark." If one places Macbeth's lines:

My thought, whose murther yet is but fantastical,   (I.iii.139)
Shakes so my single state of man . . .

together with the lines just quoted, one can see how similar Macbeth and Lady Macbeth are, and where the difference between them lies. Lady Macbeth tries to close heaven and activate all the dynamisms of hell. This is further proof that in the characterization of Lady Macbeth we do not have a separate individual, a living woman, but the personification of Macbeth's ambition and darkest possibilities. In terms of modern psychology, she is Macbeth's anima, "the illusionist, the seductress who draws him into life with her Maya." This characterization of Lady Macbeth and Macbeth agrees with and goes beyond Ludwig Jekels's concept of a composite personality, which Freud discusses:[16]

I shall not follow this hint any further, but I would add, nevertheless, a remark which strikingly confirms the idea—namely, that the stirrings of fear which arise in Macbeth on the night of the murder, do not develop further in him, but in the Lady.

The two personalities of which Macbeth is composed, are Lady Macbeth and himself—in narrower psychological terms, Macbeth's ego and his anima. The invasion by the unconscious (the encounter with the Witches) causes a change in Macbeth's ego, a regression into the maternal world, an uncanny openness of the ego to the unconscious.

[16] *Collected Papers,* edited by Ernest Jones (Hogarth Press, London, 1925), Vol. IV, p. 332.

Macbeth arrives and Lady Macbeth uses their few moments alone to instill her thoughts into him. Although the word "murder" is never exchanged between them, her advice and especially her line, "You shall put this night's great business into my dispatch" (I.v.67), are full of double meaning. It is a well-known fact that criminals and particularly murderers never name their crime by its proper name; they could not face it. (Cf. the "pale criminal" in Nietzsche's *Thus Spake Zarathustra.*) Therefore, Hitler and his henchmen used such euphemisms as "final solution," "work camps," etc.

vi

Scene 6 brings the arrival of Duncan and a large number of Scottish nobles. To an amazing degree the King again displays complete unawareness of the real situation. As an antagonist of Macbeth, he symbolizes not only goodness, royalty and order in the realm, but also complete unconsciousness.

vii

Scene 7 begins with a long monologue which gives us a deep insight into Macbeth's psychic condition. By this time the idea of murder has taken a firm hold upon him, but the arguments against it are most vivid. He realizes that every action has effects in this world. If it were not so, he would be willing to forego eternal life. In very strong terms he tells himself that there is "even-handed justice" also in the world and that what evil he does will return to him. He enumerates to himself all the good reasons why the murder he plans would be a particularly heinous one. The strongest argument against such a vile deed is Duncan's purity and great virtue. They "will plead like angels"

> . . . trumpet-tongu'd, against   (I.vii.19)
> The deep damnation of his taking-off;
> And Pity, like a naked new-born babe,
> Striding the blast, or heaven's Cherubins, hors'd
> Upon the sightless couriers of the air,
> Shall blow the horrid deed in every eye,
> That tears shall drown the wind.

But Macbeth's ambition is stronger than all the arguments and the monologue reaches its conclusion with these crucial lines:

> I have no spur   (I.vii.25)
> To prick the sides of my intent, but only
> Vaulting ambition, which o'erleaps itself
> And falls on th' other—

The image used in this passage is taken from horsemanship. Kenneth Muir explains it:[17]

> "I have no spur to stimulate my guilty intention except ambition—ambition which is like a too eager rider, who in vaulting into the saddle o'erleaps himself and falls on the other side of the horse." Hunter: "lights on the opposite side of what was intended; that is, dishonor and wretchedness, instead of glory and felicity."

In other words, Macbeth cannot stimulate his murderous intent any further, and ambition, the only motive for his crime, would go beyond the goal and "o'erleap itself." Therefore, his reasoning has convinced him that he should do no more about the murder. At this moment, Lady Macbeth enters and he tells her briefly that he has dropped his plans, which again he does not name as murder but euphemistically calls "this business" ("We will proceed no further in this business"). He gives none of the reasons he has just enumerated in his monologue, but refers only to "golden opinions from all sorts of people." (He has created an image in the minds of many people and does not want to disturb it.) Such an argument, which has nothing to do with his real self, is of course very weak and gives Lady Macbeth ample opportunity to attack. She mocks him for not being able to look at his contemplated crime without being shaken. In typically feminine fashion she tells him also that now she doubts his love, and then she uses the strongest argument of all: she questions his masculinity. We already know, from his monologue in Act I, Scene 3, that Macbeth has doubts about his masculinity. He

[17] Arden, p. 41.

spoke then of the "swelling act to the imperial theme," and was afraid that murder would shake his "single state of man." We noted that there was uncertainty in him about his sexual potency, and furthermore that the integrity of consciousness was endangered by the contemplated murder. But his manhood is threatened in other ways too, as can be seen from the taunts with which Lady Macbeth assails him:

> Art thou afeard   (I.vii.39)
> To be the same in thine own act and valour
> As thou art in desire?

In Lady Macbeth's opinion, to be a man means to have the ability to execute what one sets out to do. The gap between desire and deed is always great. Great deeds cannot always be accomplished. The heroic attempt characterizes the man and frequently suffices. The situation becomes complicated if moral issues are involved. An evil deed, even if very hotly desired, will emasculate the man. Macbeth fervently wishes to be king, he would do a great deal to achieve it, but he knows that murder would undo him. Lady Macbeth muddles up the issues. As the Witches exclaimed in their first appearance: "Fair is foul, and foul is fair. Hover through the fog and filthy air" (I.i.11), so acts Lady Macbeth now.

She calls Macbeth's hesitation cowardice, while in fact it would require great courage for Macbeth to resist his wife. His protestation that he dares "do all that may become a man" elicits a further taunt, in which she uses still another opposite to "man":

> What beast was't then   (I.vii.47)
> That made you break this enterprise to me?

She proceeds to tell him that he would even be "more a man" if he were more than he was. By putting it this way, she cleverly instills in him her conviction that were he king he would be very much the *man*. She is probably quite right when she reminds him that when he originally worked out his plans for attaining kingship he included murder and made arrangements for it. Now that "time and place adhere," he is frightened. Thus she puts a "blanket of the dark" around his intention to call off the murder. Enveloping him in the "dunnest smoke of hell," she ends her argument with these terrifying lines:

> I have given suck, and know　　　　　　　　　(I.vii.54)
> How tender 'tis to love the babe that milks me:
> I would, while it was smiling in my face,
> Have plucked my nipple from his boneless gums
> And dashed the brains out, had I so sworn as you
> Have done to this.

On first hearing, these words sound like perfect support for Macbeth's original murderous plan. Their impact is tremendous. Even if we have heard them many times on the stage, or read them over and over again, they hit our feelings like a sledge-hammer. The reason for the horror and alarm in our experience is due to direct and immediate juxtaposition of two intense images: the helpless baby, smiling and nursing at the breast in fullest trust—and against it the complete betrayal, the mother dashing the babe's brains out. And why? Well, because she had "so sworn"! Of course, this is not an actuality, but the image of the heartless, murderous mother is there. Macbeth's unconscious registers the terrible threat. Lady Macbeth has called up the archetype of the wrathful Magna Mater, best represented by the goddess Kali in Eastern religion. At this moment, Lady Macbeth is a Kali. Macbeth who, as we saw in his encounter with the Witches, was invaded by the feminine in its destructive aspect, succumbs now to the demonic nature of his wife because she speaks with the voice of the destructive mother archetype. All that he can set against this terrible onslaught of Lady Macbeth is:

> If we should fail,—　　　　　　　　　(I.vii.59)

His metaphysical deliberations are forgotten; not even the "golden" opinions he had bought are remembered. On the other hand, it is not really clear in *what* he might fail: to execute the murder? to do it without being found out? to achieve kingship? or, in a general human sense, to be a failure as a human being?

Lady Macbeth's answer, "We fail?" can be pronounced with many different accents, giving it many shades of meaning. It is this multiplicity of meanings which shakes Macbeth's weak defenses. But the last bastion falls when she proposes how they should go about the murder. Again she would not use words like "kill" or "murder," although it is very clear what she means. Macbeth now has only questions about the practical details. Will he be found out? And so, the dark anima with her dream world of murder and deceit has conquered Macbeth and now he is ready to perform the deed.

Act Two

i

The second act begins with a short midnight talk between Banquo and his son Fleance. From our point of view, it is important to note how conscious Banquo is of the darkness that has descended upon his soul. The unconscious fills him with "cursed thoughts" and will not allow him to sleep. We never hear whether he suspects that Macbeth might consider committing a foul deed in order to gain the kingship promised by the Witches. Whatever his thoughts, we recognize that in Banquo a gate is open to the unconscious but that he has strength enough to contain the pressure. The pressure of the unconscious, however, is so strong that it forces him to call upon the "merciful powers." He cannot help but mention, when Macbeth appears, that he "dreamt last night of the three weird sisters." He would like to talk more about it with Macbeth, with whom he shared the experience, but Macbeth, in an ambiguous way, postpones any such conversation and in just as ambiguous and dark a manner proposes to Banquo some participation in his scheme:

> If you shall cleave to my consent,[1] when 'tis,   (II.i.25)
> It shall make honour for you.

[1] Arden, p. 48—*"to be of consent:* to be an accessory."

As before, Banquo is willing to play along with Macbeth so long as he can keep a clear conscience:

> So I lose none (II.i.27)
> In seeking to augment it, but still keep
> My bosom franchis'd and allegience clear,
> I shall be counsell'd.

When Banquo and Fleance exit and Macbeth is alone, we are able to observe his inner condition from a monologue. We know that at the end of Act One the sinister image of the mother-anima, in the form of Lady Macbeth, had gained possession of Macbeth. Now the murder fantasy, the destructive content of the negative mother, rises in him in the image of a dagger. Curry[2] suggests the dagger is

> an hallucination caused immediately, indeed, by disturbed bodily humours and spirits but ultimately by demonic powers, who have so controlled and manipulated these bodily forces as to produce the effect they desire.

Macbeth has quite often been spoken of as the "visionary" Macbeth because of this scene, later scenes on the heath, the banquet scene, et al. It is important, however, to understand that on the heath an inner process was set in motion in Macbeth in which ego and unconscious approach each other dangerously. Lady Macbeth then broke, as it were, the last wall between Macbeth's consciousness and the unconscious. The murderous intentions now step over the threshold in the form of an autonomous symbol, the dagger. Immediately the ego confronts this image and there follows a discussion between ego and activated image, which the Germans call an *Auseinandersetzung*. The image is not a hallucination in the strict psychiatric sense because a hallucination is a voice heard or an image seen which is assumed without question to exist in the environment. For a moment, when he says, "Come, let me clutch thee," Macbeth believes the dagger to be real, but then he becomes aware that it *is* an image,

[2] Arden, p. 49.

for he says, "I have thee not, and yet I see thee still." He addresses himself to the image-dagger:

> Art thou not, fatal vision, sensible   (II.i.36)
> To feeling as to sight? or art thou but
> A dagger of the mind, a false creation
> Proceeding from the heat-oppressed brain?
> I see thee yet, in form as palpable
> As this which now I draw.

So he makes a very clear distinction here between a real dagger and the image, which he knows comes from within. He believes, of course, that it is due to some pathology ("false creation . . . heat-oppressed brain"). Then he understands it as a psychological symbol, something that directs him ("marshal'st me the way I was going"). He recognizes an important effect of this invasion by a commanding image:

> Mine eyes are made the fools o' the other senses,   (II.i.44)
> Or else worth all the rest.

While he is looking at it the image undergoes a change. Suddenly there are "gouts of blood" on the blade. In discussing "active imagination," Jung once related an experience he had as a child when looking at the picture of one of his ancestors standing on a staircase. If he looked long enough at the picture, he saw the ancestor *walking down* the steps. This experience led to an important method for initiating an active imagination. If we do the same thing—that is, if we concentrate intensively on an image or a picture—the libido thus given over to the unconscious will affect the image and will start a further flow of images. Macbeth of course is in a state of great excitement; all his libido is concentrated on the image of the dagger which has suddenly dropped into his consciousness. The alteration of the image from a simple dagger to a bloody dagger corresponds to the intensification of his murderous thoughts. What Macbeth does here is nothing less than active imagination. But with him it has disastrous effects. It need not be destructive however. Much depends on the conscious attitude of the one who practices this method, and perhaps even more on the condition of his unconscious and the images which are stimulated.

The method is simple: the patient takes any image he likes, usually one from a dream, and looks at it for a certain length of time. It will then move spontaneously, and contents of the unconscious will make their appearance. However, just as in Macbeth's monologue, it is important to confront these images and converse with them. Jung used this method widely and describes it at length in the second part of his *Mysterium Coniunctionis*. The present writer has published a short article on active imagination entitled *Journey to the Moon*.[3]

Active imagination—that is, the concentration of consciousness on an unconscious image and the participation of the ego in the changing images of the unconscious—is, however, a two-edged method. It always activates the unconscious, whether for good or ill. In analytical practice this method is used of course for healing purposes. The analyst recommending the method to a patient must be reasonably sure that healing images are dormant in the unconscious before they are awakened. The case of Macbeth is an outstanding example of the activation of destructive elements—because Macbeth's unconscious was "top-full" of murderous fantasies:

> Fill me from the crown to the toe top-full   (I.v.43)
> Of direst cruelty.

The following lines in this monologue show how much Macbeth is aware of the darkness of the unconscious, and especially of the bloodthirsty aspects of the mother archetype:

> Now o'er the one half-world   (II.i.49)
> Nature seems dead, and wicked dreams abuse
> The curtained sleep; witchcraft celebrates
> Pale Hecate's offerings; and wither'd murder,
> Alarum'd by his sentinel, the wolf,

[3] See p. 212fn.

> Whose howl's his watch, thus with his stealthy pace,
> With Tarquin's ravishing strides, toward his design
> Moves like a ghost.

In contrast to Banquo, Macbeth has by now no objections to this condition. Thus an important element is missing which would be present in genuine active imagination: a real confrontation between ego and unconscious, a discussion between them and the ability of the ego to make a choice, to take a different course than that which the unconscious proposes. As we already observed in the first act, Macbeth's ego is weak, it has never quite separated from the maternal unconscious, and now, because of the fascination of the mother archetype, it is completely enveloped in bloodthirsty fantasies. In Shakespeare's terms: "Witchcraft celebrates pale Hecate's offerings." Therefore, without any further conflict, Macbeth decides he will commit the crime. He prayerfully addresses another symbol of the mother archetype, "Thou sure and firm-set earth," and begs that his dark steps might not be detected. That there is an ego still present can be deduced from the fact that he feels the "present horror."

ii

Lady Macbeth enters. Macbeth is, of course, exceedingly tense and believes he hears a noise when there is none: "Who's there?" Lady Macbeth describes how she has prepared everything:

> I laid their daggers ready;   (II.ii.13)
> . . . Had he not resembled
> My father as he slept I had done't.

Freud quotes these lines on page 327 of the fourth volume of his *Collected Papers,* but does not immediately comment on them. Later, on page 330, he says, "The murder of the kindly Duncan is little else than parricide." Undoubtedly, Duncan is a father figure to Macbeth, but he is also much more. He is in many ways a contrasting figure to Macbeth. As his monologue in Scene 7 of Act I demonstrated, Macbeth's deepest conflict was not so much whom he would murder as whether to murder or not. As we have seen from the preceding discussions of the weird Sisters and of Lady Macbeth as his mother-anima, it was the invasion of the unconscious with its destructive feminine forces that created these murderous desires. Duncan is a suitable victim for this crime because the murder of the King would also satisfy Macbeth's ambition. That Macbeth was Duncan's "kinsman and his subject," his "host," and that Duncan "had great virtues," serve to make the crime especially revolting, but the important question is: Will Macbeth transpose his fantasies into reality? He will—and does. The murder is committed behind the scenes.

Now that the fantasies have become an irreversible reality, the psychological situation for Macbeth and Lady Macbeth is radically altered. Up to this point hell has been a dark potential which exerted terrible pressure on both of them. Now that the deed is done, the psychological development of each of them takes a very different course. The relationship which each of them had to the unconscious before the murder determines what happens to each of them, and the guilt they share inevitably separates them from each other. This fact has been commented on frequently and I do not want to expand it further. We have seen that Macbeth is quite open to the unconscious, while Lady Macbeth disregards it and actively represses it. Correspondingly, the reaction of one is the exact opposite of the other. Their talk is dialogue only on the surface, inasmuch as only concrete facts are mentioned between them. Macbeth, with his fascination by the unconscious, is now deeply gripped by the memory-image his deed has created: "This is a sorry sight." In killing Duncan, he has also killed something in himself and the image of his violated psyche returns when he remembers the prayers of the two attendants sleeping with Duncan:

One cried 'God bless us!' and 'Amen' the other.   (II.ii.28)

But Macbeth could not say "Amen" or "God bless us!" The image of the actual murder will haunt him forever because it incarnates the terrible moment in which he cut himself off from

God. This is the injury he did to his own soul. "This blow" was not "the be-all and the end-all." The "life to come" (I.vii.1-7) was a reality he had forfeited. There is a German proverb which says: "When things are at their worst, God is nearest to you." Macbeth knows he is now in dire distress, that in this moment he has "most need of blessing," but God does not come to his rescue. His wish, "and take the present horror from the time," has not been fulfilled. On the contrary, the horror increases, because the guilt of the bloody deed has irreversibly isolated him from God and, as we shall see later, from man as well.

Lady Macbeth, in her attempt to repress the unconscious, interrupts his thoughts with:

> Consider it not so deeply.   (II.ii.31)
> . . .
> These deeds must not be thought
> After these ways; so, it will make us mad.

It is a popular idea that to take the unconscious seriously will make us mad. At this moment, Lady Macbeth seemingly succeeds in suppressing the image of the bloody deed, but we will see later, in the sleepwalking scene, that the unconscious does take its revenge and plagues her with the memory of the murder night.

The more deeply Macbeth becomes involved in the thoughts that rise from his unconscious, the more Lady Macbeth becomes psychologically removed from her partner-in-crime. The dynamism of Macbeth's thoughts, however, is so powerful that nothing can stop it. Now the realization that he has killed more than Duncan dawns upon him. A voice from the unconscious tells him, with the symbol of sleep:

> Methought I heard a voice cry 'Sleep no more!   (II.ii.36)
> Macbeth does murther Sleep.'

Freud notices that[4]

---

[4] *Collected Papers,* Vol. IV, p. 333.

. . . we never hear that King Macbeth could not sleep, while we see that the Queen rises from her bed and betrays her guilt in somnambulistic wanderings.

He is not quite accurate, however, since in III.iv.141 Lady Macbeth says:

You lack the season of all natures, sleep.

This line and Macbeth's affliction of "terrible dreams" indicate that after his deed Macbeth has little sleep, and what he has of it is never the restful healing sleep of unburdened human beings. On one level, sleep here has the ordinary meaning ("the death of each day's life"), but it is also a symbol;[5] it refers to the healing capacity of the unconscious into which our consciousness submerges every night:

. . . sore labour's bath,   (II.ii.39)
Balm of hurt minds, great nature's second course,
Chief nourisher in life's feast.

Macbeth has violated nature and with that has added an intolerable burden to the unconscious ("innocent sleep"—innocent = unconscious). His guilt is deeply imprinted on his unconscious by the bloody image of his deed:

'Glamis hath murdered sleep, and therefore   (II.ii.44)
    Cawdor
Shall sleep no more! Macbeth shall sleep no
    more!'

He speaks as if he were three different personalities. He himself (in the figure of Glamis) has violated (murdered) the unconscious. In so doing he has split the unconscious in two and de-

---

[5] Jung: "The images in dreams and spontaneous fantasies are symbols, that is, the best possible formulation for still unknown or unconscious facts, which generally compensate the content of consciousness or the conscious attitude." —*Mysterium Coniunctionis*, p. 540.

prived it of its healing capacity. From now on the unconscious will be nothing but an enemy to Macbeth.

The more the talk progresses, the more outspoken and markedly opposed the attitudes of Macbeth and Lady Macbeth become. Since they represent a composite personality (consciousness and the anima of Macbeth), we can see two conflicting trends in the image of this composite:

(1) Macbeth's consciousness, overwhelmed by the image of the deed and unable to face it:

> I am afraid to think what I have done;　　　(II.ii.52)
> Look on't again I dare not.

(2) Lady Macbeth, describing his thinking as "brainsickly" and brazenly daring to go into the murder chamber again. Her attitude is the exact opposite of Macbeth's; she deprecates it:

> The sleeping and the dead　　　(II.ii.55)
> Are but as pictures; 'tis the eye of childhood
> That fears a painted devil.

It is Shakespeare's crowning imagination that at this moment a knocking is heard which brings violently home to Macbeth the realization that his guilt is unredeemable. Not even "all great Neptune's ocean will wash this blood clean" from his hand. While Lady Macbeth says, "A little water clears us of this deed," Macbeth's terrible conflict, his inability to live with himself, is significantly expressed in the one line:

> To know my deed, 'twere best not know myself.　　(II.ii.73)

In the analysis of *Hamlet*[6] mention was made that every one of Shakespeare's plays contains lines which refer to *knowing oneself*. Individuation, as defined by C. G. Jung, represents the process by which self-knowledge may be gained. Macbeth's words prove that originally he had had the capacity to know

[6] Pp. 29-30.

himself, but his deed and his inability to carry the guilt have irrevocably destroyed it. Since individuation is no longer possible for him, the opposite of individuation is forced upon him. From now on, he must pretend to be what he is not. He must wear masks and clothes to cover up what he really is. He must equivocate. The further the action develops, the wider becomes the gap between his pretense and his true being. Inevitably, in this split, his anima, as symbolized by Lady Macbeth, fails, deteriorates, becomes mentally disturbed and dies a suicide (" 'tis thought, by self and violent hands took off her life"—V.vii.99). It is even said of Scotland, "Alas! poor country; almost afraid to know itself" (IV.iii.164).[7]

iii

Since our principal interest is Macbeth's relationship to the unconscious, I will pass over much of the third scene. It brings the discovery of the murder. We attach great significance to Lennox's description of the terrible conditions which existed during the murder night. It is as if chaos were ruling in the universe. Hell has taken over not only in Macbeth's soul, but in the whole of Scotland:

> The night has been unruly: where we lay,   (II.iii.60)
> Our chimneys were blown down; and, as they say,
> Lamentings heard i' the air; strange screams of
>   death,
> And prophesying with accents terrible
> Of dire combustion and confus'd events
> New hatch'd to the woeful time. The obscure bird
> Clamour'd the livelong night: some say the earth
> Was feverous and did shake.

Lennox feels very strongly the frightful disturbance in the unconscious.

Macbeth's lines:

[7] For a thorough analysis of this theme of equivocation, particularly in the Porter scene, see the Arden Shakespeare, p. xxxix.

> Had I but died an hour before this chance   (II.iii.97)
> I had liv'd a blessed time; for, from this instant,
> There's nothing serious in mortality,
> All is but toys; renown and grace is dead,
> The wine of life is drawn, and the mere lees
> Is left this vault to brag of.

express his sorrow and would be understood by his listeners as genuine grief for the sudden and terrible loss of Duncan, but it is also an acknowledgment that he has lost much more; through his deed life has lost all meaning, the very spirit of life is drained out of him. This is repeated in several images:

> The wine of life is drawn, and the mere lees   (II.iii.102)
> Is left this vault to brag of.

> The spring, the head, the fountain of your blood   (II.iii.106)
> Is stopp'd; the very source of it is stopp'd.

Lady Macbeth faints. Kenneth Muir[8] cannot decide whether it is real or pretended, but I believe it quite possible that this lady who could go into the murder chamber and take the dagger back, seemingly unmoved, would now, when everyone is deeply shaken by the gory discovery, be genuinely overwhelmed by the unconscious and really faint.

iv

The last scene carries the story further but also brings new evidence that nature herself is deeply disturbed by the murder. Or was it this disturbance in nature which overtook Macbeth and led him to the fateful deed?

> Thou seest, the heavens, as troubled with man's act   (II.iv.5)
> Threaten his bloody stage; by the clock 'tis day,
> And yet dark night strangles the traveling lamp.

The following three lines show clearly that this image also expresses the condition of the unconscious:

[8] Arden, p. 69.

Is't night's predominance, or the day's shame,   (II.iv.8)
That darkness does the face of earth entomb,
When living night should kiss it?

The darkness of the unconscious has extinguished the light of
consciousness, has even made a "tomb" of Scotland, as we hear
later from Ross:

It cannot be call'd our mother, but our grave.   (IV.iii.165)

The result of the hidden murder is a reversal of natural behavior in the animal kingdom. Both the Old Man and Ross
express their horror of the uncanny mood in nature by stories
which have a strange, legendary quality, though they have only
recently happened: one, that a falcon was killed by a mousing
owl; the other, that Duncan's horses "broke their stalls" as if
they would make war on mankind. Chaos and conflict rage in
the universe just as in human affairs. The strangest thing about
the horses, however, is the unheard of event which Ross, as an
eyewitness, confirms: "They eat each other." In this image of
wild horses devouring each other, we see the split in Macbeth's
soul as it continues to deepen in him, to consume him, and to
affect his environment.

We now hear from Macduff that Macbeth has already been
named King, and since he is the King this terrible illness will
now also envelop the whole country.

Act Three

i

At the beginning of Act III, Macbeth has already been crowned
King. We hear it first from Banquo who in a monologue medi-
tates on the weird women's promises. He also strongly suspects
Macbeth is the murderer of Duncan: "I fear thou play'dst most
foully for't."

Macbeth enters as King, and Lady Macbeth as Queen. They

invite Banquo to attend a great feast they are preparing. In spite of his suspicions, Banquo not only accepts this invitation but fully acknowledges Macbeth as his King, with full powers over him. Macbeth's questions and Banquo's answers are full of ambiguity and hidden meaning. Banquo furnishes enough details about his evening ride for Macbeth to prepare an ambush for killing him. In relating these details Banquo also conveys that he has become a participant in Macbeth's darkness:

> . . . go not my horse the better,   (III.i.26)
> I must become a borrower of the night
> For a dark hour or twain.

The weird Sisters have affected Banquo, enveloped him in the same darkness as Macbeth. Though his attitude is royal and independent, Banquo is quite willing to cooperate with the new King:

> Let your highness   (III.i.15)
> Command upon me; to the which my duties
> Are with a most indissoluble tie
> For ever knit.

Indeed he "borrows" from Macbeth's darkness and is thereby doomed. No sooner has Banquo left than Macbeth is ready to make the arrangements necessary for his murder.

Before the two men whom Macbeth wants to charge with this grim task enter, a long monologue gives us profound insight into Macbeth's conflicts. Now that he has achieved everything the weird Sisters foretold, he feels his present royal position means nothing to him. For one reason, it has not given him any real security. He is even more insecure than before and feels threatened by Banquo. Now that he is King, he realizes Banquo's natural superiority. Banquo has "wisdom." Macbeth is "under him." Banquo's "dauntless temper of mind" and his "valor" are a reproach to Macbeth. He specifically remembers Banquo's strength of ego in his encounter with the weird women: "He chid the sisters." He realizes the tragic irony that now that he has achieved kingship there is no permanence to it. He also feels quite inadequate as a man, since he knows from the "sisters" that his crown is "fruitless" (III.i.61), his scepter "barren" (62). Macbeth suffers from sexual incompetence, especially from his inability to produce children. Though named and crowned a king, he knows that he is king in name only. He lacks true royalty, that peculiar nature in kingship which from primitive times, well into the Elizabethan age, was felt as grace given by God to the King. It made the King inviolable.

Macbeth's tragedy is so moving because he knows exactly what has happened to him:

> For Banquo's issue have I fil'd my mind.　　(III.i.65)
> For them the gracious Duncan have I murder'd;
> Put rancours in the vessel of my peace
> Only for them; and mine eternal jewel
> Given to the common enemy of man,
> To make them kings, the seed of Banquo kings!

"The vessel of my peace" is a feminine symbol and is a poetic expression for his soul. Those insights which began immediately after the murder and were climaxed in the symbol of sleep, he here faces with great clarity. The "eternal jewel" may be just another symbol for his soul, like "the vessel of my peace." However, in contrast to the vessel which might break, the jewel emphasizes the incorruptibility of the Self,[1] and a quality which is always associated with the Self, that of not being temporal. Therefore I think the jewel represents the essential content of the soul rather than the soul itself. If this is so, Macbeth might have decided to give up his kingship and, by penitence and whatever religious means he might have chosen, to regain his eternal jewel from the devil and return to God. At least this would be possible if he had taken his insights absolutely seriously. But as before and in spite of these insights, his ambition and his attachment to the world are much stronger. Therefore he takes the opposite direction. He attempts to attain his "safety"

---

[1] Cf. Jung, *Pyschology and Alchemy,* pp. 37, 458.

by challenging fate. In this sense fate is not only the course of events as foretold by the weird women, but also the natural healing powers in the collective unconscious which always try to establish wholeness. By making this decision to challenge fate Macbeth rejects any truly religious attitude. He attempts to fight God and therefore surrenders to hell itself. (Cf. p. 380.) In this sense, hell psychologically represents the utmost hubris of the ego, the willful pride and arrogance of man.

The balance of Scene 1 is taken up with Macbeth's successful efforts to persuade the two men to commit the murder of Banquo and his son Fleance. He uses these men's grievances for his purpose. He attacks them in their weak spots by accusing them of not being men. His own profound doubts about his own masculinity make him exceedingly eloquent and exert an almost magic influence on both the Murderers. At the same time he admits that he must mask "the business from the common eye for sundry weighty reasons." As usual, he cannot call it murder, but *"that business . . .* whose execution takes your enemy off," or, in referring to Fleance, he remarks that his "absence is no less material to me than is his father's, (and) must embrace the fate of that *dark hour."*

In the Second Murderer, Macbeth finds a man who is like himself but who, for different reasons, is "reckless what I do to spite the world." With Macbeth, of course, the recklessness goes much deeper. He spites God to gain the world.

ii

The following scene gives us an insight into the extent to which the relationship between the royal couple has deteriorated. Lady Macbeth knows that the fulfillment of her desires has been destructive. But she maintains the same attitude toward the unconscious as before—that "those thoughts" should be forgotten:

Things without all remedy (III.ii.11)
Should be without regard; what's done is done.

However, Macbeth, now on his path to utmost hubris, feels that he is not safe. What truly disturbs him is the unconscious, but as usual the enemy is perceived only as an outer object. Banquo with good reason has carried this projection since the time they encountered the Sisters on the heath. As in mythology, and in many dreams, the unconscious is symbolized by the snake:

> We have scorch'd [2] the snake, not kill'd it: (III.ii.13)
> She'll close and be herself.

The ego ("our poor malice") "remains in danger of her former tooth." One can frequently hear the masculine gender attributed to the snake, but for Macbeth the snake is definitely feminine, which of course agrees with his whole psychology. The unconscious is not dead for him. It still has the same poison it always had, its numinosity combined with its power to overwhelm consciousness; briefly, its capacity for making man crazy. There is no human being who is not afraid of losing his mind, and Macbeth, who as we saw from the beginning has had natural access to the unconscious more than most humans, suffers this activity of the unconscious nightly. It continually plagues him with "terrible dreams that shake us nightly." It is this terrible psychic condition which calls up in him the fiercest spite and destructiveness. He would rather "let the frame of things disjoint" than continue in this condition. But he also knows that since he cannot give up his worldly gains, only death can give him this peace:

> Better be with the dead,   (III.ii.19)
> Whom we, to gain our peace, have sent to peace,
> Than on the torture of the mind to lie
> In restless ecstasy. Duncan is in his grave;
> After life's fitful fever he sleeps well.
> . . . nothing, can touch him further.

---

[2] Arden, p. 84: *"scorch'd:* slash'd, as with a knife. Theobald's emendation is unnecessary."

Lady Macbeth is quite out of touch with the terrible affliction of Macbeth's soul:

> Be bright and jovial among your guests to-night.   (III.ii.27)

And Macbeth agrees to do so, just in order to destroy Banquo the more effectively:

> And make our faces vizards to our hearts,   (III.ii.34)
> Disguising what they are.

Yet another symbol of the terrible condition of his mind is revealed:

> O! full of scorpions is my mind, dear wife.   (III.ii.36)

As before, we find that in spite of so much insight into the anguished and hopeless condition of his soul, Macbeth suddenly changes his trend of thought and conjures up some hope: "There's comfort yet." He does not tell Lady Macbeth what this comfort might be, but in symbolic terms he tells her, addressing the "seeling night":

> Scarf up the tender eye of pitiful day,   (III.ii.47)
> And with thy bloody and invisible hand
> Cancel and tear to pieces that great bond
> Which keeps me pale!

By trusting the hellish powers of night, that is, of unconsciousness, he can free himself of this terrible affliction of his soul.

It seems to be impossible for a human ego to face so much guilt and darkness in itself. The full truth of Macbeth's situation would be intolerable to him, as it usually is to murderers. So he turns to an easy deceptive optimism when he tells Lady Macbeth:

> Things bad begun make strong themselves by ill: (III.ii.55)
> So, prithee, go with me.

iii

The next scene brings the murder of Banquo. Fleance escapes. Thus an important part of the three women's prophecy is fulfilled in an unexpected way:

> Not so happy, yet much happier. (I.iii.66)
> Thou shalt get kings, though thou be none.

With the escape of Fleance, the possibility of a line of kings is introduced, about which we hear more later.

The presence of a Third Murderer in this scene is most puzzling and effectively adds to the atmosphere of mystery in the play. I agree with Wilson[3] that

> Shakespeare introduces the Third Murderer to show that Macbeth, "tyrant-like, feels he must spy even upon his chosen instruments."

Of symbolic significance is Banquo's calling for a light, as do the Murderers, but somehow the light is extinguished:

THIRD MURDERER: Who did strike out the light? (III.iii.17)

In Kenneth Muir's opinion, this is the turning point of the play. The forces of darkness have done their worst but Fleance's escape is a promise of the return of the light and of the eventual defeat of the forces of darkness. Though the full fury of the tyrant is felt more and more after this deed, the forces of light begin to assemble and gain strength from this moment on in the drama.

This is an opportune moment to discuss briefly the dramatic justification for Banquo's death. We could assume that since the weird Sisters predicted it, it would have to happen sometime, but Shakespeare almost always gives us the psychological motivation. Banquo represented a threat to Macbeth because the weird

---

[3] Arden, p. 90.

Sisters had told him: "Thou shalt get kings, though thou be none." Macbeth could never accept this prediction. But the deeper reason for Macbeth's need to murder is his necessity for gaining "safety," for becoming whole. What was it in *Banquo* that necessitated his own death? What was *his* guilt? What led dramatically and psychologically to his violent death? We saw that in dealing with the three Sisters he acted in a manly and independent way. He even was aware that

> The instruments of darkness tell us truths,   (I.iii.124)
> Win us with honest trifles, to betray's
> In deepest consequence.

He also suspected that Macbeth might use foul means to achieve his end. In spite of all this, he was willing to cooperate with Macbeth because he thought that by careful maneuvering, and as long as he personally was not involved, his integrity might not be tainted:

> So I lose none (honor)   (II.i.27)
> In seeking to augment it, but still keep
> My bosom franchis'd and allegiance clear,
> I shall be counsell'd.

When Duncan's murder was first discovered and Banquo appeared with the other Lords, he must have apprehended at once that Macbeth was the murderer, without yet having any concrete evidence, but he did not speak up or try to substantiate his suspicions. He did not wish to examine anything further. On the contrary! He was a true collaborator. His promise to appear at the banquet and his attitude in his talk with Macbeth (III.i.1-44) show that he had successfully concealed all his doubts. His active cooperation with the murderer-king was quite in evidence. The lines:

> Let your highness   (III.i.15)
> Command upon me; to the which my duties
> Are with a most indissoluble tie
> For ever knit.

demonstrate that he did not maintain his manly independence in the face of the *fait accompli*. When he continued: "Go not my horse the better, I must become a borrower of the night," he betrayed his inner condition as well. He had "borrowed" some of Macbeth's darkness, and by tacitly condoning the murder had become a partner to the deed after the fact. Since Banquo took no stand against evil, the darkness that had descended on Macbeth and the whole of Scotland enveloped him too and involved him in guilt. It is particularly meaningful for him then that before his "soul's flight" found "heaven," he called for a light (III.ii.8), but it was too late. While on the surface Banquo evidently did not know that he had only a short time to live, his unconscious seemed to know that the fateful hour was near, for to Macbeth's question, "Goes Fleance with you?" he replied:

Ay, my good lord: our time does call upon's.   (III.i.37)

iv

There are many places in the play where Macbeth's ambition is described as ravenous hunger. In contrast, Duncan had felt quite satisfied:

True, worthy Banquo; he is full so valiant,   (I.iv.54)
And in his commendations I am fed;
It is a banquet to me.

The banquet scene which now follows shows us Macbeth at the zenith of his power and fulfillment. Now, as it were, his hunger may be stilled. He may perhaps be satisfied when the Murderers return and inform him of Banquo's death. But a strange thing happens: he sees blood on one of the Murderer's faces. Kenneth Muir comments:[4] "Absurd from a naturalistic point of view, but proper to a murderer in a poetic play." I believe, however, that it is part of Macbeth's stimulated unconscious. Just as he saw, quite realistically, a dagger before his eyes even though he

4 Arden, p. 92.

could acknowledge it as a creation of his mind (II.i.33), he now sees blood on the Murderer's face. When he wants to verify whether his vision corresponds to reality, he carefully avoids the word "murder" in his question. Instead he must use the ambiguous: "Is he dispatched?"—a question which the Murderer answers with unusual directness:

> My lord, his throat is cut; that I did for him.   (III.iv.16)

The escape of Fleance is a great failure in his plan and disturbs Macbeth deeply. This becomes understandable, however, if we remember that although Macbeth had easy access to the unconscious he was deprived of its healing qualities. His unconscious was split; it contained dangerous poison, was full of "scorpions." His easy optimism, his illusion that by the deaths of Banquo and Fleance he will have recovered wholeness, is now shattered:

> Then comes my fit again: I had else been perfect;   (III.iv.19)
> Whole as the marble, founded as the rock,
> As broad and general as the casing air.

Now he is "cabin'd, cribb'd, confin'd, bound in to saucy fears and doubts." This aggregation of verbs, all meaning approximately the same thing, with its use of alliteration, powerfully demonstrates how the ego, at the acme of its power, is also imprisoned and a victim of "doubts and fears." The "snake," the image Macbeth had used in III.ii.13, returns, strong evidence that Banquo and Fleance are the "serpent" for him. Again he projects. The unconscious remains his real enemy and appears in the image of "the worm." Fleance's escape proves that the unconscious has not been killed:

> The worm that's fled   (III.iv.29)
> Hath nature that in time will venom breed,
> No teeth for the present.

On the contrary, it maintains its unceasing vitality and fertility. Lady Macbeth calls her husband back to the banquet. Dissembling his deep disturbance, he returns and wishes his guests:

> Now good digestion wait on appetite,   (III.iv.39)
> And health on both!

He can hope for satisfaction of his intensive desires, but this ravenous appetite of his can never be satisfied. The moment he wishes for Banquo's presence, the unheard of occurs. Banquo's ghost enters. Macbeth had just heard from one of the Murderers:

> Safe in a ditch he bides,   (III.iv.26)
> With twenty trenched gashes on his head.

His strong imagination must have seized on this image and transformed it into a powerful, uncanny wraith. It flows easily into consciousness. Macbeth is overwhelmed by it. His wife and his guests at the banquet become merely a backdrop; the Ghost is all he sees. Of course nobody else sees this Ghost. Macbeth's manner changes completely and he behaves in an astonishing fashion. To the guests his action must appear as a mental fit. Courteously, Ross asks the guests to rise and leave, but Lady Macbeth, never taking the unconscious seriously, and believing that the fit will pass quickly, asks the Lords to remain:

> My lord is often thus,   (III.iv.53)
> And hath been from his youth; pray you, keep seat.

She turns to Macbeth, hoping that by talking strongly to him she can quickly bring him out of his fit. It would appear that she asks the wrong questions, however. Husband and wife are now quite out of touch with each other. She, who had so powerfully incited him to murder Duncan by questioning his manhood (I.vii.46-51), repeats the same question, but in this grim situation it assumes a new and troubled meaning:

Are you a man? (III.iv.58)

He answers:

> Ay, and a bold one, that dare look on that
> Which might appal the devil.

Two opposite opinions on what it is to be truly a man collide here. As we see throughout the play, Lady Macbeth, who has no access to the unconscious, represses it and despises anyone who pays attention to it. In contrast, for Macbeth the channel between consciousness and the unconscious is always open. Therefore, calling for Banquo brings up that image for him and it has more reality than does the banquet—and to be able to face this terrible image requires truly great courage. He knows that he is quite manly, even heroic, if he can withstand such a supernatural apparition. Therefore, from his viewpoint he is quite right when he answers: "Ay, and a bold one." Of course, for Lady Macbeth his vision is nonsense. It is an illusion which has no reality whatsoever:

> . . . When all's done (III.iv.68)
> You look but on a stool.

Her talk does not tear Macbeth from the grip of the terrible ghost image. He continues to speak to the Ghost, but the apparition only nods. I have mentioned before that active imagination is a method in which there is an exchange between consciousness and the unconscious. Specifically, the ego is confronted with an unconscious content which assumes "personality." In such an encounter between the ego and an inner figure, it frequently occurs that the inner vis-à-vis speaks. But it is extremely rare that in active imagination the inner figure is personified in the image of a ghost. As a rule, the unconscious content represents an archetype; it usually communicates through the spoken word. That a ghost speaks in a Shakespearean play is not unheard of. In Act I and Act III of *Hamlet,* the Ghost does speak, but one of the points in *Hamlet* is that the Ghost does not speak to

Marcellus or Horatio, but only to Hamlet himself when no one else is present. The reason the Ghost in *Hamlet* was able to converse with a human being was because of the close, personal relationship which had existed between Hamlet and his father, and the complete absence of any guilt in their mutual relationship. In *Macbeth* the purpose of the apparition is to remind Macbeth of his bloody crime and terrible guilt. Lady Macbeth does not understand her husband at all. She thinks his strange behavior is something to be ashamed of. For him, Banquo's return is a terrible experience. He is particularly shocked because he now knows that life after death exists. This has more significance to him than even the murder. His jumping the "life to come" (I.vii.7) has been of no avail.

The subject of immortality occupied Shakespeare's mind a great deal. It is most beautifully discussed in Hamlet's monologue, "To be or not to be" (III.i.56-87), especially in the lines:

> For in that sleep of death what dreams may come   (III.i.66)
> When we have shuffled off this mortal coil,
> Must give us pause.

Macbeth now comes to the conclusion:

> . . . but now they rise again,   (III.iv.80)
> With twenty mortal murders on their crowns,
> And push us from our stools: *this is more strange*
> *Than such a murder is.*

Once the ghost image lets go, Macbeth quickly regains his composure. He equivocates and makes light of it to all his guests. He returns to the banquet table believing that with a slight excuse the banquet can at last begin. He cannot help mentioning his dear friend Banquo ("whom we miss, would he were here"). Immediately, the Ghost reappears and Macbeth is once more seized with panic—only more strongly than before.

Again Lady Macbeth declares that her husband is in a fit which unfortunately "spoils the pleasure of the time," but Macbeth feels profoundly challenged in his manhood. If the Ghost were a living being, even though terribly armed, Macbeth would fight him as a man, but he must admit that this second appearance of a vision from the netherworld, this "horrible shadow" which deprives him of his manhood, weakens him so much that it makes him feminine, changes him into "the baby of a girl." This transformation agrees very well with modern psychiatric experience. There are men who on the field of battle perform marvels of courage, but at the sight of a mouse fall into a state of terror. It makes all the difference whether the danger appears from without or within. As a rule, human beings are not prepared for a surprise attack by an unconscious content and we can profoundly sympathize when Macbeth exclaims, after the Ghost's appearance:

> Can such things be   (III.iv.111)
> And overcome us like a summer's cloud,
> Without our special wonder?

He also notices the peculiar effect the Ghost has on him. The ego, as it were, has dissolved and is alienated from what it considers to be its proper nature:

> You make me strange   (III.iv.113)
> Even to the disposition that I owe,
> When now I think you can behold such sights,
> And keep the natural ruby of your cheeks,
> When mine are blanch'd with fear.

I would like to remark parenthetically that in *King Lear* Shakespeare describes the effect of a terrible experience on the ego:

> O most small fault,   (I.iv.290)
> How ugly didst thou in Cordelia show!
> Which, like an engine, wrench'd my frame of nature
> From the fix'd place.

This is a description of the *violent separation* of an ego from all its conscious convictions. In *Macbeth* we have an *alienation* of the ego from its conscious convictions. The difference is due to the difference in causes. In *King Lear* the cause is a violent affect, in *Macbeth* a numinous image.

Only Lady Macbeth knows that Macbeth must have seen some apparition, but by now she has had all she can take. She fears quite rightly that more of these shaking visions may fall upon her husband, and so, without further ado, she ends the banquet—and we never hear that anyone had a chance to eat!

As a rule, the function of such a vision as Macbeth's is compensatory. It adds knowledge to consciousness so that with the increase of knowledge it can handle the situation more adequately. But Macbeth does not really reflect on his insights in order to draw the proper conclusions. His reaction to "these terrible dreams that shake us nightly" is to commit another murder, so now, instead of changing his ways, his literal-mindedness and unappeased thirst and hunger incite him to murder again:

> It will have blood, they say; blood will have blood.
>
> (III.iv. 122)

And so he plots the next murder. He feels slighted because Macduff has not attended the banquet. We can imagine that Banquo might also have stayed away had he been more outspoken in his reaction to Duncan's murder. Macduff knows less, as far as facts are concerned, but during the murder night he evidently drew the proper conclusion and subsequently has avoided any association with Macbeth that could be taken as silent approval of Duncan's murder. Nor can Macduff be appeased. He has refused to have any dealing with the tyrant and therefore quite naturally becomes the center of all the forces assembling against Macbeth.

In plotting this further murder, Macbeth can only state the true weakness of his ego. All that matters now is his own advantage:

> For mine own good   (III.iv.135)
> All causes shall give way.

Murder has become the only way to solve problems:

> I am in blood   (III.iv.136)
> Stepp'd in so far, that, should I wade no more,
> Returning were as tedious as go o'er.

It is worth mentioning that the Hebrew word for repentance, *T'shuvah,* means *return.* It would be just too much effort for Macbeth "to return," to change his ways. His soul is so engulfed in blood that he cannot possibly repent. So he decides to give free rein to all his murderous thoughts, to become finally and completely unconscious:

> Strange things I have in head that will to hand,   (III.iv.139)
> Which must be acted ere they may be scann'd.

v

Since Scene 5 is probably not Shakespeare's,[5] I feel justified in omitting it from psychological considerations.

vi

The sixth scene carries the action further and indicates the growing discontent with Macbeth's reign. Lennox reports in a sarcastic manner the general belief that Macbeth murdered Duncan, and informs us that Macduff has fled to England:

> Macduff is gone to pray the holy king, upon his aid (III.vi.29)
> To wake Northumberland and war-like Siward:
> That, by the help of these—(with Him above
> To ratify the work)—we may again
> Give to our tables meat, sleep to our nights,
> Free from our feasts and banquets bloody knives,
> Do faithful homage and receive free honours;
> All which we pine for now. And this report
> Hath so exasperate the king that he
> Prepares for some attempt at war.

---

[5] G. Wilson Knight defends this scene as being genuinely Shakespeare's. *The Shakespearian Tempest* (Oxford Univ. Press, London, 1932), p. 326.

Act Four

i

Like the first act, the fourth act begins with a scene in hell. The Three Witches are assembled again, this time not on the heath but in a dark cave—if we accept Rowe's stage direction. J. Dover Wilson follows the edition of Edward Capell (1768) and considers the locality to be "The pit of Acheron," for which he gives good reasons.[1] Whichever place we accept, it appears as a symbol of the dark aspect of the Great Mother, as a womb out of which life originates or is destroyed. As in the first act, the three women are alone in the first part of the scene. In their opening speeches they refer to their respective familiars: "brinded cat," "hedge-pig" and "Harpier." It is now time to begin their magical work. The center of the scene is taken up by a boiling cauldron into which they throw a large number of ingredients, accompanying their sinister activity with magical incantations. According to the laws of demonology in Elizabethan times, the objects used by the Sisters have a powerful destructive effect: "poisoned entrails," "a toad," "sweltered venom," "fillet of a fenny snake," "eye of newt," etc. With the exception of the toad, they are all portions of some animal or of a human being. What matters is the magical purpose. Through magic, this "hell-broth" becomes destructive. Its particular emphasis is making new life impossible:

> Finger of birth-strangled babe   (IV.i.30)
> Ditch-deliver'd by a drab.

Images which belong to the negative aspect of the mother archetype, like "sow's blood that hath eaten her nine farrow," abound in these speeches.

The difference between this scene and the hellish scene in Act I (iii.37-88) does not lie so much in content as in emotional impact. Compared with the earlier scene, the maternal destruc-

---

[1] See the Cambridge University Press edition of 1960, p. 146.

tiveness of the present scene is highly intensified, a fact which corresponds to the psychological changes which have occurred in Macbeth and in the whole of Scotland. The atmosphere is much thicker, as it were, the "charm of powerful trouble" much more effective: "The charm is firm and good." Macbeth seems to be part of this world when he addresses the Witches:

> How now, you secret, black, and midnight hags! (IV.i.48)
> What is't you do?

To which all answer: "A deed without a name." While in Act I Macbeth and Banquo happened to come upon the Witches, this time Macbeth has deliberately sought them out. It is Macbeth's insecurity, his arrogant decision to fight even God, and his complete surrender to hell (cf. p. 366), which lead him to probe the mantic powers of the Witches. He has no doubt that they truly know the future. He therefore appeals to them to use their black art to tell him about his future:

> I conjure you, by that which you profess,— (IV.i.51)
> Howe'er you come to know it,—answer me.

He could not make the Ghost speak to him, but he succeeds in conversing with the weird Sisters. He can handle them because he is now one of their kind. He acts as if he were their master, but he is truly their victim. He has become evil incarnated. He knows their almost unlimited power of destruction and wants to use them for his own purposes. They can "untie the winds and let them fight against the churches"—that is, they can upset the divine order in human society. They can confuse all human orientation, raze nature and overthrow social order. But their greatest potency lies in their power to destroy all creativity in nature:

> . . . though the treasure (IV.i.58)
> Of Nature's germens[2] tumble all together,

[2] Curry (Arden, p. 113): Nature's germens are the *rationes seminales,* "the material essences which correspond to the exemplars in God's mind."

Even till destruction sicken: answer me
To what I ask you.

Wilson's perceptive comment on these lines is very helpful:[3]

> The culminating image here, and one upon which the speaker
> obviously dwells in delight, seems to envisage a stage even be-
> yond the triumph of Hell and the destruction of 'both the
> worlds', namely the discovery, through that catastrophe, of the
> hidden seeds of life whether in heaven or earth; seeds which,
> originating in the mind of God, could not themselves be de-
> stroyed but might be rendered for ever barren, or productive
> of mere monstrosity, if tumbled all together in devilish confu-
> sion. In other words, Macbeth speaks of a time when the Devil
> will not only have made an end of God's world, but have ren-
> dered its re-creation for ever impossible. After the contempla-
> tion of so dreadful a contingency, the words: 'I 'gin to be a-
> weary of the sun, and wish the estate o' th' world were now
> undone' (V.i.49) sound almost tame, and are, I think, intended
> to mark the sinking of the volcanic fires before the end.

I doubt whether Macbeth "dwells in delight" on the image. I
rather agree with Kenneth Muir's statement:[4]

> It is rather the *reductio ad absurdum* of the principle that the
> end justifies the means, of which the equivocator in the Porter
> scene provides a mild example. Macbeth is willing to sacrifice
> the future of the universe to his own personal and temporary
> satisfaction.

In *The Wheel of Fire,*[5] G. Wilson Knight says of these same
lines:

> He (Macbeth) is living in an unreal world, a fantastic mock-
> ery, a ghoulish dream; he strives to make this single nightmare

[3] Cambridge edition, p. lxiii.
[4] Arden, p. 113.
[5] Meridian Books (World Publishing Co., Cleveland, 1957), pp. 154-
156.

to rule the outward things of his nation. He would make all
Scotland a nightmare thing of dripping blood. He knows he
cannot return, so determines to go o'er. He seeks out the Weird
Sisters a second time. Now he welcomes disorder and confusion, would let them range wide over the earth, since they
range unfettered in his own soul:

> . . . *though the treasure*
> *Of nature's germens tumble all together,*
> *Even till destruction sicken; answer me*
> *To what I ask you.*

So he addresses the Weird Sisters. Castles, palaces, and pyra-
mids—let all fall in general confusion, if only Macbeth be
satisfied. He is plunging deeper and deeper into unreality, the
severance from mankind and all normal forms of life is now
abysmal, deep. Now he is shown Apparitions glassing the future. They promise him success in terms of natural law; no
man 'of woman born' shall hurt him, he shall not be van-
quished till Birnam Wood come against him. He, based firmly
in the unreal, yet thinks to build his future on the laws of reality. He forgets that he is trafficking with things of nightmare
fantasy, whose truth is falsehood, falsehood truth. That success
they promise is unreal as they themselves. So, *once having can-
celled the bond of reality he has no home: the unreal he understands not, the real condemns him. In neither can he exist.* He
asks if Banquo's issue shall reign in Scotland: most horrible
thought to him, since, if that be so, it proves that the future
takes its natural course irrespective of human acts—that prophecy need not have been interpreted into crime: that he would in
truth have been King of Scotland without his own 'stir'. Also the
very thought of other succeeding and prosperous kings, some
of them with 'two fold balls and treble sceptres,' is a madden-
ing thing to *him who is no real king but only monarch of a
nightmare realm.* The Weird Sisters who were formerly as the
three Parcae, or Fates, foretelling Macbeth's future, now, at
this later stage of his story, become the Erinyes, avengers of
murder, symbols of the tormented soul. They delude and mad-
den him with their apparitions and ghosts. Yet he does not
give way, and raises our admiration at his undaunted sever-

ance from good. He contends for his own individual soul against the universal reality. Nor is his contest unavailing. He is fighting himself free from the nightmare fear of his life. He goes on 'till destruction sicken'; he actually does 'go o'er,' is not lost in the stream of blood he elects to cross. It is true. He wins his battle. He adds crime to crime and emerges at last victorious and fearless:

> *I have almost forgot the taste of fears:*   (V.v.9)
> *The time has been, my senses would have cool'd*
> *To hear the night-shriek; and my fell of hair*
> *Would at a dismal treatise rouse and stir*
> *As life were in't; I have supp'd full with horrors;*
> *Direness, familiar to my slaughterous thoughts,*
> *Cannot once start me.*

In this lengthy quotation we meet with profound insights into the changing psychology of Macbeth, but I feel that by considering this great theme of Act IV, Scene 1, together with lines occurring much later in Act V, the picture of Macbeth becomes somewhat distorted. We gain a better understanding of what happens to him when we accompany the process as it unfolds through the fourth and fifth acts. For example, I cannot agree with Knight that Macbeth "welcomes disorder and confusion." It is rather the extreme *hubris* of the ego that wishes and wants to use the destructive powers of nature to the utmost, and that expresses his total hostility to all creation. Certainly Macbeth goes "o'er" but we know that what he is really seeking is to be "perfect, whole as the marble, founded as the rock, as broad and general as the casing air." He desires *wholeness* and *security* —the very aim of individuation. For this purpose, he uses the powers of destruction, of hell. Being so committed to the powers of darkness, he must fight God, if we take creativity as the very life of God. He cannot succeed, not only because he cuts himself off from common humanity and from all good, but just because this arrogance of the ego, the hubris, makes him blind, literal-minded, deprives him of all feeling and destroys his soul. That the weird Sisters, formerly the three Parcae or Fates,

now become the Erinyes, figures who persecute him, as Knight
states, appears to be doubtful. For one thing, the feminine here
is not seen as the ultimate; the Witches are under the control of
masculine factors, "masters." There exists a hierarchy of powers
in the unconscious. The First Witch asks:

> Say if thou'dst rather hear it from our mouths,   (IV.i.61)
> Or from our masters'?

Macbeth prefers to hear it from the "masters." The masters are
the deepest portion of the unconscious accessible to Macbeth.
Though Macbeth calls, "Let me see 'em!" they do not materialize. Rather, their presence is felt, as they produce a series of
apparitions. This is in contrast to the theory[6] that the masters
can "only mean the demons who assume the shape of the apparitions."

One would expect a passively receptive attitude from Macbeth but the opposite occurs. Twice he addresses the Witches
and each time has to be told:

> He knows thy thought: (IV.i.70)
> Hear his speech, but say thou nought.

> He will not be commanded.   (IV.i.75)

By trying to command the Witches, he interferes with the autonomous activity of the unconscious. His intentional interrupting
of the emergent visions could stop the "show" completely, but
fortunately it does not. In spite of his interference, the inner
process continues and proves the close connection that Macbeth
has with the unconscious, the lack of walls between him and the
unconscious—but it also emphasizes the autonomy of unconscious contents.

The "show" actually speaks in two different ways to him. The
visual appearances are symbols that need to be interpreted but
Macbeth does not react to the first two apparitions as to a sym-

6 Arden, p. 115.

bol. He only listens to the second form of communication: to speech. In our analysis, we will have to pay attention to both forms of communication.

The First Apparition is that of an "armed Head," which has been thought to represent Macbeth's head.[7] Wilson even adds the stage direction: "like Macbeth's, rises from the cauldron." Crawford and Kittredge[8] both think the first apparition is Macduff. I agree with Knight, however, who points out in *The Imperial Theme:* [9]

> The vivid destruction-birth sequence in this scene. . . . The Armed Head, recalling Macdonwald's head . . . blends with the 'chaos' and 'disorder' thought throughout . . . and suggests both the iron force of evil and also its final destruction.

The stage direction in the Folio does not specify the armed Head as that of a particular person. A symbol always has many meanings but never refers to any specific person. It indicates a content not known, or unknowable. It personifies a feature in the psychic structure, for which it is the best possible representation. I therefore agree with Knight that the armed Head "suggests both the iron force of evil and also its final destruction." Without detracting from Knight's interpretation, I would add that the armed Head might refer to other psychological qualities, for example, Macbeth's imperviousness to the higher powers.

The armed Head addresses Macbeth three times by name and warns him most solemnly:

Beware Macduff; Beware the Thane of Fife.   (IV.i.71)

—but without any further specific details. Macbeth accepts this warning gratefully and adds, "Thou hast harped my fear aright," indicating that the apparition is born out of his fear of Macduff.

---

[7] Upton (Furness edition, p. 256): "The Armed Head represents symbolically Macbeth's head cut off and brought to Malcolm by Macduff."

[8] Arden, p. 114.

[9] Methuen & Co., London, 1961, pp. 150-151.

He wants to know more, but a new image arises—that of a bloody Child. Again Knight's symbolism is most fitting:[10]

> The blood-agony of birth that travails to wrench into existence a force to right the sickening evil.

Since the child is a factor in Macbeth's unconscious, it would also represent his own creativity. It is a symbol of ever-recurring birth which, in spite of all violence and murder, survives.[11] As such, it knows of facts which exist outside of nature. It knows the "metaphysical" powers which enter history and overcome evil. Therefore it can inform Macbeth:

> . . . laugh to scorn   (IV.i.80)
> The power of man, for none of woman born
> Shall harm Macbeth.

In his blindness, Macbeth takes this prophecy literally. Actually, the bloody Child gives him more information, thus responding to his request as addressed to the armed Head: "But one word more." The message is at the same time factual and symbolic:

> Be bloody, bold and resolute . . .   (IV.i.79)

But Macbeth is only concerned with the concrete meaning of the Second Apparition's speech:

> Then live, Macduff: what need I fear of thee?   (IV.i.81)
> But yet I'll make *assurance double sure,*
> And take a bond of Fate.

Kittredge's comment is to the point:[12]

---

[10] *Ibid.,* p. 151.

[11] Cf. Jung, "The Psychology of the Child Archetype," in *The Archetypes and the Collective Unconscious,* p. 151.

[12] *Macbeth,* ed. by George Lyman Kittredge (Ginn & Co., New York, 1939), p. 190.

By killing Macduff, Macbeth will put it out of Fate's power to harm him unless Fate is ready to break two of her fixed laws: the law of birth and the law of death; she must bring forward a man who was never born, and must bring back a man (not a mere ghost) from the dead.

Macbeth's ultimate motive in his decision to do away with Macduff is to find peace from the attacks of the unconscious:

> Thou shalt not live;   (IV.i.84)
> That I may tell pale-hearted fear it lies,
> And *sleep*[13] in spite of thunder.

The Third Apparition follows immediately and is similar to the Second in presenting an image of a Child. However, it is not bloody; it wears a crown and holds "a tree in his hand." Macbeth's reaction is different too. Although he does not interpret all of what he sees, he at least describes it. He is deeply shocked:

> What is this,   (IV.i.88)
> That rises like the issue of a king;
> And wears upon his baby brow the round
> And top of sovereignty?

We accept the armed Head as a genuine symbol. Again, it would be a mistake to see a specific person in the crowned Child. Kittredge does this when he identifies the Child with "Malcolm as King." [14] The image is a genuine symbol and points to many more meanings than the first Child. Like the first, it also symbolizes the victorious renewal of life, but it has the added meaning of royalty since it wears the appropriate insignia of kingship. It has no mark of injury. This whole, royal Child is truly a symbol of the Self. It represents totality, that royal quality which Macbeth wants more than anything. (We remember that he

---

[13] Cf. pp. 358-359, III.ii.22.
[14] *Op. cit.,* p. 190.

wants to be "whole as the marble, founded as the rock.") The reference to the "round and top of sovereignty," which might strike us as redundant, actually points to two different aspects of the Self.

Let us, however, first hear what older commentators have had to say about this particular line. Johnson wrote:[15]

> The *round* is that part of the crown that encircles the head. The *top* is the ornament that rises above it.

R. G. White says:[16]

> Shakespeare makes Macbeth call the crown 'the round of sovereignty' here and elsewhere—first, obviously, in allusion to the form of the ornament. That is prose; but immediately his poetic eye sees that a crown is the external sign of the complete possession of the throne. It is the visible evidence that the royalty of its wearer lacks nothing, but is '*totus, teres, atque rotundus*'—that it is finished, just as 'our little life is *rounded* with a sleep.' But the crown not only completes (especially in the eye of Macbeth, the usurper) and rounds, as with the perfection of a circle, the claim to sovereignty, but it is figuratively the top, the summit, of ambitious hopes. Shakespeare often uses 'top' in this sense—e.g., 'the top of admiration,' 'the top of judgment,' 'the top of honor,' 'the top of happy hours.' All this flashed upon Shakespeare through his mind's eye, as he saw the circlet upon the top of the child's head.

However, it is necessary to understand that these symbols—child, king, round, top and tree—are archetypal symbols which express important facets of the totality. This combination of images rose in the poet out of the common ground of human experience, the collective unconscious, as a means of expressing that perfection and totality which Macbeth is seeking, and which would be the aim of individuation. R. G. White, with his amazing sensitivity, therefore quite rightly associates these four Latin

---

[15] Furness, p. 258.
[16] Furness, p. 259.

words, *"totus, teres, atque rotundus,"* with the line in *Macbeth*.
Let us hear what C. G. Jung, the outstanding explorer of archetypal symbolism, has to say:[17]

> Because the king in general represents a superior personality
> exalted above the ordinary, he has become the carrier of a
> myth, that is to say, of the statements of the collective un-
> conscious. The outward paraphernalia of kingship show this
> very clearly. The crown symbolizes his relation to the sun. . . .
> The further we go back in history the more evident does the
> king's divinity become.

In regard to the archetype of the *child,* and also of the *tree,* I
would refer readers to Jung's articles on these two archetypes,
where one will find a rich discussion of these symbols of totality.
I would like to quote from *Aion* in regard to the *round* as a
symbol of spirit, which Jung discusses there at length:

> The *rotumdum* connotes a transcendent entity.[18]

> The *rotundum* is a highly abstract, transcendent idea, which
> by reason of its roundness and wholeness refers to the Original
> Man, the Anthropos.[19]

Such visions as Macbeth beholds here are compensatory. The
unconscious is trying to convey to him the idea that the wholeness and security he is seeking is not in this world but lies in a
transcendental realm. But, as we saw in the beginning, Macbeth
is lacking in the essential quality which makes a king. He has
usurped kingship and, more than that, wants to acquire wholeness, perfection. Now it appears to him in this beautiful symbol
of a "Child crowned, with a tree in his hand." Like the first
Child, it also speaks to him. It admonishes him to be reckless,
"lion-mettled, proud," and adds the prophecy:

[17] *Mysterium Coniunctionis,* p. 258.
[18] *Aion,* p. 249.
[19] *Ibid.,* p. 246.

> Macbeth shall never vanquished be, until (IV.i.91)
> Great Birnam Wood to high Dunsinane Hill
> Shall come against him.

To which Macbeth reacts with:

> That will never be: (IV.i.94)
> Who can impress the forest, bid the tree
> Unfix his earth-bound root?

Kittredge comments:[20]

> Macbeth, in eager acceptance of the oracle, continues it in the
> same rhymed form. In effect, he makes himself his own
> prophet: he identifies himself, as it were, with the lying spirits
> whom he has consulted, and whom he trusts to the end.

Kittredge's observation on the rhymed form emphasizes Macbeth's identity with this Child, but I cannot agree that these spirits are "lying spirits." On the contrary, they are speaking true. It
is Macbeth who misunderstands. He again misinterprets a
prophecy because of his belief that transcendental forces cannot
affect the laws of nature. This Apparition is another opportunity
for Macbeth to find himself but of course the narrowness of his
mind, his egotistical murderous ego, has long ago lost the ability
to understand such a revelation of the unconscious.

In our psychiatric practice we find quite often that a dream
will present a schizophrenic with extraordinary healing symbols
although the suffering ego has no chance of understanding and
integrating them. Although Macbeth is no schizophrenic, he
shares with the schizophrenic the inability to understand his unconscious. The reason for this in a schizophrenic is his "split" of
consciousness. In Macbeth it is guilt and *hubris* which force him
to take symbols only concretely. The revelations are wasted on
him. They increase and intensify his blood-thirst. He wants to
know "one thing" more. They all warn him, but he insists—and
now the cauldron sinks. The cauldron is a feminine symbol, rep-

[20] *Op. cit.,* p. 190.

resenting the mothers and the anima in an abstract form. What characterizes these three visions is that they all have some reference to Macbeth and present him with a healing possibility for his own good.

The fourth vision, as is so often the case, is of a totally different nature. In *Psychology and Alchemy*,[21] Jung discusses the numbers three and four. He quotes Maria Prophetissa:

> "One becomes two, two becomes three, and out of the third comes the one as the fourth."

He remarks that the number four is a number of wholeness. According to him:

> The number three is not a natural expression for wholeness, since four represents the minimum number of determinants in a whole judgment. . . . there is always a vacillation between three and four which comes out over and over again. Even in the axiom of Maria Prophetissa the quaternity is muffled and alembicated . . . This uncertainty has a duplex character— in other words, the central ideas are ternary as well as quaternary. The psychologist cannot but mention the fact that a similar puzzle exists in the psychology of the unconscious: the least differentiated or "inferior" function is so much contaminated by the collective unconscious that, on becoming conscious, it brings up among others the archetype of the self as well. . . . Four signifies the feminine, motherly, physical; three the masculine, fatherly, spiritual. Thus the uncertainty as to three or four amounts to a wavering between the spiritual and the physical—a striking example of how every human truth is a last truth but one.

However, when a four is clearly established and differentiated, then the character of wholeness is unmistakable and indubitable. It is also a regular occurrence that *three* aspects are more or less of one character, while the fourth is something essentially different. In order to establish wholeness our orientation

[21] Pp. 23, 26.

toward the sensual world needs, for example, the division of time in three—past, present, future—and adds the fourth as something essentially different, that is, space. Or we have the three dimensions of space but need the essentially different dimension of time to establish reality, a fact which modern physics expresses by the so-called time-space continuum.

I cannot mention all the examples in Jung's writings to establish that the number four is the archetype of totality, but I gladly refer the reader to his many works. The number three occurs in this scene in the "three witches," and the fourth would be the totally other one, the "masters." The "show" consists of four separate apparitions, in which the fourth has a very different character from the preceding three. They perfectly express the pattern which the archetype of totality imposes. Shakespeare, in using this fourfold division, was instinctively guided by the archetype, a function of the unconscious. The fourth and essentially different experience is characterized by two facts: the "cauldron sinks," and it is accompanied by a particular noise:[22]

Why sinks that cauldron? and what noise is this?   (IV.i.106)

"Hautboys" is added as stage direction.[23]

I believe that the sinking of the cauldron indicates that the images which now arise are in no way produced by magic, but are the free flow of the unconscious. The number four appears here as a multiple—"A show of eight Kings"—thus expressing again a totality.[24] Kittredge says:[25]

> The cauldron sinks to give the audience a clear view of the kings, as each passes rapidly across the lighted doorway at the back of the inner-stage.

[22] Arden, p. 117: "A concert or company of musicians, usually three in number, who attended taverns, etc., was called a 'noise.'"

[23] Kittredge, p. 191: "Hoboyes (Hautboys) play in F. *Ham.* as here."

[24] I am of course familiar with Chambers' statement (Furness, p. 262): "The 'eight Kings' are Robert II (1371), Robert III, and the six Jamses. Those in the glass are the successors of James."

[25] *Op. cit.,* p. 191.

Well, this might also be correct, but the principal reason for the sinking cauldron is certainly the inner psychological necessities. These, of course, very often agree with the requirements of stage production. Undoubtedly the archetypal patterns, eight, royalty and mirror, impressed themselves on Shakespeare's mind and determined his choice. The mirror has many different meanings. I believe it reflects the eight Kings and points to the infinite sequence of productive life. It could also symbolize consciousness and would then be a hint to Macbeth to reflect more deeply on these visions.

Banquo, as an identifiable person, stands outside the archetypal symbol of the eight Kings. He represents a historical link between the archetypal vision and Macbeth's personal life. The "show" is mute.[26] Whatever comment we have about it comes from Macbeth's highly affective exclamations. We have to remember that Macbeth reacts to this show out of his own intense emotional involvement. He would naturally emphasize all those qualities and facts which portend the limited time of his reign. It is just this cool objective presentation of the future which so profoundly disturbs him: "Thy crown does sear mine eye-balls," and makes him curse: "filthy hags!" with utter desperation:

What! will the line stretch out to th' crack of doom?

(IV.i.117)

The "two-fold balls and treble sceptres" are variously interpreted. In the Furness edition we find:[27]

> *Warburton:* This was intended as a compliment to King James the First, who first united the two islands and the three kingdoms under one head; whose house too was said to be descended from Banquo.—*Clarendon:* The 'two-fold balls' here mentioned probably refer to the double coronation of James,

[26] Cf. *The Tempest* (III.iii.37):
Such shapes, such gesture, and such sound, expressing—
Although they want the use of tongue—a kind
Of excellent dumb discourse.
[27] P. 263.

at Scone and at Westminster.—*Manly:* The style and title assumed by James I, after October 24, 1604, was: 'The Most
High and Mightie Prince, James, by the Grace of God, King
of Great Britaine, France, and Ireland, Defender of the Faith.'
This is the treble sceptre, and not that of the three kingdoms
of England, Scotland, and Ireland.

The Arden edition comments in this way:[28]

> The two-fold balls are usually taken to refer to the double
> coronation of James at Scone and at Westminster.

Dr. Barron, however, introduces the psychological point of view
when he says:[29]

> . . . Besides the idea of political power we are undoubtedly
> justified in believing sexual power to be symbolized in the
> "two-fold balls and treble sceptres." This is but one example
> of Shakespeare's ability to obtain concentration of meaning
> through over-determined use of symbols.

Not only sexual power but all the royal attributes of kingship
and of the outstanding personality are contained in the symbol
of the balls and scepters. With other commentators, I hold that
the lines spoken by the First Witch (IV.i.125-132) are interpolated.[30] It appears to me more in keeping with the whole mood of
the drama and the phenomenology of such visions that this
"show" suddenly vanishes. Considering the entire extraordinary
sequence of visions, we should not be surprised that Macbeth
cannot stand the confrontation with truth and that to him it was
"a pernicious hour":

> Stand aye accursed in the calendar! (IV.i.133)

Reality breaks in upon Macbeth when Lennox enters. For
Macbeth the visions have been so real that he has to ask Lennox

---

28 P. 118.
29 *Op. cit.,* p. 142fn.
30 Arden, p. xxvii.

whether he has also seen the weird Sisters. His affect still rejects that which was his greatest gift—the openness to the unconscious. In rejecting it he also rejects himself most thoroughly. We cannot deny our sympathy to him because the influx of unconscious contents is too much of a burden for him. His mind is too narrow to understand his own visions. Under the impact of the unconscious, his ego deteriorates. His greatest gift has become an evil spirit to him, as it once was for the Israelitic king, Saul:[31]

> But the Spirit of the Lord departed from Saul, and an evil spirit from the Lord troubled him. And Saul's servants said unto him, Behold now, an evil spirit from God troubleth thee.

By the grace of God, the first Israelitic king was a prophet *and* a king. But this burden was too much for him. He did not completely obey the Lord and thus the spirit of the Lord changed from good to bad. Macbeth, however, never received the grace of God. His gift, his openness to the unconscious, connected him with the negative mother archetype in various shapes. He never had a chance to maintain himself against them.

Of all Shakespeare's dramas, *Macbeth* contains the greatest number of monologues. The drama takes place in Macbeth's soul and therefore finds its only suitable expression in the monologue. And so, this grand scene also ends with a monologue. Macbeth becomes harder than ever, more stubborn in his will to help fate along:

> . . . I'll make assurance double sure, (IV.i.83)
> And take a bond of fate.

The advice of the "bloody Child"—"Be bloody, bold and resolute"—is taken up with a characteristic emphasis:

> . . . from this moment (IV.i.146)
> The very firstlings of my heart shall be
> The firstlings of my hand.

[31] I Samuel 16:14, 15.

Macbeth now makes it a definite principle to avoid any reflection. From now on consciousness is finally and absolutely excluded. There will be no time between thought and act:

> And even now, (IV.i.148)
> To crown my thoughts with acts, be it thought and done.

With this he gives up the last thread of humanness. He will act like an animal that falls upon its prey. He will not seek visions any more—"But no more sights"—not so much because they terrify him as because they inevitably convey truth and force reflection upon him. With this statement, the independence, isolation and satanic hubris of the ego is expressed in absolute form.

ii

I omit an analysis of all of Scene 2 because it does not bear on our particular theme. I also omit an analysis of the long Scene 3 which takes place in England and shows the gathering force of Macbeth's antagonists. It is a profoundly moving scene in which Ross tells Macduff of the murder of his entire family. Macduff's reaction:

> O hell-kite! All? (IV.iii.217)
> What! all my pretty chickens and their dam
> At one fell swoop?

emphasizes and brings out in strong relief Macbeth's hatred of life, fertility—in brief, of all the positive aspects of the mother archetype. This foul deed proves that by now Macbeth has put all his dire resolutions into action.

German commentators find that the intensity of the dramatic action usually is highest in the first three acts of Shakespeare's tragedies, but declines sharply in the fourth and fifth. In contrast, G. Wilson Knight's commentary speaks of "the gathering poetic force of Macbeth's speeches, culminating in the supreme pieces of Act V." [32] In the Furness edition, Fletcher comments: [33]

[32] *Wheel of Fire,* p. 159.
[33] P. 267.

It mars the whole spirit and moral of the play to take anything
from that depth and liveliness of interest which the dramatist
has attached to the characters and fortunes of Macduff and
his Lady. They are the chief representatives in the piece, of the
interests of loyalty and domestic affection, as opposed to those
of the foulest treachery and the most selfish and remorseless
ambition. . . . It is not enough that we should hear the story
in the brief words in which it is related to Macduff by his
fugitive cousin, Ross. The presence of the affectionate family
before our eyes,—the timid lady's eloquent complaining to her
cousin, of her husband's deserting them in danger,—the grace-
ful prattle with her boy, in which she seeks relief from her
melancholy forebodings,—and then the sudden entrance of
Macbeth's murderous ruffians,—are all requisite to give that
crowning horror, that consummately and violently revolting
character to Macbeth's career, which Shakespeare has so evidently studied to impress upon it.

While there may be contrasting opinions on the dramatic intensity of the last two acts of *Macbeth,* there certainly is none in
regard to their psychological interest. Shakespeare's concern
with self-knowledge is possibly at its highest when this great
drama finds its resolution. The character of the play as a *Seelendrama* (literally, drama of the soul: a play in which the dramatic events occur in the soul, not in outward reality) reveals
itself movingly just in its conclusion. Among the many terrible
things which Macbeth's reign has brought to suffering Scotland
and her people is the cruel human condition in which we cannot
be true to ourselves:

> But cruel are the times, when we are traitors   (IV.ii.18)
> And do not know ourselves.

This state of mind—not knowing oneself—transcends the individual and even applies to the country:

> Alas! poor country;   (IV.iii.164)
> Almost afraid to know itself.

Act Five

i

Everything that has been germinating and developing in the preceding four acts now arrives at its meaningful solution. This is
particularly true of the fate of the two main characters, Macbeth
and Lady Macbeth. Among the many fascinating moments
which Shakespeare's vast imagination has brought to life, Lady
Macbeth's sleepwalking has been one of the strangest, most
mysterious, and deeply moving scenes in all his plays. The
lighted taper, the eerie, sightless eyes, the mumbled spasmodic
words—these have never failed to cast an uncanny spell,
coupled with a feeling of compassion, a sense of *tat twam asi*
(thou art that) in sympathy for this lonely tortured human being. John Russell Brown[1] reproduces the feeling of tragedy in
this scene by a masterful description, from which I quote freely:

> Lady Macbeth is a strange and precarious figure on the nearly
> empty stage so caught in her own imagination that she alone
> carries a light with her. . . . Her talk moves alarmingly from
> one idea to another, as quickly as they occur to her mind. . . .
> She speaks in spurts, to relapse into silences that may be more
> frightening than her words, for there is no indication which
> way her imagination will move. . . . She is caught in the real-
> ity of a past moment, when they were together in guilt and
> when she could control Macbeth; only, as she re-lives that
> crisis, she calls now for his hand and, aware that they are
> doomed ('What's done cannot be undone'), calls him to their
> bed, repeatedly. She goes 'directly' as if leading him: so the
> audience's last view of Lady Macbeth emphasizes her delusion
> of closeness to her husband, together with her sense of guilt,
> hopelessness and determination.

This scene has 76 lines only, of which Lady Macbeth speaks
approximately 20. All of the other lines belong to the Doctor of

---

[1] *Shakespeare: The Tragedy of Macbeth* (Edward Arnold, Ltd., London, 1963), pp. 56-57.

Physic and the waiting Gentlewoman. The structure of the scene is actually quite simple, which helps to bring out its profound significance for the fates of Macbeth and Lady Macbeth. A short remark by Max Lüthi points this up:[2]

> Thus the insanity scene of Lady Macbeth has become a kind of play within a play; as such it is announced and commented upon. The lady becomes a "she" from an "I" or "thou"; from a person speaking and addressed, she becomes a person discussed, a fact which in this case is particularly meaningful: She has lost herself.

Truly, this scene is a play within a play. In this "play" Lady Macbeth is the only principal figure on the stage, therefore the center of attention and the carrier of the dramatic movement. The Doctor and the Gentlewoman comment upon and discuss the tragic woman and her condition from their contemporary, and to a degree, objective point of view. In turn, we, the spectators, removed in time and space, look at her as she acts and as she is mirrored in the view of her contemporaries. It is just this double distance which brings her close to us and makes her such a powerful symbol of frail and guilty man.

So far I have avoided discussing the literary or poetic qualities of Shakespeare's masterpiece, but I feel I should quote at least one poet's opinion on the style and poetry of this scene, because poetry is the anima's essence and is naturally her language when a great artist laments a soul's deterioration. Edith Sitwell [3] quotes from Bayfield:

> 'Lady Macbeth's speeches, which have always been printed in prose are really verse, and very fine verse too. The reader . . . will see how enormously they gain by being delivered in measure, and that the lines drawn out in monosyllabic feet are as wonderfully effective as any that Shakespeare wrote.'

[2] "Shakespeare, Dichter des Wirklichen und des Unwirklichen," *Dalp. Taschenbücher,* No. 373, p. 62.

[3] *A Notebook on William Shakespeare* (Beacon Press, Boston, 1961), pp. 44-45.

and adds her own comment:

> The speeches in the sleep-walking scene, if spoken as verse,
> have a great majesty. They drag the slow weight of the guilt
> along as if it were the train of pomp. But they have not the
> infinite pathos of the speeches when they are in prose, they do
> not inspire the same pity for this vast being, her gigantic will
> relaxed by sleep, trying to draw that will together, as she wan-
> ders through the scenes of her crime. The more relaxed sound
> of the prose produces that effect. The beat of the verse should
> be felt rather than heard, underlying the speeches.

This short scene has a profound effect upon the audience,
partly due to an intense concentration on Lady Macbeth's sleepwalking and talking. The result is that she appears quite real, as
something belonging to this world, and at the same time belonging to another world, living in a different category of reality.

We remember Lady Macbeth as the wife of the Thane; we
remember her gigantic monologue in which she addressed the
spirits (I.v.44: "Come you spirits . . ."), her being willing
even that they "unsex" her; we remember her part in the crime
of Duncan (II.ii.54-68), her inability to understand her husband after the murder (II.ii.45-47), her utter dissatisfaction
with the results of her "success" (III.ii.4-7), her alienation from
Macbeth (III.ii.8-10). We see her now for the last time—a sick
woman. The Gentlewoman describes her illness:

> I have seen her rise from her bed, throw her   (V.i.5)
> night-gown upon her, unlock her closet, take
> forth paper, fold it, write upon't, read it,
> afterwards seal it, and again return to bed;
> yet all this while in a most fast sleep.

This beautiful prose is at the same time a complete and valid
psychiatric description. Her actions are orderly and purposeful.
The pathology arises from the peculiar state of consciousness
with which these "normal" actions are associated. One expects
such well-coordinated activity from a state of *full* consciousness.

Nevertheless, she is not awake. Such will-directed actions are impossible without some consciousness. Ample clinical observation shows that such coordinated activity is only possible if a minimum of consciousness exists. Shakespeare's "doctor" is correct in his critical analysis when he calls her state of mind "a great perturbation" (constitutional disorder[4]). The whole ego is not present—just a small portion. A partial ego has a channel open to a fully active unconscious ("her eyes are open . . . but their sense is shut"). Lady Macbeth suffers from a psychic dissociation. The unconscious is cut off, but in this *abaissement du niveau mental* the unconscious succeeds in reaching consciousness again. How much of the unconscious is active is difficult to say; only those parts function, and that in a lively fashion, which Lady Macbeth has repressed.

As Freud and Jung have demonstrated with much clinical material, the unconscious, with the libido contained in it, always becomes destructive when it is not allowed to see the light of day. Like a mole, it burrows and undermines the psychic fundaments. Since Duncan's murder, the repressed unconscious has had a certain amount of time to do its destructive work; the repressed complex has forced its way back into consciousness and has manifested itself in symbolic actions. Shortly after the murder, Lady Macbeth had said, "A little water clears us of this deed" (II.ii.66). Now this need for cleansing her guilt returns in a compulsive action, as a long-continued washing of her hands. Yet this washing ceremonial brings her no peace. It does not cleanse her soul; on the contrary, it increases her agony. Instead of enlightenment of her consciousness, she has to have actual light:

> She has light by her continually;   (V.i.25)
> 'tis her command.

The thoughts and images which occupy her mind come up in fragments but in such a way that we, the audience, who know all the facts of the murders, can easily fill in the missing parts and,

---

[4] Wilson, Arden, p. 142.

just because we have the whole picture, we can be the more aware of how broken up is Lady Macbeth's mind. The Doctor and the Gentlewoman are surprised and shaken to hear snatches which make it clear that Lady Macbeth was implicated in the murders of Duncan and Banquo. To the audience these facts are not surprising, but rather the pitiful condition of Lady Macbeth which compels her to reveal them.

Some of the memory images (the bits and pieces of her guilty conscience) are of sight ("damned spot"), some of smell ("Here's the smell of the blood still: all the perfumes of Arabia will not sweeten this little hand"). There are even some of hearing ("there's knocking at the gate"), a memory which intensifies the horror and moves us deeply to compassion for this tortured soul. Only one thing has brought about this condition: the repression of her guilt.

If we compare Macbeth's and Lady Macbeth's attitudes toward the unconscious, we find a decisive difference: Macbeth did not resist the unconscious, *could* not resist it: he had to submit to its powerfully-emerging images (cf. the dagger monologue or his reaction immediately after Duncan's murder, his reaction to Banquo's ghost in the banquet scene and, most strongly, in his confrontation with the weird Sisters). The images did not repeat some actual experience but were fresh, new and unexpected, always associated with his destiny. When he met the Witches for the second time (IV.i), the unconscious presented him with a "show of eight Kings," images which pointed even beyond his personal life into a distant future. In contrast, Lady Macbeth tried to suppress any image or discussion of what had happened. From the beginning, she made light of guilt and therefore to a large extent kept it bottled up. The resulting repressed complexes psychologically isolated her from her husband and all other human beings. In the end these locked-up memory images literally exploded into her consciousness, causing a clouding and fragmenting of consciousness. The images all belong to her past, representing facts and actual occurrences which she could not face and therefore could not integrate. Macbeth, however, consciously dealt with his crime. But he did not *act* according to his insight into his guilt; he attempted to keep and increase the harvest resulting from his crimes, thus also preventing a redemption of his guilt. The images which came from his unconscious had to do with the future; Lady Macbeth was overwhelmed by fragmented images recalling the past. The weight of her images forces her weakened ego to commit suicide. Macbeth could maintain almost to the very end the illusion that the powers of evil would bring about his final and complete victory. His problem was the interpretation of the numinous images which so easily found entrance into his consciousness, and their application to reality. He never even guessed at their compensatory or healing function. He never sought redemption, but only success and power, and he used the revelations of the unconscious for this purpose. Lady Macbeth's problem had been the repression of the unconscious. Now it has invaded her against her will. It has no positive aspect for her at all. On the contrary, it is only destructive. Her consciousness has decidedly changed. It has lost its sharpness, its ability to focus and its cohesiveness. Though this is definitely an abnormal state of mind, one cannot call it "insanity" as Max Lüthi does. Shakespeare does not call her state of mind "insane" or "mad"—as he does with telling effect in *Hamlet* and *King Lear*.

Lady Macbeth's sleepwalking, and especially her sleeptalking, are something very different from what we observe under clinical conditions in our time. Dr. James C. Coleman gives the most concise description of somnambulism in his textbook, *Abnormal Psychology and Modern Life*,[5] as well as modern views on the causation, motivations and conflict-situations which lead to somnambulism:

> Dissociative reactions, often classified as one type of hysteria, include amnesia, fugue, multiple personality, and somnambulism. . . . The ideas blocked off from consciousness are strong enough to determine the patient's behavior, though only during sleep. . . . (Somnambulistic) episodes are most common

[5] Third edition (Scott, Foresman & Co., New York, 1964), pp. 212, 217-218.

in adolescence, but apparently are much more frequent in adult life than is generally realized. . . . Sleepwalking is much more common among females than males. . . . *Symptoms,* The patient usually goes to sleep in a normal manner, but sometimes during the night arises and carries out some act. This may take him to another room in the house or even outside and may involve rather complex activities. He finally returns to his bed and to sleep and in the morning remembers nothing that has taken place. During the sleepwalking the patient's eyes are usually partially or fully open, he avoids obstacles, hears when spoken to, and ordinarily responds to commands such as to return to bed. Shouting or shaking the patient will usually awaken him, and he will be surprised and perplexed at finding himself in his strange and unexpected position. Usually such sleepwalking episodes last from fifteen minutes to a half-hour. . . . Contrary to popular opinion, many sleepwalkers injure themselves, sometimes quite seriously, as a result of activities they undertake in their sleep. . . . These patients usually evidence other neurotic symptoms. Sandler (Sandler, S.A., *Somnambulism in the Armed Forces,* "Mental Hygiene," (1945)) reports that in his study of 22 successive cases of somnambulism occurring in the armed forces, 18 had been referred for psychiatric attention because of somatic complaints rather than because of their somnambulism. . . . In general, sleepwalking seems to be a symbolic escape from some conflict situation. . . . Adult somnambulism also represents an escape, although the precipitating cause was usually some traumatic experience that had just occurred or was expected in the very near future. The somnambulism represented to the patient an attempt to escape from threatened danger. . . . The personality structure of the adult somnambulist is usually that of the typical hysteric—an immature, egocentric, overly suggestible individual with exaggerated needs for affection, approval, and security.

In an older book, by Dr. William B. Carpenter,[6] I found the description of a case which seems to be much closer to that of

---

[6] *Principles of Mental Physiology* (D. Appleton & Co., New York, 1887). In this case, actual guilt in a sleep-walking woman creates neurotic symptoms but is definitely not the cause of her somnambulism.

Lady Macbeth. But of course, although Shakespeare always tries to stay as close as possible to nature, the observable facts are only the material which he transforms, in the furnace of his imagination, into new creations, eternally valid. Therefore, though there has never been and never will be a medical case of sleepwalking which is quite like that of Lady Macbeth's, it is completely true and reveals the great truth underlying the whole of his masterwork. There is no case known in medical literature in which the repression of real guilt can be seen as the only, or principal, cause of somnambulism. And yet Lady Macbeth's sleepwalking is true on the higher level of poetry. There is no other and no truer way to demonstrate the change and the specific deterioration of consciousness in Lady Macbeth than through sleepwalking, and through betraying her guilty secrets in sleeptalking. Shakespeare could use certain elements of reality, even sleepwalking, to express the full truth of his inner vision.

Curry believes that Shakespeare, in writing this scene, followed the universally accepted ideas of the Renaissance in regard to possession. To substantiate his belief he quotes Cassian and adds:[7]

> We must not imagine that this possession of spirit is accomplished by the infusion of the demonic substance in such a way that it actually penetrates the substance of the soul—only the spirit of God may be fused in this manner with the spirit of man. Rather the unclean spirits overwhelm the intellectual nature of man only when they are permitted to seize upon those members in which the vitality of the soul resides. This is what happens to Lady Macbeth. . . . Apparently there is a steady deterioration of her demon-possessed body until, at the beginning of Act V, the organs of her spirit are impaired to the point of imminent dissolution. . . . Her symptoms in these circumstances resemble those of the ordinary somnambulist, but the violence of her reactions indicates that her state is what may be called 'somnambuliform possession,' or 'demoniacal somnambulism.'

[7] *Op. cit.,* pp. 88-89.

As in many other instances, I do not believe that Shakespeare simply applied the knowledge and conceptions current in his time, but that he had his own experience of the unconscious (without the scientific terminology of our time, of course) and gave poetic expression to his great vision. Each play represents a step in the growth of his consciousness. If we understand this, we do not need to congratulate ourselves, as Curry does, when he says that[8]

> Shakespeare has spared us in the case of Lady Macbeth, a representation of the more disgusting physical symptoms of the diabolically possessed, such as astounding contortions of the body and fantastic creations of the delirious mind.

So far we have looked at this scene from the objective level and have discovered essential differences between Macbeth and Lady Macbeth. Lady Macbeth, however, is not only the wife of the Thane, she is more; Levy-Schucking called her "a figure like Medea." I consider her a personification of the negative mother-anima archetype. In this scene she is shown in a state of complete disintegration. The great significance of the sleepwalking scene would then consist in bringing out in greatest clearness the downfall and destruction of the hero's soul. His crime first destroys his soul and later his body. This is usual in Shakespearean tragedy. The woman always dies first. So it is, dramatically, in *Romeo and Juliet, Othello* and *King Lear.* In this respect the greatest similarity exists between *Hamlet* and *Macbeth,* since Ophelia represents distinctly the type and specific psychic quality of the hero's deterioration and ultimate destruction. Hamlet's soul drowns in the unconscious, Macbeth's suffers a change of consciousness caused by indissoluble guilt. Even in the so-called romances written in Shakespeare's later creative years the woman undergoes terrible dangers before she is reinstated in her proper kingdom (Imogen, Hermione, Perdita and Miranda).

The most conspicuous and astounding fact would then be that the hero's consciousness and his soul take divergent paths after

[8] *Ibid.,* p. 92.

the murder. Macbeth's male consciousness takes a very different path from that of his anima, who is his unconscious personified. (As is usual in a man, the unconscious has feminine characteristics.) It appears strange to speak of the consciousness of the unconscious, but as Jung has shown in his essay, "On the Nature of the Psyche," [9] consciousness is always surrounded by a varying amount of unconsciousness and, on the other hand, the archetypes (the organs of the unconscious) always have an indeterminate amount of consciousness, which in dreams is symbolized by certain luminosities. For example, the collective unconscious can be symbolized as a "city at night with many lights," or the "night sky with its innumerable stars." The lights of the "city" or the "night sky" represent the consciousness of the unconscious. In discussing Lady Macbeth's sleepwalking, we stated that though she appeared totally unconscious to the observer, a minimal amount of consciousness still existed, an amount just great enough for coordination of motor activity. The anima, even at this stage of disintegration, contains a certain amount of consciousness. Macbeth, we know, always had a certain amount of consciousness. Even when he was "rapt," that is, engrossed, in the activity of the unconscious, he could quickly tear himself out of it. He was never simultaneously in both worlds.

Another critical point is the attitude to guilt. Macbeth knew his guilt immediately after the murder (symbolized in the image: the murdering of "sleep"). The anima, on the contrary, avoided knowing her guilt; she "repressed" it. As a result, her consciousness and her conscience gradually became paralyzed. The sleep-walking is a most adequate symbol for the twilight consciousness of Macbeth's anima. It allows us to see that although Macbeth knew of his guilt, it was in no way integrated into his consciousness. Therefore, in his anima, the bloody events of his career appear in fragmented, incoherent pieces and break through into a consciousness which, due to the same conflict of forces, has become murky.

After this scene, Lady Macbeth disappears from the play as

[9] *Structure and Dynamics of the Psyche,* p. 159.

an active figure. From here on Macbeth's consciousness and that of his anima move in diametrically opposite directions. The sleepwalking of Macbeth's anima reveals the profound split in his personality. The two are so far apart that a reconciliation between them appears utterly impossible. After this scene we hear about her only indirectly: when Macbeth is informed of her death, and when her suicide is mentioned in Malcolm's final speech. This indicates that after the sleepwalking scene, the anima loses her autonomous function. She becomes dissolved and is assimilated into Macbeth's personality. From then on the features of her psychology can be directly observed in Macbeth himself—in the fading, deteriorating and disintegrating quality of his soul during the last scenes of the play.

ii

The balance of the fifth act (Scenes 2-7) is largely determined by the disintegration and death of Macbeth's soul, and the corresponding rise of the forces against the tyranny of evil. Scottish and English forces join; Macbeth strongly fortifies the castle of great Dunsinane. It is apparent that the outcome of the battle will depend on the result of this siege.

Scene 2 shows the condition of Scotland and of Macbeth (they are identical to a large degree) at that moment when Macbeth's power has reached its utmost limits. Macbeth's enemies cannot see him with detachment and so cannot observe the intimate details which we, the audience, have become acquainted with, but their opinions round out the picture. Caithness begins by repeating hearsay:

> Some say he's mad; others that lesser hate him   (V.ii.14)
> Do call it valiant fury; but, for certain,
> He cannot buckle his distemper'd cause
> Within the belt of rule.

It appears that everyone is aware of Macbeth's condition. He is a man brimful of affects; he is therefore constantly in a bad mood. The affects spill over. The Arden Shakespeare gives two possible interpretations for the lines, "He cannot buckle . . . rule":[10]

> It may mean that Macbeth, like a man with dropsy who cannot get his belt on (cf. Falstaff), cannot restrain his passions (cf. "mad"). Or, it may mean that the kingdom which he rules is sick and rebellious.

Both interpretations are based on the image of a "belt" which cannot hold a content. Essentially it is a psychological image of his inability to contain affects. The belt "contains," rules the abdomen, the seat of emotions according to primitive and medieval traditions. "Belt of rule" can also refer to an area. We thus realize that Macbeth can neither control his emotions, nor his kingdom. Now that the forces of resistance are being organized against him, it can at last openly be said of him:

> Now does he feel (V.ii.16)
> His secret murders sticking on his hands.

Again using a clothing image, Shakespeare characterizes Macbeth's inadequacy as a king, the misproportion between ego and royal function, when he puts the following words into Angus's mouth:

> Now minutely revolts upbraid his faith-breach; (V.ii.18)
> Those he commands move only in command,
> Nothing in love; now does he feel his title
> Hang loose about him, like a giant's robe
> Upon a dwarfish thief.

Macbeth's enemies realize that it is not only they who fight him but his own unconscious:

> Who then shall blame (V.ii.22)
> His pester'd senses to recoil and start,
> *When all that is within him does condemn*
> *Itself for being there?*

[10] P. 148.

iii

The third scene is somewhat longer. Macbeth is in a room in the castle. The Doctor is present during the entire scene. At one point a servant enters, bringing news of 10,000 soldiers marching against Dunsinane. Seyton is called in by Macbeth and given orders. John Russel Brown remarks: [11]

> There are a few passages of reflective and deeply-felt speech. . . . The role is now full of sudden and intense transitions, as from instinctive guilt to 'valiant fury'. In the transitions are new explorations of his most inward nature, revealing despair in suicide or flight, loneliness, fear and courage, blind hatred of his enemies, suspicion of his friends and, perhaps, love on the death of his wife.

These "sudden and intense transitions" are characteristic of the anima, especially when she has degenerated to such a degree as was demonstrated by Lady Macbeth's twilight consciousness in the sleepwalking scene. These changes of mood indicate that the anima has been dissolved into Macbeth's personality. He is no longer the brave hero in battle, but at times behaves rather womanish. At the beginning of this scene he is arrogant, sure, bombastic:

> I cannot taint with fear. What's the boy Malcolm?   (V.iii.3)
> Was he not born of woman?

His stubborn belief in his cause is based on the Witches' prophecies. They alone sustain him in his defense against an overwhelming superiority:

> The spirits that know   (V.iii.4)
> All mortal consequences have pronounc'd me thus;
> 'Fear not, Macbeth; no man that's born of woman
> Shall e'er have power upon thee.'

[11] *Op. cit.,* p. 57.

It is this prophecy, the second one actually, which imbues Macbeth with a conviction of invulnerability and fortifies his supreme hubris. Ironically, it is at this moment that the servant informs him of the vast superiority of his enemies.

Macbeth plays the fearless one, but for a moment he admits he is "sick at heart" and reveals how he truly feels:

> I have liv'd long enough: my way of life   (V.iii.22)
> Is fall'n into the sear, the yellow leaf.

These words issue directly from his anima, who as we know is in a condition of twilight consciousness. Instead of growing, maturing and harvesting the fruits of life, the usual course of human existence, Macbeth's crimes and unredeemable guilt rot his soul. Instead of intensity and beauty, he experiences a dying in the midst of life. Life has no meaning for him. There is no goal. The juices of his life are soaked out. The Doctor is not much help. He is not a medicine-man who treats both body and psyche of his patients, although he is somewhat nearer to some modern concepts of medicine. At least he recognizes the psychological causes of Lady Macbeth's illness and diagnoses her condition as the effect of "thick-coming fancies, that keep her from her rest."

Macbeth is quite right in demanding help in his present condition. This physician is inadequate if he cannot "minister to a mind diseas'd." Only recently have physicians taken it upon themselves to cure diseased minds, and it is even more recent that drugs have been used to treat the psyche. Macbeth's demand was natural and justified:

> Pluck from the memory a rooted sorrow,   (V.iii.41)
> Raze out the written troubles of the brain,
> And with some sweet oblivious antidote
> Cleanse the stuff'd bosom of that perilous stuff
> Which weighs upon the heart.

But the time has not yet arrived for psychotherapy or psychopharmacology. However, it appears more than questionable that at this late stage any modern form of therapy could help Macbeth or Lady Macbeth. Murder, and in particular secret murder, poisons the soul so completely that only under the most extraordinary circumstances can a human being be redeemed of it. We have seen before how the images of the unconscious tried to show Macbeth a path leading to redemption, but his concretistic and literal thinking was a thick wall against any penetration of insight.

Now, at the end of Scene 3, Macbeth demands this insight from the unfortunate Doctor:

> . . . If thou couldst, doctor, cast   (V.iii.50)
> The water of my land, find her disease,

and even the cure:

> And purge it to a sound and pristine health.

For Macbeth, the disease is the invasion by the English—but not his own deeds. He must outshout his inner doubt by referring to the Witches' first prophecy:

> I will not be afraid of death and bane   (V.iii.59)
> Till Birnam forest come to Dunsinane.

In spite of all his crimes, we cannot help but feel a great deal of sympathy with Macbeth because we know his doom is now inevitable; there is no escape for him. Something in him knows it too but his trust in the Witches and their prophecies is unshakeable. Although we realize how badly he has misunderstood these prophecies when they were given to him, we must appreciate that Macbeth's faith in the pronouncements was a religious conviction, though of a satanic nature.

iv

Scene 4 takes place before the wood of Birnam. It is Malcolm who, for the sake of camouflage, orders every soldier to carry a bough:

> Let every soldier hew him down a bough (V.iv.5)
> And bear't before him; thereby shall we shadow
> The numbers of our host, and make discovery
> Err in report of us.

v

In Scene 5 Macbeth is again inside the castle. As before, his words are defiant and bombastic; he is sure of victory. But this is only one side of the coin. A cry of women interrupts and we now see the other side:

> I have almost forgot the taste of fears. (V.v.9)
> The time has been my senses would have cool'd
> To hear a night-shriek, and my fell of hair
> Would at a dismal treatise rouse and stir
> As life were in't. I have supp'd full with horrors;
> Direness, familiar to my slaughterous thoughts,
> Cannot once start me.

For Macbeth, ambition was a kind of insatiable hunger, and his murders were an attempt to satisfy it. Now he realizes he has "supp'd full with horrors." Instead of nourishing his soul, he has eaten poison and killed her with his "slaughterous thoughts." Closely associated with hunger, of course, is the sense of taste: he almost "forgot the taste of fears." The sense of taste (as well as all the other senses) has been completely dulled. The loss of sensation is an outstanding symptom of his mortally poisoned anima. She is the psychological organ in man which *experiences,* irrespective of whence the stimulus issues. Her mode of function is very similar to that of the retina. If the retina is destroyed by poison, blindness is the inevitable result. In the case of the psyche, psychological poison causes death of the soul; its inevitable result is psychic blindness, that is, inability to experience. In Macbeth's case, his crimes cause the death of the anima. He, who was a most sensitive man ("my senses would have cool'd to hear a night-shriek"), "feels" nothing now, and therefore the report that his Queen is dead only serves to emphasize the death of his sensitivity and perceptivity. Without a vital anima, life is quite meaningless. Not even "death" is meaningful to him, and the word for it does not convey signification:

> She should have died hereafter; (V.v.17)
> There would have been a time for such a word.

For Macbeth, "tomorrow" is not an image which includes growth, unfoldment, but endless, meaningless repetition; the end is extinction, "dusty death"; what is between birth and death is not life, not light-increasing consciousness, but a vague, two-dimensional nothingness, a "walking shadow," a "poor player upon the stage," forgotten immediately after his exit. Life has no reality for him and no goal transcending itself:

> It is a tale (V.v.26)
> Told by an idiot, full of sound and fury,
> Signifying nothing.

This nihilism is the philosophy naturally issuing from a dying anima. It is the more tragic since in the beginning his soul was very much alive, and knew of a life to come. The murder cut Macbeth off from immortality and from all hope for an unbroken existence. His suffering is particularly intense because he *knows* of the death of his soul and can express it.

Macbeth is not allowed to remain in this mood of utter nihilism for very long. A messenger brings the news that the Birnam "wood began to move." With that, one of the two pillars (the prophecies) on which Macbeth's security has rested collapses. His first reaction naturally is a tremendous rage. Any sudden removal of ego support releases a strong affect in a psychic system and overwhelms the ego with it. The messenger's firmness in reporting the fact calms Macbeth sufficiently to allow reflection. In typical tyrant's fashion, he threatens the messenger with torture-laden execution, but is just as willing to accept such dire fate for himself should Birnam wood now really be a "moving grove." His ego attitude changes and for the first time he doubts the Apparitions' declarations:

I pull in resolution and begin   (V.v.42)
To doubt the equivocation of the fiend
That lies like truth: 'Fear not, till Birnam wood
Do come to Dunsinane'; and now a wood
Comes toward Dunsinane. Arm, arm, and out!
If this which he avouches does appear,
There is nor flying hence, nor tarrying here.
I 'gin to be aweary of the sun,
And wish the estate o' the world were now undone,
Ring the alarum-bell! Blow, wind! come, wrack!
At least we'll die with harness on our back.

I accept Kittredge's explanation of "I pull in resolution":[12]

> *pull in:* rein in, check. 'I can no longer give free rein to con-
> fidence and determination.' Or the figure may be from a bird
> that pulls in its wings.

Either one of these two images beautifully describes the withdrawal of the ego defense. Psychological destruction precedes
the physical end. For the first time Macbeth realizes that
the utterances of the Apparitions have more than one meaning.
He, of course, blames the weird Sisters and their show: he
speaks of "equivocation of the fiend that lies like truth." The
trouble, however, is not with the unconscious, but with Macbeth's limited understanding. He cannot see that the unconscious speaks in symbols and needs careful interpretation and
meditation. The most dangerous thing always is to take a symbol only literally and concretely. But this is exactly what Macbeth does. He only interprets it concretely and disregards any
other possible meaning of the images. So he repeats the prophecy to himself:

'Fear not, till Birnam wood   (V.v.44)
Do come to Dunsinane'.

The impossible occurs. Both physically and psychologically the
forces that be close in on him; he knows he is trapped. Again,

---

[12] *Op. cit.,* p. 224.

as in the Witches' scene (IV.i.50), he wishes the state of the world were now undone ("though the treasure of nature's germens tumble all together . . ."). This time his wish does not come out of hubris and defiance, but rather out of deathly weariness. At last he is willing to give in to his fate, to accept death and defeat: "At least we'll die with harness on our back!"

vi

Scene 6 is the last scene printed in the Folio, but most editors follow Pope and Johnson by introducing two further scene divisions, since place and event change considerably. The battle takes a rapid course. Shakespeare does not give much emphasis to the actual battle, but rather to the inner events. Macbeth meets an individual, not an army.

The short monologue with which the seventh scene begins expresses Macbeth's full surrender to fate:

> They have tied me to a stake; I cannot fly,   (V.vii.1)
> But bear-like I must fight the course.

—in spite of which he cannot give up the second prophecy. First, Shakespeare shows us the fight between Macbeth and young Siward. This is the first time since the battles mentioned in I.ii that Macbeth, in fighting, is face to face with his opponent. Siward's fall renews and encourages Macbeth's faith in the one last prophecy. After all, Siward is a "man that's of a woman born."

Macduff is seeking Macbeth, but misses him. We hear: "the castle's gently rendered." The battle is over. Macbeth alone remains to fight. In this utterly hopeless situation, he considers suicide for a moment but, being a warrior, rejects it as "Roman foolishness." At last he meets Macduff, and seeing him loses his determination to live out his fate—because he remembers the warning given by the First Apparition (the armed Head):

> Macbeth! Macbeth! Macbeth! beware Macduff;   (IV.i.72)
> Beware the Thane of Fife.

But, aloud, Macbeth tells him:

> Of all men else I have avoided thee. (V.vii.33)
> But get thee back, my soul is too much charg'd
> With blood of thine already.

Macduff's determination to fight and kill Macbeth is absolute. He who has lost his loved ones to Macbeth's hirelings is sustained in this last struggle by a divine power. For a while the fight goes on—indecisively, mercilessly. Now Macbeth does not consider the warning of the armed Head. He has greater faith in the pronouncement of the Second Apparition (the bloody Child):

> . . . laugh to scorn (IV.i.80)
> The power of man, for none of woman born
> Shall harm Macbeth.

Encouraged by the long drawn-out joust, he mocks Macduff:

> Thou losest labour: (V.vii.37)
> As easy mayst thou the intrenchant air
> With thy keen sword impress as make me bleed.

And then he tosses out his last trick, which he thinks will cow his adversary:

> I bear a charmed life, which must not yield (V.vii.41)
> To one of woman born.

Whereupon Macduff, guessing Macbeth's secret intercourse with the powers of evil, trumps him and, just as triumphantly, pierces his fantastic inflation:

> Despair thy charm; (V.vii.42)
> And let the angel whom thou still hast serv'd
> Tell thee, Macduff was from his mother's womb
> Untimely ripp'd.

At last Macbeth knows he has found his victor; Macduff is going
to kill him. Like any other creature, he does not want to die. His
ego wants to run away from this intolerable situation. Nothing is
left of that which made him the bloody tyrant, the "hell-hound"
(V.vii.32). His murderous career has been the direct result of
his relationship with the three weird Sisters. Up to the very end
his course has depended on the utterances of the unconscious,
which he interpreted in only one way. Now he calls the weird
Sisters "juggling fiends." Banquo's warning about them in the
first act:

> But 'tis strange: (I.iii.22)
> And oftentimes, to win us to our harm,
> The instruments of darkness tell us truths,
> Win us with honest trifles, to betray's
> In deepest consequence.

is finally realized by Macbeth as perfect truth:

> . . . these juggling fiends   (V.vii.48)
> That palter with us in a double sense;
> That keep the word of promise to our ear,
> And break it to our hope.

He is now a man stripped of all faith in non-human powers. Still,
he believes that his fate is in his own hands:

> I'll not fight with thee.   (V.vii.51)

Only the taunt of "coward" and Macduff's promise to exhibit
him in a show ("as our rarer monsters are") cause him to continue the fight in which he is finally killed.

I give such a detailed analysis of Macbeth's ferocious duel
with Macduff in order to show clearly the final human condition
of the hero. After the battle which the Sergeant reported in I.ii,
Macbeth never again encountered his foe "on the front" until he
met Macduff. In this final moment he is forced to be himself, to

fulfill the Witches' prophecies, and to confront his enemy who, he knows, is the only one who can defeat him. He has lost everything, including his belief in the Witches. The defilement of his "jewel" (his soul) has made a monster of him. He regains a last thread of human dignity in preferring death to captivity and humiliation.

This is perhaps the proper place to add some amplifications to the images which occurred in the prophecies. The key symbols were "wood" and "womb," both outspoken mother symbols. They point to the strength and protectiveness of nature as mother. They emphasize the immutable character of the laws of nature. When these pronouncements become a reality in the here and now, it becomes manifest that these laws are unexpectedly changed or suspended for the time being. Thus the "moving wood" and the "man not born of woman" appear as true miracles. The events demonstrate that a power from beyond nature is using natural occurrences for its own purposes. It is a miracle that the wood moves, though we are let in on the secret of how it is done. It is a miracle that Macduff lives. His unusual entrance into existence ("from his mother's womb untimely ripp'd"), though perfectly possible and natural, at this crucial moment becomes a miracle. The two men who are the principal instruments in defeating Macbeth are extra-ordinary, though in all other respects as human as the next one. It was Malcolm who gave the command to cut down the boughs. Malcolm is Duncan reborn, but fully aware of the dark world of murder and treason. The unusual fact about him is that he has not yet known woman. The extraordinary fact about Macduff is that he was born without the mother's "taint." According to Barron: [13]

> Macduff was thus triply separated in that he was ripp'd from his mother's womb, he left his wife and children behind, and they were murdered by the hirelings of Macbeth.

What these two men had in common was that they were not subject to "Nature," i.e., feminine nature. Macbeth's commerce

[13] *Op. cit.*, p. 157.

with the powers of evil required as opponents men who were not
yet, or no longer, linked to the feminine. Scotland's healing
could only be brought about by a power transcending nature,
invested in a man who was not subject to the ordinary rules of
nature, and was guided and aided by divine power:

> What's more to do, (V.vii.93)
> Which would be planted newly with the time,
> . . . this, and what needful else
> That calls upon us, by the grace of Grace
> We will perform in measure, time, and place.

Conclusion

The tragedy of Macbeth is not so much his fate and final destruction, as the contrast between his potential and what he
made of it. At all times he knew that a very different possibility
lay in him, but from the very beginning destructive feminine
forces arose in him which he could not deal with. From the moment of his surrender to the Witches, his destruction as a human
being was unavoidable. That this change of Macbeth into an
inhuman monster was Shakespeare's intention can be seen from
the indignity piled on Macbeth's head after his death—his head
is ignominiously carried in by Macduff, thus fulfilling Lady Macbeth's threat:

> I would . . . have . . . dash'd the brains out, had I so
> sworn as you (I.vii. 56)
> Have done to this.

Malcolm's final speech confirms this impression when he speaks
of the tyrant:

> . . . this dead butcher and his fiend-like queen. (V.vii.98)

Of *Macbeth,* Dover Wilson once said: "It is almost a morality
play." Though it appears that in some way Shakespeare went

back to medieval modes of thinking, in fact he used the given forms of the Elizabethan theater to experiment with the utmost extremes of opposites in the human soul. In one of his sonnets (cxxxvii) he could still address his soul:

> For I have sworn thee fair, and thought thee bright
> Who art as black as hell, as dark as night.

In his play, the dark Lady can pray:

> Come, thick night,   (I.v.51)
> And pall thee in the dunnest smoke of hell,
> That my keen knife see not the wound it makes,
> Nor heaven peep through the blanket of the dark,
> To cry, 'Hold, hold!'

And his hero can go all the way from being a valiant and admired fighter to utter destruction and damnation because he completely, and without reflection, surrenders to evil in the form of feminine transcendental forces.

Through the action of his characters, Shakespeare freed and redeemed himself from the one-sided oppressive power of the feminine and could so return to a dynamic balance of his own soul. He experienced the archetypal world as a realm in which the opposites—male and female, good and evil—were constantly attempting to gain possession of him. But by maintaining his determination to "live in doubt" he sustained the freedom of his soul.

> Two loves I have of comfort and despair,
> Which like two spirits do suggest me still:
> The better angel is a man right fair,
> The worser spirit a woman color'd ill.
> To win me soon to hell, my female evil
> Tempteth my better angel from my side,
> And would corrupt my saint to be a devil,
> Wooing his purity with her foul pride.

And whether that my angel be turn'd fiend
Suspect I may, yet not directly tell;
But being both from me, both to each friend,
I guess one angel in another's hell:
    Yet this shall I ne'er know, but live in doubt,
    Till my bad angel fire my good one out.

—Sonnet cxliv